Commodore 128 Reference Guide for Programmers

Commodore 128 Reference Guide for Programmers

David L. Heiserman

Howard W. Sams & Co.
A Division of Macmillan, Inc.
4300 West 62nd Street, Indianapolis, IN 46268 USA

FIRST EDITION
FIRST PRINTING—1986

International Standard Book Number: 0-672-22479-8
Library of Congress Catalog Card Number: 86-60936

Acquisitions Editor: *Greg Michael*
Editor: *Katherine Stuart Ewing*
Designer: *T. R. Emrick*
Illustrators: *Don Clemons* and *Ralph E. Lund*
Cover Artist: *Gregg Butler*
Compositor: *Shepard Poorman Communications, Indianapolis*

Printed in the United States of America

Trademark Acknowledgments

All terms mentioned in this book that are known to be trademarks or service marks are listed below. In addition, terms suspected of being trademarks or service marks have been appropriately capitalized. Howard W. Sams & Co. cannot attest to the accuracy of this information. Use of a term in this book should not be regarded as affecting the validity of any trademark or service mark.

CP/M is a registered trademark of Digital Research, Inc.

Amiga, Commodore 64, and Commodore 128 are registered trademarks of Commodore Electronics, Limited.

Contents

Preface

Like the Commodore 128 Computer, this book can mean a lot of different things to different people. And like the Commodore 128, this book is assembled so that it can be used by a variety of users who possess a wide range of skills and computer know-how.

- Beginners with no previous programming experience can benefit immediately from the elemental topics presented in the first two chapters—how to operate the computer and how to write programs in BASIC.
- Readers already familiar with other personal computers and BASIC can note in the first two chapters the differences and move quickly to special applications topics in the remaining chapters.
- Readers who have already mastered BASIC and 6502 machine language programming from other sources can note the enhancements built into the new version of DOS (Chapter 3) and the machine-language monitor (Chapter 4).
- Readers who have the desire to use CP/M in a Z-80 or 8080A environment will be pleased to find that the Commodore 128 supports it. A Z-80 microprocessor is built into the system and is fully dedicated to the CP/M features that are briefly described in Chapter 5.

Chapters 2 through 5 deal with the eight programming formats available on the "stock" Commodore 128—BASIC (actually both BASIC 2.0 and 7.0), DOS (the new Commodore disk operating system), the machine language monitor and 8502 machine/assembly language, and CP/M and Z-80/8080A machine language programming.

Chapters 6 through 12 describe the individual features of the Commodore 128 system. A reader who wishes to study sprite animation or RS-232-C communications procedures, for example, will find complete descriptions of those subjects in Chapters 8 and 12, respectively.

Chapter 13 is a memory map of the Commodore 128 system. This chapter outlines the principal blocks of memory, describes the most important registers, and summarizes the built-in Kernal routines that are readily available to the programmer.

Chapter 14 deals with procedures for managing the entire 128K of memory. Wherever possible, each principle cited in the book is first demonstrated in a format that should be familiar to most readers—in BASIC; then the same principle is illustrated in terms of monitor and machine-language programming.

The use of many examples written in 8502 assembly language directly reflects the fact that the Commodore 128 is designed to encourage machine-language programming and calls to Kernal subroutines.

Unlike much of the early literature dealing with the Commodore 128, no underlying assumption is made that the reader is already familiar with the features and quirks of the earlier Commodore personal computers, notably the Commodore 64.

I believe that paying twice the suggested retail price for this system would be a bargain. The Commodore 128 is a powerful system that stands on its own merits and promises to engage a lot of users who have no previous experience with earlier Commodore systems.

DAVID L. HEISERMAN

1

General Operating Procedures

The minimum Commodore 128 system consists of a console-keyboard unit, an external power supply for the console, a display unit, and a disk or cassette-tape unit. The power supply is included with the console, and the remaining items are available separately.

You should count on using one of Commodore's own disk or cassette-tape units. Most discussions in this book assume you are using the Commodore 1571 disk drive, but you will find references to other Commodore disk drives and cassette-tape units where such references are particularly relevant.

Unlike the disk and cassette-tape units, you are not strictly bound to use a Commodore display (monitor). If you choose not to use a Commodore display, you can get the full benefit of the video features by using a high-resolution color monitor that includes both composite-video and RGB (separate red-green-blue) inputs. The RGB connection is absolutely necessary for displaying text in the 80-column format.

A color monitor that uses only the composite-video connection is less expensive than the models that include the RGB feature, but composite video units are adequate for all 40-column text and graphics applications.

You can use an ordinary color TV set as the display unit. The video quality is not quite as good as that of a composite-video monitor, and TVs lack the RGB feature that is necessary for displaying 80-column text.

The connectors on the Commodore equipment are clearly and meaningfully labeled as shown in Figure 1-1.

Understand that the grooves cut across the housings for the console and disk drive are air vents. Although you may be tempted to stack disks, papers and books on those attractive, flat surfaces, do not do so. Blocking the vents can cause serious overheating problems that will greatly reduce the working life of the units.

The Three Main Operating Modes

Many of the features of the Commodore 128 computer can be described in the context of its three main operating modes:

- C128 mode
- C64 mode
- CP/M mode

These three operating modes are so distinctly different that you may be convinced that they represent three entirely different computer systems.

C128 mode is the default operating mode. That is, the Commo-

Fig. 1-1 Arrangement of connectors on Commodore 128 console units

(A) Commodore 128 right side view.

(B) Commodore 128 rear view.

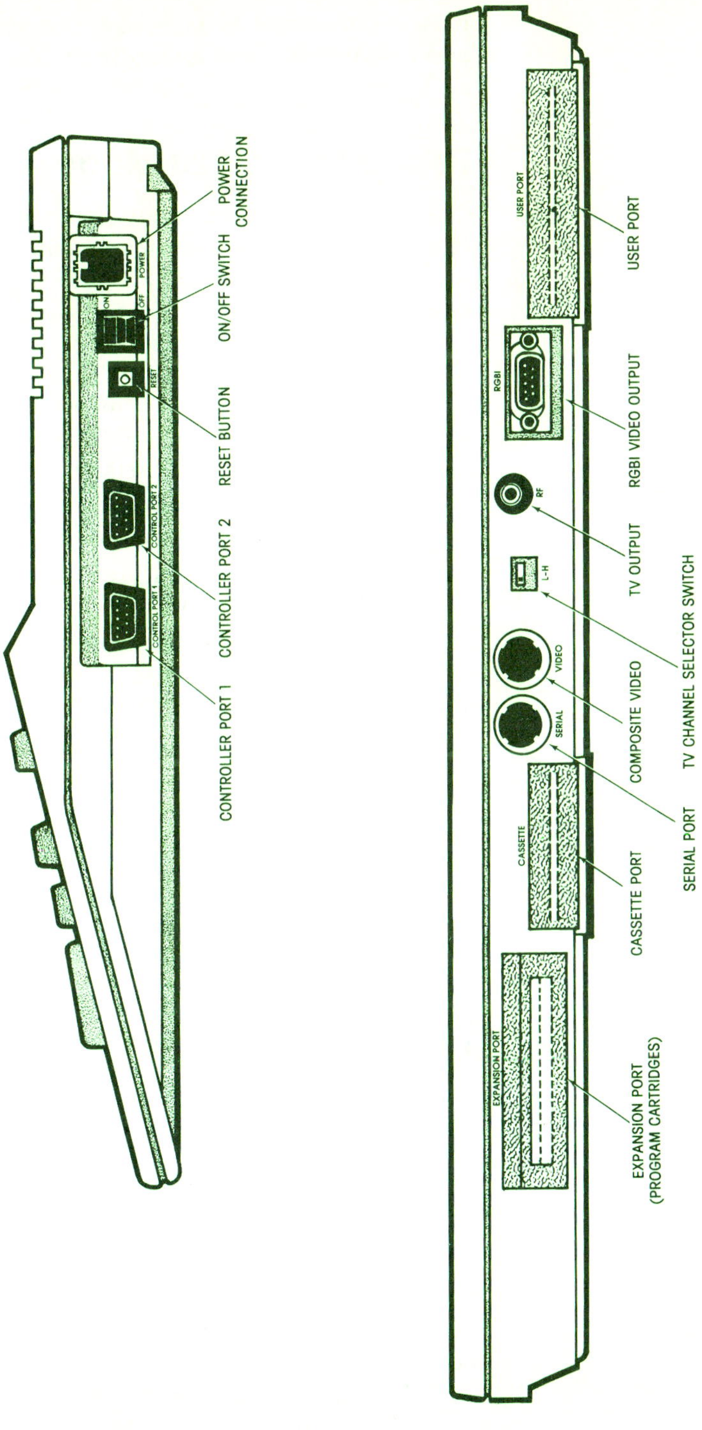

dore 128 computer starts and runs in C128 mode unless directed otherwise—either from the keyboard or programmed commands. If you have any intention of using or writing programs that function in C64 and CP/M modes, understanding their essential features and how to switch from one mode to another is vital.

Features of C128 Mode

C128 mode is unique to the Commodore 128 personal computer system. This mode is the system's default mode and is the subject of most of the discussions in this book. In fact, you can assume any discussion concerns C128 mode unless clearly stated otherwise.

One essential feature of C128 mode is Commodore's enhanced BASIC interpreter, version 7.0. That language is built into the system as non-destructible, read-only memory (ROM) and is readily available without having to load any kind of external programming. Turning on the computer automatically sets up the system for running BASIC 7.0 in C128 mode and so does operating the Reset pushbutton. Both operations bring up a screen display similar to the one shown in Figure 1-2.

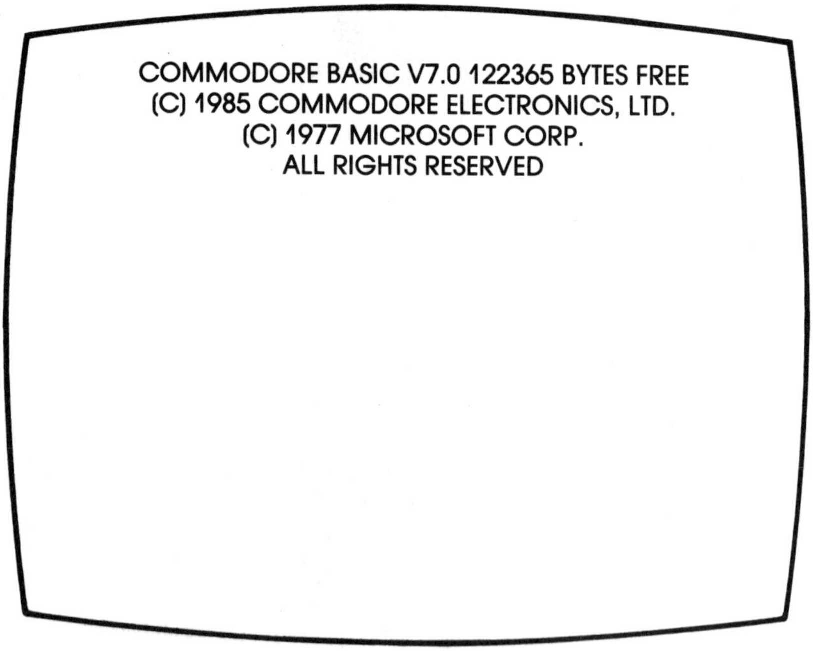

Fig. 1-2 Heading message that appears when system is first set to C128 mode. Border and characters are light green and background is dark gray

This display confirms that the system is running BASIC 7.0 and, by inference, in C128 mode as well. The screen also indicates that the C128 mode takes advantage of the full range of built-in random-access memory (RAM).

C128 mode also supports:

- the full range of keyboard operations
- a choice of 40- or 80-column text screens
- a machine-language monitor mode, including a disassembler and a mini-assembler
- high-speed, double-sided 1571 disk drives
- RGB video
- a mouse
- joysticks and game paddles
- a light pen
- RS-232-C I/O, including telephone communications via an external modem accessory
- Commodore Datasette tape player-recorder
- serial output for other accessories such as a line printer

In short, C128 mode takes full advantage of all features built into the Commodore 128 console unit. The two other major operating modes, C64 and CP/M, are actually subsets of the C128 mode.

C64 Mode

C64 mode reconfigures the Commodore 128 to work like its predecessor, the Commodore 64 personal computer. The internal workings of the Commodore 128 are significantly different from those of the older Commodore 64, and a good many programs developed for the 64 cannot run properly on the 128. Rather than allow all Commodore 64 software to become instantly obsolete, Commodore decided to include the C64 mode—one that properly runs all software developed over the years for the Commodore 64 system. C64 mode is built into the system and does not have to be loaded from an external source of programming.

Commodore didn't forget about the disk drive, either. The 1571 disk drive recommended for the Commodore 128 computer is quite different from the 1541 model commonly used with the older Commodore 64. The 1571 disk drive is "smart" enough to know what kind of disk your computer is using. If your disk happens to be one that was originally formatted on a 1541 drive, the computer automatically makes appropriate adjustments. (The 1571 disk drive actually is a small, microprocessor-based computer in its own right.)

The Commodore 128 does not enter C64 mode unless the computer is directed to do so. As described previously, the system always starts in C128 mode. Getting into C64 mode is a simple matter of executing this command:

```
GO64
```

When you type GO64 and press the RETURN key, the system prompts ARE YOU SURE? If you do indeed want to go to C64 mode, press the Y key and then the RETURN key.

After a short delay, the screen changes to the blue colors that characterized the Commodore 64 system and displays the heading shown in Figure 1-3.

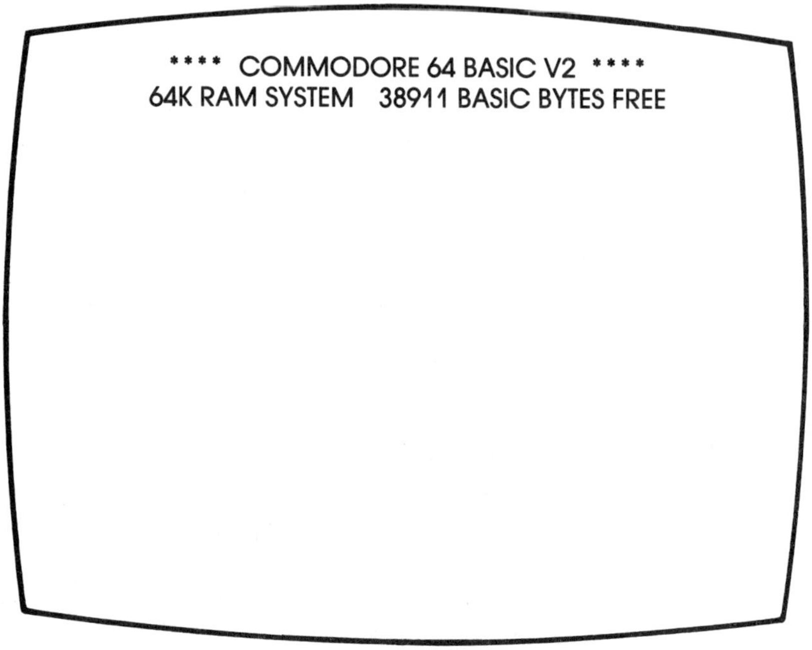

Fig. 1-3 Heading message that appears when system is first set to C64 mode. Border and characters are light blue and background is dark blue

The heading confirms that the system is operating as a Commodore 64 and shows that the amount of available memory has been reduced to the level of the older system.

An alternative way to go to C64 mode is to hold down the "Commodore key" (the C= key in the lower-left corner of the keyboard) when you turn on the power to the computer. This procedure takes the system directly to C64 mode.

The material in this book is directed toward the wider range of features available in C128 mode. Users who want to use C64 features should consult other resources such as *Commodore 64 Programmer's Reference Guide* (Sams #22056).

The simplest and most effective way to return to C128 mode from C64 mode is by operating the Reset pushbutton.

CP/M Mode

CP/M mode configures the Commodore 128 to run as an entirely different kind of computer. This mode bypasses the 8502 microprocessor used for the other operating modes and switches in an entirely different microprocessor, Z-80.

Unlike C128 and C64 modes, CP/M is not an integral part of the system. CP/M must be loaded into RAM from the *CP/M System Disk.* Assuming that the system is currently operating in C128 mode, the general procedure for getting into CP/M mode is as follows:

1. If you can run 80-column text on your system, set the monitor for RGB input and latch down the 40/80 DISPLAY key. CP/M can be run on a 40-column screen, but you can see only half the display at any given time.
2. Insert the *CP/M System Disk* into the disk drive.
3. Operate the system Reset pushbutton or enter the BOOT command.

After a short delay and some changing screen displays, the system settles in to CP/M mode. The screen generally has a brown border, black background, and purple characters. The heading shown in Figure 1-4 and the A> prompt characters confirm that the system is ready.

Fig. 1-4 Heading message that appears when system is operating in CP/M mode. Border is brown, background is black, and characters are purple

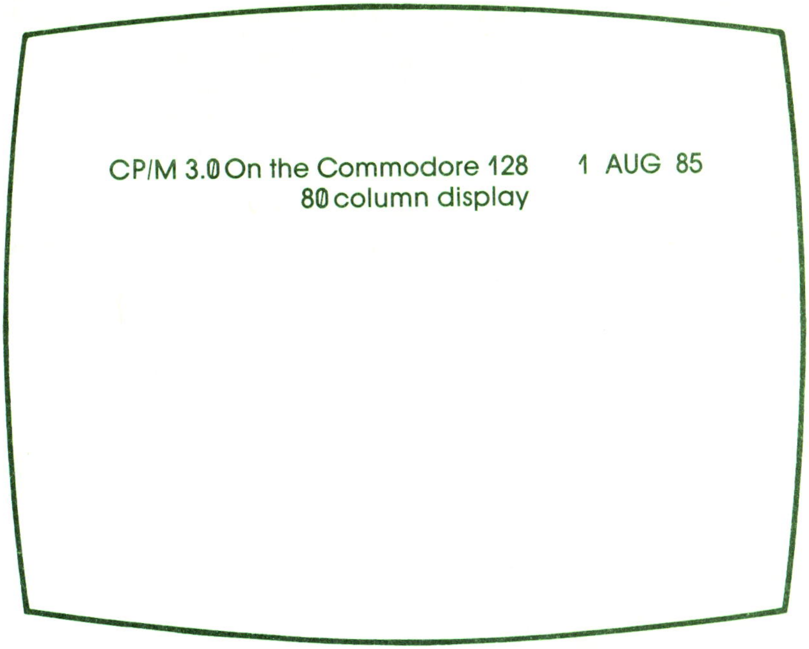

Bear in mind that CP/M mode transforms the Commodore 128 into a different kind of system. Many of the key functions are quite different, and the I/O functions are defined in entirely different ways. Chapter 5 in this book can help you become oriented in the CP/M

environment, but you will have to consult other sources for additional information. Consider, for instance, the CP/M order card that is included in your *Commodore 128 Personal Computer System Guide*.

You can return to C128 mode by first removing any sort of CP/M disk from the drive, then operating the Reset pushbutton.

Getting Familiar with the Keyboard

After the computer is properly started in the C128, BASIC 7.0 mode, the system prints the following prompt:

```
READY.
```

followed by the text cursor—a blinking rectangle. Those two elements on the screen indicate that the system is ready to accept BASIC commands and other key functions from the keyboard.

Much of the material in this book deals with the nature of BASIC commands. The computer is virtually useless without some commands. Unless they are loaded in the form of prescribed programs from a disk, commands must come directly from typing operations at the keyboard.

As indicated in Figure 1-5, most of the keys on the Commodore 128 keyboard are identical to those of a conventional typewriter, and can serve the same general purpose. However, some keys are irrelevant for ordinary typing operation but are quite important for operating the computer.

The RETURN key is perhaps the most frequently used computer key. You must press this key when you want the computer to execute a command that you've typed. When you are ready to execute a BASIC program, for example, type RUN on the keyboard, then press the RETURN key, and the computer reads and executes that program.

The keyboard includes 26 keys for the letters of the alphabet. The top surfaces of the keycaps show those letters in an uppercase form. When the computer is turned on, pressing the alphabetic keys prints uppercase characters on the screen.

The two SHIFT keys serve much the same function as the shift keys on an ordinary typewriter. Pressing the 3 key while not holding down either SHIFT key prints that numeral to the screen. Pressing the same key while holding down one of the shift keys prints the uppercase character shown on the keycap, a pound sign (#), to the screen.

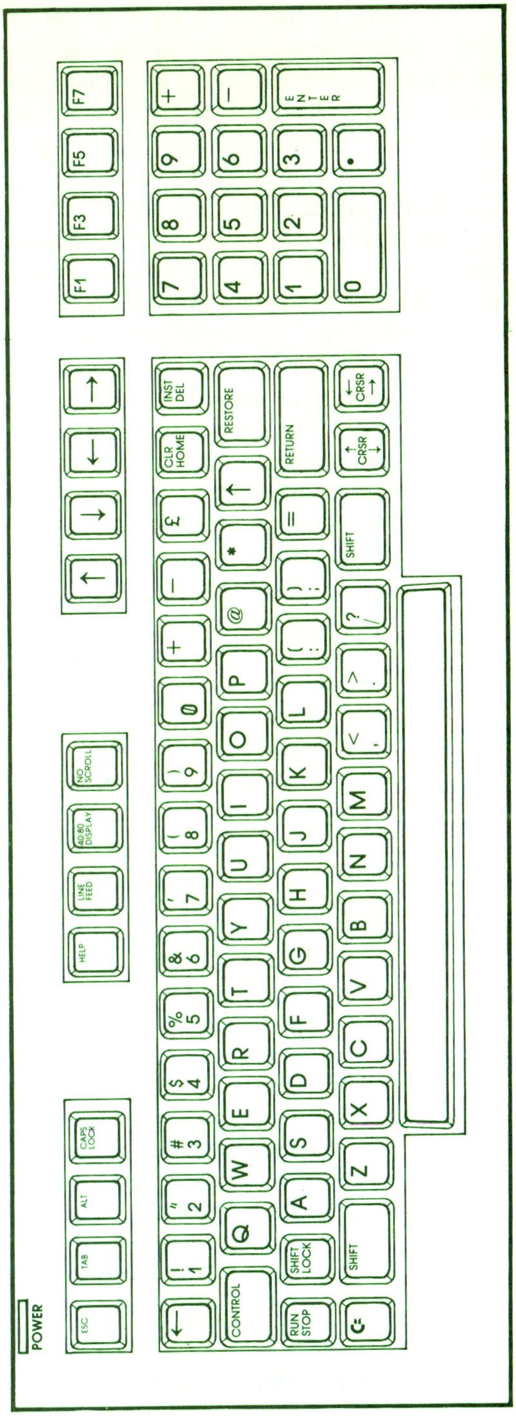

Fig. 1-5 Commodore 128 keyboard

Pressing alphabetic keys without holding down one of the SHIFT keys normally prints uppercase letters, so you might suppose that holding down a SHIFT key while pressing one of the alphabetic keys would print a lowercase character, which is not necessarily the case. In fact, holding down a SHIFT key while pressing alphabetic keys prints special graphics characters to the screen—one of the graphics characters appearing on the front surfaces of the keycaps.

The system can print both uppercase and lowercase letters, but only after you press the C= key (located at the lower-left corner of the keyboard) while holding down one of the SHIFT keys. Once you've done that, you can print both upper- and lowercase letters of the alphabet in the same way as you do with a typewriter. Pressing the C= key while holding down a SHIFT key returns the system to the normal uppercase/graphics format.

When operating in the 40-column mode, switching the character-set format changes all characters currently on the screen as well as those subsequently written to it. The 80-column mode supports both character sets at the same time, so changing the character-set format does not affect any text already printed to the screen. This change affects only the characters printed after the change takes place.

Using ESC, CONTROL, and C= Functions

The ESC, CONTROL, C=, and ALT keys greatly multiply the number of key functions that is available. These keys do nothing when used alone. They must be used in conjunction with a second key. The CONTROL key, for example, works in a fashion similar to a SHIFT key: it has no effect unless you press it while pressing another key.

As a simple example of how the CONTROL key works, hold it down while pressing the G key. This combination of keystrokes produces the system's bell sound.

CONTROL-*key*

where *key* is some other key operation. For example, the technique for sounding the bell—holding down the CONTROL key while pressing the G key—is presented as:

CONTROL-G

The Commodore key, C=, works the same way: hold down this key while pressing some other key. Consider the following notation:

C=-8

The notation instructs you to hold down the C= key while pressing the 8 key. C=-8 instructs the system to plot all subsequent characters in light gray. You can return to the normal light green by pressing a C=-6.

> ***NOTE:*** Invoke CONTROL and C= functions by holding down the key while pressing some other designated key.
>
> The general notation used throughout this book is:
>
> CONTROL-*key* and C=-*key*
>
> where *key* is some other designated keystroke.

The ESC key is used in a somewhat different manner. Instead of holding down the key while pressing another, the procedure is divided into two separate steps: press the ESC key, release it, then press a second key. The general notation used in this book is:

ESC/*key*

where *key* is some other designated key.

The following ESCape function, for example, forces the system to show the text cursor as a non-blinking rectangle:

ESC/E

First press the ESC key, release it, then press the E key. This operation disables the cursor's normal blinking mode. Use the following ESC function to restore the normal blinking effect:

ESC/F

> ***NOTE:*** Invoke an ESCape function by first pressing the ESC key, releasing it, then pressing some other designated key.
>
> The general notation used throughout this book is:
>
> ESC/*key*
>
> where *key* is some other designated keystroke.

The ALT (ALTernate) key is not an integral part of the normal operating system. This key serves no purpose until you run a program that happens to make use of it. As described in Chapter 5, CP/M mode uses the ALT key but only because the disk-loaded CP/M system programming refers to it.

Using the Cursor-Control Keys

The blinking text-cursor symbol indicates exactly where the next character will be printed on the screen. While entering data from the keyboard and modifying information on the screen, you often need to move the cursor from its present position. That sort of operation is best handled with the cursor-control keys.

The Commodore 128 has two different sets of cursor-movement keys, which are shown in Figure 1-6. In C128 mode, they perform the same set of tasks: move the cursor up, down, left, or right. These keys move the cursor through text material on the screen without disturbing it in any way.

Fig. 1-6 Two sets of cursor control keys

(A) Four gray arrow keys located along top row of keys on console unit.

(B) Two light-colored CRSR keys located near lower-right corner of keyboard.

Referring to the cursor-control, arrow keys shown in Figure 1-6A, the arrows indicate the direction of motion. Pressing one of these keys moves the cursor one space in the indicated direction. Holding down one of the keys makes the cursor move any number of spaces in succession. These keys are not active in C64 mode, and they perform a different sort of function in the CP/M mode.

Figure 1-6B shows a pair of cursor-control (CRSR) keys. Each key shows two different arrows that indicate a direction of cursor motion. The direction of cursor movement depends on whether or not a SHIFT key is pressed at the time: the upper CRSR arrows indicate the direction of cursor motion when a SHIFT key is pressed, whereas the lower arrows indicate the direction of motion when a SHIFT key is not pressed. The two CRSR keys are active in C64 and CP/M modes as well as C128 mode.

There are two additional arrow keys: a left-arrow key located just above the CONTROL key and an up-arrow key above and to the left of the RETURN key. Those are *not* cursor-control keys. Rather, they print the designated arrow figure to the screen.

The TAB and LINE FEED keys also move the text cursor without affecting any text that might be in its path. The TAB key performs the same task as its counterpart on a typewriter—advance the cursor a fixed number of spaces to the right (normally eight column locations). The LINE FEED key moves the cursor down one line.

Pressing the CLR/HOME key returns the text cursor to the upper-left corner of the screen (a location that is commonly known as the *home* position). Pressing the CLR/HOME key while holding down a SHIFT key not only homes the cursor but clears the entire screen as well.

Controlling the Printing Rate on the Screen

Certain kinds of computer operations and programs print long lists of information. When such a listing reaches the bottom of the screen, the material begins scrolling upward. The problem is that it often becomes virtually impossible to read the information as it is presented. A couple of different keys and key operations can slow down the listing for closer inspection.

The Commodore key (C=) is usually used in conjunction with other keys. But when the computer is printing long lists of information, holding down the C= key slows the scrolling rate by inserting a time delay between the printing of each line. Releasing C= restores the normal printing rate.

Pressing the NO SCROLL key stops the printing operation altogether. This keypress does not interrupt the program or computer function that is generating the material on the screen but simply puts the program "on hold" until you press the NO SCROLL key again.

The NO SCROLL key represents a simplification of an older but equally effective technique for stopping and starting listings on the screen:

- Do a CONTROL-S operation to stop the listing.
- Do a CONTROL-X operation to resume the listing.

Using the RUN/STOP and RESTORE keys

Matters sometimes get a bit out of hand during the normal course of developing new BASIC and machine-language programs—musical sounds don't stop, sprites keep moving all over the screen, links between the keyboard and screen get scrambled, and the program generally flies off into some endless and confusing loop.

Of course you can regain control by operating the Reset pushbutton. The only problem is that BASIC programming is lost in the process.

A more satisfactory way to get things under control and to do so without losing any of the programming is to hold down the RUN/

STOP key while pressing the RESTORE key. As long as the system is still in C128 mode, the STOP-RESTORE operation resets the default C128, BASIC 7.0 format. This method generally only works for BASIC programming however, and commercial software sometimes disables the RUN/STOP and RESTORE keys.

Using the 40/80 DISPLAY Key

Generally speaking, the purpose of the 40/80 DISPLAY key is to set the system for displaying 40- or 80-column text (40 or 80 columns per line). Latching down or releasing that key does not directly change the column format however.

The 40/80 DISPLAY key must be set to the desired position prior to turning on the computer, operating the Reset pushbutton, doing a STOP-RESTORE operation, or booting the CP/M system disk.

Chapter 6 illustrates some procedures for switching between 40- and 80-column displays within programs and without using the 40/80 DISPLAY key.

Using the Calculator Keypad

Figure 1-7 shows a block of keys that are arranged in the format traditionally used on adding machines and calculators. The numerals, decimal point, plus, and minus signs do exactly the same job as their counterparts elsewhere on the keyboard. The ENTER key is really nothing more than an additional RETURN key.

Fig. 1-7 Numeric keypad

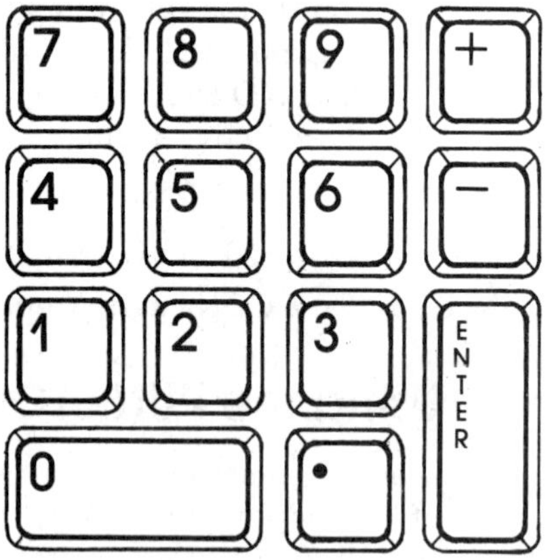

Inserting and Deleting Text with the INST/DEL Key

Consider an instance where you have already typed some text to the screen, and you find that you want to make some minor revisions. If all that is necessary is to change a character or two, use the cursor-control keys to position the text cursor over the character to be changed and overstrike it with the correct character. But if you need to insert additional characters within a line or to delete characters, use the INST/DEL key.

Holding down a SHIFT key while pressing the INST/DEL key inserts spaces in the line. The insertion begins at the current cursor location and shifts the remaining characters on the line to the right. Doing one INST key operation inserts one space, doing it twice in succession inserts two spaces, and so on. The general idea is to do INST key operations until the number of inserted spaces equals the number of successive characters you want to add to the line. Once you've inserted that string of spaces, type the characters that belong in those locations.

Deleting one or more characters from a line of text is a matter of doing a DEL operation—pressing the INST/DEL key alone. Deletion takes place from right to left. Use the cursor-control keys to place the text cursor over a character and press the INST/DEL key. You will see that the operation takes the character under the cursor and moves it one space to the left. An INST/DEL operation deletes the character immediately to the left of the cursor, replaces the deleted character with the cursor and character under the cursor, and moves the remaining portion of the line to the left also.

Using the Function Keys: F1-F8, HELP, and RUN

The console keyboard includes four function keys that are labeled F1 through F8. Functions F1 through F4 are invoked by pressing the key while *not* holding down a SHIFT key. Functions F5 through F8, those indicated on the front surfaces of the keycaps, are invoked by pressing the key while holding down a SHIFT key.

The computer normally assigns certain BASIC commands to these function keys. The general idea is to make more convenient the execution of those commands. The default assignments are:

F1—GRAPHIC

F2—DLOAD"

F3—DIRECTORY

F4—SCNCLR

F5—DSAVE"

F6—RUN

F7—LIST

F8—MONITOR

Displaying the directory of the current disk is usually a matter of typing the DIRECTORY command and pressing the RETURN key. The function-key feature makes it possible to execute the same command in a much more convenient fashion, namely by pressing the F4 function key. Likewise, F4 clears the screen and homes the cursor, F6 runs the BASIC program that is currently loaded in the system, F7 lists a resident BASIC program, and F8 switches the system to the machine-language monitor mode.

Function keys F1, F2, and F5 do not immediately execute their designated commands but at least handle most of the preliminary keyboard work for you. GRAPHIC, for instance, is not a complete command and must be concluded with a graphics screen number, 0 through 5, and a RETURN keystroke. In the same way, the DLOAD" and DSAVE" functions need a file name and a RETURN keystroke.

The computer automatically assigns the group of BASIC commands listed previously to the eight function keys. You can change the function-key assignments to suit your needs. See the description with the KEY statement in Chapter 2.

The HELP and RUN keys are configured internally to do their tasks in the same way as the function keys, F1-F8. Pressing the HELP key emulates the keyboard operation where you type HELP and press the RETURN key. See a description of the HELP command in Chapter 2.

The RUN function is invoked by holding down the SHIFT key and pressing the RUN/STOP key. RUN actually executes a DLOAD"* command followed by a RUN, which instructs the system to load and run the first program on the current disk.

The commands assigned to the HELP and RUN keys cannot be altered by the KEY command. You can change those assignments, however, using the technique described in Chapter 10.

Quote-Mode Operations

BASIC 2.0 and 7.0 (C64 and C128 modes, respectively) support a special kind of PRINT statement that is particularly relevant to most of the keyboard commands described in the previous section of this chapter.

A PRINT statement, as described in Chapters 2 and 6, can print a message to the screen if that message is enclosed in quotation marks. The general form of that sort of statement is

PRINT "*string*"

where *string* is any combination of printable characters.

The following example prints HELLO to the screen:

```
PRINT "HELLO"
```

The so-called "quote mode" allows you to perform just about any sort of screen-control operation by including keystrokes within the quotes of a PRINT statement.

Suppose that you want to perform a series of BASIC operations that begins with clearing the screen, homing the cursor, then printing HELLO. You can do so by entering a command that begins with PRINT ". After typing the first quotation mark, press the CLR/HOME key while holding down the SHIFT key. Normally the SHIFT-CLR/HOME operation clears the screen and homes the cursor. Using this operation in the quote mode prints a dark-on-light heart character. Type HELLO immediately after the heart character and close the sequence with another quote. When you press the RETURN key to execute the operation, you see that the screen is cleared, the cursor is homed, and HELLO is printed.

Most sources of Commodore 64 and 128 information would specify the SHIFT-CLR/HOME quote-mode operation in this way:

```
PRINT "{1 SHIFT-CLR/HOME}HELLO"
```

The information enclosed in the braces is the instructions for the special quote-mode operation. Consider this example:

```
PRINT "{1 SHIFT-CLR/HOME}{4 CRSR down}{1 TAB}HELLO"
```

The statement instructs the system to clear the screen, home the cursor, move the cursor down four lines, tab the cursor to the right, then print HELLO. On the screen, this appears as a series of reverse-colored characters—one heart, four Qs, and an I.

Quote-mode routines make easy the inclusion of all sorts of control operations into a program. The technique makes the program quite difficult for others to read, though. For that reason, the examples in this book do not cite quote-mode operations. Instead, the examples use alternative techniques, such as POKE and CHR$ statements, to do the same operations in a format consistent with a broad range of varied personal computer systems.

The quote-mode feature can be troublesome, however, when you are attempting to edit characters that are enclosed in quotation marks for other reasons. You can cancel the quote mode for the current operation by doing an ESCAPE/O key combination—holding down the ESCAPE key while pressing the O key.

Essential Disk Operations

Although you can work with the Commodore 128 without using any disk operations, you lose a good many advantages and opportunities when you don't use disks. The following discussions deal with the disk procedures required for the most elementary operations. Chapter 3 deals with a far wider range of procedures.

The discussions in this book assume that you are using the Commodore 1571 disk drive. It uses a double-sided, double-density format, and you should purchase disks that have those specifications. Attempting to save a few dollars by using single-sided disks invites the loss of valuable data because such disks are, by nature, of lesser quality than their double-sided counterparts.

Displaying the Disk Directory

Once the computer is turned on and operating under C128 BASIC, you can display a listing of the programs on a disk by executing one of two commands from the keyboard: CATALOG or DIRECTORY.

By way of an example, insert into the drive unit the *TEST/ DEMO DISKETTE* supplied with the Commodore disk drive. Close the latch and enter this command:

```
DIRECTORY
```

Figure 1-8 shows the first part of the directory display that should appear on the screen. (Remember that you can stop the display at any time by pressing the NO SCROLL key.)

Fig. 1-8 First few lines of the directory listing for TEST/DEMO DISKETTE

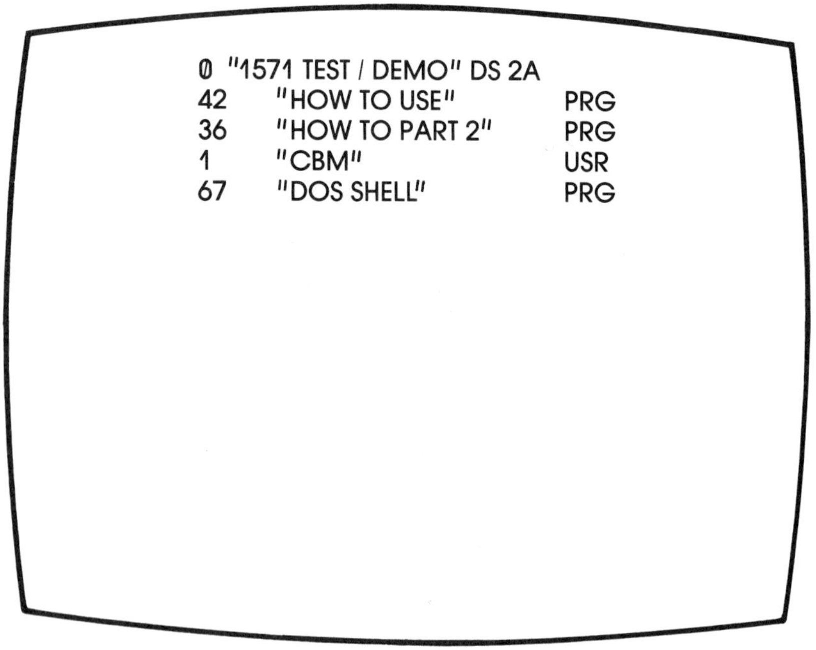

The first line in the display is the disk's *header* . The first digit in that line indicates the disk drive number being used—Drive 0 in this case. The characters enclosed in quotes are the disk's header name, the DS expression is the disk's identification code, and the 2A is a system-identification code common to all disks made for the C128/1571 system.

The remaining lines show information regarding each program or file saved on the disk. The numbers in the first column show how many blocks—how much disk space—the file occupies. Generally speaking, the larger the number of blocks, the larger the program.

The items enclosed in quotation marks are the file names for the individual programs and files. They are the names you use for loading the programs into the computer, and they are the kinds of names you can use for saving your own material on a disk.

The final column in the main listing shows the file type. The computer supports a number of different file types, but the ones shown here are PRG (program file) and USR (special user file).

The partial directory listing in this example does not show the comment that appears at the end of such a display. When you allow the system to display the entire directory for the *TEST/DEMO DISKETTE* , you see a notation that looks like this:

```
281 BLOCKS FREE.
```

which provides a good idea of how much space is available on the current disk.

Formatting a Disk

New disks must be properly formatted before any information can be written to them. Previously used disks can be formatted, too, but the operation destroys all data and programming that they contain.

The C128 BASIC command for formatting a disk has this general form:

HEADER "*diskname*",I*idno*

where *diskname* is the disk name (up to 15 characters) and *idno* is the identification number (any two alphanumeric characters).

Find a new disk, or one that contains no useful information, and insert it into the disk drive. Close the latch and enter this HEADER command:

```
HEADER "SEE IT WORK",I01
```

This example assigns the disk name, SEE IT WORK, and uses an identification code of 01.

When you have entered the command and pressed the RETURN key, the system asks:

```
ARE YOU SURE?
```

Respond by entering a Y response.

The computer handles the rest of the formatting job. When the system is done, it prints the READY prompt.

Saving a BASIC Program on Disk

A BASIC program residing in memory can be saved on disk by entering this general command:

DSAVE "*filename*"

where *filename* is a name, up to 15 characters long, that you want to assign to the program.

Suppose that you have developed a BASIC program and want to save it on disk as POPS. Enter the following command and press the RETURN key:

```
DSAVE "POPS"
```

The system has some built-in protection against saving more than one program with the same file name. For example, if POPS is already in the disk directory when you execute the DSAVE command, the green light on the 1571 disk drive begins blinking on and off to inform you that a disk-related problem exists. In that case, you have two options: either DSAVE the program with a different file name or write over the old disk program by beginning the file name with an at (@) character:

```
DSAVE "@POPS"
```

In either case, you can do a DIRECTORY or CATALOG command to see the new name in the directory.

Loading a BASIC Program from Disk

A BASIC program currently residing on a disk can be loaded into the computer by means of this general command:

DLOAD "*filename*"

where *filename* is the name of the program to be loaded. To load a program named POP, for example, type the following command and press the RETURN key:

DLOAD "POP"

If POP is a BASIC program that resides on the disk, DLOAD" loads the program into the system. The program can be executed by entering the RUN command.

If POP is not on the current disk, the system returns a **FILE NOT FOUND** error message and blinks the green light on the 1571 disk drive. Whenever that happens, do a CATALOG or DIRECTORY command to double check the spelling of the file name. (Executing the CATALOG or DIRECTORY command also clears the disk error condition.)

The DLOAD command loads a BASIC program from the current disk to the computer. As described earlier, you have to enter a RUN command to begin running the program. An alternative disk command makes possible the loading of a BASIC program and the running of that program without having to do the RUN command. The general form of the load-and-run command looks like this:

RUN "*filename*"

where *filename* is the file name of the program.

2

BASIC Operations and Programming Procedures

The BASIC programming language and the Commodore 128 personal computer go together quite well. In fact the language is built into the machine as ROM (read-only memory) firmware, so the discussions in this chapter assume that the system is operating under the C128-mode's BASIC 7.0. Programmers who wish to prepare programs that run in the C64 mode should follow the descriptions of BASIC 2.0 in the book, *Commodore 64 Programmer's Reference Guide*.

It is not appropriate to deal with the fundamental principles of BASIC programming in a book of this type. The discussions thus assume that you have at least a rudimentary understanding of the subject. If you do not, consult any one of a number of good books that are devoted exclusively to BASIC programming.

Although you can work with BASIC without the aid of DOS (disk-operating system), you rarely have any good reason to do so. Among other things, you use DOS to save and load BASIC programs and files. Like BASIC, DOS is built into the machine—some of the system in the Commodore 128 console and some in the disk-drive unit.

The purpose of this chapter is to summarize the essential features of BASIC, DOS commands, and error messages generated by those systems. The discussions of DOS for the Commodore 128 computer are limited to the ways it interacts with BASIC. Chapter 3 deals with DOS in a more complete fashion.

Numeric and String Constants for Basic

In terms of BASIC programming, a *constant* is a specific numeric value or a set of meaningful text characters. Constants can be classified as either *numeric* or *string*.

Numeric Constants

A numeric constant always takes the form of a fixed numerical value such as:

23 −212 1.6888 9.9999 1432000

Numeric constants can be very small or very large numbers, they can be positive or negative, and they can be whole numbers or numbers having decimal parts.

A few special rules, limitations, and forms of notation apply to numeric constants in BASIC. For example, large numbers must not use commas in the conventional fashion. In fact, large numbers must not use commas at all. If you wish to express a value of one million in BASIC, you must enter it as 1000000, *not* as 1,000,000.

In keeping with the usual arithmetic convention, negative-valued numeric constants are preceded by a minus sign, whereas positive values can be expressed with a plus sign or no sign at all. If you enter a PRINT −128 command, for example, BASIC responds by printing −128 on the screen. But if you enter a PRINT +128 command, BASIC exercises its "no-sign" option and prints 128.

BASIC uses a number format called *floating-point notation*. Among other things, being a floating-point number means that it expresses very large and very small values in terms of powers of 10 *(scientific notation)*. To see how BASIC handles very large values, enter this command:

PRINT 12345678901

and you will see this response:

```
1.23456789E+10
```

The PRINT statement specifies a positive constant that has more than nine significant digits, and BASIC responds by converting the value to a form of scientific notation. The E+10 in that response represents $\times 10^{10}$—ten to the tenth power.

The same general idea applies to small numeric values. Enter this command:

PRINT 0.00012345

and BASIC shows this version:

```
1.2345E-04
```

This value in the PRINT statement is less than 0.01, so BASIC automatically converts it to scientific notation, where E−04 means 10^{-4}.

Generally speaking, BASIC invokes scientific notation whenever a numeric value has more than nine digits to the left of a decimal point or more than two significant digits to the right of a decimal point.

There are some limitations on the range of numeric values that can be expressed in BASIC, even when using scientific notation, and that range is:

−1.701411834E+38 through 1.701411834E+38

Attempting to assign values outside that range causes the system to halt ongoing operations with a **?OVERFLOW ERROR** message.

And finally, BASIC allows only nine significant digits that are not zero, it accepts numbers having more than nine significant digits, but it sets all digits beyond the ninth to zero. The constant 123456789123456789, for example, has 18 significant digits, but BASIC deals with it as 123456789000000000. Eighteen significant digits still are present, but only the first nine have non-zero values. As described earlier, the system converts such values to scientific notation: 1.23456789E+17.

The same principle applies to fractional numbers. A constant such as 0.00123456789123456789 has 20 significant digits to the right of the decimal point. Eighteen of them are non-zero digits, so BASIC treats the number as 0.00123456789 and displays it as 1.23456789E−03.

Summarizing the limitations and conventions required for numeric constants in BASIC:

- Large numeric values must not include commas.
- A negative sign (−) must precede a negative-valued constant, but a plus sign (+) is optional for positive-valued constants (BASIC always prints positive values *without* the plus sign.)
- BASIC uses scientific notation for expressing very large and very small numeric constants.
- BASIC deals with only nine non-zero significant digits. Any digits beyond the ninth are set to zero.

String Constants

Whereas numeric constants must be composed of meaningful numeric values, string constants can be constructed of combinations of letters, punctuation marks, graphics symbols, and numerals. What's more, string constants usually must be enclosed within quotation marks.

The following BASIC statement prints a string constant HELLO:

```
PRINT "HELLO"
```

The string constant in this instance is composed entirely of uppercase letters of the alphabet and, as is usually the case, the constant is enclosed in quotation marks. When you execute this PRINT command, however, BASIC prints HELLO without the quotes.

As implied earlier, a string constant can be built from all sorts of letters and punctuation. The only character that doesn't work is the quotation mark because it is used to mark the beginning and end of a string constant and therefore cannot appear within the string. Most programmers cope with that little difficulty by using apostrophes where quotes would normally appear within a string.

Numerals included in a string constant are treated as literal characters rather than numeric values. You can prove this point with a simple demonstration. First, treat the expression 1+2 as a string constant. In other words, execute this statement:

```
PRINT "1+2"
```

The fact that you enclosed the expression in quotation marks means that the computer will interpret the numerals as part of a string and will respond by printing out a literal version of your string:

```
1+2
```

Next, execute this command:

```
PRINT 1+2
```

Omitting the quotation marks suggests that the numerals are to be treated as numeric constants, and the computer responds by printing the result of the summation operation:

```
3
```

A string constant can contain between 0 and 255 characters. Incidentally, a string that contains no characters is called a *null* string and is specified by successive quotation marks, "".

Summarizing the rules and limitations for expressing string constants:

- In most instances, string constants must be enclosed in quotation marks. (The primary exceptions concern the use of string constants with INPUT and DATA statements that are described later in this chapter.)
- String constants may be composed of any characters except a quotation mark.
- Numerals appearing within a string constant are treated as literal characters rather than numeric values.
- The maximum length of a string constant is 255 characters.

Numeric and String Variables in Basic

Most arithmetic and control operations in BASIC make reference to variables and, particularly, variable names. A *variable* is an expression that can take on a wide variety of different values—values that are assigned to variables through the normal execution of a program. A *variable name* is a set of one or more alphanumeric characters that you, the programmer, devise according to a few simple rules.

BASIC uses two principal kinds of variables: *numeric variables* and *string variables*. However, as described in the following discussions, variations of those two types of variables exist.

Numeric Variables and Variable Names

Numeric variables and numeric variable names refer to numbers or quantities. They are used in much the same way that variables are used in ordinary algebra. This two-line program illustrates the use of a particular numeric variable:

```
10 AX=200
20 PRINT AX
```

Line 10 assigns a *numeric constant*, 200, to a numeric variable, AX. Line 20 then prints the value currently assigned to variable AX, a value of 200 in this case. You could get the same overall result by executing

```
PRINT 200
```

but that limits the operation to printing a single value. The advantage of using variables is that you can get this program to print some other number by assigning a different constant to AX in line 10. You don't need to adjust the PRINT statement in line 20 because that statement refers to the variable name in a general way and makes no specific reference to the constant value assigned at an earlier time.

A BASIC programmer has a great deal of latitude and only a few rules to follow when making up numeric variable names. First, a numeric variable name can be composed of letters of the alphabet and numerals 0 through 9. Punctuation, including spaces and periods, is not accepted and the first character in the variable name must be a letter of the alphabet.

Second, a variable name must include at least one character but can have as many characters as practical applications require. *BASIC only considers the first two characters in a name,* however. Thus, the system cannot distinguish a variable name such as DETERM from one such as DECREASE.

Third, variable names must not include certain combinations of letters that are shown in the reserved-word lists in Figure 2-1. TI, for instance, cannot be used as a variable name because TI is reserved for use by the BASIC interpreter. And BEFORE cannot be used as a variable, because the reserved word, FOR, is used within it. Inadvertently using a reserved word within a variable name causes the system to generate a syntax-error message: **?SYNTAX ERROR**.

Fig. 2-1 BASIC reserved word list

ABS	DELETE	HEX$	PRINT	SPC
AND	DIM	IF	PRINT USING	SPRCOLOR
APPEND	DIRECTORY	INPUT	PRINT#	SPRDEF
ASC	DLOAD	INPUT#	PRINT# USING	SPRITE
ATN	DO	INSTR	PUDEF	SPRSAVE
AUTO	DOPEN	INT	QUIT	SQR
BACKUP	DRAW	JOY	RCLR	SSHAPE
BANK	DSAVE	KEY	RDOT	ST
BEGIN	DS$	LEFT$	READ	STASH
BEND	DVERIFY	LEN	RECORD	STEP
BLOAD	EL	LET	REM	STOP
BOOT	ELSE	LIST	RENAME	STR$
BOX	END	LOAD	RENUMBER	SWAP
BSAVE	ENVELOPE	LOCATE	RESTORE	SYS
BUMP	ER	LOG	RESUME	TAB
CATALOG	ERR$	LOOP	RETURN	TAN
CHAR	EXIT	MID$	RGR	TEMPO
CHR$	EXP	MONITOR	RIGHT$	THEN
CIRCLE	FAST	MOVSPR	RND	TI
CLOSE	FETCH	NEW	RREG	TI$
CLR	FILTER	NEXT	RSPCOLOR	TO
CMD	FNxx	NOT	RSPPOS	TRAP
COLLECT	FOR	OFF	RSPRITE	TRON
COLLISION	FRE	ON	RUN	TROFF
COLOR	GET	OPEN	RWINDOW	UNTIL
CONCAT	GETKEY	OR	SAVE	USR
CONT	GET#	PAINT	SCALE	VAL
COPY	GO64	PEEK	SCNCLR	VERIFY
COS	GOSUB	PEN	SCRATCH	VOL
DATA	GOTO	PI	SGN	WAIT
DCLEAR	GRAPHIC	PLAY	SIN	WHILE
DCLOSE	GSHAPE	POKE	SLEEP	WIDTH
DEC	HEADER	POS	SLOW	WINDOW
DEF FN	HELP	POT	SOUND	XOR

Unless clearly specified otherwise, numeric variable names refer to floating-point *(real)*, values. You can, however, force a numeric variable to treat any value assigned to it as integer values. All you need to do is end the variable name with a percent symbol, %.

The primary advantages of using integer values are that they take up less memory space and allow calculations to take place much faster.

Integer values are limited to whole-number values between −32767 and +32767, inclusively. A numeric variable that ends with a percent sign is forced to work in that format. The following demonstration illustrates this feature:

```
10 A%=1.2345
20 PRINT A%
```

BASIC responds to this routine by printing the integer version of 1.2345, or 1.

> ***NOTE:*** A numeric variable name that ends with a percent sign (%) forces that variable to work only with integer values. The advantage of using integer values is that they require less memory space and are handled faster by the BASIC interpreter than floating-point values.

String Variables and Variable Names

String variables and string-variable names refer mainly to literal expressions, but they also can refer to special control operations. The following routine illustrates the use of a particular string variable:

```
10 AX$="HELLO"
20 PRINT AX$
```

Line 10 assigns a *string constant* HELLO to a string variable AX$. Then line 20 prints the constant that is currently assigned to variable AX$—HELLO in this case. You could get the same result on the screen by executing:

```
PRINT "HELLO"
```

but that limits the operation to printing a single string constant. The advantage of using string variables is that you can get this program to print some other string by assigning a different constant to AX$ in line 10. You don't have to adjust the PRINT statement in line 20 because that statement refers to the variable name rather than a specific string constant that is assigned at an earlier time.

As with numeric variable names, a BASIC programmer has a great deal of latitude and only a few rules to follow when making up string variable names. First, every string variable name must end with a dollar-sign ($) character. This symbol distinguishes it from numeric variable names.

Second, a string variable name is composed of letters of the alphabet and numerals 0 through 9 but must begin with a letter of the alphabet and end with a dollar sign.

Third, the shortest allowable string variable name is one that is composed of a letter of the alphabet and a dollar sign. The names can be about as long as you choose, but BASIC regards only the first two characters and the dollar sign as significant.

Finally, string variable names must not include combinations of letters appearing in the reserved words list in Figure 2-1. If you inadvertently use a reserved word in a string variable name, the system responds by interrupting the program and printing the **?SYNTAX ERROR** message.

Here are some examples of valid string variable names:

TRY$ AXIS$ MODEL1$ NAMESFROMTABLE10$

And here are some *invalid* string variable names:

1TRY$ (begins with a numeral)
DARLING.SET$ (includes punctuation)
MIX$MONEY$ (includes $ as punctuation)
ACHR$ (uses a reserved word)
SALT (does not end with $)

Subscripted Variables

Subscripted variables offer an alternative technique for naming and using variables.

Ordinary modern algebra often uses a similar kind of subscript notation. For example, a geometry text might show this sort of equation:

$$Y = x_1+x_2+x_3+x_4$$

where the four different *x* variables are distinguished by the *subscript* numerals assigned to them. Few computers can directly print those subscript numerals a half line below the variable name, however, so the notion has to be expressed in some other way—by enclosing the subscript numerals in parentheses.

Thus the BASIC version of that equation looks like this:

Y = X(1)+X(2)+X(3)+X(4)

where the X terms and their subscript numerals each represent a subscripted variable name.

One of the powerful advantages of subscripted variables is that the subscript numerals can be treated as numeric variables. The following routine illustrates that notion.

FOR N = 0 TO 10:X(N) = N+1:NEXT N

This routine uses two kinds of variables: an ordinary numeric variable N and a set of eleven subscripted variables X(0) through X(10). The assignment statement in this instance happens to add a value of 1 to the current value of N.

If you were to use ordinary variables throughout, the same sort of job would have to be done this way:

```
10 X0=1:X1=2:X2=3:X3=4:X4=5:X5=6
20 X6=7:X7=8:X8=9:X9=10:X10=11
```

The advantages of using subscripted variables ought to be clear, even from those simple examples.

BASIC supports the use of subscripted string variables as well. The next example assigns some simple words to a group of subscripted string variables NA(0)$ through NA(4)$:

```
10 FOR X=0 TO 4
20 READ A$:NA$(X)=A$
30 NEXT X
40 DATA CAT,DOG,RAT,BIRD,FISH
```

After executing this routine, the five strings in the DATA listing are assigned to subscripted string variables NA$(0) through NA$(4), where NA$(0) = CAT, NA$(1) = DOG, NA$(2) = RAT, NA$(3) = BIRD, and NA$(4) = FISH.

The variable names for subscripted variables are identical to ordinary variable names but must end with a numeric value or expression enclosed in parentheses.

BASIC automatically sets aside enough RAM for coping with subscript numerals 0 through 10. Whenever you need to use larger-valued subscripts, DIMension that variable prior to using it in the program. (The subscripted variables in the previous examples were not DIMensioned because none of them used subscripts larger than 10.)

The general form of a DIMension statement is:

```
DIM var(n)
```

or

```
DIM var$(n)
```

or

```
DIM var%(n)
```

where *var*, *var$*, and *var%* specify numeric, string, or integer variable names, and *n* is the largest subscript value to be used in the program.

Executing a NEW, CLR, or RUN command automatically sets all elements of subscripted numeric values to 0 and subscripted string values to the null string. Thus, if the initial values of a set of subscripted variables must be initialized at some value other than 0, use this sort of initialization routine:

```
10 DIM FE(50),GEG(25)
20 FOR N=0 TO 50:FE(N)=1:NEXT N
30 FOR N=0 TO 25:GEG(N)= - 1:NEXT N
```

Line 10 DIMensions two different subscripted numeric variables FE and GEG. The first is dimensioned for 51 elements, the second for 26. Line 20 sets all 51 elements of FE to a value of 1, and line 30 initializes all values of GEG to −1.

Array Variables

A *variable array* is an extension of subscripted variables. Instead of using just one subscript numeral, arrays use two or more. The traditional foundation for arrays in BASIC are the matrices of modern algebra.

A 3 x 3 algebraic matrix is often organized this way in math-oriented books:

$$\begin{matrix} a_{1,1} & a_{1,2} & a_{1,3} \\ a_{2,1} & a_{2,2} & a_{2,3} \\ a_{3,1} & a_{3,2} & a_{3,3} \end{matrix}$$

The two subscripted numerals separated by a comma indicate the *row,column* locations. So variable $a_{2,3}$ indicates the third element in the second row.

Such elements are expressed in BASIC by including the subscript numerals—also separated by a comma—within a set of parentheses. For example:

A(1,1) A(1,2) A(1,3)
A(2,1) A(2,2) A(2,3)
A(3,1) A(3,2) A(3,3)

Those are examples of a two-dimensional array for variable A. Because none of the subscript values exceeds 10, you don't need to DIMension the array prior to using it.

Arrays can grow quite large very easily. If, for example, you see a three-dimensional string array DIMensioned this way:

```
DIM M$(20,15,25)
```

it implies that the program will be using 21 times 16 times 26 (or 8400) elements! A program using such a large array would work, though, as long as a sufficient amount of RAM is available for saving BASIC values.

Arrays, like subscripted variables, are zeroed or set to the null string automatically upon executing RUN, NEW, or CLR statements. If you have a need to initialize that gigantic three-dimensional string array to CAT, this brief routine does the job in a couple of minutes:

```
10 DIM M$(20,15,25)
20 FOR I=0 TO 20:FOR J=0 TO 15:FOR K=0 TO 25
30 M$(I,J,K)="CAT"
40 NEXT K,J,I
```

Operators for Commodore BASIC

Much of the computing and control activity of a computer is determined by the nature of *operators* that are written into the programs. Just three families of operators exist: arithmetic, relational, and logical operators. This section describes and compares those three families.

Arithmetic Operators

Arithmetic operators are well-defined symbols that indicate a mathematical operation to take place between two numeric constants or variables. Table 2-1 lists the arithmetic operators that apply under C128 BASIC and most other versions of BASIC as well.

You can easily confirm the function of those operators by entering some simple commands that use them. The computer, in effect, works like a calculator.

PRINT 2+3 shows the sum, 5, on the screen.
PRINT 2−3 shows the difference, −1, on the screen.

PRINT 2*3 shows the product, 6, on the screen.
PRINT 3/2 shows the quotient, 1.5, on the screen.
PRINT 3↑2 evaluates 3^2 and shows 9 on the screen.
PRINT 2↑3 evaluates 2^3 and shows 8 on the screen.
X=2:PRINT −X negates the value originally assigned to variable X and shows −2 on the screen.

Table 2-1
BASIC Arithmetic Operators

Operator	Function
+	addition (sum)
−	subtraction (difference)
*	multiplication (product)
/	division (quotient)
↑	exponentiation (power)
−	negation (change of sign)

Relational Operators

Relational operators suggest the relative magnitudes of numeric values or the values assigned to numeric variables. The operations apply equally well to string values and variables, but their applications in that case are rather different. In either case, the operators are generally meaningful only when used in conditional IF. . .THEN statements. Table 2-2 shows BASIC's family of relational operators.

Table 2-2
BASIC Relational Operators

Operator	Function
<	less than
>	greater than
=	equal to
<= or =<	less than or equal to
>= or =>	greater than or equal to
< > or > <	not equal to

Like arithmetic operators, relational operators look like their math-oriented text counterparts. The *not-equal* operator is the only one that is different. It most often is shown as ≠ in non-computer literature.

Consider the following programming routines that demonstrate the features of relational operators as applied to numeric values and variables.

1. The *less-than* operator:

```
10 X=1
20 IF X<10 THEN 40
```

```
30 END
40 PRINT X;
50 X=X+1
60 GOTO 20
```

The *less-than* conditional statement in line 20 allows the program to print the current value of X as long as that value is less than 10. In other words, the program prints integers 1 through 9, inclusively.

2. The *greater-than* operator

```
10 X=1
20 IF X>9 THEN END
30 PRINT X;
40 X=X+1
50 GOTO 20
```

This program also prints integer values of X in the range of 1 through 9. Line 20, however, uses a *greater-than* operator to determine when the current value of X exceeds 9 and consequently brings the program to an end.

3. The *equal-to* operator

```
10 X=1
20 IF X=10 THEN END
30 PRINT X;
40 X=X+1
50 GOTO 20
```

The routine prints integers 1 through 9 and comes to an end when the *equal-to condition* in line 20 is satisfied.

4. The *less-than-or-equal-to* operator

```
10 X=1
20 IF X<=10 THEN 40
30 END
40 PRINT X;
50 X=X+1
60 GOTO 20
```

This is yet another way to print integers from 1 through 9. In this case, the program continues printing those integers as long as X is less than 10—as determined by the *less-than-or-equal-to* conditional statement in line 20.

5. The *greater-than-or-equal-to* operator

```
10 X=1
20 IF X>=10 THEN END
30 PRINT X;
40 X=X+1
50 GOTO 20
```

This routine prints integers 1 through 9. The routine ends when the *greater-than-or-equal-to* operator in line 20 finds the current value of X is 10 or more.

6. The *does-not-equal* operator

```
10 SCNCLR
20 X%=10*RND(1)
30 PRINT
40 INPUT "GUESS A NUMBER BETWEEN 0 AND 9";N%
50 IF N%<>X% THEN PRINT "NOPE":GOTO 30
60 PRINT "THAT'S IT!";CHR$(7)
70 END
```

Line 20 assigns a randomly generated integer value, 0 through 9, to variable X. Line 40 prompts you to enter a number in the same range and subsequently assigns the number to integer variable N. Line 50 compares the two integer values and if they are *not* equal, the program prints NOPE and loops back to line 30 to give you another chance to guess the correct value of X. When you correctly guess the value, the *does-not-equal* condition in line 50 fails, and the program concludes by printing THAT'S IT! and sounding the bell.

The foregoing examples refer to relational operators as they apply to numeric constants and variables. The examples apply equally well to string constants and variables, however.

The notion of using relational operators to test relationships between strings might seem obscure at first. It might seem curious, for example, to question whether HELLO is *greater-than-or-equal-to* GOOD-BYE. But there is a clear rationale behind the notion.

Relational operators, when applied to strings, "regard" the characters in the strings in terms of their individual ASCII code numbers. The decimal ASCII code for *A*, for example, is 65; and the code for *B* is 66. Bearing the codes in mind, you can appreciate the fact that A>B—and BASIC relational operators do indeed "view" the situation in that way.

The notion extends to strings of more than one character. Consider this simple example:

IF "BRAT" > "BROTHER" THEN PRINT "YES"

The first two characters in these two strings are identical, and the *less-than* decision is based on the third character. The BRAT string is indeed *less than* the BROTHER string.

When working with relational operators between strings, BASIC compares the pattern of ASCII values in a left-to-right fashion.

Logical Operators

Table 2-3 shows the logical operators that are directly available from BASIC. Just three of them—AND, OR, and NOT—are available, but they are sufficient to perform any desired logical operation.

Table 2-3 BASIC Logical Operators

Operator	Function
AND	Logical AND
OR	Logical OR
NOT	Logical negation

Used in conjunction with IF. . .THEN conditional statements, the AND and OR operators connect two or more expressions in explicit ways. Consider this general type of AND statement:

IF *expr1* AND *expr2* THEN *expr3*

The literal interpretation of this statement is IF *expr1* is true AND if *expr2* is also true, THEN execute *expr3*. IF either *expr1* or *expr2* is not true, the implication is that computer operations should ignore the action prescribed by *expr3* and go to the next statement in the program.

By way of a specific example:

IF A>=0 AND A<=9 THEN PRINT A

When executing this statement, the computer prints the value currently assigned to variable A only if that value is between 0 and 9, inclusively.

A conditional statement that uses AND operators is satisfied only when *all* of the ANDed expressions are true at the same time.

Consider this general form of a conditional statement that uses an OR operator:

IF *expr1* OR *expr2* THEN *expr3*

The literal interpretation of this statement is IF *expr1* is true, if *expr2* is true, OR if both are true, THEN execute *expr3*. IF both *expr1* and *expr2* are not true, then the implication is that computer operations should ignore the action prescribed by *expr3*, and go to the next statement in the program.

Here is a specific example:

```
IF A<0 OR A>9 THEN END
```

When executing this statement, the program ends if the value currently assigned to variable A is less than 0 or greater than 9.

A conditional statement that uses OR operators is satisfied when one or more of its ORed expressions is true.

The AND and OR operators are both *binary* logical operators in the sense that they connect at least two different expressions. The NOT operator, on the other hand, is an *unary* operator—it applies to a single expression.

The NOT operator reverses the logic of the expression to which it applies. For instance,

```
IF NOT A>10 THEN END
```

This statement literally says, IF the value currently assigned to variable A is NOT greater than 10, then END the program.

Each of the foregoing examples used one particular logical operator, but you often need to use various combinations of them within the same conditional statement.

Boolean Operators

BASIC offers four operators that perform Boolean logical operations on numeric values: NOT, AND, OR, and XOR. The first three also serve as logical operators, as described in the previous section of this chapter. The fourth operator, however, is unique to Boolean operations.

Boolean functions are based on a set of well-defined rules for manipulating binary numbers. Table 2-4 illustrates those rules. Columns A and B represent the given binary values, and C shows the result of the Boolean operation.

Table 2-4 Summary of Essential Boolean Rules

NOT	AND	OR	XOR
A C	A B C	A B C	A B C
0 1	0 0 0	0 0 0	0 0 0
1 0	0 1 0	0 1 1	0 1 1
	1 0 0	1 0 1	1 0 1
	1 1 1	1 1 1	1 1 0

The Boolean NOT operator switches, or inverts, values; it changes a 0 to 1 and switches a value of 1 to 0. The result of the AND operation is 0 in every instance except when the given values are both 1. On the other hand, the result of an OR operation is 1 in every case except where the given values are both 0. And the XOR operation is nearly the same as the OR operation but excludes the situation where both terms are 1.

BASIC can deal with Boolean functions for numeric values of eight bits or less, and that translates into single-byte hexadecimal values or decimal values in the range of −256 through 255. Attempting to apply Boolean operators to larger values results in an **?ILLEGAL QUANTITY** error message.

As indicated in the table of Boolean rules, Boolean functions are designed to work with the binary number system. BASIC, however, is heavily oriented toward the decimal system, and that tends to obscure applications of Boolean functions in BASIC programming. Consider the following comparisons.

Problem:

> Use the Boolean AND operation to set the four leading bits of a binary value to 0 but leave the four lower-order bits unchanged.

Approach to the Solution:

> Logically AND the given value with 00001111—a value that forces the first four bits to 0 and leaves the remaining bits unchanged.

Applying the Solution:

> Let the value to be manipulated be 11011001. ANDing that with 00001111 looks like this:

```
11011001
00001111
--------
00001001
```

The foregoing is a straightforward procedure for anyone who is familiar with the binary number system and the rules of Boolean logic.

Fitting the same application into the context of decimal-oriented BASIC requires converting the relevant binary values to their binary equivalents.

Problem:

> Use the Boolean AND operation to set the four leading bits of a binary value to 0 but leave the four lower-order bits unchanged.

Approach to the Solution:

Logically AND the given value with 15—the decimal equivalent of binary 11110000.

Applying the Solution:

Let the value to be manipulated be 217, the decimal equivalent of binary 11011001. ANDing that value with decimal 15 looks like this on the screen:

```
PRINT 217 AND 15
9
```

In other words, 217 AND 15 is equal to 9. That might seem rather obscure, but the decimal result is equal to the binary result obtained with the first phase of this scenario.

The table of decimal, hexadecimal, and binary values in Appendix A can be helpful when it comes to selecting decimal values to be used for Boolean operations.

It is beyond the scope of the current discussion to suggest the relevant applications of the Boolean operators in the context of the Commodore 128 system. The meaningful and important applications, however, are cited at appropriate places in other parts of this book.

Order of Precedence for Operators

Many programming situations call for including more than one operator within a statement—combinations of more than one arithmetic, relational, and logical operator. This situation is handled by some conventions built into BASIC.

Table 2-5 shows the *order of precedence* for the execution of BASIC's operators. Those having a higher order of precedence are always executed before others having a lower order. Operators having the same order of precedence are executed in a left-to-right sequence.

Suppose that you have written a BASIC statement of this form:

```
A = B+2 – C/16*D
```

The division and multiplication operators have equal but higher precedence than the addition and subtraction operators. Working with the division and multiplication operations in a left-to-right fashion, the computer first divides C by 16, then multiplies the result by D.

Table 2-5 Order of Precedence of BASIC Operator

Operator	Function	Precedence Level
( )	Sign of grouping	8 (Highest precedence)
NOT	Negation (logical)	7
NOT	Inversion (Boolean)	7
−	Negation (arithmetic)	7
↑	Exponentiation	6
*	Multiplication	5
/	Division	5
+	Addition	4
−	Subtraction	4
=	Equal	3
<	Less than	3
>	Greater than	3
<=	Less than or equal to	3
>=	Greater than or equal to	3
< >	Not equal	3
AND	Logical/Boolean AND	2
OR	Logical/Boolean OR	1
XOR	Boolean EXCLUSIVE-OR	0 (Lowest precedence)

Having taken care of the higher-precedence operations, the computer deals with the addition and subtraction operations. These are of equal precedence, so the computer handles them from left to right: add 2 to the value of B, then subtract the result of the earlier division-multiplication operation from the result of the summation.

The same idea applies to all of the operators cited in the table. Notice that all of the relational operators have the same level of precedence, meaning that they will be regarded in a strict left-to-right sequence. Logical operators AND and OR are at the bottom of the list, thereby giving them the lowest level of precedence.

Perhaps a need for setting up BASIC statements according to those fixed orders of precedence seems troublesome for a programmer. That isn't quite the case, however. BASIC includes signs of grouping (parentheses) that take precedence over all other operators. This means that you can specify the operators in any convenient or meaningful sequence, then use sets of parentheses to establish the order of execution.

Recall this statement:

```
A = B+2 − C/16*D
```

You can avoid any troublesome references to the orders of execution by expressing it this way:

```
A = B+2 − (C/(16*D))
```

Knowing that *nested* parenthetical expressions are always executed from innermost to outermost levels, the form of the statement shown in the preceding equation more clearly suggests this literal interpretation: multiply 16 times D, divide the result into C, subtract the result from 2 and add variable B. Having to recall the orders of precedence is far less important when using parentheses to dictate the sequence.

BASIC 7.0 Commands, Statements, and Functions

This section describes, in alphabetical order, all Commodore 128 BASIC commands, statements, and functions. The purpose is to show the proper syntax and, in some instances, suggest typical applications. Most of the descriptions are complete. Others refer to details in other chapters.

Readers who learned BASIC from other sources will find this a handy guide for dealing with differences between Commodore BASIC (actually a version of Microsoft BASIC) and other versions. It is beyond the scope of this book to deal with the general principles of BASIC programming on an elementary level, however, so if you are not already acquainted with the essential elements of programming in BASIC, refer to an appropriate beginner's book.

ABS(*x*) The ABS function returns the absolute, or unsigned, value of *x*, where *x* is a numeric constant, variable, or expression.

Example:

```
PRINT ABS(−3)
```

This statement prints 3 to the screen.

Example:

```
10 FOR K= −5 TO +5
20 PRINT ABS(K);
30 NEXT K
```

Although K takes on this series of values:

−5 −4 −3 −2 −1 0 1 2 3 4 5

the ABS function in line 30 causes the program to print:

5 4 3 2 1 0 1 2 3 4 5

AND AND is used as both a logical and Boolean operator. As a logical operator, it usually is fit into conditional statements such as:

```
IF X=FE AND Y>40 THEN END
```

Both conditions X = FE and Y greater than 40 must be satisfied in order to execute the END statement.

The Boolean AND operator logically ANDs two numeric values. For example:

```
PRINT 3 AND 2
```

This statement prints 1 to the screen. The justification is that binary 11 ANDed with binary 10 is equal to binary 01.

APPEND *#fileno,"filename"* APPEND is a DOS statement that makes possible the addition of more information to the end of an existing disk file, where *fileno* is a logical file number and *filename* is the name of the file to be appended.

Executing the APPEND statement first opens the designated file, then sets the file pointer to the end of the file. By contrast, an OPEN command opens a file but sets the pointer to the beginning of the designated file.

The APPEND feature allows only writing operations to the designated file. You can close an appended file by means of the CLOSE, DCLOSE, or DCLEAR statements.

Example:

```
APPEND #1, "NAMES OF FOLKS"
```

This example opens an existing disk file, NAMES OF FOLKS, for output as file #1. The example also illustrates setting the file pointer to the location immediately following the last item in the file.

See Chapter 3 for more details, examples, and extended versions of the statement.

ASC(*x$*) ASC is a string function that returns the ASCII code number for the first character in *x$*, where *x$* is a string constant, variable, or expression. If *x$* is the null character, the function returns 0.

Example:

```
PRINT ASC("M")
```

This statement prints 77 (the ASCII value for the letter M) to the screen.

Example:

```
M$="HELLO":PRINT ASC(M$)
```

This example first assigns string HELLO to string variable M$, then prints the ASCII value of the first character in that string. The ASCII value of letter H, 72, is printed.

Example:

```
10 M$="HELLO"
20 FOR N=1 TO LEN(M$)
30 PRINT ASC(MID$(M$,N,1))
40 NEXT N
```

This routine prints the ASCII codes for each letter in the string assigned to M$ in line 10.

ATN(*x*) ATN(*x*) is a numeric function that returns the arctangent (inverse tangent) of *x*, where *x* is a numeric constant, variable, or expression.

The ATN function always returns an angular value in units of radian measure. You can convert the result to units of degrees, however, by multiplying it by $180/\pi$.

AUTO *incr* AUTO is a programming aid that automatically generates and prints BASIC line numbers to the screen in increments of *incr*. The idea is to save you the trouble of having to type new line numbers during the keyboard entry process.

The operation is invoked in two steps:

1. Type and enter AUTO *incr* (*incr* being the desired increment between successive line numbers in the program).
2. Enter the line number and BASIC programming for the first line to be AUTO numbered.

Auto-numbering begins after you complete the second step.

While the AUTO feature is enabled, entering a line of BASIC programming and pressing the RETURN key automatically brings up the line number for the next line. When you are done programming, respond to the current line number by pressing the RETURN key. Disable the AUTO feature by entering the AUTO command without specifying the increment, *incr*, parameter.

BACKUP D*source* TO D*dest* BACKUP is a DOS command that is used for making a complete backup copy of a disk, where *source* is the number of the disk drive that contains the disk to be copied and *dest* is the number of the disk drive that contains the disk that is to become the backup copy. Any data residing on the *dest* disk is destroyed during the backup process.

Example:

```
BACKUP D0 TO D1
```

This example copies the entire contents of a disk in drive 0 to a disk in drive 1.

BACKUP works only for systems having two or more disk drives. See Chapter 3 for further details.

BANK *bankno* BANK is a memory-management statement that provides a convenient means for configuring the memory, where *bankno* is a code number between 0 and 15. The default configuration for C128-mode BASIC is one where *bankno* is equal to 15, which makes available the Kernal and BASIC ROM, bank-0 RAM, and the system's I/O features.

Table 2-6 is a summary of bank numbers and the memory configurations associated with each of them. As described in Chapter 14, some of the bank configurations are redundant.

Table 2-6 Summary of Bank Numbers and Corresponding Bank Configurations

bankno	**Bank Configuration**
0	RAM bank 0 only
1	RAM bank 1 only
2	RAM bank 2 only
3	RAM bank 3 only
4	Internal ROM, RAM bank 0, I/O
5	Internal ROM, RAM bank 1, I/O
6	Internal ROM, RAM bank 2, I/O
7	Internal ROM, RAM bank 3, I/O
8	External ROM, RAM bank 0, I/O
9	External ROM, RAM bank 1, I/O
10	External ROM, RAM bank 2, I/O
11	External ROM, RAM bank 3, I/O
12	Kernal, internal ROM (low), RAM bank 0, I/O
13	Kernal, external ROM (low), RAM bank 0, I/O
14	Kernal, BASIC ROM, RAM bank 0, character ROM
15	Kernal, BASIC ROM, RAM bank 0, I/O

BEGIN. . .BEND BEGIN and BEND mark the beginning and end of a series of BASIC statements that are to be executed until a specified condition is met. Mainly used in conjunction with IF. . .THEN statements where the THEN clause is overly complicated, BEGIN . . .BEND is also a valuable structuring tool for programmers who are inclined to use highly structured programming formats.

Compare the examples in Listings 2-1 and 2-2. Line 50 in Listing 2-1 uses a moderately complicated THEN clause composed of five BASIC statements. The version in Listing 2-2 uses a BEGIN. . .BEND statement to simplify the programming structure, BEGIN marks the beginning of the THEN clause and BEND marks its end.

Listing 2-1

```
10 SCNCLR
20 M$="WHAT'S THE POINT IN MAKING HAY IF THE BARN IS EMPTY?"
30 FOR K=0 TO 1
40 IF K=0 THEN PRINT M$:PRINT
50 IF K=1 THEN PRINT:FOR N=LEN(M$) TO 1 STEP
   -1:PRINT MID$(M$,K,1):NEXT N:PRINT
60 NEXT K
70 PRINT:PRINT "-- PENNY LOGIC"
```

Listing 2-2

```
10 SCNCLR
20 M$="WHAT'S THE POINT IN MAKING HAY IF THE BARN IS EMPTY?"
30 FOR K=0 TO 1
40 IF K=0 THEN PRINT M$:PRINT
50 IF K=1 THEN BEGIN
51 PRINT
52 FOR N=LEN(M$) TO 1 STEP -1
53 PRINT MID$(M$,K,1)
54 NEXT N
55 PRINT
56 BEND
60 NEXT K
70 PRINT:PRINT "-- PENNY LOGIC"
```

BEND See BEGIN. . .BEND

BLOAD "*filename*",*devno* BLOAD is a DOS command that loads a binary-coded file, *filename*, from device, *devno*. Load a file from the current disk drive by setting *devno* to 8. Omit the *devno* parameter to load the file from cassette tape.

The following example loads a binary file called LETON for the current disk drive:

```
BLOAD "LETON",8
```

Use the BOOT command to load and run binary (machine language) program files.

This chapter has more details, including procedures for loading the file to alternate RAM addresses and bank configurations.

BOOT "*filename*" The BOOT command loads and initiates the execution of a machine-language program, *filename*, that exists on the current disk.

See Chapter 3 for details about creating auto-BOOT programs.

BOX *x1,y1,x1,y2* BOX is a bit-mapped graphics statement that makes it quite easy to plot a rectangular figure on the screen. Arguments *x1* and *y1* mark the coordinate of one corner of the rectangle, whereas *x2* and *y2* represent the coordinate of the opposite corner.

Chapter 7 describes extensions of the statement that make it possible to select the source of color for the rectangle, rotate it, and fill it with a specified color.

BSAVE "*filename*",P*strtaddr* TO P*endaddr* BSAVE is a DOS statement that saves a block of memory to the current disk drive. The block is saved under the name, *filename*. The decimal starting address of the block is *strtaddr* and the end is defined by *endaddr*—the last byte to be saved, plus 1.

Example:

```
BSAVE "PICTURE", P1024 TO P2024
```

This example saves the contents of memory locations 1024 through 2023 to the current disk as PICTURE.

See Chapter 3 for extended versions of the statement that allow the specification of alternative device numbers, drive numbers, and bank configurations.

BUMP(*x*) BUMP is a sprite-graphics function that returns a value indicating the nature of the most recent collision. When *x* is set to 1, the function deals with sprite-to-sprite collisions. When you set *x* to 2, the function deals with collisions between sprites and any other object on the screen.

The value returned by BUMP is a decimal version of an eight-bit binary number where bit positions 0 through 7 correspond to collisions involving sprites 0 through 7. The collision condition must be evaluated by means of Boolean AND expressions that isolate the relevant bit.

Executing the BUMP function automatically restores the BUMP value to 0.

See examples and more details in Chapter 8.

CATALOG CATALOG is a DOS command that displays the file directory on the current disk drive. This command produces the same result as the DIRECTORY command.

CHAR *,x,y* The CHAR statement sets the text/bit-map cursor to a screen location determined by the values of *x* and *y*.

The value that you assign to the *x* parameter determines the column location, 0 through 79. (When you work with the 40-column screen, specifying *x* values larger than 39 wraps around the cursor to the next-lower line.)

The *y* parameter determines the row location, 0 through 24.

Example:

```
CHAR ,10,15:PRINT "X"
```

This routine fixes the text/bit-map cursor to column 10, row 15 and prints an X at that place.

You can simplify the routine in the foregoing example by taking advantage of an extension of the CHAR statement:

CHAR, *x,y,string*

where *string* is a string constant, variable, or expression to be printed at the designated *x,y* location.

```
CHAR ,10,15:,"X"
```

A further extension lets you select whether *string* is printed in the normal or reverse-color format:

CHAR, *x,y,string,rvsflg*

where *rvsflg* is set to 0 (normal color) or 1 (reverse color).

When you work in a bit-mapped mode, the CHAR statement can be extended to specify the color source—background or foreground:

CHAR *colrsrc,x,y*

where setting *colrsrc* to 0 selects the background color and setting *colrsrc* to 1 selects the foreground color.

See Chapters 6 and 7 for more examples.

CHR$(*x*) CHR$(*x*) returns the string value represented by ASCII codex, where *x* is a numeric constant, variable, or expression that has a value between 0 and 255.

Example:

```
10 SCNCLR
20 FOR K=33 TO 95
30 PRINT CHR$(K);
40 NEXT K
```

This BASIC routine uses the CHR$ function to print the main alphanumeric character set on the screen.

CIRCLE *,x,y,xrad,yrad* CIRCLE is a graphics statement that makes rather easy the plotting of elliptical figures, including circles and arcs, to a bit-mapped screen. Arguments *x* and *y* specify the coordinate of the center of the figure, whereas *xrad* and *yrad* specify the maximum radii in horizontal and vertical directions, respectively.

See Chapter 7 for extensions of the CIRCLE statement that allow further options, such as selecting the color source, plotting arcs, rotating the figure, and transforming it to a regular polygon.

CLOSE *#fileno* CLOSE is a DOS statement that closes a file which was originally opened as *fileno* under the OPEN, DOPEN, or APPEND statements.

See more details and examples in Chapter 3.

CLR The CLR statement resets all numeric variables to zero and nulls all strings. The statement is especially useful for filling large, multidimensioned arrays with zeros or null characters. You also can use this statement when you need to reDIMension an array or subscripted variable.

CLR also clears the return lines for any GOSUB, FOR. . .NEXT, BEGIN. . .BEND, and DO loops that might be in effect. For this reason, you must exercise care when using the CLR statement in a BASIC program.

CMD *fileno* CMD sends characters normally printed to the screen to a device previously opened with file number, *fileno*. Follow the routine with a PRINT#*fileno* statement in order to restore the screen as the designated output device.

Example:

```
10 DOPEN#1,"THISCAT,S",W
20 CMD 1
```

```
30 CATALOG
40 PRINT#1
50 CLOSE 1
```

This example opens a sequential disk file, THISCAT, for writing to the disk under file number 1. The CMD command in line 20 directs subsequent screen operations to the disk file. The screen operation in this instance is a catalog of the current disk. Line 40 redirects data to the screen and line 50 closes the file. The overall result is that the current disk catalog is saved on disk as a sequential text file.

Extended version:

CMD *#fileno [,string]*

where *string* is a string constant or variable sent to the designated device the moment the CMD statement is executed. This version is often used as a header or title in text-related operations.

See Chapters 3 and 12 for examples and more information.

COLLECT COLLECT is a DOS "housekeeping" command that removes references to improperly closed files from the current disk. Such files, called *splat files*, are virtually useless and are marked on the directory with an asterisk (*) preceding the file-type designation. Entering the COLLECT command from the keyboard eliminates splat files and makes space available for more useful information.

COLLISION *type,lineno* COLLISION is a sprite-graphics statement that specifies a subroutine to be executed when a specified collision occurs. The collision *type* codes are:

1—sprite-to-sprite collision

2—sprite-to-object collision

3—light-pen contact

The *lineno* parameter indicates the beginning of a collision-handling subroutine.

When the designated type of collision occurs, the system completes the execution of the current BASIC statement, then does a GOSUB to the collision handler. A RETURN statement in the collision-handling subroutine returns program execution to where it left off.

Omitting the *lineno* parameter from the COLLISION statement turns off the corresponding collision-interrupt feature.

Use the BUMP statement where necessary to determine which sprites were involved in a collision situation.

See Chapter 8 for more details and examples.

COLOR *srce,colr* BASIC's COLOR statement is the primary color-setting operation. It assigns any of 16 different colors, *colr*, to a specified color source *srce*. Subsequent references to the source number automatically imply the use of the color assigned to it.

Table 2-7 lists the full range of sources and colors. Notice that the colors differ somewhat for the 80- and 40-column screen formats.

Table 2-7 Source and Color Codes

(A) Color Sources

srce	**Source**
0	40-column background
1	40-column foreground
2	Multicolor 1
3	Multicolor 2
4	40-column border
5	40-80-column character
6	80-column background

(B) Color Codes for 40- and 80-Column Screens

40-Column Colors		**80-Column Colors**	
colr	**Color**	*colr*	**Color**
1	Black	1	Black
2	White	2	White
3	Red	3	Red
4	Cyan	4	Cyan
5	Purple	5	Purple
6	Green	6	Green
7	Blue	7	Blue
8	Yellow	8	Yellow
9	Orange	9	Dark Purple
10	Brown	10	Dark Yellow
11	Light Red	11	Light Red
12	Dark Gray	12	Dark Cyan
13	Medium Gray	13	Medium Gray
14	Light Green	14	Light Green
15	Light Blue	15	Light Blue
16	Light Gray	16	Light Gray

See further details and examples in Chapters 6, 8 and 9.

CONCAT "*filename1*" TO "*filename2*" CONCAT is a DOS command that merges (concatenates) one disk-based data file, *filename1*, to the end of another, *filename2*. You cannot use the procedure with program (PRG) files.

See Chapter 3 for further information, including extensions that allow options for different drive and device numbers.

CONT CONT is a command that can be used for resuming the execution of a BASIC program halted under the following circumstances:

- Execution of a STOP statement within the program
- Execution of an END statement within the program
- Execution of a STOP keystroke

CONT is normally used as a program debugging tool. When a program is interrupted in one of the three ways just listed, you can enter the CONT command to resume operations from the beginning of the next program line.

If the program cannot be resumed in this fashion, the system prints the **?CAN'T CONTINUE** error message.

You cannot use CONT as a statement within a BASIC program.

COPY "*srcfilename*" TO "*desfilename*" This form of the COPY command copies one disk file called *srcfilename* to the same disk but under file name, *desfilename.*

See Chapter 3 for more details and an extended version of COPY that supports different combinations of drive and device numbers.

COS(*x*) COS(*x*) is a numeric function that returns the trigonometric cosine of angle *x*, where *x* is expressed in units of radian measure.

In instances where it is more convenient to express the angle in degrees, convert it to radians by multiplying it by $\pi/180$.

Example:

```
PRINT COS(A*π/180)
```

This routine prints the cosine of angle A as expressed in degrees.

DATA *item list* DATA is a non-executable statement that contains the *list* of constants to be read by a READ statement. The items in the list can be numeric or string constants that are separated by commas. You don't need to enclose in quotes the string constants in a DATA listing.

You can mix numerical and string constants within the same DATA list but only if the corresponding READ operation specifies the correct variable type.

Example:

```
10 FOR N=1 TO 5
20 READ A:PRINT A
30 NEXT N
40 DATA 100,200,300,400,500
```

This example reads and prints the numeric constants, one at a time, from the DATA list.

Example:

```
10 FOR N=1 TO 5
20 READ A$:PRINT A$
30 NEXT N
40 DATA HARRY,GEORGE,RALPH,CINDY,JUDY
```

The example reads and prints the string constants in the DATA list.

Example:

```
10 FOR N=1 TO 4
20 READ N$,A:PRINT N$,A
30 NEXT N
40 DATA SUSAN,20,JENNIFER,18,MIKE,22,TED,21
```

Line 20 in this example reads a string constant as N$, followed by a numeric value read as A. Notice that the DATA listing carries variable types in the same sequence—string followed by numeric value.

You can place DATA listings at any convenient location in a BASIC program.

See the READ and RESTORE statements for more examples and relevant details.

DCLEAR DCLEAR is a DOS statement that closes all files and clears the disk channels. See also Chapter 3.

DCLOSE DCLOSE is a DOS statement that closes all files for disk device 8. You can use an extension of the statement to close selected files:

DCLOSE#*fileno*

See Chapter 3 for examples and more details.

DEC(*string*) The DEC function returns the decimal value of a string constant or variable that represents a hexadecimal value in the range of $0000 through $FFFF.

Example:

```
PRINT DEC("F000")
```

This example prints 61440—the decimal version of $F000.

See the HEX$ function for converting decimal values to hexadecimal notation.

DEF FN *name*(*numvar*)=function DEF FN is a powerful function with which you establish custom arithmetic functions for later use in the program. Once the function is defined, it is called *name* and uses a numeric variable, *numvar*, as an argument. In the definition statement, *function* specifies the exact nature of the custom function.

Example:

```
DEF FNRAD(ANG)=ANG*π/180
```

This example defines a function to be cited as RAD(*var*), where *var* is a numeric constant, variable, or expression. The function is one that converts angles from units of degrees to units of radian measure. Later in the program, the following function returns the radian form of any angle, *var*, that is expressed in degrees:

FN RAD(*var*)

Failing to define the function before calling it in the program results in an **?UNDEF'D FUNCTION** error message.

DELETE *strtline-endline* Use the DELETE command to delete a range of BASIC line numbers and their programming from an existing program. Deletion begins with line number *strtline* and ends at *endline*, inclusively. Here are some variations:

DELETE *strtline*: delete single line, *strtline*
DELETE *strtline-*: delete lines from *strtline* through the end of the program
DELETE *-endline*: delete lines from the beginning through line *endline*

DELETE is a direct command and thus cannot be applied to a statement within a program.

DIM *var* (*x*[,*y*. . .]) Use the DIM statement for DIMensioning numeric and string arrays, where *var* is the variable name and *x*, *y*. . . are the DIMension parameters.

Example:

```
DIM N(10,20)
```

This statement DIMensions variable N as an 11 x 21 numeric array: 0 through 10, 0 through 20.

Example:

```
DIM M$(2,2,4)
```

This statement DIMensions a 3 x 3 x 5 string array, M$. The next example DIMensions two different arrays.

Example:

```
DIM N(20,5),M$(14,10)
```

BASIC automatically DIMensions subscripted variables up to an index of 10. The following operation, for example, does not require a DIM statement because the subscript values do not exceed 10:

```
FOR K=0 TO 5:L(K)=2:NEXT
```

On the other hand, the DIM statement is quite necessary in the next example:

```
DIM L(20):FOR K=0 TO 20:L(K)=2:NEXT K
```

Arrays that specify the same variable name cannot be DIMensioned more than one time in the course of a program, unless a CLR statement precedes the subsequent DIM statement. For that reason, most programmers DIMension arrays within the first few lines of a program.

DIRECTORY DIRECTORY is a DOS command that displays the contents of the directory file for the disk in the current disk drive. This command is identical to the CATALOG command.

See Chapter 3 for extended versions of the command that allow for alternative drive numbers, device numbers, and wildcard listings.

DLOAD "*filename*" DLOAD is a DOS command that loads a BASIC program, *filename*, from the current disk drive.

See Chapter 3 for extended versions of DLOAD that allow for alternative drive and device numbers.

DO. . .LOOP Statements DO and LOOP work together to define the beginning and ending of a series of programmed statements to be executed in a repetitive fashion. The following example prints an unlimited number of X characters to the screen:

```
10 DO
20 PRINT "X";
30 LOOP
```

This example loops indefinitely and illustrates the notion that such primitive DO. . .LOOP statements are worthless. Such statements have to be extended to include provisions for terminating the looping action under a specified set of circumstances.

One such extension uses an UNTIL expression. The general idea is to DO a set of steps and LOOP UNTIL a given condition is met. The routine in Listing 2-3 keeps track of the number of characters printed to the screen and LOOPs only UNTIL there are 10 of them.

Listing 2-3

```
10 N=0
20 DO
30 PRINT "X";
40 N=N+1
50 LOOP UNTIL N=10
60 PRINT:PRINT "DONE"
```

Rather than running a DO. . .LOOP until a given condition is met, often it is more convenient to run the loop WHILE a specified condition exists. Consider the version of the X-printing routine that is shown in Listing 2-4.

Listing 2-4

```
10 N=0
20 DO
30 PRINT "X";
40 N=N+1
50 LOOP WHILE N<10
60 PRINT:PRINT "DONE"
```

Finally, the family of DO. . .LOOP statements offers a brute-force technique for breaking out of the loop: EXIT. The program in Listing 2-5 prints ten X characters but uses the EXIT option to end the procedure.

Listing 2-5

```
10 N=0
20 DO
30 PRINT "X";
40 N=N+1
50 IF N=10 THEN EXIT
60 LOOP
70 PRINT:PRINT "DONE"
```

The EXIT option is rarely used as the primary mechanism for terminating a DO. . .LOOP operation. UNTIL and WHILE are far more meaningful and convenient. EXIT is more often used as a secondary, or "emergency," technique for breaking away from a LOOP UNTIL or LOOP WHILE operation, responding to disk-system error, for example.

DOPEN#*fileno,"filename"* DOPEN is a general-purpose DOS command used for opening a disk file to be read or write to sequential and relative text files. The desired logical file number is *fileno*, and *filename* is the file-directory name.

To open a sequential file for reading operations, use:

```
DOPEN#fileno,"filename"
```

then apply GET# and INPUT# statements to read the text information.

To open a sequential file for writing operations, use:

```
DOPEN#fileno,"filename",W
```

and apply the PRINT# statement to write text information to the file.

To open a relative file for writing operations, use:

```
DOPEN#fileno,"filename",Lreclen,W
```

where *reclen* is the number of bytes set aside for each record in the file.

See Chapter 3 for examples and more information about using sequential and relative text files.

DRAW *,x1,y1* TO *x2,y2* DRAW is a bit-mapped graphics statement that plots a straight line between two points, from a point having coordinate *x1,y1* to one having coordinate *x2,y2*.

Omitting the reference to the second coordinate plots a single point at *x1,y1:*

```
DRAW ,x1,y1
```

Extend the command to plot straight lines between more than two points in succession. The following example plots a triangle on the screen:

```
DRAW ,25,10 TO 50,50 TO 0,50 TO 25,10
```

See Chapter 7 for a complete discussion of the DRAW statement.

DSAVE *"filename"* DSAVE is a DOS command that saves a program file, *filename*, to the current disk drive.

See Chapter 3 for extensions of the command that allow alternative drive and device numbers.

DS DS is a reserved numeric variable that is assigned a decimal value which indicates the current DOS block status. When a DOS error occurs, as signaled by the blinking green light on the disk-drive unit, any reference to DS clears the error condition.

DS is most useful for trapping DOS error conditions. Executing a PRINT DS prints the status code on the screen.

See the DS$ reserved string variable for an extended version of the DOS block status feature. Also see Chapter 3 for more details, additional examples, and a complete listing of DOS status numbers.

**DS$** DS$ is a reserved string variable that is assigned a literal version of the current DOS block status. When a DOS error occurs, as signaled by the blinking green light on the disk-drive unit, any reference to DS$ clears the error condition.

Executing a PRINT DS$ statement shows that the string has this general form:

status code,literal comment,trackno,sectorno

where

status code is a decimal number indicating the current status of the disk-drive block and the value assigned to reserved numeric variable, DS.

literal comment is a literal rendition of the current DOS error or block status.

trackno is a two-digit decimal value usually set to 00 and indicates the number of tracks involved in certain kinds of DOS operations.

sectorno is a two-digit decimal value usually set to 00 and indicates the number of disk sectors involved in certain kinds of DOS operations.

When the 1571 disk drive is first turned on, for example, executing the PRINT DS$ statement prints the following information on the screen:

```
73,CBM DOS V3.0 1571,00,00
```

which indicates comment number 73 and shows that the system is operating under CBM DOS version 3.0 on a 1571 disk drive.

By way of another example, remove the disk from the drive and execute the CATALOG command. Follow that operation with a PRINT DS$ command to clear the error condition and print this sort of comment line:

```
74,DRIVE NOT READY,00,00
```

See Chapter 3 for more details, additional examples, and a complete listing of DOS comments and error conditions.

DVERIFY "*filename*" DVERIFY is a DOS command that compares a file which has been loaded into RAM against the version saved on disk. Select the file with *filename*. DVERIFY runs a byte-by-byte comparison and generates a **?VERIFY ERROR** message in the event that a comparison fails.

See Chapter 3 for more details and examples.

EL EL is a reserved numeric variable that has meaning only when a BASIC error condition occurs, in which case, EL is assigned the line number where the error occurs. EL is most often used as part of a custom error-handling routine.

ELSE ELSE is an optional part of the IF. . .THEN statement.

END BASIC's END statement brings a program to a smooth conclusion. END is especially useful in instances where the last statement to be executed is not included in the last line of the program.

ENVELOPE *envno* ENVELOPE is a sound/music statement that defines the shape of a sound waveform, where *envno* specifies one of ten different envelopes numbered 0 through 9.

The default ENVELOPE sounds mimic certain musical instruments as shown in Table 2-8.

Table 2-8
Default Values for ENVELOPE Statements as Used in Sound and Musical Routines

envno	**Instrument**
0	Piano
1	Accordion
2	Calliope
3	Drum
4	Flute
5	Guitar
6	Harpsichord
7	Organ
8	Trumpet
9	Xylophone

See Chapter 9 for more details and information about extensions of the ENVELOPE statement that allow the programmer to specify customized parameters, such as attack rate, decay rate, sustain duration, release rate, overall waveform, noise content, and pulse width.

ER ER is a reserved numeric variable that has meaning only when a BASIC error condition occurs, in which case, ER is assigned the BASIC error number. See details in a subsequent section of this chapter dealing with custom error-handling routines.

**ERR$** ERR$ is a reserved string variable that has meaning only when a BASIC error condition occurs, in which case, ERR$ is assigned the text rendition of the error message. Find more information in the subsequent section of this chapter dealing with BASIC error-handling procedures.

EXIT EXIT is an optional part of a DO. . .LOOP statement.

EXP(*x*) EXP is a numeric function that returns the value of constant *e* (2.71828182) to the power of *x*, where *x* is a numeric constant, variable, or expression.

FAST The FAST command doubles the operating speed of the system's 8502 microprocessor from the normal 1 MHz rate to 2 MHz. Text and graphics operations can be included in the FAST mode of operation but results are blanked from the screen until the system is returned to SLOW, the 1 MHz rate.

See the SLOW command.

FETCH *#nobytes,instrt,exbno,exstrt* The FETCH statement transfers a block of data from an optional external memory-expansion module to internal RAM, where

nobytes is the number of bytes in the block to be transferred.

instrt is the starting address of the block of internal RAM.

exbno is the external memory bank number (0 through 3).

exstrt is the starting address of the block in external memory.

The STASH statement copies a block of internal RAM/ROM data to external RAM.

See more details and other memory-management procedures in Chapter 14.

FILTER FILTER is a sound music statement that makes possible the filtering of the frequency elements of current sounds. See Chapter 9 for FILTER parameters that allow the selection of cut-off, low-pass, high-pass, band-pass, and resonant qualities.

FN See the DEF FN statement.

FOR. . .NEXT The general form of the FOR. . .NEXT routine is:

FOR *numvar=begin* TO *end:statements:*NEXT *numvar*

The FOR portion of the routine initiates a counting action from value *begin*. The NEXT statement causes the counting action to continue until it reaches the value specified by *end*. The BASIC *statements* inserted between the FOR and NEXT expressions are executed with each count.

While the FOR. . .NEXT loop is counting and executing the statements included in the loop, the current count is assigned to a numeric variable, *numvar*. The *numvar* associated with the NEXT term is optional.

Unless you direct otherwise (as described below), FOR. . .NEXT counts increments in steps of 1. Variable *numvar* is left with a value of *end* + 1 at the conclusion of the looping operation.

Example:

```
10 FOR N=0 TO 9
20 PRINT N
30 NEXT N
```

This example prints integer values 0 through 9.

A variation of the FOR. . .NEXT statement uses a STEP term to adjust the increment between successive counts. The following example uses a STEP value of 2 to print only the even integers between 0 and 100:

```
10 FOR X=0 TO 100 STEP 2
20 PRINT X;
30 NEXT X
```

The following example shows how you can use the STEP feature to increment backwards:

```
10 FOR DWN=10 TO -10 STEP -1
20 PRINT DWN
30 NEXT
```

Many practical applications call for *nesting* one or more FOR . . .NEXT loops. The next example increments and prints values of N but uses a second loop to generate a time delay:

```
10 FOR N=0 TO 9
20 PRINT N;
30 FOR T=0 TO 100
40 NEXT T
50 NEXT N
```

The *outer* FOR. . .NEXT loop increments values of N and executes the statements in lines 20 through 40. The *inner* FOR. . .NEXT loop increments the value of T. Because the inner loop is inserted within the N-loop, the inner loop is executed each time N is incremented. Notice that the FOR statements refer first to variable N and then T, whereas the NEXT statements refer to variable T and then N.

FRE(*x*) FRE is a numeric function that returns the number of bytes of RAM available for BASIC operations. Setting argument *x* to 0 returns the amount of RAM available for BASIC programming. Setting *x* to 1 returns the RAM available for storing BASIC variables.

GET *strvar* The GET statement instructs the system to scan the keyboard for a pressed key. If a key is pressed when the GET statement is executed, the key's character is assigned to string variable, *strvar*. If no key is pressed, the GET statement assigns the null character to *strvar*.

Unlike the INPUT and GETKEY statements, GET does not halt execution of the program until a key is pressed. GET is most useful in routines in which certain sequences of operations repeat until the operator presses a certain key. The following example counts and prints numerals to the screen until you press the S key.

```
10 DO UNTIL K$="S"
20 GET K$
30 PRINT N;
40 N=N+1
50 LOOP
```

You can use the GET statement with a numeric variable, but that combination is not recommended because pressing a non-numeric key causes a **?TYPE MISMATCH** error. You are better off to GET the keystroke as a string variable, test to see whether or not the keystroke represents a numeric key, and if so, use the VAL function to convert the string version to its numeric counterpart.

GETKEY *strvar* The GETKEY statement instructs the system to halt program execution and scan the keyboard until the user presses a key. When a key is pressed, the key's character is assigned to string variable, *strvar*, and program execution resumes from the next BASIC statement.

Unlike the INPUT statement, GET does not require that you press the RETURN key to stop the statement's execution.

The following example deals with a common interactive situation:

```
10 PRINT CHR$(7)
20 PRINT "WANT TO RING THE BELL AGAIN (Y/N)?"
30 GETKEY K$
40 IF K$="Y" THEN 10
50 IF K$="N" THEN END
60 GOTO 30
```

Program line 10 sounds the bell. Line 20 prompts the user to press the Y or N key. Line 30 halts program execution until the user presses any key. If the user responds by pressing the Y key, program line 40 loops the program to the beginning where the bell is sounded and the prompting message is printed again. If the user responds to the prompt by pressing the N key, line 50 brings the program to an end. Line 60 handles the situation where the user presses a key other than Y or N: operations loop back to the GETKEY statement in line 30.

The GETKEY statement can be extended to accept a sequence of keystrokes:

GETKEY *var1,var2,var3,. . .*

where *var* arguments are variable names, preferably string variable names.

GET#*fileno,var* GET fetches a single byte of string or numeric data from a file opened as *fileno* and assigns it to variable, *var*. GET is normally used in instances where an INPUT# statement is inadequate.

See Chapter 3 for more details and specific examples.

GO64 The GO64 command invokes the C64 mode of operation, making possible the running of any program originally written for the Commodore 64 personal computer.

GOSUB *lineno* GOSUB is a program-control statement that directs the execution of a program to a subroutine that begins at the specified line number, *lineno*. Unless the subroutine ends the entire program with an END statement, you must conclude GOSUB with a RETURN statement that returns program execution to the statement that follows the GOSUB.

GOTO *lineno* GOTO is a program-control statement that directs the execution of a program directly to a specified line number, *lineno*.

GRAPHIC *n* The GRAPHIC statement establishes one of the six available graphics modes shown in Table 2-9.

Table 2-9
Summary of GRAPHIC Modes

GRAPHIC *n* Value	Graphic Format
0	40-column text
1	Standard full-screen, bit-mapped graphics
2	Standard split-screen, bit-mapped graphics
3	Multicolor full-screen, bit-mapped graphics
4	Multicolor split-screen, bit-mapped graphics
5	80-column text

See Chapters 6, 7, and 8 for specific applications.

GRAPHIC CLR The Commodore 128 operating system normally allocates a 9K section of RAM for bit-mapped graphics. Executing the GRAPHIC CLR statement opens (deallocates) this area so that it is available for BASIC programming.

Reallocate the area for bit-map usage by executing a GRAPHIC statement that sets up a bit-map mode of operation.

GSHAPE *strvar x,y* GSHAPE is a graphics statement that plots a pre-defined graphic to the screen. You defined the graphic in terms of a string variable, *strvar*, usually by means of an SSHAPE or SPRSAV statement. GSHAPE plots the figure within a rectangular area on the screen, where *x,y* is the coordinate of the upper-left corner of that rectangle.

See Chapter 7 for more details and examples.

HEADER "*diskname*",I*idno* HEADER is a DOS command that formats a disk under the specified disk name and identification number. The *diskname* parameter can be up to 16 characters long, and *idno* can be any two alphanumeric characters.

Example:

```
HEADER "SILLY STUFF",IXX
```

This example formats a disk in the current drive giving the disk the overall name SILLY STUFF and using an identification number, XX.

Omitting the *idno* parameter makes much faster the reformatting of Commodore 128 disk. Specify the *idno* when formatting a new disk or one that was previously formatted on a different kind of computer.

> ***WARNING:*** Formatting a disk destroys access to any information that the disk contains.

HELP The HELP command helps you identify the location of a programming mistake that has just resulted in an error message. Error messages generated during the execution of a BASIC program usually indicate the nature of the error and the line number where the error occurred. Entering the HELP command, or pressing the HELP key, prints the line that contains the error and highlights the faulty statement.

HEX$(*x*) The HEX$ function returns the four-byte hexadecimal version of a decimal value, *x*. The range of decimal values is all integers from 0 through 65535.

The converse operation is DEC.

See Appendix A for more information about computer number systems.

IF. . .THEN IF. . .THEN is BASIC's primary conditional statement. One general form is:

IF *condition* THEN *statement*

This version literally says: IF a given *condition* is met, THEN execute the given *statement*, implying that if the *condition* is not met, the system ignores the given *statement* and goes to the next available statement in the program.

Example:

```
IF X=6 THEN PRINT "6"
```

You can extend the *statement* portion of IF. . .THEN to include a sequence of statements to be executed, each separated by a colon. For example:

```
IF X=6 THEN PRINT "SIX":PRINT:PRINT "DONE":END
```

If variable X is equal to 6 when the routine is executed, it prints SIX, a blank space, and DONE, then the program ends.

You can extend the IF. . .THEN statement to include an ELSE clause. When *condition* fails (X is not equal to 6, for example), the system ignores any following *statement* routines and resumes execution from the next line in the program. Add an ELSE clause to provide an alternative procedure for citing what is to be done if the given *condition* fails. The general form of such a statement is

IF *condition* THEN *statement1* :ELSE *statement2*

If the *condition* is met, the system executes *statement1* then goes to the next line of programming. If the given *condition* is not met, the system skips *statement1* but executes *statement2* before going to the next program line.

Compounded IF. . .THEN statements can become awkward and difficult for other programmers to follow. When your IF. . .THEN statements are becoming complex, take advantage of the BEGIN . . . BEND statements.

INPUT *var* An INPUT statement halts the execution of a program, prints a question mark, awaits a series of key responses from the user, then assigns the keyboard information to string or numeric variable, *var*. The user must press the RETURN key to complete the operation.

The nature of the information entered from the keyboard must match the variable type. A statement such as INPUT X, for example, requires input of a numeric value, whereas INPUT M$ requires a string constant. When the user fails to enter the correct variable type, the system automatically prints a **REDO FROM START** message followed by the question-mark prompt symbol. Unlike most other error-handling routines, **REDO FROM START** does not interrupt the program.

You can enter more than one numeric or string constant from the keyboard under a single INPUT statement. An example of a compound INPUT statement looks like this:

INPUT X,W$,Z

This example expects a numeric constant, a RETURN keystroke, a string constant, a RETURN keystroke, a second numeric constant, and a final RETURN keystroke. Whatever the number of variables cited in a compound INPUT statement, those variables must be separated with a comma and must match the type of constant to be entered from the keyboard.

You can extend the INPUT statement further to include a prompting message that is printed to the screen. The general form of such a statement is:

INPUT "*prompt*";*var*

INPUT#*fileno,var* INPUT# fetches a series of strings or numeric data from a file that has been opened as *fileno*, and the command assigns the data to variable *var*. The data thus fetched must end with a carriage-return character, ASCII 13, or $0D, and include no more than 188 characters.

The system returns a DOS error message, **STRING TOO LONG**, if the data shows more than 188 characters without a carriage return. The screen displays a **FILE DATA ERROR** message if the specified variable type assigned to *var* does not match that of the data to be fetched from the file.

See Chapter 3 for more details and specific examples.

INSTR (*string1,string2*) INSTR is a function that searches *string1* for the first occurrence of a substring, *string2*, and returns the character position where the matchup begins.

Example:

```
PRINT INSTR("PARENTHETICAL","THE")
```

prints the numeral 6 to the screen.

INT(*x*) The INT function returns the next-smaller integer value of any numeric constant, variable, or expression, *x*.

Examples:

`PRINT INT(3.8)` prints 3 to the screen
`PRINT INT(8.3)` prints 8 to the screen
`PRINT INT(−1.2)` prints −2 to the screen

The result of this example is justified on the grounds that negative values farther from zero are considered smaller than those closer to zero.

JOY(*x*) The JOY function is dedicated to external joystick operations, Joystick 1 when *x* is set to 1 and Joystick 2 when *x* is set to 2.

Values greater than 128 indicate that the pushbutton on the joystick assembly is being pressed. The position is then determined by subtracting 128 from the value returned by JOY.

See Chapter 11 for further details and specific examples.

KEY *keyno,string* Use the four function keys located in the upper-right corner of the console for printing up to eight different string expressions to the screen, including BASIC statements and commands. The unSHIFTed versions return strings assigned to keys F1 through F4, and the SHIFTed versions return strings assigned to keys F5 through F8.

Executing the KEY command without including the *keyno* and *string* parameters displays the current string assignments. Using the parameters makes it possible to assign any string expression, *string*, to function-key, *keyno*.

Example:

```
KEY 1,"LIST"+CHR$(13)
```

After entering this command, pressing the F1 key lists the BASIC program currently in RAM. The *string* emulates the keyboard operation: type LIST and press the RETURN key.

The total number of characters for all key assignments must not exceed 241.

See Chapter 10 for more details.

LEFT$(*string,x*) LEFT$ is a function that returns the first *x* characters in the designated string constant, variable, or expression.

Example:

```
PRINT LEFT$("HELLO",3)
```

This example prints HEL—the first three characters in string, HELLO—to the screen.

LEN(*string*) The LEN function returns the number of characters in the designated string constant, variable, or expression.

LET *var=expr* LET is a variable assignment that assigns the value of a constant or expression, *expr*, to a variable name, *var*. Variable types must match—string expressions to string variable names and numeric expressions to numeric variable names.

The LET expression is optional and rarely appears in BASIC programming.

Examples:

```
LET X=1+Y
LET X$="FLIP YOUR WIG"
Z=ABS(E)
MM$=X$+CHR$(32)
```

LIST The LIST command is used for listing to the current output device (usually the screen) a BASIC program that currently resides in RAM. Used alone, LIST displays the entire program listing from beginning to end.

The extended version of the command looks like this:

LIST [strtline][– lastline]

where *strtline* is the line number for the first line to be listed and *lastline* is the last line number. You can use the extended version to list selected portions of a program.

Examples:

LIST lists the entire program
LIST 20 lists line 20 only
LIST 10–100 lists lines 10 through 100
LIST 500– lists from line 500 through the end of the program
LIST -100 lists from the beginning of the program through line 100

LOAD "*filename*",*devno* The LOAD command loads a file, *filename*, from disk or tape into RAM. Setting *devno* to 8 specifies a loading operation from disk. If you set *devno* to 1, the system searches for *filename* on cassette and loads the file into the system. A LOAD command with no file name or device number instructs the system to search for the beginning of the next file on the cassette and load that file into RAM.

An extension of the LOAD command includes a relocate flag:

LOAD "*filename*",*devno,reloflg*

Setting *reloflg* to 0 (the default value) loads the file from the beginning of the current BASIC RAM space. Setting the flag to 1 loads the file beginning from the address where the file was originally saved.

See Chapter 3 for more details and examples.

LOCATE *x,y* Locate is a bit-mapped graphics statement that places the pixel cursor at a desired coordinate on the screen, where *x* represents the horizontal component and *y* equals the vertical component.

You can designate the location parameters, *x* and *y*, as absolute or relative values. If no signs (+ or –) precede a parameter, it is taken as absolute. For example:

LOCATE 60,100

sets the pixel cursor to location 60,100 on the screen.

A sign preceding a location parameter indicates relative relocation: where + indicates a positive direction and − indicates a negative direction. For instance:

```
LOCATE +10,-8
```

This relative-LOCATE expression moves the pixel cursor 10 units to the right and 8 units up from the current location.

You can combine relative and absolute parameters in the same LOCATE statement:

```
LOCATE 100,+20
```

A literal interpretation of this statement is "set the pixel cursor to absolute horizontal position 100 and move it down 20 locations from its current vertical position."

> ***NOTE:*** The negative relative parameter does not function properly on the earlier production models of the Commodore 128. Programmers preparing software for commercial distribution should either avoid the relative-positioning format or use an error-handling routine to deal with relative positioning.

See Chapter 7 for more details and examples.

LOG(*x*) LOG is a numeric function that returns the natural, or base-*e*, logarithm of *x*, where *x* is a numeric constant, variable, or expression that is greater than zero.

LOOP See DO. . .LOOP

MID$(*string,firstchar,numchar*) The MID$ function returns a segment of string characters from a designated string variable or constant, *string*. The segment returned begins from character number *firstchar* and is *numchar* characters long.

Example:

```
PRINT MID$("HELLO",2,3)
```

This statement prints ELL—three consecutive characters, beginning from character number 2 in the string constant HELLO.

Example:

```
10 INPUT "ENTER A SHORT MESSAGE:";G$
20 FOR K=1 TO LEN(G$)
30 PRINT ASC(MID$(G$,K,1));
40 NEXT K
```

This routine prompts the user to enter a string message, which is assigned to variable G$. As K increments from 1 through the length of the string, the statement in program line 30 prints the ASCII code values for each of the characters in succession.

The *numchar* parameter in the MID$ function is actually optional. If you omit *numchar* the function returns character number *numchar* and all remaining characters to the right of it.

Example:

```
PRINT MID$("HELLO",2)
```

This statement prints HELLO to the screen.

MONITOR The MONITOR command switches the Commodore 128 from the BASIC interpreter to the monitor operating system. See details and examples in Chapter 4.

MOVSPR *sprnum,param* MOVSPR is a sprite-positioning statement where *sprnum* is a sprite number (1 through 8) and *param* is a parameter that determines the nature of the operation. The parameters make possible the use of MOVSPR in four different ways:

1. Position the upper-left corner of the designated sprite at absolute screen coordinate *x,y*:

   MOVSPR *sprnum,x,y*

2. Position the upper-left corner of the designated sprite *xdist* and *ydist* pixel locations relative to the current pixel-cursor location:

   MOVSPR *sprnum,+xdist,+ydist*

3. Position the upper-left corner of the designated sprite distance *d* at angle *ang* relative to the current pixel-cursor location:

   MOVSPR *sprnum,d;ang*

4. Move (animation) the designated sprite at angle *ang* relative to the original coordinate, at speed *speed*:

MOVSPR *sprnum,ang #speed*

Angle *ang* is reckoned in degrees and in a clockwise direction. Speed values are 0 through 15, with 15 being the highest speed.

Example:

```
MOVSPR 2,90 #15
```

This statement moves sprite 2 horizontally from left to right at the highest speed.

See Chapter 8 for further details and examples.

NEW NEW is a command that clears existing BASIC programming from RAM and initializes internal BASIC operations. Execute the NEW command before typing a new BASIC program from the keyboard.

You can execute NEW as a statement from a BASIC program but obviously you want to exercise a great deal of care and forethought when doing so.

NEXT See the FOR. . .NEXT statement.

NOT NOT is a high-priority, logical Boolean operator. As a logical operator, NOT reverses the sense of a conditional statement: IF NOT(A = B), for example, is the same as A ≠B. As a Boolean operator, NOT inverts binary bit values—changes 0 to 1 and 1 to 0.

ON *x* GOSUB *line1,line2* . . . ON. . .GOSUB is a control statement that calls a subroutine beginning at one of a list of line numbers, *line1*, *line2*, ... The line number is determined by the current value of integer expression, *x*. If *x* has a value of 1, the statement calls the subroutine specified by the first line-number designation. If *x* is equal to 2, the statement calls the subroutine that begins at the second line number in the list. If *x* is equal to 8, the statement calls the subroutine indicated by the 8th line number in the list.

After executing a given subroutine, program execution resumes from the statement that follows the ON. . .GOSUB that called the subroutine.

If the current value of *x* is 0 or if its value exceeds the number of line numbers in the list, BASIC ignores the ON. . .GOSUB statement and goes to the next program statement.

Example:

```
10 FOR N=1 TO 5
20 ON N GOSUB 100,110,135,100,150
30 NEXT N
```

As the value of N increments from 1 through 5, line 20 calls subroutines that begin at lines 100, 110, 135, 100, and 150 in that order. (You can call the same subroutine more than one time within the list.)

ON *x* GOTO *line1,line2* . . . ON. . .GOTO is a control statement that jumps program execution to one of a list of line numbers, *line1*, *line2*, and so on. The line number is selected by the current value of integer expression, *x*. If *x* has a value of 1, program execution jumps to the first line-number designation. If *x* is equal to 2, the statement forces a jump to the second line number in the list.

If the current value of *x* is 0 or if its value exceeds the number of line numbers in the list, BASIC ignores the ON . . . GOSUB statement and goes to the next program statement.

OPEN *fileno,devno* The OPEN statement is the primary mechanism used to set aside files for input and output operations, including those for the disk drive, cassette recorder, printer, monitor screen, and so on. The *fileno* parameter cites a logical file number, 0 through 128. The device number, *devno*, specifies the kind of device to use the opened file. Table 2-10 summarizes the device numbers for the Commodore 128.

Table 2-10 Summary of Devices and Device Numbers

devno	Device
0	Keyboard
1	Cassette drive
2	RS-232-C communications
3	Screen
4 through 7	Printers
8 through 11	Disk drives
12	(Available for custom applications)

Example:

```
OPEN 1,4
```

This statement opens logical file 1 for output to the line printer.

Certain kinds of file operations, especially those used with cassette and disk drives, require a second element of information that is often called a *secondary address*. This form of the statement looks like

OPEN *fileno,devno,secaddr*

Table 2-11 shows the secondary address parameter, *secaddr*, as relevant to files for certain devices.

Table 2-11 Summary of Relevant Secondary Addresses

Cassette drive

secaddr	**Operation**
0	Open a file for reading operations.
1	Open a file for writing operations.
2	Open a file for writing operations and conclude with an EOT (end-of-table) character.

Disk drive

secaddr	**Operation**
0	Open a file for loading to the computer.
1	Open a file for saving to the disk.
15	Open the disk command channel.

Example:

```
OPEN 15,8,15
```

This statement literally says, OPEN file number 15 to the disk drive as a command channel.

In a manner of speaking, OPEN statements are as important to I/O operations as PRINT statements are to text-screen operations. OPEN offers far more extensions and enhancements than are described here. See more details and examples in Chapters 3 and 12.

OR OR is used as both a logical and a Boolean operator. As a logical operator, OR is usually fit into conditional statements such as:

```
IF X=FE OR Y>40 THEN END
```

The condition is satisfied if X=FE, Y is greater than 40, or both.

The Boolean OR operator logically ORs two numeric values. For example:

```
PRINT 1 OR 2
```

This statement prints a 3 to the screen. The justification is that binary 01 ORed with binary 10 is equal to binary 11.

PAINT *srce,x,y* PAINT is a bit-mapped graphics statement that fills an enclosed area of the screen with a color specified by source, *srce*. The *x* and *y* terms are the coordinate of any point *within* the area to be PAINTed.

See Chapter 7 for more details and specific examples.

PEN(*n*) PEN is a screen-coordinate function that returns the status of a light pen used with the Commodore 128 computer. The parameter returned by the function depends on the integer value assigned to *n* (see Table 2-12).

Table 2-12 Light Pen Parameters Returned by Pen *(n)* Function

n Value	Parameter Returned
0	X component of 40-column, light-pen coordinate
1	Y component of 40-column, light-pen coordinate
2	X component of 80-column, light-pen coordinate
3	Y component of 80-column, light-pen coordinate
4	Pen trigger (any value other than 0 indicates pen contact)

PLAY "*param*" PLAY is a versatile music statement described in detail in Chapter 9.

POS(*x*) The POS function returns the column number of the text cursor's current location. Argument *x* is a "dummy value," has no real significance to the function, and can be any numeric value or numeric variable name.

POT(*x*) POT is an I/O function that returns an integer value between 0 and 255. The number indicates the rotated position of game paddle *x* (1 through 4). The larger the value, the greater the amount of clockwise turn. Pressing the "fire" pushbutton on the game-paddle assembly causes POT to return values of 256 plus the rotation value.

PRINT *expr* PRINT is a statement used for printing information contained in *expr* to the current output device—usually the screen. PRINT also can print lists of numeric constants and strings as well as string constants and expressions.

If you separate the items in a list of expressions with semicolons, the printing of one item begins immediately after the end of a previous one. If you separate the items with commas, each item is printed at the beginning of the next tab-stop column on the screen.

PRINT USING "*format*";*x* PRINT USING is a text-formatting statement that specifies the arrangement of items printed to the screen, where *format* determines the printing format of a constant, variable, or expression, *x*.

Define the *format* string in terms of a series of characters. Figure 2-2 shows the default formatting characters and their relevant variable types.

PRINT#*fileno,item* The PRINT# statement is the primary mechanism for writing numeric and string items to a file previously opened with file number *fileno*.

See examples in Chapters 3 and 12.

Fig. 2-2 Summary of characters relevant for PRINT USING statement

#	Pound sign (U.S.): Fixes the length of a printed numeric or string constant.
+	Plus sign: Forces a + signs to appear ahead of positive numeric values. Force + and − signs to appear in the first column location of the field.
−	Minus sign: Forces a − sign to appear in the first column location of a field for negative-valued numbers.
.	Decimal point: Aligns numeric values with decimal points in the specific column location.
,	Comma: Inserts a comma at designated places in a numeric field specifier.
$	Dollar sign: Inserts a dollar sign in numeric values with the option of fixed or floating dollar signs.
↑↑↑↑	Four up-arrows: Forces all numeric values to be printed in the exponential format.
=	Equal sign: Centers all strings within a specified field.
>	Greater-than: Right justifies strings in a field.

PRINT#*fileno* USING "*format*";*x* The PRINT# USING statement combines the features of PRINT# and PRINT USING described above. PRINT# USING prints numeric or string values, *x*, to an opened file, *fileno*, using the field specified as *format*.

PUDEF"*string*" The PUDEF statement replaces the standard characters in PRINT USING statements with other kinds of characters. The changes are specified by characters in the *string* argument.

The *string* argument can be up to four characters long, where

1. The first character replaces the filler blanks.
2. The second character redefines the comma character.
3. The third character redefines the decimal point.
4. The fourth character redefines the dollar sign.

See the PRINT USING statement.

RCLR(*srce*) RCLR is a function that returns the code for the color currently assigned to color source, *srce*. See the source and color codes as described for the COLOR statement in Table 2-7.

RDOT(*param*) The RDOT function returns numeric information regarding the location of the graphics pixel cursor and its color source. The parameter that is returned depends on the value you assign to the argument of the function, *param*.

param	Parameter
0	Horizontal coordinate of the pixel cursor
1	Vertical coordinate of the pixel cursor
2	Color source of the pixel cursor

See the description of the COLOR statement for a listing of color-source code numbers.

READ *var* READ statements must be used in conjunction with DATA lists. A READ statement sequentially reads items in DATA listings and assigns them to the specified numeric or string variable, *var*.

The variable types must match; that is, READ A$ expects to read string constants from the DATA list, whereas READ X reads only numeric constants. Bear in mind that numbers can be regarded as either numeric or string constants, but string values can be regarded only as strings.

READ statements can be extended to read sequences of items. For example, READ X,Y,M$ reads three items at a time in the designated, left-to-right sequence—two numeric values and a string value.

RECORD#*fileno, recno* RECORD is a DOS statement that sets the position of the file pointer to record number, *recno*, in open file, *fileno*. You can extend the statement to point to a byte within designated logical file and record:

RECORD#*fileno,recno,byteno*

where *byteno* is the byte number.

The allowable range of *fileno* values is 0 through 255, *recno* is 0 through 65535, and *byteno* is 1 through 254.

See the discussion of relative files in Chapter 3.

REM REM is a non-executable statement. You use REM to insert printed text, or REMarks, within a program listing. The text of a REM statement appears on the screen only when the program is LISTed.

Example:

```
10 REM ** COUNT TO TEN **
20 FOR K=1 TO 10:PRINT K:NEXT K
30 END:REM END THE PROGRAM
```

RENAME "*oldname*" TO "newname" RENAME provides a simple means for changing the name of a file that resides on the current disk. The first parameter, *oldname*, refers to the current file name, and the second, *newname*, specifies its new name.

Example:

```
RENAME "FISH" TO "STUFF"
```

Assuming that a file named FISH is on the current disk, this statement renames it STUFF.

RENUMBER The RENUMBER command renumbers the lines in a BASIC program that currently resides in RAM. In its simple form, RENUMBER renumbers the entire program, begins the new numbering format from line 10, and uses increments of 10.

The extended version of the command looks like this:

RENUMBER [*newstart*][,*incr*][,*oldstart*]

where *newstart* is the new starting line number, *incr* is the increment between successive line numbers, and *oldstart* is the old line number where the renumbering is to begin. Default values are 10,10,0—begin renumbered listing with line 10, use increments of 10 between successive line numbers, and renumber the entire program.

Example:

```
RENUMBER 1000,2,100
```

This command literally says, renumber the program so that the renumbered segment begins with line number 1000, uses increments of 2 between lines, and begins the renumbering from line 100 in the current version.

Example:

```
RENUMBER ,5
```

This version renumbers the entire program, begins the renumbered version with line 10, and uses increments of 5 between successive lines.

RESTORE RESTORE makes it possible to reREAD a DATA list, beginning from the first item in the lowest-numbered DATA line.

An extended version provides an opportunity to resume READ operations from the first item in any DATA line:

RESTORE *lineno*

where *lineno* is the DATA line number where the next READ statements are to begin.

Executing a RUN command automatically RESTOREs the item pointer to the first item in the lowest-numbered DATA line.

Listing 2-6

```
10 FOR J=1 TO 2
20 FOR K=1 TO 5
30 READ D$:PRINT D$
40 NEXT K
50 RESTORE
60 NEXT J
70 DATA TOM,DICK,HARRY,SALLY,MUFF
```

The example in Listing 2-6 reads and prints the list of DATA items twice. If it were not for the RESTORE statement in program line 50, the program would run out of data and display an **?OUT OF DATA** error message.

RESUME RESUME is always used in conjunction with a custom BASIC error-handling routine. (See the TRAP statement.) The RESUME statement returns program execution to the instruction that initiated the error-handling routine in the first place.

One alternative version is:

```
RESUME NEXT
```

This version resumes normal program execution from the statement immediately following the one that initiated the error-handling operation.

A third version returns program control to a designated line number:

```
RESUME lineno
```

See discussions of custom error-handling operations in the closing sections of this chapter.

RETURN RETURN is a program-control command that returns operations from a subroutine to the statement following the corresponding GOSUB. The command is meaningless without calling GOSUB or ON. . .GOSUB statement.

RGR(*x*) RGR is a function that returns the current GRAPHIC code number. Argument *x* is a "dummy" argument that can be any valid numeric constant or variable name. See the listing of codes and graphics modes described for the GRAPHICS statement in Table 2-9.

RIGHT$(*str,x*) The RIGHT$ function returns the last *x* characters from a string constant or variable, *str*.

Example:

```
PRINT RIGHT$("HELLO",3)
```

This example prints LLO—the last three letters in the string, HELLO.

RND(*x*) RND is a numeric function that returns a random-number value equal to or greater than 0 but less than 1. The value of argument *x* determines the exact nature of the operation.

Whenever argument *x* is any positive value, RND returns a different random number each time the function is executed. RND(1), for example, represents the most commonly used form of the function.

Setting the argument to 0 *seeds* the pseudo-random number generator. This operation generally is necessary only in programs that use many different randomly chosen numbers.

Using an argument that is less than 0 (a negative number) causes RND to repeat its previous value.

Programs that use randomly generated numbers most often require integer values that are equal to or greater than 1. The programming procedure in such instances has this general form:

```
INT(modulus*RND(1))+lownum
```

where *modulus* is the number of integers to be included in the random series, and *lownum* is the lowest-valued integer in the series. Therefore, if you have an application that calls for generating random integer values in the range of 1 through 9, set *modulus* to 10 and *lownum* to 1.

RSPCOLOR(*reg*) RSPCOLOR is a sprite-graphics function that returns the color value in the designated sprite multicolor register, *reg*. Allowable values for *reg* are 1 and 2, where RSPCOLOR(1) returns the color from multicolor register 1 and RSPCOLOR(2) returns the color from register 2.

You set the color codes returned by this function with the SPRCOLOR statement.

See more details and examples in Chapter 8.

RSPPOS(*sprno,par*) RSPPOS is a sprite-graphics function that returns important animation parameters, position, and speed of a specified sprite, *sprno*. Numeric values assigned to the *par* argument determine which of three sprite parameters is returned:

0—Sprite X position

1—Sprite Y position

2—Sprite speed

See Chapter 8 for more details and specific examples.

RSPRITE(*sprno, par*) RSPRITE is a sprite-graphics function that returns the sprite parameters currently assigned under the SPRITE statement. The *sprno* argument specifies the sprite number and *par* specifies the characteristic shown in Table 2-13.

Table 2-13 Sprite Parameters Returned by RSPRITE Function

***par* Value**	**RSPRITE Value and Interpretation**
0	0 = sprite is disabled 1 = sprite is enabled
1	sprite color (1–16)
2	0 = sprite is displayed in front of objects 1 = sprite is displayed behind objects
3	0 = X-direction is not expanded 1 = X-direction is expanded
4	0 = Y-direction is not expanded 1 = Y-direction is expanded
5	0 = multicolor is not used 1 = multicolor is used

See more details and examples in Chapter 8.

RUN RUN is both a BASIC and DOS command. Used without any parameters or extensions, it begins the execution of a BASIC program from the lowest line number. Used with a line number, RUN begins execution of a BASIC program from that line number.

Example:

```
RUN 100
```

Assuming that a BASIC program is resident in the current RAM bank and that line number 100 is part of the program, this example begins execution of the program at line 100.

As a DOS command, RUN loads a BASIC program from the current disk and begins execution from the lowest-numbered line. The simplest form of the DOS version of RUN is:

RUN "*filename*"

where *filename* is the name of a BASIC program residing on the current disk.

See more details in Chapter 3.

RWINDOW (*param*) RWINDOW is a function that returns the parameters of the current text window, depending on the value that you assign to the argument, *param*:

***param* = 0**—the function returns the number of lines in the current text window

***param* = 1**—the function returns the number of rows in the current text window

***param* = 2**—the function returns the column format of the current text screen, 40- or 80-column screen.

See examples in Chapter 6.

SAVE "*filename*",*devno* SAVE is a statement that saves a program file, *filename*, to disk or cassette tape. Setting *devno* to 8 saves the file to the current disk drive. Setting *devno* to 1 (or omitting it altogether) saves the program on the current cassette drive.

See specific examples of the disk-drive application in Chapter 3.

SCALE *flg,xmax,ymax* Use the sprite-graphics statement, SCALE, for changing the scaling of bit maps in the standard bit-map and multicolor modes. If you set *flag* to 0, the scaling is set to the normal dimensions. The two remaining parameters are thus irrelevant and can be omitted from the statement.

Setting the *flg* term to 1 adjusts the scaling of the graphics screen to suit the horizontal and vertical values specified in software for other computer systems.

In the standard bit-map mode:

xmax values are in the range of 230 through 32767 (default value is 1023)

ymax values are in the range of 200 through 32767

In the multicolor mode:

xmax values are in the range of 160 through 32767 (default value is 511)

ymax values are in the range of 160 through 32767 (default value is 511)

The following example makes the coordinates for an IBM PC high-resolution graphics program wholly compatible with the Commodore 128:

```
SCALE 1,640,200
```

This operation compensates for the fact that the IBM PC's high-resolution screen has a 640-by-200 format.

SCNCLR *mode* SCNCLR clears the screen specified by the *mode* parameters shown in Table 2-14.

Table 2-14 Screens Selectively Cleared by SCNCLR Statement

mode	Screen-Clearing Function
0	Clears the 40-column text screen
1	Clears bit-mapped screen
2	Clears split bit-mapped screen
3	Clears multicolor, bit-mapped screen
4	Clears split multicolor, bit-mapped screen
5	Clears the 80-column text screen

Executing the SCNCLR command without specifying a *mode* parameter clears the current screen.

SCRATCH "*filename*" SCRATCH is a DOS command that deletes a file, *filename,* from the current disk directory.

See Chapter 3 for more details and specific examples.

> ***WARNING:*** Do not attempt to SCRATCH splat files—those marked with an asterisk (*) on the disk directory. Use the COLLECT command instead.

SGN(*x*) SGN is a numeric function that returns integer value −1, 0, or 1, depending on the sign of *x*, where *x* is any numeric constant, variable, or expression.

If *x* is negative, SGN(*x*) returns a value of −1.
If *x* is 0, SGN(*x*) returns a value of 0.
If *x* is positive, SGN(*x*) returns a value of 1.

SIN(*x*) SIN(*x*) is a numeric function that returns the trigonometric sign value of angle *x*, where *x* is an angle expressed in units of radians.

In instances where angles are more conveniently expressed in degrees, you can convert them to units of radian measure by multiplying by $\pi/180$.

Example:

```
PRINT SIN(A*π/180)
```

where A is an angle expressed in units of degrees.

SLEEP *t* SLEEP executes a time delay of a specified period, *t*, where *t* is expressed in seconds.

SLOW The slow command sets the operating speed of the 8502 microprocessor to its default 1MHz rate. The system must be operating at the SLOW rate in order to display any information on the screen.

Also see the FAST command.

SOUND *voice,freq,dur* The SOUND statement sets the key parameters for special sound and musical effects. The simplest version of the statement sets the sound frequency, *freq,* and tone duration, *dur,* for a designated voice register, *voice*.

The sound-interface device (SID) in the Commodore 128 can deal with up to three voices at the same time, so the range of values you can assign to the *voice* parameter is integers 1 through 3. The audio output frequency is proportional to the value that you assign to the *freq* parameter—an integer value from 0 through 65535. The duration of the tone is proportional to the value that you assign to the *dur* parameter (0 through 32767).

You can extend the SOUND command to include a number of waveform options:

SOUND *voice,freq,dur*[,dir][,fmin][,sstep][,wfrm][,pw]

dir—step direction (0 through 2):

0 = up (default)
1 = down
2 = oscillate

fmin—minimum frequency for sweep applications (0 through 65535). Default is 0.

sstep—step value for sweep applications (0 through 32767). Default is 0.

wfrm—waveform (0 through 3)

0 = triangle
1 = sawtooth
2 = variable (default)
3 = noise

pw—pulse width (0 through 4095). Default is 2048.

See Chapter 9 for more details and applications examples.

SPC(*x*) Used with PRINT and PRINT# statements, SPC prints a designated number of spaces, *x*, in succession.

Example:

```
PRINT "X";SPC(8);"Y"
```

This example prints X, eight spaces, and Y.

SPRCOLOR *mcolor1,mcolor2* SPRCOLOR is a sprite statement that assigns colors (1–16) to the two additional color sources available for multicolor sprites. See details and examples in Chapter 8.

SPRDEF The SPRDEF command evokes a utility routine that you can use to define sprites and sprite parameters in an interactive fashion. The routine uses a set of keyboard commands to define a sprite within a gridwork on the screen.

See Chapter 8 for detailed operating instructions.

SPRITE *num,flg,colr,pri,xexp,yexp,mode* SPRITE sets the main characteristics of sprite number, *num*. The remaining parameters are defined in Figure 2-3.

Fig. 2-3 Summary of parameters for SPRITE statement

flg—0 = turn sprite off
1 = turn sprite on

color—sprite color (1–16)

pri—0 = sprite moves in front of objects
1 = sprite moves behind objects

xexp—0 = horizontal expansion off
1 = horizontal expansion on

yexp—0 = vertical expansion off
1 = horizontal expansion on

mode—0 = standard sprite
1 = multicolor sprite

Executing a simplified version, SPRITE *num*, sets the parameters of SPRITE *num* equal to those assigned to the most recently specified sprite.

See more details and examples in Chapter 8.

SPRSAVE *srce,dest* SPRSAVE is a sprite-graphics statement that copies sprite image data from a designated source, *srce*, to a destination, *dest*. You can specify the sources and destinations as sprite numbers (1 through 8) or valid string-variable names.

Examples:

**SPRSAVE 1,S$**—Copy sprite image data from sprite 1 to variable, S$

**SPRSAVE X$,2**—Copy sprite image data from string variable, X$, to sprite 2

SPRSAVE 3,1—Copy sprite image data from sprite 3 to sprite 1

You cannot use the SPRSAVE statement for copying sprite image data from one string to another. You can more easily accomplish copying by a statement such as X$ = S$, anyway.

SQR(*x*) SQR is a numeric function that returns the square-root of *x*, where *x* is any positive-valued numeric constant, variable, or expression.

ST ST is a reserved numeric variable that indicates the status of the most recent I/O operation with external devices. You normally use ST only as part of custom error-handling procedures as described subsequently in this chapter.

STASH ***nobytes,instrt,extstrt,extbank*** STASH is a memory-management command that copies data from a range of internal memory to expansion RAM, where

nobytes—number of bytes to be copied
instrt—starting address of the internal block of memory
extstrt—starting address in the external block
extbank—bank number in external RAM

Before using STASH, you must define by means of a BANK statement the bank number for the internal memory block.

STEP See the FOR. . .NEXT statement.

STOP The STOP command halts the execution of a program and causes the computer to return a message indicating the current line number. You can resume running the program by entering the CONT command.

STOP is often inserted temporarily into a program to halt operations for debugging purposes. This is rarely included in programs intended for use by anyone but the programmer.

STR$(*x*) The STR$ function converts any numeric value, *x*, to a string format.

Example:

```
N$=STR$(128)
```

This statement assigns a string version of 128 to string variable N$. STR$ is the inverse of the VAL function.

SWAP ***nobytes,instrt,extstrt,extbank*** SWAP is a memory-management command that exchanges data between blocks of internal memory and expansion RAM, where

nobytes—number of bytes to be copied
instrt—starting address of the internal block of memory
extstrt—starting address in the external block
extbank—bank number in external RAM

The bank number for the internal memory block must be defined previously by means of a BANK statement.

SYS ***addr*** The SYS statement is used for calling a machine-language routine or Kernal operation that begins at decimal address *addr* in the current memory bank—0 through 65535.

You can invoke the C128 monitor by executing the MONITOR command from BASIC. However, because the monitor begins in ROM address $B000 (decimal 45056) of bank 15, you also can invoke the system monitor by executing this sort of routine:

```
BANK 15:SYS 45056
```

The allowable extensions of the SYS statement make it an especially powerful programming tool for integrating BASIC and faster-running Kernal and machine-coded routines. The general form of the statement is:

SYS *addr*[,*a*][,*x*][,*y*][,*s*]

where *a* is a value to be loaded directly to register A in the 8502 microprocessor; *x*, a value to be loaded to register X; *y*, a value for register Y; and *s*, a value to be loaded to the status register. All these optional values are between decimal 0 and 255.

See the USR function for an alternative technique for executing machine-coded routines from a BASIC program.

TAB(*x*) TAB is a PRINT-formatting function that advances the text cursor *x* columns to the right, where *x* is an integer value between 1 and 255, inclusively.

Example:

```
PRINT TAB(5)"HELLO"
```

This example prints HELLO five column locations to the right of the current cursor position.

When a TAB function carries the cursor beyond the right end of a line, the effect resumes from the beginning of the next line.

Unlike the SPC function, TAB does not print spaces in its path.

TAN(*x*) TAN is a numeric function that returns the trigonometric tangent of an angle *x*, where *x* is expressed in units of radians.

In instances where angles are more conveniently expressed in degrees, you can convert angles to units of radian measure by multiplying each by $\pi/180$.

TEMPO *x* TEMPO sets the tempo of a musical routine generated by PLAY statements. Argument *x* is a numeric constant, variable, or expression in the range of 1 through 255. The larger the value, the faster the tempo. The default value is 8.

See Chapter 9 for examples and more details.

THEN See the IF. . .THEN statement.

TI TI is a reserved numeric variable that indicates the value in the real-time clock counter. Turning on the computer or doing a RESET operation initializes TI at 0. It then increments at a 60Hz rate to a maximum count of 5183999.

The reserved string variable, TI$, uses the value of TI to determine the status of the time-of-day clock. TI is equal to 0 when TI$=000000 and 5183999 when TI$="235959".

See the TI$ reserved variable described below.

**TI$** TI$ is a reserved variable that deals with the time-of-day clock. The first pair of characters indicates the hour (00 through 23); the second pair indicates the minute (00 through 59); and the third, the second (00 through 59).

TI$ is initialized at 000000 when the computer is turned on or RESET. You can set the correct time by assigning the appropriate string value to TI$.

Example:

```
TI$="123148"
```

This example sets the time-of-day clock for 12:31:48. This string also sets the time-of-day counter, represented by reserved numeric constant TI, to the corresponding count.

Having thus set the time-of-day clock, the time can be determined by a simple PRINT TI$ statement.

TO See the FOR. . .NEXT statement.

TRAP *lineno* TRAP *lineno* detects errors in the execution of BASIC programs and jumps to customized error-handling routines that begin at the designated line number, *lineno*. As described in a subsequent section of this chapter, the general idea is to keep a program running in the face of errors that would normally interrupt it.

> ***NOTE:*** TRAP does not work with DOS errors. DOS errors have to be detected by referring to the current value of reserved numeric variable, DS. See the descriptions of the DS and DS$ reserved variables in this section and refer to Chapter 3 for more details and specific examples.

TRON The TRON command enables the system's program-debugging trace feature. After executing the TRON command, BASIC displays line numbers as they are executed.

Use the TROFF command to disable the trace feature.

TROFF The TROFF command disables the trace feature that is turned on by executing the TRON command.

See the TRON command described above.

UNTIL See the DO. . .LOOP statement.

USR(*x*) The primary purpose of the USR function is to pass a value, *x*, to a machine-language subroutine and return a value to BASIC. The USR function cannot stand alone—you must set it up in advance.

The first step is to specify the starting address (entry point) of the machine-language subroutine. Do so by POKEing the LSB of the address to RAM location 4633 ($1219) and the MSB to 4634 ($121A).

When the system executes the USR*(x)* function, the value of *x* is passed to Floating-Point Accumulator #1 (FAC1). Then you can use the value in machine-language programs. At the conclusion of such a program, a value can be returned to the USR function by placing it in FAC1. See the FAC jump table described at addresses $AF00-$AFA2 in Chapter 13.

VAL(*str$*) The VAL function returns a true numeric version of numerals that are expressed in a string format, *str$*. Val*(str$)* is the inverse of the STR$ function.

VERIFY "*filename*",*devno* The VERIFY command compares a disk- or tape-based program, *filename,* against the version previously loaded into RAM. Setting *devno* to a value of 1, or omitting it altogether, verifies a cassette tape file. Setting *defno* to 8 verifies a disk file.

If the two versions mismatch, the system prints the **?VERIFY** error message.

See variations of the command as described in Chapter 3.

VOL *x* The VOL statement sets the volume level for sounds created by the SOUND and PLAY statements. Argument *x* can be any integer value between 0 and 15, with 15 specifying the highest volume level.

WAIT *addr,mask* The WAIT statement completely halts the execution of a program until the data at *addr* satisfies the criteria specified by *mask*. Because the statement halts all internal operations, *addr* must refer to an I/O register that is influenced by activity external to the BASIC interpreter—certain VIC, SID, and CIA operations, for example.

WHILE See the DO. . .LOOP statement.

WIDTH *x* The WIDTH statement sets the width (Y dimension) of graphics lines to single or double width.

***x* = 1**—sets single-line width (default)

***x* = 2**—sets double-line width

WINDOW *topcol,toprow,botcol,botrow* The WINDOW statement provides a means for defining custom text windows. The location of the upper-left corner is specified by column-row values *topcol* and *toprow* and the lower-right corner by *botcol* and *botrow*.

The range of values is:

topcol—0 through 38 for a 40-column screen (default is 0)
0 through 78 for an 80-column screen (default is 0)

toprow—0 through 23 (default is 0)

botcol—1 through 39 for a 40-column screen (default is 39)
1 through 79 for an 80-column screen (default is 79)

botrow—1 through 24 (default is 24)

See Chapter 6 for more details and examples.

XOR(*x1,x2*) XOR is a Boolean operator that returns the EXCLUSIVE-OR value of numeric constants, variables or expressions *x1* and *x2*. Whereas the OR operator returns a binary 1 when either or both terms are equal to 1, XOR returns a binary 1 only when either term is equal to 1—not both.

Keyboard Abbreviations of Basic Operations

Most BASIC commands, statements, and functions can be abbreviated when entered directly from the keyboard. Table 2-15 lists those abbreviations.

Table 2-15 Summary of BASIC Text Abbreviations

Abbreviation	Meaning
ABS	A followed by SHIFT B
APPEND	A followed by SHIFT P
ASC	A followed by SHIFT S
ATN	A followed by SHIFT T
AUTO	A followed by SHIFT U
BACKUP	BA followed by SHIFT C
BANK	B followed by SHIFT A

Table 2-15 (cont.)

Abbreviation	Meaning
BEGIN	B followed by SHIFT E
BEND	BE followed by SHIFT N
BLOAD	B followed by SHIFT L
BOOT	B followed by SHIFT O
BOX	none
BSAVE	B followed by SHIFT S
BUMP	B followed by SHIFT U
CATALOG	C followed by SHIFT A
CHAR	CH followed by SHIFT A
CHR$	C followed by SHIFT H
CIRCLE	C followed by SHIFT I
CLOSE	CL followed by SHIFT O
CLR	C followed by SHIFT L
CMD	C followed by SHIFT M
COLLECT	COLL followed by SHIFT E
COLLISION	COL followed by SHIFT L
COLOR	COL followed by SHIFT O
CONCAT	C followed by SHIFT O
CONT	none
COPY	CO followed by SHIFT P
COS	none
DATA	D followed by SHIFT A
DEC	none
DCLEAR	DCL followed by SHIFT E
DCLOSE	D followed by SHIFT C
DEF FN	none
DELETE	DE followed by SHIFT L
DIM	D followed by SHIFT I
DIRECTORY	DI followed by SHIFT R
DLOAD	D followed by SHIFT L
DO	none
DOPEN	D followed by SHIFT O
DRAW	D followed by SHIFT R
DSAVE	D followed by SHIFT S
DVERIFY	D followed by SHIFT V
EL	none
END	none
ENVELOPE	E followed by SHIFT N
ER	none
ERR$	E followed by SHIFT R
EXIT	EX followed by SHIFT I
EXP	E followed by SHIFT X
FAST	none

Table 2-15 (cont.)

Abbreviation	Meaning
FETCH	F followed by SHIFT E
FILTER	F followed by SHIFT I
FOR	F followed by SHIFT O
FRE	F followed by SHIFT R
FN	none
GET	G followed by SHIFT E
GETKEY	GEK followed by SHIFT E
GET#	none
GOSUB	GO followed by SHIFT S
GO64	none
GOTO	G followed by SHIFT O
GRAPHIC	G followed by SHIFT R
GSHAPE	G followed by SHIFT S
HEADER	HE followed by SHIFT A
HELP and HEX$	H followed by SHIFT E
IF. . .GOTO	none
IF. . .THEN. . .ELSE	none
INPUT	none
INPUT#	I followed by SHIFT N
INSTR	IN followed by SHIFT S
INT	none
JOY	J followed by SHIFT O
KEY	K followed by SHIFT E
LEFT$	LE followed by SHIFT F
LEN	none
LET	L followed by SHIFT E
LIST	L followed by SHIFT I
LOAD	L followed by SHIFT O
LOCATE	LO followed by SHIFT C
LOG	none
LOOP	LO followed by SHIFT O
MID$	M followed by SHIFT I
MONITOR	MO followed by SHIFT N
MOVSPR	M followed by SHIFT O
NEW	none
NEXT	N followed by SHIFT E
ON. . .GOSUB	GO followed by SHIFT S
ON. . .GOTO	G followed by SHIFT O
OPEN	O followed by SHIFT P
PAINT	P followed by SHIFT A
PEEK	PE followed by SHIFT E
PEN	P followed by SHIFT E
PI	none
PLAY	P followed by SHIFT L

Table 2-15 (cont.)

Abbreviation	Meaning
POKE	PO followed by SHIFT K
POS	none
POT	P followed by SHIFT O
PRINT	?
PRINT#	P followed by SHIFT R
PRINT USING	?US followed by SHIFT I
PUDEF	P followed by SHIFT U
RCLR	R followed by SHIFT C
RDOT	R followed by SHIFT D
READ	RE followed by SHIFT A
RECORD	R followed by SHIFT E
REM	none
RENAME	RE followed by SHIFT N
RENUMBER	REN followed by SHIFT U
RESTORE	RE followed by SHIFT S
RESUME	RES followed by SHIFT U
RETURN	RE followed by SHIFT T
RGR	R followed by SHIFT G
RIGHT$	R followed by SHIFT I
RND	R followed by SHIFT N
RREG	R followed by SHIFT R
RSPCOLOR	RSP followed by SHIFT C
RSPOS	R followed by SHIFT S
RSPR	none
RSP;RITE	RSP followed by SHIFT R
RUN	R followed by SHIFT U
RWINDOW	R followed by SHIFT W
SAVE	S followed by SHIFT A
SCALE	SC followed by SHIFT A
SCNCLR	S followed by SHIFT C
SCRATCH	SC followed by SHIFT R
SGN	S followed by SHIFT G
SIN	S followed by SHIFT I
SLEEP	S followed by SHIFT L
SLOW	none
SOUND	S followed by SHIFT O
SPC(	none
SPRCOLOR	SPR followed by SHIFT C
SPRDEF	SPR followed by SHIFT D
SPRITE	S followed by SHIFT P
SPRSAV	SPR followed by SHIFT S
SQR	S followed by SHIFT Q
SSHAPE	S followed by SHIFT S
STASH	S followed by SHIFT T

Table 2-15 (cont.)

Abbreviation	Meaning
ST	none
STEP	ST followed by SHIFT E
STOP	ST followed by SHIFT O
STR$	ST followed by SHIFT R
SWAP	S followed by SHIFT W
SYS	none
TAB(	T followed by SHIFT A
TAN	none
TEMPO	T followed by SHIFT E
TI	none
TI$	none
TO	none
TRAP	T followed by SHIFT R
TROFF	TRO followed by SHIFT F
TRON	TR followed by SHIFT O
UNTIL	U followed by SHIFT N
USR	U followed by SHIFT S
VAL	none
VERIFY	V followed by SHIFT E
VOL	V followed by SHIFT O
WAIT	W followed by SHIFT A
WHILE	W followed by SHIFT H
WIDTH	WI followed by SHIFT D
WINDOW	W followed by SHIFT I
XOR	X followed by SHIFT O

Dealing with BASIC Error Conditions

Commodore BASIC includes a built-in, error-handling protocol. When the interpreter encounters certain kinds of error conditions, the error-handling routine interrupts execution of the statement, prints out a descriptive error message, and shows a relevant line number. For example, running a program that attempts to execute a FOR statement without a corresponding NEXT statement stops the program and brings up the **FOR WITHOUT NEXT** error message.

The built-in, error-handling protocol is mainly intended to be a programming aid—a debugging tool. As annoying as it might seem at times, this protocol stops execution of a program before a disastrous ''crash'' can occur.

BASIC Error Messages and Error Code Numbers

The following paragraphs describe, in alphabetical order, the 41 error conditions, messages, and corresponding error code numbers supported by Commodore BASIC, version 7.0. The disk-operating system (DOS) is an integral part of the BASIC interpreter, and a number of the error messages reflect that fact. See Chapter 3 for other kinds of error conditions unique to the disk I/O channel.

BAD DISK BASIC Error #36

The current disk is damaged or improperly formatted.

BAD SUBSCRIPT BASIC Error #18

This error indicates an improperly DIMensioned array or an attempt to use a subscript larger than specified in the corresponding DIM statement.

BEND NOT FOUND BASIC Error #37

A BEGIN statement is used without a corresponding BEND.

BREAK BASIC Error #30

The BREAK message indicates that either the program has encountered a STOP command within an operating program or that the user has pressed the STOP key during execution of a program.

CAN'T CONTINUE BASIC Error #26

The CONT (CONTinue) command normally is used for resuming the execution of an interrupted program. Certain kinds of interruptions cannot be resumed, however; namely cases where a program has already ended, where the program was interrupted by some other error condition, or where the programmer has done some program editing.

CAN'T RESUME BASIC Error #31

This error occurs only when the program uses a RESUME statement without a valid TRAP scenario.

DEVICE NOT PRESENT BASIC Error #5

Statements that refer to I/O operations for a device not present or improperly connected to the system produce this error condition.

DIRECT MODE ONLY BASIC Error #34

This error condition occurs when the BASIC interpreter encounters a command to be used only in the direct (immediate) keyboard mode. Examples of such commands include AUTO, RENUMBER, TRON, and TROFF.

DIVISION BY ZERO BASIC Error #20

The division-by-zero error occurs whenever an attempt is made to divide any numeric value or expression by 0.

FILE DATA BASIC Error #24

This error condition arises when garbage or meaningless data is read from a disk or tape.

FILE NOT FOUND BASIC Error #4

This error occurs when the system cannot find a designated file name.

FILE NOT OPEN BASIC Error #3

A file must be opened in some fashion before you read or write data to it.

FILE OPEN BASIC Error #2

Once a file is opened, it must be closed before attempting to open it again. Otherwise the FILE OPEN error occurs.

FILE READ BASIC Error #41

The FILE READ error occurs whenever the system encounters a problem after a disk-reading operation begins (such as removing the disk while reading is taking place).

FORMULA TOO COMPLEX BASIC Error #25

This error condition arises when an arithmetic or logical statement is so complex that the individual components overflow the execution stack.

ILLEGAL DEVICE NUMBER BASIC Error #9

This error occurs when you attempt to apply a designated device improperly, such as loading data to read-only devices or reading data from write-only devices.

ILLEGAL DIRECT BASIC Error #21

Certain BASIC statements can be executed only from programmed statements. An ILLEGAL DIRECT results from attempting to execute such statements directly from the keyboard. Examples include INPUT, GET, DEF FN, and READ.

The DIRECT MODE ONLY is the complement of this error.

ILLEGAL QUANTITY BASIC Error #14

This error condition occurs under several different classes of numeric errors: illegal quantities assigned to mathematical functions (such as assigning a value of 0 or a negative value to a LOG function), illegal or nonsense values assigned to certain BASIC statements, and out-of-range values for graphics operations.

LINE NUMBER TOO LARGE BASIC Error #38

The largest BASIC line number is 63999. Typing line numbers of 64000 or greater returns a SYNTAX error message. The LINE NUMBER TOO LARGE error condition occurs only when a RENUMBER command attempts to create line numbers that are larger than 63999.

LOAD BASIC Error #29

Certain classes of data-loading errors yield this error condition. They are not as clearly defined as some of the other loading errors, and the Commodore literature suggests retrying the loading operation.

LOOP NOT FOUND BASIC Error #32

This error condition occurs when you attempt to execute a DO statement without a corresponding LOOP. See the DO. . .LOOP statement.

LOOP WITHOUT DO BASIC Error #33

This error condition occurs when the BASIC interpreter encounters a LOOP statement without a corresponding DO. See the DO. . .LOOP statement.

MISSING FILE NAME BASIC Error #8

Certain file-manipulation routines return this error message when no file name is provided.

NEXT WITHOUT FOR BASIC Error #10

This error condition arises when the BASIC interpreter encounters a NEXT statement without a corresponding FOR. See the FOR. . .NEXT statement.

NO GRAPHICS AREA BASIC Error #35

The NO GRAPHICS AREA error occurs when you attempt to execute graphics statements prior to executing an appropriate GRAPHIC statement.

NOT INPUT FILE BASIC Error #6

Many files have to be specified as input files or output files. The NOT INPUT FILE error condition arises when you attempt to read data from a file opened for write-only operations.

NOT OUTPUT FILE BASIC Error #7

Many files have to be specified as input files or output files. The NOT OUTPUT FILE error occurs when you attempt to write data to a file opened for read-only operations.

OUT OF DATA BASIC Error #13

The OUT OF DATA error results from an attempt to READ more items than exist in the current DATA listings.

OUT OF MEMORY BASIC Error #16

This error occurs when certain kinds of program routines attempt to use more memory space than is normally allocated for them. Examples include:

- The program is using more RAM than is currently allocated for BASIC programming.
- FOR. . .NEXT, DO. . .LOOP, BEGIN. . .BEND, or GOSUB routines are nested too deeply

OVERFLOW BASIC Error #15

The OVERFLOW condition occurs when the result of an arithmetic operation generates a value larger than 1.701411834E +38.

REDIM'D ARRAY BASIC Error #19

Arrays should be DIMensioned only one time during the execution of a program or, alternatively, only after executing the CLR command. Otherwise this error condition occurs.

RETURN WITHOUT GOSUB BASIC Error #12

This error condition arises when the BASIC interpreter attempts to execute a RETURN statement where no corresponding GOSUB is found.

STRING TOO LONG BASIC Error #23

Strings may be up to 255 characters long. Attempting to create a longer string brings up the STRING TOO LONG error.

SYNTAX BASIC Error #11

Usually the most-often encountered error situation, SYNTAX, indicates that the BASIC interpreter is unable to "interpret" the meaning of an element in the program. The message usually results from a typing error.

The SYNTAX error condition also occurs when you assign variable names that include reserved words and after typing BASIC line numbers greater than 63999.

TOO MANY FILES BASIC Error #1

The Commodore 128 can deal with no more than 10 open files at any given time. Attempting to open an eleventh file brings up the TOO MANY FILES error condition.

TYPE MISMATCH BASIC Error #22

Numeric values must be assigned to numeric variables, and string values must be assigned to string variables. Violating that rule brings up the TYPE MISMATCH error.

UNDEF'D FUNCTION BASIC Error #27

This error condition occurs when you attempt to implement a user-defined function, FN, that has not been previously defined by means of a DEF FN.

UNDEF'D STATEMENT BASIC Error #17

This applies where you attempt to branch or loop to a line number that does not exist in the current BASIC program.

UNIMPLEMENTED COMMAND BASIC Error #40

Commodore BASIC, version 7.0, is a variation of standard Microsoft BASIC. The Microsoft BASIC interpreter table includes a few statements not actually implemented by the current version of Commodore BASIC. Examples include OFF and QUIT. Attempting to use these statements returns the UNIMPLEMENTED COMMAND error.

UNRESOLVED REFERENCE BASIC Error #39

BASIC's RENUMBER feature cannot deal with statements that refer to line numbers which do not exist in the current program. The UNRESOLVED REFERENCE error interrupts the renumbering operation and cites the line that contains the unresolved line number.

VERIFY BASIC Error #28

This error condition arises when using the VERIFY command fails to confirm that a file on disk or tape matches the version in RAM.

Reserved Variables for BASIC Error-Handling Routines

BASIC's error-handling protocol assigns information to several reserved variables:

ER—numeric variable that indicates the BASIC error-code number

ERR$(*errno*)—subscripted string variable that contains the text for printing the error message, where *errno* is the error number through 41)

EL—numeric variable that indicates the BASIC line number where the most recent error occurred

A couple of simple demonstrations clearly illustrate the way BASIC uses these reserved variables. First, create a one-line BASIC program guaranteed to bring up a syntax error. For example, enter and run this nonsense program:

```
10 XXXX
```

When you run this program, BASIC's error-handling protocol responds by printing the following sort of message:

```
?SYNTAX ERROR IN 10
```

The message indicates the nature of the error and shows the line number where the error is detected.

Next enter the following command:

```
PRINT ER,ERR$(ER),EL
```

and you will find this sort of response on the screen:

```
11          SYNTAX          10
```

The first number shows the value assigned to ER—the error code number. The listing of BASIC error conditions shows that 11 is indeed the error-code number for the SYNTAX error.

The second item indicates that SYNTAX is assigned to subscripted string variable, ERR$(11), and the final item shows that variable EL has been set to 10, the line number in the program where the error occurred.

Regarding the ERR$ variable, you can print out all of the error messages by running this brief program:

```
FOR K=1 TO 41:PRINT ERR$(K);SPC(2):NEXT K
```

Creating Customized BASIC Error-Handling Routines

BASIC's built-in, error-handling routines are intended to be programmer's aids, and a finished piece of software should be written in such a way that the normal error-handling protocol is never used. It is not enough to make sure that the software contains no programming errors.

Suppose that you are writing a piece of BASIC software which requires the user to type the name of a file to be loaded into the system from the current disk drive. It is naive to assume that the user will always enter a file name that actually resides on the disk and, even less likely, never make a typing error in an entry. If the normal error-handling protocol is in effect, such errors on the part of the user cause the program to "crash." The printed error message might provide some meaningful information about the nature of the error, but the user is forced to restart the program before having another opportunity to set matters right.

Responsibly prepared BASIC software includes provisions for dealing in a far more elegant fashion with all potential errors. That is a matter of overriding the built-in, error-handling protocol and preparing customized routines that are more appropriate.

The general procedure goes like this:

1. Use the TRAP *lineno* statement to disable BASIC's built-in, error-trapping routine and point to the beginning of your own error-handling routines.
2. Write BASIC routines that determine the nature of the potential error conditions and specify how they are to be handled.
3. Use one of several versions of the RESUME statement to resume normal program execution.

TRAP *lineno* This form of BASIC's TRAP statement disables the system's built-in, error-handling features and substitutes the programmer's own routines—routines that begin at program line *lineno*.

```
TRAP
```

The TRAP statement, used without the *lineno* parameter, restores the system's built-in, error-handling features.

RESUME This form of BASIC's RESUME statement causes the system to leave an error-handling routine and resume program execution from the statement where the most recent error condition occurred.

```
RESUME NEXT
```

RESUME NEXT also provides the path out of an error-handling routine, but RESUME NEXT resumes program execution from the statement that follows the one where the most recent error condition occurred.

RESUME *lineno*

This form of the RESUME statement directs the system out of

an error-handling routine to normal programming, beginning at line number *lineno*.

The following routine illustrates a classic programming situation that requires careful error-handling procedures:

```
10 SCNCLR
20 FOR K= -5 TO 5
30 PRINT 1/K
40 NEXT K
```

The intent of the routine is to print the arithmetic inverse of numerals −5 through 5. Everything progresses in good form until K is assigned a value of 0. When that happens, the statement in line 30 interrupts the program and prints **?DIVISION BY ZERO** error message.

The BASIC error number in this case is 20. You can determine this error-code number from the previous list of error messages and code numbers or by executing PRINT ER. The version of the program shown in Listing 2-7 uses TRAP and an error-handling routine to deal with error number 20 in a more elegant and meaningful fashion.

Listing 2-7

```
 5 TRAP 60
10 SCNCLR
20 FOR K= -5 TO 5
30 PRINT 1/K
40 NEXT K
50 END
60 IF ER=20 THEN PRINT "INFINITY":RESUME NEXT
```

The TRAP statement in line 5 instructs the system to jump to line 60 in the event of any BASIC error condition. Line 60 represents an error-handling routine that is executed only if the error happens to be error-number 20—the division-by-zero error. In this example, the routine prints INFINITY on the screen (a reasonable response to a divide-by-zero situation). The RESUME NEXT statement completes the error-handling routine by sending the system to the statement immediately following the one that created the error condition. This happens to be the statement in program line 40.

So the program divides numerals −5 through 5 into 1 and prints INFINITY at the point where K = 0.

The error-handling could be considered complete at this stage of development, but bear in mind that the TRAP *lineno* statement disables *all* of the normal BASIC error-handling operations. You should not consider the scheme finished until it deals with all possible BASIC errors. The version of the program in Listing 2-8 demonstrates the nature of the difficulty by including a syntax error in line 11.

Listing 2-8

```
 5 TRAP 60
10 SCNCLR
11 Z
20 FOR K= -5 TO 5
30 PRINT 1/K
40 NEXT K
50 END
60 IF ER=20 THEN PRINT "INFINITY":RESUME NEXT
```

Run this version. You will see line 10 clearing the screen but no other information. The program simply comes to an end. The TRAP statement detects the syntax error in line 11 and responds by sending operations to program line 60. The error-code number for a BASIC **SYNTAX** error is 11, so line 60 fails. And because there is no further programming, the program simply comes to an end.

Dealing with the problem is a matter of adding a line that handles all other errors, including the syntax error. See line 70 in Listing 2-9.

Listing 2-9

```
 5 TRAP 60
10 SCNCLR
11 Z
20 FOR K= -5 TO 5
30 PRINT 1/K
40 NEXT K
50 END
60 IF ER=20 THEN PRINT "INFINITY":RESUME NEXT
70 TRAP:GOTO EL
```

Program line 70 uses the TRAP statement without the *lineno* parameter to turn off the custom error-handling feature, then it does a GOTO statement that refers to the line where the error occurred, line 11 in this example. The syntax error is thus executed once again, but the TRAP feature is disabled this time and the system responds by printing the familiar **?SYNTAX** error message.

Delete line 11 to eliminate the syntax error. You will see that the program runs smoothly once again.

Tokenized BASIC Formats

BASIC is an interpretive language. It is executed in a statement-by-statement, line-by-line fashion. In order to speed up execution, the text for BASIC's statements and functions is crunched into simple one- or two-byte codes called *tokens*. Table 2-16 summarizes the tokens for BASIC 7.0.

Table 2-16
Summary of BASIC Keywords and Tokens

Keyword	Token Hex	Token Dec	
ABS	B6	182	
AND	AF	175	
APPEND	FE 0E	254	14
ASC	C6	198	
ATN	C1	193	
AUTO	DC	220	
BACKUP	F6	246	
BANK	FE 02	254	2
BEGIN	FE 18	254	24
BEND	FE 19	254	25
BLOAD	FE 11	254	17
BOOT	FE 1B	254	27
BOX	E1	225	
BSAVE	FE 10	254	16
BUMP	CE 03	206	3
CATALOG	FE 06	254	6
CHAR	E0	224	
CHR$	C7	199	
CIRCLE	E2	226	
CLOSE	A0	160	
CLR	9C	156	
CMD	9D	157	
COLLECT	F3	243	
COLLISION	FE 17	254	23
COLOR	E7	231	
CONCAT	FE 13	254	19
CONT	9A	154	
COPY	F4	244	
COS	BE	190	
DATA	83	131	
DCLEAR	FE 15	254	21
DCLOSE	FE 0F	254	15
DEC	D1	209	
DEF FN	96 A5	150	165
DELETE	F7	247	
DIM	86	134	
DIRECTORY	EE	238	
DLOAD	F0	240	
DO	EB	235	
DOPEN	FE 0D	254	13
DRAW	E5	229	
DSAVE	EF	239	
DVERIFY	FE 14	254	20
ELSE	D5	213	
END	80	128	
ENVELOPE	FE 0A	254	10
ERR$	D3	211	
EXIT	ED	237	
EXP	BD	189	
FAST	FE 25	254	37
FETCH	FE 21	254	33

Table 2-16 (cont.)

Keyword	Token		
	Hex	Dec	
FILTER	FE 03	254	3
FN	A5	165	
FOR	81	129	
FRE	B8	184	
GET	A1	161	
GETKEY	A1 F9	161	249
GET#	84	132	
GO64	CB	203	
GOSUB	8D	141	
GOTO	89	137	
GRAPHIC	DE	222	
GSHAPE	E3	227	
HEADER	F1	241	
HELP	EA	234	
HEX$	D2	210	
IF	8B	139	
INPUT	85	133	
INPUT#	84	132	
INSTR	D4	212	
INT	B5	181	
JOY	CF	207	
KEY	F9	249	
LEFT$	C8	200	
LEN	C3	195	
LET	88	136	
LIST	9B	155	
LOAD	93	147	
LOCATE	E6	230	
LOG	BC	188	
LOOP	EC	220	
MID$	CA	202	
MONITOR	FA	250	
MOVSPR	FE 06	254	6
NEW	A2	162	
NEXT	82	130	
NOT	A8	168	
ON	91	145	
OPEN	9F	159	
OR	B0	176	
PAINT	DF	223	
PEEK	C2	194	
PEN	CE 04	206	4
PI	FF	255	
PLAY	FE 04	254	4
POINTER	CE 0A	206	10
POKE	97	151	
POS	B9	185	
POT	CE 02	206	2
PRINT	99	153	
PRINT#	98	152	
PUDEF	DD	221	

Table 2-16 (cont.)

Keyword	Token		
	Hex	Dec	
RCLR	CD	205	
RDOT	D0	208	
READ	87	135	
RECORD	FE 12	254	18
REM	8F	143	
RENAME	F5	245	
RENUMBER	F8	248	
RESTORE	8C	140	
RESUME	D6	214	
RETURN	8E	142	
RGR	CC	204	
RIGHT$	C9	201	
RND	BB	187	
RREG	FE 09	254	9
RSPCOLOR	CE 07	206	7
RSPPOS	CE 05	206	5
RSPRITE	CE 06	206	6
RUN	8A	138	
RWINDOW	CE 09	206	9
SAVE	94	148	
SCALE	E9	233	
SCNCLR	E8	232	
SCRATCH	F2	242	
SGN	B4	180	
SIN	BF	191	
SLEEP	FE 0B	254	11
SLOW	FE 26	254	38
SOUND	DA	218	
SPC	A6	166	
SPRCOLOR	FE 08	254	8
SPRDEF	FE 1D	254	29
SPRITE	FE 07	254	7
SPRSAV	FE 16	254	22
SQR	BA	186	
SSHAPE	E4	228	
STASH	FE 1F	254	31
STEP	A9	169	
STOP	90	144	
STR$	C4	196	
SWAP	FE 23	254	35
SYS	9E	157	
TAB	A3	163	
TAN	C0	192	
TEMPO	FE 05	254	5
THEN	A7	167	
TO	A4	164	
TRAP	D7	215	
TRON	D8	216	
TROFF	D9	217	
UNTIL	FC	252	
USING	FB	251	

Table 2-16 (cont.)

Keyword	Token		
	Hex	Dec	
USR	B7	183	
VAL	C5	197	
VERIFY	95	149	
VOL	DB	219	
WAIT	92	146	
WHILE	FD	253	
WIDTH	FE 1C	254	28
WINDOW	FE 1A	254	26
XOR	CE 08	206	8

The text for a BASIC program normally begins at $1C00 or $4000, depending on whether or not the block of RAM beginning at $1C00 is allocated for bit-mapped graphics operations. Each line of BASIC programming, as portrayed in RAM, begins with two bytes that indicate the actual address of the start of the next line. The next two bytes represent the line number of the current line. The remainder of non-zero bytes carry the BASIC tokens and ASCII versions of numerical and string variable names and constants. The line always concludes with a $00 byte.

3

DOS Operating and Programming Procedures

The combination of a Commodore 128 personal computer and the 1571 disk drive provides a powerful and dynamic disk-operating system (DOS). Unlike many other personal computers, most of the programming for the disk drive operations is contained in the drive unit rather than the host computer. The disk-drive is actually a small computer in its own right. It is run by its own 6505 microprocessor and is supported by 32K of ROM and 2K of RAM. None of that steals any operating time or memory space from the host computer.

The purpose of this chapter is to outline the procedures for using the C128/1571 system. It is impossible to describe all of the features in full detail in a book of this scope. The subject is worthy of a book of its own. The discussions are limited to the 1571 disk drive. Although many of the suggested procedures apply equally well to the Commodore 64 and C64 operating mode, the material is specifically prepared for the Commodore 128 operating in its C128 mode. Furthermore, the descriptions of disk formatting apply only to the GCR disk format.

Preliminary Considerations

A good many Commodore-128 users do not expect much from the disk system beyond formatting new disks, loading and running BASIC and machine-language programs, saving their own BASIC programs, and perhaps cleaning up a disk by scratching unwanted programs. Chapter 1 provides most of the information necessary for operating the system to that extent.

This chapter also describes those procedures but offers a number of alternatives and refinements as well. The material is organized generally according to the kinds of tasks that most programmers would like to use: formatting a disk, working with the disk directory, saving programs, loading programs, erasing them, copying material from one disk to another, and generally manipulating the data.

Subtopics are included within some of those categories. The procedures for saving and loading programs, for example, depend on whether the program is a BASIC program or a machine-language program. Both kinds of programs appear on a disk directory as PRG files. BASIC programs are more conveniently saved and loaded from BASIC, but machine-language programs can be saved from BASIC or in the system monitor with equal ease.

These topics and their variations deal just with PRG files. Other kinds of files contain text data. Data files cannot be executed as program files. Rather, they are recordings of information, such as a list of telephone numbers and coordinates of stars in the sky, that are used by PRG files. Two kinds of data (text) files exist: sequential (SEQ) and relative (REL).

DOS-Related Commands, Functions, and Statements

The highest-level DOS commands are executed under BASIC 7.0—the BASIC that is inherent to C128 mode. Being the highest-level DOS commands implies they are the simplest to use. One simple command often executes a handful of different, lower-level commands in an automatic fashion.

You pay a price for that convenience, though. Someone has decided what they think you want to do, and they devise the high-level commands accordingly. Their ideas might not line up exactly with yours, and if you use the BASIC 7.0 commands exclusively, you are missing out on some other opportunities.

Chapter 2 describes the entire family of BASIC commands in detail. The following summaries of BASIC commands are limited to those most directly related to DOS operations. Some commands are specific to disk operations, whereas others apply to serial I/O operations in general.

This section also lists the Kernal routines most useful for executing DOS operations from machine language programming. Direct-access disk commands, those working on the most primitive track-and-sector levels, are described in the closing section of this chapter.

BASIC Commands Specific to DOS

The following BASIC commands are specifically designed for DOS operations and, in a few instances, cassette operations. Forthcoming discussions cite applications of most of these commands.

APPEND—Open an existing sequential text file for adding more text information.

BACKUP—Duplicate a disk in one disk drive to a disk in a second drive.

BLOAD—Load a binary file.

BOOT—Load and run a binary file.

BSAVE—Save a binary file.

CATALOG—Display the current disk directory.

COLLECT—Deallocate disk space previously allocated for improperly closed (splat) files.

CONCAT—Add one disk-based text file to the end of another on the same disk.

COPY—Copy a specified file from one disk to another.

DCLEAR—Clear all channels and close all disk files.

DCLOSE—Close specified disk files.

DIRECTORY—Display the current disk directory.

DLOAD—Load a BASIC program file.

DOPEN—Open a disk file.

DSAVE—Save a BASIC program file.

DVERIFY—Compare a disk file against the version loaded in RAM.

HEADER—Format a disk.

LOAD—Load a specified program file.

RECORD#—Adjust the position of the record pointer in a relative file.

RENAME—Change the name of a current disk file.

SAVE—Save a program file.

SCRATCH—Erase a file name from the disk directory and deallocate the disk space originally devoted to the file.

VERIFY—Compare a disk file against the version loaded in RAM.

BASIC Serial I/O Commands Relevant to DOS Operations

The following BASIC statements apply to serial I/O operations in general but are limited to those most useful for DOS operations. CLOSE and OPEN often can be replaced with their simpler counterparts, DCLOSE and DOPEN. The remaining statements—GET#, INPUT#, and PRINT#—are absolutely essential, however.

CLOSE—Close a specified file.

GET#—Fetch a single character from a file and advance the file pointer.

INPUT#—Fetch a string of data from a file and advance the file pointer.

OPEN—Open a specified file.

PRINT#—Print a string of data to a specified file and advance the file pointer.

DOS-Related Kernal Routines

The system Kernal provides the most convenient means for implementing DOS commands from machine-language programs. In principle, you can do anything in BASIC from a machine-language routine that takes advantage of disk-related Kernal subroutines.

The system Kernal is the key to executing disk-related machine language programs. The following list of Kernal routines includes the ones most useful for DOS procedures. Discussions throughout this chapter cite specific examples of how most of the Kernal routines can be used. See the Kernal jump tables in Chapter 13 for complete descriptions of all Kernal routines.

BOOT $FF53 (65363)—Load and execute an auto-boot binary program on the current disk.

CHKIN $FFC6 (65478)—Specify an open file as an input channel.

CHKOUT $FFC9 (65481)—Specify an open file as an output channel.

CHRIN $FFCF (65487)—Fetch a byte from the current input channel.

CHROUT $FFD2 (65490)—Send a byte to the current output channel.

CLOSE $FFC3 (65475)—Close a file.

CLRCHN $FFCC (65484)—Restore default channels.

GETIN $FFE4 (65508)—Fetch a byte from an input buffer.

LOAD $FFD5 (65493)—Load or verify a binary file.

OPEN $FFC0 (65472)—Open a logical file.

READST $FFB7 (65463)—Fetch the block status error condition of the previous operation.

SAVE $FFD8 (65496)—Save a binary file.

SETLFS $FFBA (65466)—Specify file, device, and secondary-address numbers.

SETNAM $FFBD (65469)—Specify a file name.

DOS-Related Error Conditions

DOS returns errors from three different kinds of sources, sometimes more than one at a time. Assuming that a file named FOO does not exist on your current disk directory, attempting to load a file by that name creates a couple of different error conditions under as many different operating conditions.

Using BASIC's DOS commands, for example, trying to load a file that does not exist brings up two different error conditions. The more obvious is BASIC's error message, **?FILE NOT FOUND ERROR.** That error condition is generated on one level—the BASIC level. But errors involving the disk system are frequently less forgiving than simple BASIC errors of the type described in Chapter 2. Table 3-1 summarizes the BASIC error most directly related to DOS operations.

Table 3-1 BASIC Error Conditions Most Relevant for DOS Operations Returned Through Reserved Variables ER and ERR$

Error	Message
1	TOO MANY FILES
2	FILE OPEN
3	FILE NOT OPEN
4	FILE NOT FOUND
5	DEVICE NOT PRESENT
6	NOT INPUT FILE
7	MISSING FILE NAME
24	FILE DATA
28	VERIFY
29	LOAD
36	BAD DISK
41	FILE READ

In the particular case being described, the green light on the 1571 disk drive begins flashing, which is a clear indication that the error condition runs deeper than simple BASIC. Your approach to handling it requires looking at the reserved variables DS and DS$. Executing a PRINT DS or PRINT DS$ not only provides information regarding the nature of the error, but clears the condition by turning off the annoying, blinking green light.

The DS variable returns a DOS error number that represents one of the error conditions shown in Figure 3-1. Executing PRINT DS$ shows the same error number followed by a verbal description and, where relevant, the track and sector numbers.

Fig. 3-1 Summary of DOS error conditions

Error 0 OK
The last disk operation was successful.

Error 1 FILES SCRATCHED
The last file-erasing operation was successful.

Error 20 READ ERROR
Attempt to access an invalid or non-existent sector.

Error 21 READ ERROR
Sync markers not found.

Error 22 READ ERROR
Checksum error when working with the file header.

Error 23 READ ERROR
Checksum error when working with the drive's internal memory.

Error 24 READ ERROR
Hardware read error.

Error 25 WRITE ERROR
A VERIFY command fails.

Fig. 3-1 (cont.)

Error 26 WRITE PROTECT ON
Attempt to write data to a disk that is mechanically write protected.

Error 27 READ ERROR
Checksum error while reading a block header.

Error 28 WRITE ERROR
A write was successful, but sync is lost for the next sector.

Error 29 DISK ID MISMATCH
Disk initialization is automatic for the 1571 system. The occurrence of this error suggests a defective disk in the area of the disk header.

Error 30 SYNTAX ERROR
Invalid DOS command sent through the command channel.

Error 31 SYNTAX ERROR
Invalid direct-access command sent through the command channel.

Error 32 SYNTAX ERROR
Command-channel command is too long, more than 58 characters.

Error 33 SYNTAX ERROR
Improper use of wildcard characters, * and ?

Error 34 SYNTAX ERROR
Missing file name or colon in a disk command.

Error 39 SYNTAX ERROR
Command-channel command contains data not recognizable by DOS.

Error 50 RECORD NOT PRESENT
Command specifies a relative-file record that does not exist. This is not necessarily a problem when creating new records in a file.

Error 51 OVERFLOW IN RECORD
Attempt to write data to a relative file longer than the specified record length.

Error 52 FILE TOO LARGE
Insufficient disk space for the current relative-file record.

Error 60 WRITE FILE OPEN
Attempt to open a file for reading operations when it is still open for writing.

Error 61 FILE NOT OPEN
Attempt to access a file not yet open.

Error 62 FILE NOT FOUND
Attempt to read from a file that does not exist.

Error 63 FILE EXISTS
Attempt to save to a file that already exists.

Fig. 3-1 (cont.)

Error 64 FILE TYPE MISMATCH
File name is in the current directory, but the application does not match the file type assigned to it.

Error 65 NO BLOCK
Attempt to use a Block-Allocate command for a block already allocated.

Error 66 ILLEGAL TRACK AND SECTOR
Attempt to access a track or sector that does not exist on the current disk.

Error 70 NO CHANNEL
Attempt to use a channel that is not available or to open too many files at one time.

Error 71 DIRECTORY ERROR
Directory data does not make sense.

Error 72 DISK FULL
Disk is full or using more than 144 files.

Error 73 DOS MISMATCH
Attempt to use a disk formatted in a way the 1571 cannot understand.

Error 74 DRIVE NOT READY
Attempt to access an empty drive or a disk not formatted.

Attempting to DLOAD a file that doesn't exist returns a BASIC error, **?FILE NOT FOUND.** Doing a PRINT DS returns the DOS error code 62. Doing PRINT DS$ returns this sort of message:

```
62, FILE NOT FOUND,00,00
```

A third kind of DOS error can occur. It is far less obvious, because it does not interrupt the execution of a program and does not cause the green light on the disk drive to flash on and off. It is a block-status error, which you can detect by looking at the value currently assigned to reserved variable ST or fetching the status of an open command channel. Table 3-2 shows the block status conditions relevant to DOS operations.

You need to deal with DOS error conditions in virtually all programs that refer to disk operations. Truly responsible software authors write programs that do not "crash," even when the user makes mistakes. Discussions throughout this chapter cite applications of DOS error-handling procedures, although error handling is sometimes sacrificed in the examples for the sake of clarity.

Table 3-2 Summary of DOS Error Conditions Returned Through Reserved Variable ST and from Disk Command Block

Condition	Description
ST = 0	block-status errors
ST = 16	VERIFY error
ST = 64	End-of-file error
ST = −128	Device does not exist

The Disk Directory

A disk directory is actually handled as a file in its own right. The directory is structured when a disk is first formatted, and subsequent DOS operations keep it updated with regard to current file names, file types and the number of blocks devoted to each file, and the total number of blocks that remain available on the disk.

The DIRECTORY and CATALOG commands perform the same tasks and use the same general syntactic forms. Used without any of their optional extensions, DIRECTORY and CATALOG display the entire directory for the disk in the default disk drive (device 8, drive 0). The listing is always directed to the screen. However, procedures described in following text make possible the direction of the disk directory to other kinds of output devices, including the disk itself.

A directory listing begins with a heading that shows, from left to right, the current drive number, disk name, disk identification code, and a two-character code that indicates the version of DOS being used—2A for the Commodore 128 system described throughout this book.

The system then lists the disk directory. Each line of the listing shows the number of blocks devoted to the file, the file name, and the file type. The listing ends with a notation that shows the number of unused blocks remaining on the disk.

In the case of long directory listings, there is a good chance the items will be printed too quickly to be read. When that poses a problem:

- Pressing the RUN/STOP key aborts the directory listing altogether.
- Pressing the NO SCROLL key stops the listing until you press any other key.
- Holding down the C= key slows the listing rate.

You can extend the DIRECTORY and CATALOG commands to specify a drive number, device number, and wildcard string:

DIRECTORY [D*driveno*][,U*devno*][,*wildstr*]

or

CATALOG [D*driveno*][,U*devno*][,*wildstr*]

where *driveno* is a drive number, *devno* is a disk-drive device number (usually 8), and *wildstr* is a wildcard string.

Wildcard strings generally are used for limiting the number of files printed to the screen. Suppose that you only want to know the number of blocks devoted to a program file named GEORGE. That being the case, executing CATALOG GEORGE or DIRECTORY GEORGE lists the data for that single file.

There are two special wildcard characters that can be used for listing groups of files with similar file names. A question-mark character (?) is a wildcard symbol for any single character. You use an asterisk (*) in place of any number of characters.

Suppose that a disk directory contains files having the following names:

```
STOOPID
STOOPY
1STOOGE
2STOOGE
STRIP.1
STRIP.2
STOOP
```

Executing a CATALOG or DIRECTORY command lists all of those files. The following version of a CATALOG command, however, lists only STRIP.1 and STRIP.2:

STRIP.?

This command literally says: "List all directory files beginning with STRIP followed by a period and any other single character."

Suppose, however, that you want to see a directory of all files that begin with STOO. An appropriate wildcard version would be:

DIRECTORY "STOO*"

This one lists STOOPID, STOOPY and STOOP.

A DIRECTORY* or CATALOG* command lists all directory items.

You can use DIRECTORY and CATALOG as programmed statements as well as keyboard commands.

Disk Formatting Procedures

All disks must be formatted before they can be used by a particular disk operating system. What is more, the disks must be formatted for the particular system to use them. The implications of these facts are that unused disks have to be formatted before they can be used and disks that might have been formatted on a different brand of computer must be formatted again before they can be used with the C128/1571 system.

The formatting operation assigns a disk name and identification code and defines the track sector format and disk directory.

Once a disk has been formatted as described in this section, you don't need to format it again. In fact, you shouldn't reformat a disk unless you are willing to lose track of all the data saved on it.

> ***WARNING:*** Formatting a disk destroys references to any data saved on it.

Formatting with BASIC's HEADER Command

The simplest procedure for formatting a new disk is through BASIC's HEADER command:

HEADER "*diskname*",I*idno*

where *diskname* is any name to be assigned to the disk (up to 16 characters), and *idno* is an identification code (exactly two characters). The following example formats a new disk as FUN&GAMES with an identification code, 01:

```
HEADER "FUN&GAMES",I01
```

Before executing this sort of formatting command, insert the disk to be formatted into disk drive 0. Immediately after you enter the command, the system prints this prompting message on the screen:

ARE YOU SURE?

Entering the Y character in response to this question begins the formatting operation. Entering any other character aborts the operation.

The formatting procedure requires several moments. The system returns the READY prompt message when the job is done.

Disks that have been formatted on the C128/1571 system at some earlier time can be reformatted in a much shorter period of time by omitting the I*idno* parameter:

HEADER "*diskname*"

This abbreviated version of the procedure simply clears the disk directory, bypassing the time-consuming task of setting up the soft-sectored blocks. Reformatted disks take on the specified disk name but retain the original identification number. The "quick-formatting" procedure is generally used only for clearing the directory and, in effect, wiping it clean for further use.

The HEADER command, as described thus far, assumes that the disk to be formatted is located in drive 0. That is the only choice in a single-drive system. When you are working with a multiple-drive system, you can extend the command to point to a drive other than 0:

HEADER "*diskname*",I*idno*,D*driveno*

where *driveno* is the drive number for the drive that contains the disk to be formatted.

More sophisticated C128/1571 systems might use disk-drive device numbers other than 8. The HEADER command assumes device number 8, but you can change that:

HEADER "*diskname*",I*idno*,D*driveno*,U*devno*

or

HEADER "*diskname*",I*idno*,D*driveno*,ON U*devno*

The following example tests the idea, even if you are using a single-drive system with a device number of 8:

HEADER "FUN&GAMES",I01,D0,ON U8

You can include the HEADER command as a programming statement in a BASIC routine, replacing the disk name and identification number with string variables and the drive and device numbers with numeric variables. An example of such a routine would be one that simplifies the task of formatting a series of disks by prompting the user to insert new disks and by automatically incrementing the identification numbers.

Formatting with BASIC File Commands

The procedure for formatting a disk with the older BASIC 2.0 commands:

1. Insert the disk to be formatted into the disk drive.
2. Use the OPEN command to open a command channel to the disk drive.
3. Send the NEW command and its parameters.
4. Use the CLOSE command to close the channel when the formatting is done.

   The general form of the NEW command is:

   N*driveno:diskname,idno*

where *driveno* is the disk drive number, *diskname* is the desired disk name (up to 16 characters), and *idno* is the disk's identification number (any two alphanumeric characters). The following sequence of steps represents a one-for-one implementation of the general procedure cited above.

1. Insert the disk to be formatted into the disk drive.
2. OPEN a command channel to the disk drive as channel number 15:

   ```
   OPEN15,8,15
   ```

3. Send the NEW command to the channel, specifying drive 0, disk name FUN&GAMES, and identification number 01:

   ```
   PRINT#15,"N0:FUN&GAMES,01"
   ```

4. When formatting is done and the system returns the READY prompt, CLOSE the command channel:

   ```
   CLOSE15
   ```

Using the command-string feature of the OPEN command makes possible the simplification of the procedure. The next example performs the same tasks as Steps 2 and 3 in the previous example.

```
OPEN15,8,15,"N0:FUN&GAMES,01"
```

Be sure to CLOSE the channel when the formatting operation is done.

Formatting with Kernal File Routines

The Kernal includes a couple of routines that make it possible to format a disk through a machine-language program. The programming follows this general procedure:

1. Load an ASCII version of the NEW command to a convenient RAM location.
2. Set up and execute the SETLFS Kernal routine.
   A. Logical file number to register A
   B. Device number to register X
   C. Secondary address to register Y
   D. Call SETLFS routine at $FFBA
3. Set up and execute the SETNAM Kernal routine.
   A. Load length of file name (from Step 1) to register A
   B. Load LSB of starting address of file name to register X
   C. Load MSB of starting address of file name to register Y
   D. Call SETNAM routine at $FFBD
4. Call the OPEN routine at $FFC0.
5. Set up and execute the CLOSE Kernal routine.
   A. Load logical file number to register A
   B. Call CLOSE routine at $FFC3

For all practical purposes, the NEW command cited in Step 1 is identical to the BASIC file command described in the previous section of this chapter:

N*driveno:diskname,idno*

where *driveno* is the disk drive number, *diskname* is the desired disk name (up to 16 characters), and *idno* is the disk's identification number (any two alphanumeric characters). The difference here is that the command has to be loaded into RAM in an ASCII-coded form.

The example in Listing 3-1 formats a disk in drive 0, using TRYIT as the disk name and XX as the identification code. This information is loaded as ASCII characters in addresses $F1500 through $F150A.

Listing 3-1

```
>F1500 4E 30 3A 54 52 59 49 54:N0:TRYIT
>F1508 2C 58 58                :,XX

LDA #$0F          ;LOGICAL FILE NUMBER, 15, TO A
LDX #$08          ;DEVICE NUMBER, 8, TO X
LDY #$0F          ;SECONDARY ADDRESS, 15, TO Y
JSR $FFBA         ;CALL SETLFS
LDA #$0B          ;LENGTH OF FILE NAME, 11, TO A
LDX #$00          ;LSB OF NAME ADDRESS TO X
LDY #$15          ;MSB OF NAME ADDRESS TO Y
JSR $FFBD         ;CALL SETNAM
JSR $FFC0         ;CALL OPEN
LDA #$0F          ;LOGICAL FILE NUMBER,15, TO A
JSR $FFC3         ;CALL CLOSE
```

The semicolons and text that follows them should not be typed as part of the miniassembler operations for entering this program.

Procedures for Saving Programs on Disk

Chapter 1 describes the simplest procedure for saving a BASIC program to the current disk. This section describes that procedure, extensions of it, and alternative procedures for saving BASIC programs. The following also cites a variety of techniques for saving machine-language programs and files of machine-language data.

Saving BASIC Programs with DSAVE

BASIC's DSAVE command makes rather easy the saving of a BASIC program that is currently in system RAM. The simplest form of the command is

DSAVE "*filename*"

where *filename* is the name, up to 16 characters, to be assigned to the program in the disk directory. The command assumes the program is to be saved on disk-drive 0 (device 8, drive 0). The following example saves a BASIC program on disk as WHY ME:

```
DSAVE "WHY ME"
```

You can use the DSVE command as a program statement. In that case, the file name can be shown as a string variable, *but only if the string variable is enclosed in parentheses.* The following example saves itself on disk as SILLY and lists the current directory:

```
10 F$="SILLY"
20 DSAVE (F$)
30 DIRECTORY
```

Users who have more than one disk drive can select the target drive by extending the DSAVE statement in this fashion:

DSAVE "*filename*",D*driveno*

where *driveno* is the drive number of the unit to receive the BASIC programming. You can save a BASIC program called USEFUL to the disk in drive 1 this way:

DSAVE "USEFUL",D1

For the benefit of users who have altered the device number of a disk drive, you can extend the command to specify the device number as well as drive number:

DSAVE "*filename*",D*driveno*,U*devno*

or

DSAVE "*filename*",D*driveno* ON U*devno*

where *devno* is the current device number.

The DSAVE command has a built-in mechanism that prevents saving a program with the same name as another file in the current disk directory. The disk drive runs and the system returns the READY prompt message, but the program is not saved and the flashing green light on the disk drive indicates that a disk error has occurred. Normally this feature is regarded as beneficial: It prevents the user from accidentally overwriting a file already on the disk. Sometimes, though, not being able to write over a file is a nuisance.

During the course of developing a BASIC programming, save the completed portion of the work on disk from time to time. In such instances, it is convenient to use the same file name each time.

The DSAVE command can be modified to perform that sort of save-with-replace function. You can simply begin the file name with an at (@) character. For example:

DSAVE "@NEWGAME"

This command can be executed any number of times and saves the program as NEWGAME each time. The NEWGAME file appears just one time in the directory, and the at character does not appear as part of the name.

Saving BASIC Programs with SAVE

The SAVE command is available to Commodore 128 users. This command is a bit more awkward than the DSAVE command described previously, but SAVE is compatible with the earlier C64 environment. You can use this command also to save BASIC programming to cassette tape. The general form of the command is:

SAVE"*driveno:filename*",*devno*

where *filename* is the desired file name (up to 16 characters), *driveno* is the drive number and *devno* is the device number. When saving to disk, *driveno* and *devno* are usually set to 0 and 8, respectively. Omitting those two parameters calls for a saving operation to cassette number 1.

The following example saves a BASIC program on disk as WHY ME:

```
SAVE "0:WHY ME",8
```

You can use SAVE as a program statement as long as the portion enclosed in quotes is represented in a string format and the device number is a constant or numeric variable. The following example saves itself on disk as SILLY and lists the current directory:

```
10 F$="SILLY"
20 SAVE "0:"+F$,8
30 CATALOG
```

Like DSAVE, SAVE normally does not allow you to save a new BASIC program that uses the same name as a file that already exists on the current disk. Executing SAVE with a name already in the directory creates a DOS error condition.

When you want to replace a disk file with one having the same name, simply insert an at (@) character ahead of the drive-number specification. The general form is:

SAVE "@*driveno:filename*",*devno*

A working example looks like this:

```
SAVE "@0:NEWGAME",8
```

The command can be executed any number of times without creating a DOS error. SAVE saves the program as NEWGAME each time, but NEWGAME appears as a single entry in the disk directory. The at character does not appear in the directory listing.

Saving Binary Files from BASIC with BSAVE

The BSAVE command saves the data contained in a specified block of memory. The command is not particular about the purpose or the organization of the data, which can represent a machine language program, tables of ASCII-coded data, ROM routines, or even BASIC programming. BSAVE simply sends data, byte by byte, to the disk.

The simplest form of the command looks like this:

BSAVE "*filename*",P*strtaddr* TO P*endaddr*

where *filename* is the name to be assigned the file on the disk directory, *strtaddr* is the decimal starting address of the block to be saved, and *endaddr* is the ending address of the block, plus 1.

> ***NOTE:*** The ending address in the BSAVE command must be at least one address location beyond the actual end of the file.

The following example saves a block of memory from address 1024 through 2048, assigning the block the name VIDEO1:

```
BSAVE "VIDEO1",P1024 TO P2049
```

If a file is to be saved with a file name that is identical to one already residing on the current disk, the *filename* parameter should begin with an at (@) character. Otherwise the DOS system goes into a **FILE EXISTS** error condition.

An important extension of the BSAVE command specifies the bank number of the block to be saved. Unless specified otherwise, the bank number is 15, but the bank number can be introduced in the command in this general fashion:

BSAVE "*filename*",B*bankno*,P*strtaddr* TO P*endaddr*

where *bankno* is the decimal bank number, 0 through 15.

Incidentally, the starting address parameter, *strtaddr,* is saved on disk as part of the record, but the bank number is not. The real meaning of these facts becomes apparent when working with the complementary command, BLOAD.

As is the case with most BASIC 7.0 commands that deal with DOS operations, you can extend BSAVE further to specify drives and devices other than drive 0 and device number 8. The fully extended version of BSAVE looks like this:

BSAVE "*filename*",D*driveno*,U*devno*,B*bankno*,P*strtaddr* TO P*endaddr*

where *driveno* and *devno* are the drive (0 or 1) and device (8 through 15) numbers, respectively.

You can use BSAVE as a programming statement and replace the *filename* parameter with a string variable and the other parameters with numeric variables.

Saving Binary Files from the Monitor

The file-saving command from the monitor uses this general syntax:

S "*filename*",*devno*,*strtaddr*,*endaddr*

where *filename* is the name to be assigned to the file in the disk directory, *devno* is the decimal device number (usually 8), *strtaddr* is the starting address of the file in hexadecimal notation, and *endaddr* is the address of the last byte to be saved, also using hexadecimal notation. Both address parameters should indicate the bank number as the first of a five-bit address. For example:

```
S "COOKER",8,F1500,F15FF
```

Saving Files with Kernal Routines

The Kernal's SAVE routine provides a convenient technique for saving programs and blocks of data on disk. This routine requires information regarding the starting and ending addresses of the block of memory to be saved on disk. The starting address must be loaded to a pair of adjacent zero-page RAM locations, LSB followed by MSB, and the first of the two addresses must be loaded to register A. The ending address of the block is loaded to registers X and Y, or LSB of the address to register X and MSB to register Y.

The SAVE routine does not stand alone, however. It must be preceded by a SETNAM operation that specifies the file name and a SETLFS operation that opens a disk file.

The procedure outlined below uses TEXTTAB, addresses $2D and $2E, as the zero-page locations required for running the SAVE routine. TEXTTAB also points to the beginning of BASIC programming, so the procedure suggests pushing the current contents onto the stack before setting up SAVE, then replacing the original contents before leaving the program.

1. Load the file name to a block of RAM.
2. Set up and execute Kernal's SETNAM routine.

   A. Length of file name to register A
   B. LSB of file name address to register X
   C. MSB of file name address to register Y
   D. Call SETNAM at $FFBD

3. Set up and execute the Kernal's SETLFS routine.
   A. Logical file number to register A
   B. Device number to register X
   C. Secondary address to register Y
   D. Call SETLFS at $FFBA

4. Push the current content of TEXTTAB onto the stack.
   A. Load content of $2D to register A
   B. Push register A onto stack
   C. Load content of $2E to register A
   D. Push register A onto stack

5. Set up and execute Kernal's SAVE routine.
   A. Load LSB of starting address to TEXTTAB $2D
   B. Load MSB of the starting address to TEXTTAB $2E
   C. Load TEXTTAB pointer, $2D, to register A
   D. Load LSB of ending address to register X
   E. Load MSB of ending address to register Y
   F. Call SAVE at $FFD8

5. Close all files by calling CLALL at $FFE7.

6. Restore the original TEXTTAB values.
   A. Pull MSB of old TEXTTAB from stack
   B. Load to TEXTTAB $2E
   C. Pull LSB of old TEXTTAB from stack
   D. Load to TEXTTAB $2D

7. Return from the routine.

The example in Listing 3-2 is a direct implementation of the recommended procedure for saving a block of memory to disk. The example uses the file name, @MYPROG.1 and saves a block of memory from $1300 through $13FF.

Saving BASIC Programs as ASCII Text Files

The DSAVE and SAVE commands described in preceding text save BASIC programs in their *tokenized* format. That is, the programs are saved in an abbreviated form that replaces the keywords with single-character codes (tokens). Using the tokenized format reduces the number of bytes in a BASIC program and allows it to run much faster. Sometimes, however, you want to save a BASIC program in a non-tokenized format, using the same ASCII text format that creates screen LISTings of the programs.

Listing 3-2

```
>F1403 40 4D 59 50 52 4F 47 2E:@MYPROG.
>F140B 31                     :1

LDA #$09          ;LENGTH OF FILENAME
LDX #$03          ;LSB OF FILENAME ADDR
LDY #$14          ;MSB OF FILENAME ADDR
JSR $FFBD         ;SETNAM
LDA #$01          ;FILE NO.
LDX #$08          ;DEVICE NO.
LDY #$0F          ;SECONDARY ADDR
JSR $FFBA         ;SETLFS
LDA $2D           ;GET LSB OF TEXTTAB
PHA               ;SAVE IT ON STACK
LDA $2E           ;GET MSB OF TEXTTAB
PHA               ;SAVE IT ON STACK
LDA #$00          ;LSB OF START ADDR
STA $2D           ;TO TEXTTAB
LDA #$13          ;MSB OF START ADDR
STA $2E           ;TO TEXTTAB
LDA #$2D          ;TEXTTAB POINTER
LDX #$FF          ;LSB OF END ADDR
LDY #$13          ;MSB OF END ADDR
JSR $FFD8         ;SAVE
JSR $FFE7         ;CLALL TO CLOSE FILES
PLA               ;GET MSB OF OLD TEXTTAB
STA $2E           ;REPLACE IT
PLA               ;GET LSB OF OLD TEXTTAB
STA $2D           ;REPLACE IT
RTS               ;RETURN
```

No special commands are available for saving and loading BASIC programs in an ASCII text format, but the procedure to do so is rather simple. Saving an ASCII-coded version of a BASIC program is simply a matter of directing a LISTing of that program to a disk file rather than the screen.

Suppose that the BASIC program to be saved in ASCII format looks like this:

```
10 SCNLCR
20 FOR K=0 TO 9
30 PRINT "HOWDY"
40 NEXT K
```

The program to be saved as an ASCII file clears the screen, homes the cursor, and prints HOWDY ten times in succession.

Normally, doing a LIST command displays the program on the

screen, and incidentally, so does a LIST 10-40 command. The next step is to add a routine that redirects a LIST 10-40 command to a disk file. For instance:

```
100 DOPEN#1,"@HOWDYDOO,S,W"
110 CMD 1
120 LIST 10-40
130 PRINT#1
140 DCLOSE
```

Line 100—Open a disk file for output as a sequential file.

Line 110—Redirect screen operations to the open disk file.

Line 120—List the portion of the program to be saved.

Line 130—Direct the standard output back to the screen.

Line 140—Close the file.

Listing 3-3 shows how the overall program looks. Lines 10 through 40 represent the program to be saved as ASCII text, and lines 100 through 140 actually do the job.

Listing 3-3

```
10 SCNLCR
20 FOR K=0 TO 9
30 PRINT "HOWDY"
40 NEXT K
100 DOPEN#1,"@HOWDYDOO,S,W"
110 CMD 1
120 LIST 10-40
130 PRINT#1
140 DCLOSE
```

A RUN 100 command executes the disk-save routine, creating a SEQuential text file called HOWDYDOO. As described subsequently in this chapter, you can recover the program by reading it as a sequential file and with a GET# function.

Procedures for Loading Programs from Disk

Chapter 1 describes the simplest procedure for loading BASIC programs from the current disk. This section describes that procedure, extensions of it, and alternative procedures for loading BASIC programs. This text also cites a variety of techniques for loading machine-language programs and files of machine-language data.

Loading BASIC Programs with DLOAD

BASIC's DLOAD command makes rather easy the loading of a BASIC program that resides on the current disk. When loaded in this fashion, the program can be run by executing the RUN command from the keyboard.

The simplest form of the command is

DLOAD "*filename*"

where *filename* is the name of the desired program file in the disk directory. The command assumes the program to be loaded is on disk drive 0 (device 8, drive 0). The following example loads a BASIC program named WHY ME:

DLOAD "WHY ME"

In the event that the designated file is not in the disk's file directory, the system responds with both BASIC and DOS error conditions. The BASIC error appears on the screen as a **?FILE NOT FOUND** message. The DOS version of the error condition flashes the green light on the disk drive. Executing a PRINT DS$ command prints the DOS error string and turns off the flashing green light.

Users who have more than one disk drive can select the source drive by extending the DLOAD statement in this fashion:

DLOAD "*filename*",D*driveno*

where *driveno* is the drive number of the unit that holds the desired BASIC programming. A BASIC program called USEFUL can be loaded from drive 1 this way:

DLOAD "USEFUL",D1

For the benefit of users who have altered the device number of a disk drive, the command can be extended to specify the device number as well as the drive number:

DLOAD "*filename*",D*driveno*,U*devno*

or

DLOAD "*filename*",D*driveno* ON U*devno*

where *devno* is the current device number.

Loading BASIC Programs with LOAD

The LOAD command from BASIC 2.0 is available to Commodore 128 users. This command is a bit more awkward than the DLOAD command, but it is compatible with the earlier C64 environment. You can use LOAD also to save BASIC programming to cassette tape. The general form of the command is

LOAD "*driveno:filename*",*devno*

where *filename* is the name of the file to be loaded, *driveno* is the drive number, and *devno* is the device number. When loading from disk, *driveno* and *devno* are usually set to 0 and 8, respectively. The *driveno*: parameter can be omitted when loading from drive 0. Omitting *driveno* and *devno* parameters, however, assumes the loading is from the current cassette device.

The following example loads a BASIC, disk-based program called WHY ME:

```
LOAD "0:WHY ME",8
```

or

```
LOAD "WHY ME",8
```

BASIC programs are saved sometimes from a block of RAM that is different from the default block. When this is the case, the file begins with an address that marks the starting point of that RAM location. Unless directed otherwise, a subsequent LOAD command loads the file from that starting location.

The LOAD command can be extended to indicate whether the file is to be loaded at the address specified at the beginning of the file or at the normal BASIC RAM area. That extended version looks like this:

LOAD "*driveno:filename*", *devno,relflg*

where *relflg* is set to 0 to load the program at the beginning of normal BASIC RAM space and set to 1 to start loading at the address specified at the beginning of the program file. The default value is 0.

Loading and Running BASIC Programs with RUN

The DLOAD and LOAD commands described in the two previous sections of this chapter simply load a program from disk into RAM.

The programs are executed only after you enter the RUN command. An extended form of the RUN command eliminates the two-step, load-and-run procedure:

RUN "*filename*"

This simple command first loads a program, *filename*, from the current disk drive, then automatically begins executing it.

Unless specified otherwise, the RUN *filename* command uses disk drive 0 as device number 8. This can be changed, however, by extending the command to include these parameters:

RUN "*filename*",D*driveno*,U*devno*

where *driveno* is the desired drive number and *devno* is the alternative device number.

You can also use RUN *filename* as a BASIC programming statement. This notion is especially important when you need to execute a series of programs, each loaded and run from the current disk drive.

Loading Binary Files with BLOAD

The BLOAD command loads a designated binary file from disk to Commodore 128 RAM. The simplest form of the command is

BLOAD "*filename*"

where *filename* is the name of the disk file to be loaded.

If the file is not in the disk directory, the system responds with both BASIC and DOS error conditions. BASIC prints the **?FILE NOT FOUND** message, and DOS flashes the green light on the disk drive.

The BLOAD command, as described thus far, works according to a set of assumptions. For one, the system assumes the file is to be loaded into a block of RAM that is identical to the one used at the time the file was BSAVEd. That original starting address is saved as part of the file, and the BLOAD command uses that address. However, instances exist where you would prefer to load a file into a different block of RAM. You can do this by specifying the alternative starting address in the BLOAD command:

BLOAD "*filename*",P*strtaddr*

where *strtaddr* is the alternative, decimal version of the starting address for the file.

Furthermore, the BLOAD command normally assumes that the file is to be loaded to the current memory bank (bank information is not carried as part of a disk file). An extension of the BLOAD command makes possible the loading of the file into a bank that is different from the current one:

BLOAD "*filename*",B*bankno*,P*strtaddr*

where *bankno* is the bank where the file is to be loaded, 0 through 15.

Finally, the BLOAD command assumes you are using disk drive 0 as device 8. That can be changed by extending the command as follows:

BLOAD "*filename*",D*driveno*,U*devno*,B*bankno*,P*strtaddr*

where *driveno* and *devno* are the alternative drive and device numbers, respectively.

You can use BLOAD as a BASIC programming statement. You can replace the *filename* parameter with a string variable and the remaining parameters with numeric variables.

Loading and Running Binary Programs with BOOT

BASIC's BOOT command loads and runs binary-coded programs in the same way that the RUN command loads and runs BASIC programs. BOOT assumes the program is resident on the current disk.

The simplest form is

BOOT "*filename*"

where *filename* is the name of the machine-language program that is to be loaded and run.

Extensions of the command allow you to specify alternative drive and device numbers:

BOOT "*filename*",*driveno*,U*devno*

Loading Binary Files from the Monitor

The file-loading command from the monitor uses this general syntax:

L "*filename*",*devno*

where *filename* is the name of the file on the current disk and *devno* is the device number (usually 8 for the disk drive). When you omit *devno*, the system assumes the file is to be loaded from cassette tape.

If the designated file name does not exist on the disk, the system returns the error message, **I/O ERROR #4**, and flashes the green light on the disk drive.

When you need to load the file at an address that is different from the one recorded on the file header, you can extend the command to specify an alternative loading address:

L "*filename*",*devno*,*altaddr*

where *altaddr* is the alternative loading address in hexadecimal notation. The alternative address also should begin with a character that specifies the bank, hexadecimal $0 through $F.

Loading Files with Kernal Routines

The Kernal's LOAD routine provides a convenient technique for loading programs and blocks of data from a disk. A simplified version of the routine loads the file to the same address where that file was originally saved. You can extend the routine to point to an alternative loading address. Also, you can use the LOAD routine to verify a segment of memory—comparing the disk file with the data LOAD has loaded into RAM.

The LOAD routine must be preceded by SETNAM to specify the name of the file to be loaded and by SETLFS to open a disk file and determine whether or not the file is loaded to an alternative address. Consider the following procedure:

1. Load the file name to a block of RAM.
2. Set up and execute the Kernal's SETNAM routine:
   - A. Length of file name to register A
   - B. LSB of file-name address to register X
   - C. MSB of file-name address to register Y
   - D. Call SETNAM at $FFBD
3. Set up and execute the Kernal's SETLFS routine:
   - A. Logical file number to register A
   - B. Device number to register X
   - C. Secondary address to register Y; (Use $00 if alternative loading address is to be used or use $0F if file is to be loaded at same address specified during original SAVE)
   - D. Call SETLFS at $FFBA
4. Set up and execute the Kernal's LOAD routine:
   - A. Specify a LOAD or VERIFY operation in register A—$00 = LOAD, $01 = VERIFY
   - B. If original loading address is to be used, contents of registers X and Y are not relevant. Otherwise load LSB of address to register X and MSB of address to register Y
   - C. Call LOAD at $FFD5

5. Close all files by calling CLALL at $FFE7.
6. Return from the routine.

The example in Listing 3-4 is a direct implementation of the recommended procedure for loading a file named @MYPROG.1 to its original address location.

Listing 3-4

```
>F1403 40 4D 59 50 52 4F 47 2E:@MYPROG.
>F140B 31                     :1

LDA #$09                      ;LENGTH OF FILENAME
LDX #$03                      ;LSB OF FILENAME ADDR
LDY #$14                      ;MSB OF FILENAME ADDR
JSR $FFBD                     ;SETNAM
LDA #$01                      ;FILE NO.
LDX #$08                      ;DEVICE NO.
LDY #$0F                      ;SECONDARY ADDR
JSR $FFBA                     ;SETLFS
LDA #$00                      ;SET FOR LOAD
JSR $FFD5                     ;LOAD IT
JSR $FFE7                     ;CLALL TO CLOSE FILES
RTS                           ;RETURN
```

Procedures for Copying Disk Files

The matter of copying a disk file is often considered in the context of transferring a copy of the file from one disk to another. An alternative is to make a copy of a file on the same disk but give the copy a different file name.

Using BASIC's COPY Command

The simplest form of the COPY command makes a copy of an original file on the same disk but with a different file name:

COPY "*oldname*" TO "*newname*"

where *oldname* is the name already assigned to the original version of the file and *newname* is the name to be given to the copy. The following example makes a copy of MIKE and assigns the name MIKE/C1 to it:

```
COPY "MIKE" TO "MIKE/C1"
```

The COPY command can copy a file from one disk to another

and use the same file name but only on a two-drive system. That form of the command looks like this:

```
COPY Dsrcdrive,"srcname" TO Ddesdrive,"desname"
```

srcdrive—drive number of the disk drive containing the original file

srcname—name of the original file

desdrive—drive number of the disk drive where the copy is to be made

desname—name of the copied file

The following example copies a file named MIKE from drive 0 to the disk in drive 1:

```
COPY D0,"MIKE" TO D1,"MIKE"
```

Unless specified otherwise, the device number for the COPY command is 8. By extending the COPY command, you can specify an alternative device number:

```
COPY [Ddriveno,]"oldname" TO [Ddriveno,]"newname"[,
Udevno]
```

Using COPY as a BASIC File Command

You can OPEN a command channel, then use a PRINT# operation to copy a file with a different name to the same disk. The procedure does not support directly copying files from one disk to another.

The general procedure looks like this:

```
OPEN fileno,devno,secaddr
PRINT#fileno,"Cdriveno:newname=oldname
"CLOSEfileno
```

fileno—logical file number used for the procedure

devno—disk device number, usually 8

secaddr—secondary address; always 15 for opening a disk-drive command channel

driveno—disk drive number, usually 0

newname—file name to be assigned to the copy

oldname—file name of the file to be copied

The next example uses the procedure to copy an existing file, MIKE, as SAM.

```
OPEN 1,8,15
PRINT#1,"C0:SAM=MIKE"
CLOSE1
```

The technique offers an opportunity to make backup copies of working files. Consider this example:

```
10 SCNCLR
20 OPEN 1,8,15
30 INPUT "WHAT FILE TO BACKUP";F$
40 PRINT#1,"C0:"+F$+".BAK="+F$
50 CLOSE 1
```

This routine prompts the user to enter a file name. The INPUT statement assigns the name to F$. Line 40 then does a COPY routine that copies the user's file with a .BAK extension, which indicates that the copy is a backup. If the user specifies a file name HELLO, the routine makes a copy named HELLO.BAK.

That's fine as long as two conditions are met: (1) the user's file name actually exists on the disk, and (2) the .BAK version does not. In the real world, the user occasionally specifies a non-existent file name. Being able to make backup copies with the same name is a vital part of the whole concept. Thus, the routine should use some error-handling routines to help the user get through a variety of situations in an elegant fashion. The program in Listing 3-5 suggests some techniques for making the program work more reliably.

Listing 3-5

```
10 SCNCLR
20 OPEN 1,8,15
30 INPUT "WHAT FILE TO BACKUP";F$
40 PRINT#1,"C0:"=F$+".BAK="+F$
50 IF DS<20 THEN 90
60 IF DS=62 THEN PRINT "NO SUCH FILE. TRY AGAIN. . .":GOTO 30
70 IF DS=64 THEN PRINT#1,"S0:"+F$+".BAK":GOTO 40
80 PRINT DS$
90 CLOSE 1
```

Line 60 deals with a case where the user's file name does not exist. Line 70 deals with a more likely situation where the user has already made a backup copy and wants to make another. This line actually scratches the old backup file.

Procedures for Cleaning Up Disks

BASIC supports a couple of DOS commands, SCRATCH and COLLECT, intended for keeping disks free of unwanted and irrelevant data. SCRATCH erases a specified file from the disk. COLLECT gets rid of "splat" files.

There are two different kinds of SCRATCH commands. The simpler of the two has this general form:

```
SCRATCH "filename"
```

where *filename* is the name of the file to be scratched. Of course, the file must exist on the disk, and it must not be a splat file (one marked with an asterisk on the disk directory).

When you execute this sort of SCRATCH command, the system prompts: ARE YOU SURE? Respond by entering a Y or N as appropriate.

The SCRATCH command, like the CATALOG and DIRECTORY commands described previously in this chapter, supports wildcard entries. This command thus makes possible the scratching of groups of files having similar kinds of names. The question-mark wildcard character represents any single character, whereas the asterisk wildcard can replace groups of characters. Use this command with care:

```
SCRATCH "*"
```

It deletes every file on the disk.

The default drive and device numbers are 0 and 8, respectively. Use extensions of the command to specify other drive and device numbers:

```
SCRATCH "filename",Ddriveno,Udevno
```

A second version of SCRATCH treats the command as a file command and lends itself more readily to programmed file-scratching operations:

```
PRINT#filenum,"Sdriveno:filename"
```

where *filenum* is a logical file number already used when opening a disk command file. The following example scratches a file named QUE from drive 0:

```
10 OPEN 1,8,15
20 PRINT#1,"S0:QUE"
30 CLOSE 1
```

Programmers often use SCRATCH commands within programs, and in conjunction with error-handling routines, to determine whether a disk drive is ready for saving and loading operations. Such a program can begin with the sort of routine shown in Listing 3-6. An analysis of the routine looks like this:

Line 10—Open a disk command channel.

Line 20—Check for DOS errors.

Line 30—Save the file with an unlikely name.

Line 40—Check for DOS errors.

Line 50—Scratch the trial file.

Line 60—Check for DOS errors.

Line 70—Close the command file.

Line 80—Go to your main programming. Everything is in good order.

Line 90—Beginning of error-checking routine. If there is no error, return to the test procedure.

Line 100—Eliminate the error number from DS$.

Line 110—Eliminate the track and sector numbers from DS$.

Line 120—Print the string portion of the DS$ error message.

Lines 130–160—Print a prompting message, wait for a keystroke, and return to the test procedure.

Listing 3-6

```
10 OPEN 1,8,15
20 GOSUB 90
30 SAVE "@0:%%%%",8
40 GOSUB 90
50 PRINT#1,"S0:%%%%"
60 GOSUB 90
70 CLOSE 1
80 GOTO 170
90 IF DS<20 THEN RETURN
100 EM$=MID$(DS$,4)
110 EM$=LEFT$(EM$,INSTR(EM$,",")-1)
120 PRINT EM$;"."
130 PRINT "CHECK THE DISK AND DRIVE, THEN STRIKE"
140 PRINT "ANY KEY TO CONTINUE . . ."
150 GETKEY K$
160 RETURN
170 REM ⋙ START YOUR MAIN PROGRAMMING HERE
```

The COLLECT command is useful only for getting rid of files that have been saved in some defective fashion. Usually faulty saves are caused by a power interruption during the saving operation. Such files appear on the directory as splat files marked with an asterisk beside the file-type designation.

Executing the COLLECT command is the most reliable and effective way to remove splat files from the directory and deallocate the blocks originally set aside for them. Do not attempt to SCRATCH splat files.

Using the TEST/DEMO DISKETTE and DOS Shell

The *TEST/DEMO DISKETTE* included with the DOS package provides a variety of programs for dealing with disks and files. One of the best ways to get acquainted with these *utility* programs is to insert this disk into your disk drive, close the latch, and enter this command:

```
RUN "HOW TO USE"
```

The program is a preview of the DOS utility programs contained on the disk. You cannot load and run the programs while the system is still running the HOW TO USE programming, but because the program is written in BASIC, you can get out of it at any time by pressing the RUN/STOP key.

Loading and running one of the DOS utility programs, except DOS SHELL, is a matter of executing this keyboard command:

RUN "*filename*"

where *filename* is the name on the directory listing. DOS SHELL, a machine-language program, is described in subsequent text.

Most of the utility programs are mentioned in this chapter in connection with appropriate DOS topics. Most of these programs are written in BASIC, and you can load, then LIST them to see examples of certain BASIC/DOS programming techniques.

The DOS SHELL program is included on the *TEST/DEMO DISKETTE*. Shell is a machine-language program that can be loaded into the computer and reside there unnoticed while doing other computer operations.

Insert the *TEST/DEMO DISKETTE* into the disk drive and close the latch. Load the program by entering the BOOT command—type BOOT and press the RETURN key.

When the READY prompt message appears, press the F1 function key to start the DOS SHELL program. The program initially expects you to specify the language you wish to use. Shell begins by showing ENGLISH as the language. If you wish the DOS SHELL text to be presented in English, press the space bar key immediately. Otherwise, wait about 15 seconds to see the presentation in French. Wait yet another 15 seconds and the language options change to German, then Italian.

Once you have selected the language, you will not have to redo that task until you reBOOT the program. If you intend to use one of the DOS SHELL features at this time, use the up and down cursor-movement keys to select a menu option, then press the space bar key to implement the option. Otherwise, press the F1 key to leave DOS SHELL.

> *NOTE:* Loading DOS SHELL redefines the function keys as follows:
>
> **F1**—Change DOS SHELL status
> **F2**—DLOAD"
> **F3**—DIRECTORY
> **F4**—SCNCLR
> **F5**—DSAVE"
> **F6**—RUN
> **F7**—LIST
> **F8**—MONITOR

When DOS SHELL options provide an effective means for carrying out the task at hand, they are described in this chapter.

Sequential Text Files

Text files are tables of string data that represent information meaningful to the user: names, telephone numbers, checkbook entries, and football statistics. Text files are sources of data generated and recalled by means of other programming operations.

A sequential text file is one generated in a sequential fashion, from the first piece of information (record), to the last. Such files must be read in a sequential fashion, from beginning to end. The fiftieth record in an existing sequential file, for example, can be reached only after reading through the previous 49 records in the file.

Sequential-File Statements and Functions

Like any other kind of file operation, sequential disk files must be opened in a particular fashion before you can write or read to them.

Use one of the following statements for opening a sequential file for writing operations:

```
DOPEN#filenum,"filename"[,D driveno][,Udevno],W
```

or

```
OPEN filenum,devno,channo," driveno:filename,S,W"
```

filenum—the logical file number

filename—name of the file

driveno—current disk-drive number, usually 0

devno—drive number, usually 8

channo—channel number, or secondary address, to be used (2 through 14)

S—a parameter that specifies a SEQuential file type

W—a parameter that specifies writing operations

Here is an example of using the DOPEN version to open a sequential file for writing operations:

```
DOPEN#1,"NUMS1",W
```

This command opens the file as NUMS1 and uses the default drive and device numbers, 8 and 0, respectively.

The next example uses the BASIC 2.0 version to do exactly the same job:

```
OPEN 1,8,2"0:NUMS1,S,W"
```

It is not unusual to have a situation where you need to open an old sequential text file and rewrite it with new information. Attempting to write information to an existing file creates a **FILE EXISTS** disk error message. You can get around the problem by using the scratch-and-replace character, @, in the open statement. For instance:

```
DOPEN#1,"@NUMS1",W
```

or

```
OPEN 1,8,2"@0:NUMS1,S,W"
```

The procedure for opening a sequential file for reading operations uses the same selection of OPEN statements, slightly modified, to specify Read instead of Write:

```
DOPEN#filenum,"filename"[,D driveno][,Udevno]
```

or

OPEN *filenum,devno,channo,"driveno: filename*,S,R"

This DOPEN statement differs from its write-to-file version only by the absence of the W parameter. The OPEN version in this instance replaces the W parameter with R.

No difference exists between the statements used for closing sequential files that have been opened for writing and reading purposes. Consider the following selection:

DCLOSE—close all open files.

DCLOSE#*filenum*—close only the file that has been opened with the given file number, *filenum*.

CLOSE*filenum*—same as DCLOSE#*filenum*.

The only statement used for writing data to a sequential file is

PRINT#*filenum,string*

where *filenum* is the logical file number used for OPENing the file and *string* is a string constant, variable, or expression.

If you want the data to be printed to the screen as well as the sequential file, use this combination of general statements:

PRINT#*filenum,string*
PRINT *string*

Two statements can be used for reading sequential file data:

INPUT#*filenum,strvar*

and

GET#*filenum,strvar*

where *filenum* is the file number assigned to the text-reading file and *strvar* is any valid string variable name.

The INPUT# version has a limited application because this version generally ignores control characters and can accept no more than 160 characters at a time. The GET# version is preferred in nearly all instances because its application has virtually no limitations.

Because the data in a sequential text file must be written as string data, it follows that INPUT# and GET# must read that data in a string format.

Sequential file information is often typed into the system from the keyboard. In the case of very long files, the job likely will have to be done over an extended period of time. You need, therefore, to reopen an existing sequential file in order to add more data to it.

With regard to opening sequential files, the DOPEN and OPEN statements always set the file pointer to the beginning of the file. If a thousand items already reside in a file, for instance, and you DOPEN or OPEN it for further writing operations, the new data will be written from the beginning of the file—destroying the information previously written!

The way around this difficulty is to use the APPEND statement. This statement replaces DOPEN or OPEN. APPEND opens the file but performs two additional tasks: this statement opens the file for writing operations and sets the file pointer at the end of the existing sequential file. New data can be added (appended) to an existing file without disturbing any of the old data.

The BASIC 7.0 form of the appending statement looks like this:

APPEND#*fileno*,"*filename*"[,D *driveno*][,U*devno*]

where *fileno* is the logical file number, *filename* is the name of the sequential file to be appended, and *driveno* and *devno* are optional parameters for the drive and device numbers.

The BASIC 2.0 version of the APPEND statement is

OPEN *fileno*,*devno*,*channo*,"*driveno*:*filename*,A"

This example differs from its normal, open-for-write counterpart by indicating an append operation—the A term.

Finally, there are the commands for putting together a series of two or more existing sequential files into one larger one. The procedure is usually called *chaining*, and BASIC 7.0 supports it in this way:

CONCAT "*filename2*" TO "*filename1*"

where the two sequential files, named *filename1* and *filename2*, reside on the same disk.

Executing that command adds (chains) the entire contents of *filename2* to the end of *filename1*. Both remain intact on the disk, but *filename1* is now larger than before.

BASIC 2.0 supports chaining operations for sequential disk files but in a somewhat different fashion. The procedure uses a command-channel PRINT# statement, so you need to open a command channel to the disk. The general sequence looks like this:

OPEN *filenum*,8,15
PRINT#*filenum*,"C:*newname*=*filename1*,*filename2*"

The operation creates a new disk file, *newname*, that is composed of *filename1* followed by *filename2*.

Designing Programs for Sequential-File Operations

The general procedure for creating a new sequential file looks like this:

1. Open a disk file for writing sequential text data.
2. Write the text to the file.
3. Close the file.

And the general procedure for reading data from an existing sequential file is:

1. Open the file for reading the data.
2. Read the data.
3. Close the file.

The routine in Listing 3-7 opens a text file called NUMS1, writes some data to it, and closes the file. The same routine then reopens the file, reads the data, prints the data to the screen, and ends by closing the file.

Line 10—Open file 1 for writing a sequential file, NUMS1.

Line 30—Write the following sequence of information to the file:

```
HELLO— 0
HELLO— 1
HELLO— 2
HELLO— 3
HELLO— 4
HELLO— 5
HELLO— 6
HELLO— 7
HELLO— 8
HELLO— 9
```

Notice that the PRINT# statement uses an STR$ function to transform the numeric values to a string format.

Line 50—Close the file.

Line 60—Reopen the file for reading operations.

Line 80—Use the INPUT# function to read the individual entries and assign them to string variable A$. (Techniques for using the preferred GET# function are described later.)

Line 90—Print the current data to the screen.

Line 110—Close the file.

Please notice that the listing does not include any DOS error-checking routines. They should be included in working versions of the program.

Listing 3-7

```
10 DOPEN#1,"@NUMS1",W
20 FOR K=0 TO 9
30 PRINT#1,"HELLO -- ";STR$(K)
40 NEXT K
50 DCLOSE#1
60 DOPEN#1,"NUMS1"
70 FOR K=0 TO 9
80 INPUT#1,A$
90 PRINT A$
100 NEXT K
110 DCLOSE#1
```

Sequential files do not always contain a known number of entries (records). The actual number of records, in fact, is often irrelevant. The next examples illustrate techniques for generating, then reading the information from a sequential file of indefinite length.

```
10 DOPEN#1,"STUFF",W
20 INPUT "ITEM (OR ### TO END)";I$
30 IF I$="###" THEN DCLOSE:END
40 PRINT#1,I$
50 GOTO 20
```

Line 10—Open a file number 1 as STUFF for sequential writing operations.

Line 20—Input a data item from the keyboard.

Line 30—If the item is ###, close the file and end the program.

Line 40—Print the item to the file.

Line 50—Loop back to input another item.

The file-reading counterpart of this program must use an error-checking routine to know when it has reached the end of the file:

```
10 DOPEN#1,"STUFF"
20 INPUT#1,D$
```

```
30 PRINT D$
40 IF ST=64 THEN DCLOSE:END
50 GOTO 20
```

Line 10—Open the file 1 for reading STUFF.

Line 20—Fetch a string from the file.

Line 30—Print the string to the screen.

Line 40—If the previous input operation created a block-status error of 64 (end of file), close the file and end the program.

Line 50—Loop back to fetch the next item from the file.

Relative File Procedures

Unlike sequential files, relative text files do not have to be written or read in a strict beginning-to-end fashion. Relative-file programs can go directly to a specified item or item location—record or record location, as they are properly called. You can even point directly to a specified byte within a given record.

Relative-File Statements and Functions

Relative disk files must be opened in a particular fashion before you can write or read them. You can properly infer from the nature of the OPEN statements that no difference exists between opening a relative file for reading and writing operations.

DOPEN#*filenum*,"*filename*",L*reclen*[,D*driveno*][,U*devno*]

or

OPEN *filenum*,*devno*,*channo*,"*driveno*:*filename*,L*reclen*"

filenum—the logical file number

filename—name of the file

reclen—number of bytes allocated for each record

driveno—current disk-drive number, usually 0

devno—drive number, usually 8

channo—channel number, or secondary address, to be used (2 through 14)

You can specify the record-length parameter, *reclen*, every time a given file is opened. You must specify this parameter when you originally create the file, but you can omit *reclen* from the statement thereafter.

Here are examples of opening a relative file for the first time:

```
DOPEN#1,"MASTERLIST",L40
```

and

```
OPEN 1,8,2,"0:MASTERILST,L40"
```

These examples open the file as MASTERLIST, specify record lengths of 40, and use the default drive.

The usual family of DOS commands is available for closing relative files:

DCLOSE—Close all open files.

DCLOSE#*filenum*—Close only the file that has been opened with the given file number, *filenum*.

CLOSE*filenum*—Same as DCLOSE#*filenum*.

Unlike sequential text files, reading and writing operations do not automatically advance the position of a record pointer. That, in fact, is the advantage of relative files. It is possible (in fact, necessary) to point to a record before executing any read/write operations to it. The record-pointing statement uses this general form:

RECORD #*fileno,recno,*[*byteno*]

where *fileno* is the file number assigned to the relative file, *recno* is the desired record number (0 through 65535), and *byteno* is an optional byte number within the record.

The following example points to the 10th byte within record number 55:

```
RECORD #1,55,10
```

The subsequent read or write statement refers directly to record 55, byte 10.

The only statement meaningful for writing data to relative files is

PRINT#*filenum,string*

where *filenum* is the logical file number used for OPENing the file and *string* is a string constant, variable, or expression. In instances where numeric information is to be written to a text file, the information must be converted to the string format by means of an STR$ function.

There are two statements used for reading relative file data:

INPUT#*filenum,strvar*

and

GET#*filenum,strvar*

where *filenum* is the file number assigned to the text-reading file and *strvar* is any valid string variable name.

The fact that numeric information must be converted to a string format before writing it to a relative file implies that numeric information must be read as string data as well. If data is to be later manipulated as numeric information, it can be converted to that format with the aid of the VAL function.

Direct-Access Disk Procedures

The 1571 disk drive is a microcomputer in its own right, and the Commodore 128 system allows direct access to its functions. The direct-access procedures are not recommended for beginners but provide powerful links to the disk system for programmers who understand how to take advantage of them.

How a Disk Is Organized: Tracks, Sectors, and Bytes

Commodore BASIC supports DOS commands and program statements that are adequate for carrying out any task meaningful in a BASIC operating environment. Programmers who have no need or desire to execute disk operations beyond those provided through BASIC's DOS commands have no need to delve into the way the disk-drive system organizes information stored on disk.

However, the disk-drives' operating system is readily available for fundamental operations that can be specified in both BASIC and machine-language formats. Taking full advantage of this feature demands an understanding of how data is organized.

One of the first operations in a disk-formatting procedure is to divide the disk into tracks. Tracks can be regarded as a succession of concentric magnetic circles on the surfaces of the disk. The system sets up 35 tracks on each side of the disk, for a total of 70 tracks.

Each track is then divided into sectors (blocks). A sector can be regarded as an arc-shaped segment of its circular track. Each arc is just long enough to hold 256 bytes, or 2048 bits, of data.

Still thinking of tracks as concentric circles, you can see that tracks near the outer edge of the disk have a much larger circumference than those near the middle. All sectors use much the same arc length, so it follows that more sectors are on the outer tracks than on the inner ones. Table 3-3 summarizes the distribution of tracks and sectors for a disk formatted on the 1571 disk drive.

Table 3-3 Organization of Tracks and Sectors on a Disk Formatted for Double-Sided Operation on a 5571 Drive

Track Nos.	Sector Nos.
1–17	0–20
18–24	0–18
25–30	0–17
31–35	0–16
36–52	0–20
53–59	0–18
60–65	0–17
66–70	0–16

The first 17 tracks, numbered 1 through 17, are located near the outer edge of the disk, so they contain the largest number of sectors—21, numbered 0 through 20. Tracks 18 through 24 contain 19 sectors, tracks 25 through 30 contain 18 sectors, and the innermost set of tracks, 31 through 25, contain just 17 sectors.

Notice that tracks 36 through 52 also include 21 sectors. The implication is that those tracks are near the outer edge of the opposite surface of the disk.

The track-and-sector numbering format provides the essential tools for pointing to (addressing) the beginning of any sector on the disk. The full range of addressing is from track 1, sector 0 through track 70, sector 16.

Track and sector numbers point to a block of 256 bytes of data on the disk. Most of the direct-disk commands make necessary the specification of a given byte within a block. So it is not unusual to work with a disk command that points to one of the 349,696 bytes of data on a double-sided disk. The general procedure is to cite a track number, a sector number, then a byte number in the range of 0 through 255.

NOTE: The terms *sector* and *block* mean the same thing for all practical purposes and are often used interchangeably. The prevailing literature generally uses *block* in the context of ordinary BASIC/DOS operations and reserves *sector* for the more general, direct-access disk environment.

Opening and Closing Command and Data Channels

Direct-access procedures require at least two open channels: a command channel and a data channel. The command channel is used for sending direct-access commands to the disk-drive system, and the data channel provides the data link between the disk drive and computer.

The general statement for opening a command channel is

OPEN *filenum,devicenum,secondary address*

filenum—the number to be assigned to the command channel for reference purposes

devicenum—device number of the disk drive, usually 8

secondary address—operation to be performed, always 15 for command-channel operations

The following example opens a disk-drive command channel as file 1:

OPEN 1,8,15

Opening a corresponding data channel requires a somewhat different form of the OPEN statement:

OPEN *filenum,devicenum,channelnum,"buffer"*

filenum—the number to be assigned to the command channel for reference purposes. Is different from the command-channel file number

devicenum—device number of the disk drive. Is same as the one used for opening the command channel

channelnum—a data-channel number between 2 and 14 but different from any other file or channel number open at the same time

buffer—a 1571 disk-drive internal buffer number, 0 through 3, enclosed in quotes. Substituting a pound sign (#) lets the 1571 select an available buffer on its own

The following example opens disk-data channel as file-number 2, channel 3, and lets the 1571 pick a buffer.

OPEN 2,8,3,"#"

Command and data channels are closed in the usual fashion, either by applying a CLOSE *file number* command to the two individual file numbers or by doing DCLOSE to close all channels.

Transferring a Block of Data

The computer does not have direct access to the data contained on a disk. Data communications between the disk drive and computer is through a 256-byte buffer inside the disk drive—the buffer specified by the data-channel's OPEN statement.

When it is necessary to read data from the disk, a designated sector of disk-based data must be first transferred from the disk to the disk drive buffer. Subsequent programming then can read any portion of the information. Writing data to the disk is likewise a two-step operation: write the desired information into the disk buffer, then transfer the information in the buffer to a designated sector on the disk.

The command for transferring data from a sector on the disk to the disk buffer has this general form:

"U1";*channelnum;drivenum;tracknum;sectornum*

"U1"—the block-read command expression

channelnum—the data channel number used when opening the channel

drivenum—disk drive number usually 0

tracknum—track number of the block to be transferred

sectornum—sector number of the block to be transferred

The block-read command line does not stand alone, however. It must be directed to the disk drive through the previously opened command channel. So the command takes this general form in BASIC programming:

PRINT#*filenum*,"U1";*channelnum;drivenum;tracknum;sectornum*

where *filenum* is the command-channel file number.

The example in Listing 3-8 opens command and data channels, reads track 18, sector 1 into the buffer, and prints the contents to the screen in the hexadecimal format.

Listing 3-8

```
10 SCNCLR
20 OPEN 1,8,15
30 OPEN 2,8,2,"#"
40 PRINT#1,"U1";2;0;18;1
50 FOR B=0 TO 255
60 GET#2,C$
70 PRINT MID$(HEX$(ASC(C$)),3)SPC(1)
80 NEXT B
90 DCLOSE
```

Line 10—Clear the screen and home the cursor

Line 20—Open a command channel to the disk drive as file 1

Line 30—Open a data channel to the disk drive as file 2, channel 2, and let the 1571 pick a data buffer

Line 40—Send the block-read command through the command channel. Read track 18, sector 1 from the disk in drive 0 and use channel 2 for data communications

Line 50–80—Read all 256 bytes in the buffer and print them to the screen in the hexadecimal format

Line 90—Close all files and channels

The command for transferring data to a designated sector on the disk looks like this:

"U2";*channelnum;drivenum;tracknum;sectornum*

"U2"—the block-write command expression

channelnum—the data channel number used when opening the channel

drivenum—disk drive number, usually 0

tracknum—track number where the block is to be transferred

sectornum—sector number where the block is to be transferred

Like the block-read command, you have to send the block-write command to the disk drive through the command channel:

PRINT#*filenum*,"U2";*channelnum;drivenum;tracknum;sectornum*

where *filenum* is the command-channel file number.

Obviously you have to be careful about casually writing data to sections of the disk allocated for specific purposes. Track 1, sector 1 is not allocated for any special purpose, so this section is a good place to experiment with block-write procedures. Listing 3-9 writes a little text message to that sector, via a disk buffer, of course.

Listing 3-9

```
10 C$="NOW IS THE TIME FOR ALL GOOD PROGRAMMERS
   TO HAVE A PARTY"
20 OPEN 1,8,15
30 OPEN 2,8,2,"#"
40 PRINT#2,C$
50 PRINT#1,"U2";2;0;1;1
60 DCLOSE
```

Line 10—Define a string to be saved on disk

Line 20—Open a command channel to the disk drive as file 1

Line 30—Open a data channel to the disk drive as file 2, channel 2, and let the 1571 pick a data buffer

Line 40—Write the string data to the disk buffer through channel 2

Line 50—Send the block-write command through the command channel. Write to track 1, sector 1 on the disk in drive 0 and use channel 2 for data communications

Line 60—Close all files and channels

It is left to you to compose a block-read program that will verify that the block-write indeed has taken place.

Setting the Block Pointer

The procedure for opening a data channel and setting up a disk buffer automatically initializes the block pointer to the first byte in the designated block. Subsequent GET and PRINT commands to the data channel advance the block pointer accordingly.

You may want to set the block pointer to a specific byte within the current data buffer. This can be done through the command channel, using the B-P (block-pointer) command.

The general form of the block-pointer command is:

"B-P";*channelno;byteno*

channelno—the data channel previously opened to the disk drive

byteno—the byte number for the desired pointer location (0 through 255)

The buffer-pointer command must be directed to the disk drive through a command channel in this fashion:

PRINT#*filenum,channelno,byteno*

where *filenum* is the command-channel file number.

Examples cited later in this chapter illustrate the power of the buffer-pointer command.

Allocating and Freeing Sectors of Disk Data

The higher-level DOS commands (DSAVE, DLOAD, SCRATCH, and so on) automatically allocate and deallocate disk sectors as required, and they adjust the directory accordingly. Furthermore, the system does not write over previously allocated sectors until they are deallocated (freed).

Such conveniences are not inherent in the direct-access family of commands, however. Sectors have to be allocated and deallocated by means of separate commands.

The commands are rather straightforward, and like other direct-access commands, they must be directed to the disk-drive system through a previously opened disk-command channel. The block-allocation command looks like this:

"B-A";*driveno;trackno;sectorno*

and the block-freeing command:

"B-F";*driveno;trackno;sectorno*

In both instances:

driveno—drive number of the disk; usually 0
trackno—designated track number
sectorno—designated sector number

They are both directed through an open disk-command channel as:

PRINT#*fileno*,"B-A";*driveno;trackno;sectorno*

and

PRINT#*fileno*,"B-F";*driveno;trackno;sectorno*

where *fileno* is the file number of the previously opened disk-command channel.

In principle, you can allocate and free disk sectors quite easily. In practice, however, avoid the directory track (track 18) altogether, allocating sectors already used for other purposes and freeing sectors that contain data you do not want to lose.

One built-in feature simplifies the task of locating free sectors. If you attempt to allocate a block already allocated (not free), the system returns the NO BLOCK error status and finds the next free sector for you.

Using the Direct-Access Status Block

The direct-access commands described thus far are sent to the disk-drive unit through an open disk-command channel. Reading from the disk command channel returns a disk-block status report. The operation is particularly important for determining whether or not the previous command has caused a disk-error condition and if so, providing a description of it. Reading disk status is a matter of executing this sort of command:

INPUT#*filenum,envar,emvar$,etvar,esvar*

filenum—file number of the file previously opened as a disk-command file

envar—a numeric variable assigned the disk error number

emvar—a string variable assigned the disk-error message

etvar—a numeric variable assigned a track number relevant to the error status

esvar—a numeric variable assigned a sector number relevant to the error status

Locating Disk and File Blocks

Table 3-4 shows the organization of the disk directory. The following procedure takes advantage of this information by suggesting a technique for locating the blocks in the directory.

Table 3-4
Disk Directory Block Structure

Byte (absolute)	Function
0	Track of next directory block
1	Sector of next directory block
2 through 31	File entry (30 bytes)
34 through 63	File entry (30 bytes)
66 through 95	File entry (30 bytes)
98 through 127	File entry (30 bytes)
130 through 159	File entry (30 bytes)
162 through 191	File entry (30 bytes)
194 through 223	File entry (30 bytes)
226 through 255	File entry (30 bytes)

1. Open command and data channels to the disk drive.
2. Initialize track and sector numeric variables for the first disk-directory block (track 8, sector 1).
3. Copy the disk-directory block to the buffer.
4. Set the buffer pointer to byte 0 (track for the next block).
5. Get byte 0, the track for the next disk-directory block.
6. Get byte 1, the sector for the next disk-directory block.
7. If the next track has a value of 0, no further blocks are allocated for the disk directory, so end the program.
8. Loop back to Step 3, using the newly fetched track and sector values.

Individual File Blocks

Table 3-5 shows the organization of individual file blocks on the disk and suggests a wealth of direct-access applications for customized disk-manipulation programs.

Table 3-5
Structure of Each File Entry in Directory Blocks

Byte (relative)	Function
0	File status and type Bits 0–3: File type, where 0 = Deleted (DEL) 1 = Sequential (SEQ) 2 = Program (PRG) 3 = User (USR) 4 = Relative (REL) Bit 6: File lock/unlock status, where 0 = Unlocked 1 = Locked Bit 7: File status, where 0 = Splat file 1 = Good file
1	Track number of the beginning of the file
2	Sector number of the beginning of the file
3 through 18	File name, padded with ASCII 160 ($A0) to fill the 15-byte space
19	Track number of the first side sector block for a relative file
20	Sector number of the first side sector block for a relative file
21	Length of records in a relative file
22 through 25	Not used; available for custom applications
26	Track number of replaced version of the file
27	Sector number of replaced version of the file
28	LSB of number of blocks in the file
29	MSB of number of blocks in the file

4

Monitor and Assembly Language Procedures

The heart of the Commodore 128 is the 8502 microprocessor and the ROM programming (firmware) that supports it. Of course, other powerful chips are built into the system: VIC for high-performance graphics, SID for sound and musical effects, CIAs for input/output operations, a separate 6502 in the disk-drive unit, and even a powerful competitor in the arena of microprocessors—a Z80-A chip that supports the CP/M feature. The 8502, however, is the device that pulls everything together.

That 8502 device, as well as its supporting firmware and the entire range of RAM, is completely open for inspection and manipulation through the system's monitor. The monitor provides direct access to all registers, RAM, and ROM. For anyone who already knows, or wants to know, something about direct microprocessor programming, the Commodore 128 monitor provides an open doorway to the internal workings of the system.

The Monitor's Hexadecimal Format

With the exception of a few mini-assembler operations described later in this chapter, the system monitor expresses addresses and data in hexadecimal notation. If you are unfamiliar with that notation, use Appendix A as a guide for understanding what hexadecimal notation means and how it is related to the more common decimal notation.

The monitor displays data and accepts data from the keyboard in a single-byte hexadecimal format. This is a clear reflection of the fact that the 8502 microprocessor is an eight-bit device.

Regarding the addressing format, the 8502 is a two-byte, or 16-bit, device. The monitor, however, displays and accepts addresses in a $2\frac{1}{2}$ byte format where the additional hexadecimal character indicates the current bank configuration.

The justification for using a $2\frac{1}{2}$ byte format stems from the fact that the 8502 can access roughly 64,000 (64K) address locations at any given time. The Commodore 128 features 128K of RAM in addition to the ROM and memory-mapped I/O locations. The fifth addressing character specifies which of 15 different memory-bank configurations are to be used.

Thus, a two-byte address such as 4000 is ambiguous to the monitor. This particular address represents the beginning of the ROM-based BASIC interpreter. However, this address is also RAM space that can hold any sort of data or machine-coded programming. Adding the extra half byte to the address resolves the ambiguity. Referring to address F4000, for example, establishes the address for an important segment of system ROM, whereas D4000 refers to a RAM location.

Table 4-1 summarizes the system's 16 different memory bank configurations. Numerous discussions throughout this book refer to bank configurations critical to particular operations. Unless specified otherwise, references to system addressing refer to the default bank, bank F (or decimal 15). Chapter 14 deals with bank configurations and memory management more thoroughly.

Table 4-1 Bank Configurations for the Commodore

Monitor Prefix Address	Bank Configuration
0	RAM 0 only
1	RAM 1 only
2	RAM 2 only
3	RAM 3 only
4	Internal ROM, RAM 0, I/O
5	Internal ROM, RAM 1, I/O
6	Internal ROM, RAM 2, I/O
7	Internal ROM, RAM 3, I/O
8	External ROM, RAM 0, I/O
9	External ROM, RAM 1, I/O
A	External ROM, RAM 2, I/O
B	External ROM, RAM 3, I/O
C	Kernal with internal low ROM, RAM 0, I/O
D	Kernal with external low ROM, RAM 1, I/O
E	Kernal with BASIC ROM, RAM 0, Character ROM
F	Kernal with BASIC ROM, RAM 0, I/O

Essential Monitor Operations

The system monitor uses a series of commands that give you an opportunity to examine the data at a specified range of addresses, write new data to a range of RAM addresses, save or load ranges of data from disk, transfer blocks of data between two address areas, search for specified combinations of data bytes, compare two blocks of data, fill a block of RAM with a specified data byte, and execute a handful of useful disk operations. The following discussions describe the use of these monitor operations.

The monitor also includes commands that deal with entering, disassembling, and executing 8502 assembly language programs. These are topics worthy of special consideration and are discussed later in this chapter.

Switching Between the Monitor and BASIC

Unless directed otherwise by a startup disk, turning on the C128 automatically brings up the BASIC 7.0 interpreter. Switching to the monitor from BASIC is a simple matter of entering this BASIC command:

```
MONITOR
```

Because the monitor programming begins at RAM address 45056 ($B000), you can also invoke the monitor by entering:

SYS 45056

Given the choice, however, the former technique—entering the MONITOR command—is preferred because it initializes the monitor system in a somewhat more elegant fashion.

You know the system has entered the monitor mode of operation when a summary of the content of the 8502 registers appears on the screen. For example:

```
      PC  SR AC XR YR SP
;  FB000 00 00 00 00 F8
```

You can use any of the following different ways to return to the BASIC interpreter from the monitor:

1. Execute the monitor's X command.
2. Momentarily depress the Reset pushbutton on the C128 console.
3. Execute the monitor's G command to a BASIC interpreter address, $F4000 or $F4003.

Executing the X command immediately restores the system to the BASIC interpreter. Pressing the Reset pushbutton also restores the BASIC interpreter, but only after checking the current disk drive for a startup program.

Executing a G $F4000 restores operations from the BASIC interpreter in exactly the same way that pressing the Reset pushbutton does—checking the current disk drive for a possible startup program. Executing G $4003 works like executing the X command: It restores control to the BASIC interpreter without checking the current disk drive.

Incidentally, switching between the BASIC interpreter and the monitor does not affect BASIC programming and machine-language programming that might be in RAM at the time. Operating the Reset pushbutton always brings up the BASIC interpreter and deletes any BASIC programming. Machine-language programming in RAM is not affected by that operation, however.

Reading the Contents of Memory

The monitor offers two different commands that display the content of a selected portion of RAM or ROM in a hexadecimal format. Both commands list at least one block of eight consecutive bytes of data and an ASCII plot of each byte.

The general forms of the two commands are:

M [*strtaddr*] [*endaddress*] >[*strtaddr*]

where *strtaddr* is the address of the first byte in the display and *endaddr* is the address of the last byte in the sequence. The difference between the two is that the M command is capable of displaying any number of consecutive bytes. Even if you do not specify an *endaddress* parameter, the M command shows no less than 12 lines of eight bytes each. The > command, on the other hand, displays just one line of eight consecutive bytes.

The address parameters for both commands should be preceded by a bank-configuration value, 0 through F. Otherwise the system displays data from addresses under the Bank 0 configuration.

Writing to Memory Locations

A byte of data can be written directly to a RAM address by means of a monitor command of this form:

>*addr data*

That is a *greater-than* symbol followed by an address, a space, and a byte of data to be written to the address. Pressing the RETURN key subsequently writes the data to the address.

After you press the RETURN key, the system displays eight consecutive data bytes, beginning from the specified address. The first byte in the series is the one specified by the command.

Many instances occur where it is sufficient to write a byte of data to a single address, but more often you need to write data to a succession of addresses—when entering ASCII-coded data for printing operations from a machine-language program, for example.

You can use the monitor to enter a series of data bytes (up to eight) by separating them with a single space. Press the RETURN key after typing the series of bytes to write the data to successive address locations, beginning from the one specified in the command.

The following example enters a series of eight data bytes into address locations $F4000 through $F4007:

```
>F4000 12 EE F0 60 7C 89 24 BB
```

After typing that command and series of bytes, press the RETURN key to write the data into the RAM locations.

It is no coincidence that the greater-than symbol used as a command for changing data bytes is identical to one used for examining a block of eight consecutive bytes. (See the previous section in this chapter.) The fact is that the monitor uses the same sort of screen-editing feature as BASIC. You can use the cursor-positioning keys to fix the text cursor over a data byte or address on the screen and overstrike it with other hexadecimal characters. Press the RETURN key then to enter the edited version of the information into the system.

One quick and convenient way to change a block of RAM data is to use the M command to list a block of 96 consecutive bytes. Use the cursor-positioning keys to fix the text cursor over the data to be changed and press the RETURN key before changing to a different line of data on the screen.

Of course, you cannot change the data in ROM and certain hardware output addresses. You can get the impression you are writing to such locations, but you will find that the data take on their original values after you press the RETURN key.

Moving Blocks of Memory

The Commodore 128 monitor includes a simple command that transfers a block of ROM or RAM data to an alternative RAM location. The general form of the command is:

T *srcestrt srcend destart*

where *srcestrt* is the first address in the block of data to be copied, *srcend* is the address of the last byte in the block to be copied, and *destart* is the address where the copy of the block is to begin.

The following example transfers (copies) the data from address $F1000 through $F1C00 to another area of RAM, beginning at $F2000:

```
T F1000 F1C00 F2000
```

The command begins with a T character, followed by the relevant addresses. The parameters are separated with a space, and the addresses should begin with a character that indicates the bank configuration.

You can transfer data between different memory banks. For example:

```
T F4000 FAFFF D4000
```

This simple monitor command copies the entire ROM-based BASIC interpreter into RAM that has the same general address range but in a different bank.

Comparing Blocks of Memory

The monitor's Compare command is a powerful testing tool for developing and debugging machine-language routines. The command executes a byte-by-byte comparison of two blocks of memory and prints the address of locations where the bytes are different (if any). The general form of the command is

C *addr1 addr2 addr3*

where *addr1* is the first address in one block of data, *addr2* is the address of the last byte in the same block, and *addr3* is the starting address of the second block.

The following example compares the data from address $F0000 through $F00FF with another area of RAM, beginning at $F1400:

```
C F0000 F00FF F1400
```

This command begins with a C character, followed by the addresses. The parameters are separated with a space, and the addresses should begin with a character that indicates the bank number.

Filling Blocks of RAM

Filling blocks of RAM with a single known data byte can serve as part of a useful testing and debugging tool. The monitor's Fill command does the job quickly and effectively.

The Fill command uses this general form:

F *strtaddr endaddr byte*

where *strtaddr* is the first address in the block to be filled, *endaddr* is the last address in the block, and *byte* is the hexadecimal data byte that is to fill the block.

The following example fills a block of RAM, from F1300 to F13FF, with 0A:

```
F F1300 F13FF 0A
```

Hunting for Combinations of Data Bytes

The monitor's Hunt command searches a specified block of addresses for a designated sequence of bytes. The command has this general form:

H *strtaddr endaddr data*

where *strtaddr* is the first address in the block to be searched, *endaddr* is the last address in the block, and *data* is the object of the search. The *data* can be any combination of 1 through 24 hexadecimal data bytes or string characters.

This example searches F4000 through F40FF for a series of 6 hexadecimal bytes:

```
H F4000 F40FF 68 22 AF D0 D1 EE
```

This one searches the same block for a string of ASCII characters that spell HELLO:

```
H F4000 F40FF 'HELLO'
```

Note that the text string is enclosed in apostrophes.

Saving Files on Tape or Disk

Although technically you can save any kind of data file or program with the monitor's Save command, practical considerations limit the application to binary files and machine-language programs originally entered in the monitor mode of operation. Save is similar in form and purpose to BASIC's BSAVE command.

The general form of the Save command:

S "*filename*",*devno*,*strtaddr*,*endaddr*

where *filename* is any valid file name, *devno* is the device number, and *strtaddr* is the starting address of the block to be saved. The final parameter, *endaddr*, marks the end of the block to be saved, but it must be incremented by 1. So if F14007 holds the last meaningful byte of data in the block, *endaddr* must be set to F14008.

> ***IMPORTANT:*** A file saved under the S command in the monitor must cite an ending address one location greater than the actual end of the file.

The following monitor command saves a file named SNOOPY on the current disk drive. The block begins at 01200 and ends at 012A0:

```
S "SNOOPY",8,01200,012A1
```

The starting and ending addresses are saved with the file so that it can be loaded into the system at the same addresses at any later time. As described in the next discussion, however, the Load command can be extended to alter the loading address.

Loading Files into RAM

Any kind of file—machine language, binary data, BASIC program, etc.—can be loaded into RAM from disk or tape by means of the monitor's Load command. It is similar in form and application to BASIC's BLOAD command.

The general syntax of the monitor version is:

L "*filename*",*devno*

where *filename* is the name of the file to be loaded and *devno* is the device number. The following example loads a file named SALTY from the current disk drive:

L "SALTY",8

The RAM address where the loading begins depends on the address used for saving the file in the first place. You can alter the address where the loading begins, however, by using the *altstrt* extension:

L "*filename*",*devno,altstrt*

A disk file called SALTY can be loaded at an alternative RAM address in this fashion:

L "SALTY",8,E4000

The *altstrt* parameter changes only the starting RAM address. It does not affect the starting address originally saved with the file on disk or tape.

Verifying Files and Blocks of Memory

The monitor's Verify command is a close cousin of the BASIC version of the same name. The general idea is to compare a data or program file residing on disk with the version previously loaded into system RAM. Once you have loaded a program or data file from disk, you can verify the two in this way:

V "*filename,devno*

where *filename* is the name of the file as listed in the disk directory, and *devno* is the device number—usually 8 for the disk drive.

If the two data blocks match, the system returns the blinking text cursor without further comment. Otherwise, it prints the **VERIFYING ERROR** message.

Verifying always begins at the address where the file is loaded. As describcd previously, however, you can load a file at an alternative address. When you have done so, you must extend the Verify command to indicate the alternative starting address:

V "*filename,devno,altstrt*

where *altstrt* is the alternative starting address.

Using the Monitor's Disk Status and Directory Commands

The monitor offers a versatile command that can perform several useful disk operations. The general form is

@ *devno,cmd*

where *devno* is the device number (default 8) and *cmd* is one of several disk commands:

@: Display the disk status
@,I: Initialize the disk
@,$: Display the entire disk directory
@,$0:PR*: Display directory of files beginning with PR
@,S0:*filename*: Scratch a disk file that has a file name, *filename*
@,N0:*header,id*: Format a disk with the header name, *header*, and identification code, *id* @,V: Validate the disk

All the commands have counterparts that are implemented from DOS-related BASIC commands. See Chapter 2 for definitions, examples, and more details.

The Monitor's Machine Language Aids

It is difficult to justify the presence of the monitor mode for someone who has no understanding or interest in machine language programming. You don't have much reason to work with the monitor unless you want to take advantage of the wealth of ROM-based machine routines that are readily available within the Commodore 128. Even that application is rather minor compared to the notion of being able to compose, test, debug, and run machine language programs of your own—all of which can be done through the monitor.

Using the Monitor's 8502 Disassembler

The ROM-based programming (system firmware) within the Commodore 128 is executed as 8502 machine coding. Executing the following memory-examination command can give you a real appreciation of the complexity and extent of the firmware programming:

```
M F4000 FCFFF
```

Use the C= key to slow down the listing, the NO SCROLL key to stop and restart it, and the RUN/STOP key to abort the listing when you've gotten the point of the demonstration.

The demonstration shows the BASIC interpreter, the monitor programming, and the system editor in terms of pure machine coding. Even highly skilled 6502/8502 machine-language programmers have difficulty making sense of it.

But a great deal of valuable information is included in the system's machine coding, and the useful and informative coding is not limited to the block of ROM cited in the demonstration. The monitor programming includes a disassembler function—one that translates blocks of machine coding into a source-code language far easier to read and interpret. The next monitor command examines the same area of ROM cited in the previous demonstration but in a form far more meaningful to anyone familiar with assembly language programming:

```
D F4000 FCFFF
```

Use the C= key to slow down the listing, the NO SCROLL key to stop and restart it, and the RUN/STOP key to abort the operation.

You will see the information divided into two basic groups, called *fields*. The left side of the screen shows an address column and between one and three columns of bytes. This *object-code* field is not much more meaningful than a pure machine-code listing, but at least the addresses and data contained in them are organized in a somewhat more meaningful fashion.

The *source-code* field on the right side of the screen is far more meaningful than anything else. It shows the 8502 instructions—mnemonics and operands—in a text form that a human programmer finds easier to learn and use. The closing section of this chapter describes all 8502 instructions in alphabetical order.

All of that is an example of using the monitor's disassembler mode. The general form of the disassembler command is:

D *strtaddr endaddr*

where *strtaddr* is the first address in the block to be disassembled and displayed on the screen and *endaddr* is the last address in the block.

Omitting the *endaddr* parameter instructs the system to disassemble a conveniently sized "page" of instructions, beginning from *endaddr*.

Once you have executed a disassembly command that cites a starting address, you can enter a D command (without addresses) to disassemble the next page of coding.

Using the Monitor's 8502 Mini-Assembler

The complement of a disassembly operation is an assembly operation—converting humanly understandable, text-like 8502 mnemonics and operands into pure machine code. The monitor system includes an assembler that makes easy the typing of custom machine-language routines into RAM. It is called a *mini-assembler* because it does not include some of the powerful programming tools of a full-blown assembler *macro-assembler*. Such features are available as separate software items from a number of different suppliers. The mini-assembler, however, is adequate for any sort of programming task and is particularly useful for relatively small tasks.

Starting an assembly operation is a matter of entering this sort of command:

A *strtaddr first instruction*

where *strtaddr* is the RAM address where the machine coding is to begin and *first instruction* is the first 8502 instruction in the program.

After entering that command, press the RETURN key to enter the object-code version into RAM, display the disassembled version, and move the text cursor to the beginning of the next line, where the second instruction is to be typed. Once you have started the assembly procedure, you don't have to enter the start-up command because the system keeps track of the addressing for you.

Leave the assembly routine by entering a null instruction—by pressing the RETURN key where the system is expecting the next 8502 instruction.

Working with the Monitor/8502 Registers

Initializing the monitor system brings up the following kind of display:

```
     PC  SR  AC  XR  YR  SP
; FB000  00  00  00  00  F8
```

Each item in this display represents the content of one of the critical registers within the 8502 microprocessor, where:

PC: Program counter, normally a two-byte register, but this register emulator shows the leading bank-address character
SR: Status register sometimes called the P register
AC: Accumulator, called *register A* throughout this book
XR: X index register
YR: Y index register
SP: Stack pointer

The monitor also prints this summary of the registers whenever a program encounters a BRK (break) command.

You can, however, display the summary of registers from the monitor at any time by entering the R command.

Directly changing the content of the 8502 registers can be a powerful test of a debugging tool. The content of the registers should not be changed indiscriminately. Assuming you have a clear purpose in mind, the simplest procedure is to:

1. Execute the monitor's R command to display the current content of the registers.
2. Use the cursor-control keys to position the text cursor over the characters to be changed and overstrike them with the desired values.
3. Enter the changes by pressing the RETURN key.

An alternative procedure is to type and enter your own sequence of register data. Begin with a semicolon (;), then type the desired hexadecimal data, using the same format that appears when doing the R command. Separate the register entries with a space. For example:

; F4000 FA 00 0F 00 F9

Typing this line and pressing the RETURN key changes the PC register to F4000, the SR register to FA, register A to 00, register X to 0F, register Y to 00, and the SP register to F9.

Executing Machine-Coded Programs from the Monitor

Entering a machine language program into RAM is just one step in the program-development procedure. It is also important to run the program in order to test its operation on a first-hand basis.

The most reliable monitor command for running a program is its Go command. The general form is:

G strtaddr

where *strtaddr* is the starting address of the machine language routine (including the bank-configuration nibble). The program continues execution under the monitor until it reaches a BRK instruction or the final RTS instruction.

If a BRK instruction interrupts the program, the monitor concludes the operation by displaying the current content of the emulated 8502 registers. If the machine-coded program ends with an RTS, the system automatically returns to the BASIC interpreter.

Finished machine language programs, especially those that are called and executed from BASIC's USR function or SYS statement, should conclude with an RTS. The notion of using a BRK instruction to interrupt a program is mainly a debugging and testing technique. Inserting a temporary BRK instruction gives you a chance to halt the operation of the program and verify the results to that point.

Executing the G command without specifying a starting address forces the system to begin execution at the address currently in the PC register.

So there are two ways to use the Go command to begin executing a machine language program at address $F1400. The simplest is to enter this command:

G F1400

The other procedure is to adjust the content of the PC register as described earlier in this chapter, then enter the G command without indicating a starting address.

The monitor also responds to a Jump command:

J strtaddr

This command does indeed initiate the execution of a machine language program from the specified address, *strtaddr*. It must be used with great care and forethought. If you fail to write the routine so that it ends by jumping to a meaningful address, the system most often locks up so that operating the Reset button is the only effective means for recovering.

Summary of 8502 Op Codes

Table 4-2 lists all the op codes, mnemonics, addressing modes, and bytes required for every 8502 instruction. The op codes are summarized here in numerical order, showing them in hexadecimal and decimal notation.

The hexadecimal notation is most useful when entering machine-language programming directly into RAM from the monitor. The decimal notation can be a valuable aid when POKEing short machine-language routines from DATA lists in BASIC programs.

The nomenclature used for the mnemonics and addressing modes are those generally displayed by the monitor's disassembler. The exception is the form of the address indicated by *relative*-addressed operations. The table shows the one byte relative-addressing format actually used by the 8502. The C128 disassembler, however, shows the absolute target address in those instances.

Table 4-2
Summary Op Codes, Mnemonics, Addressing Modes, and Number for Bits for Each 8502 Instruction

Op Code Hex	Dec	Mnemonic	Addressing Mode	Number of Bytes
$00	0	BRK	implied	1
$01	1	ORA	(indirect,X)	2
$02	2		not used	
$03	3		not used	
$04	4		not used	
$05	5	ORA	zero page	2
$06	6	ASL	zero page	2
$07	7		not used	
$08	8	PHP	implied	1
$09	9	ORA	immediate	2
$0A	10	ASL	accumulator	1
$0B	11		not used	
$0C	12		not used	
$0D	13	ORA	absolute	3
$0E	14	ASL	absolute	3
$0F	15		not used	
$10	16	BPL	relative	2
$11	17	ORA	(indirect),Y	2
$12	18		not used	
$13	19		not used	
$14	20		not used	
$15	21	ORA	zero page,X	2
$16	22	ASL	zero page,X	2
$17	23		not used	
$18	24	CLC	implied	1
$19	25	ORA	absolute,Y	3
$1A	26		not used	
$1B	27		not used	
$1C	28		not used	
$1D	29	ORA	absolute,X	3

Table 4-2 (cont.)

Op Code Hex	Dec	Mnemonic	Addressing Mode	Number of Bytes
$1E	30	ASL	absolute,X	3
$1F	31		not used	
$20	32	JSR	absolute	3
$21	33	AND	(indirect,X)	2
$22	34		not used	
$23	35		not used	
$24	36	BIT	zero page	2
$25	37	AND	zero page	2
$26	38	ROL	zero page	2
$27	39		not used	
$28	40	PLP	implied	1
$29	41	AND	immediate	2
$2A	42	ROL	accumulator	1
$2B	43		not used	
$2C	44	BIT	absolute	3
$2D	45	AND	absolute	3
$2E	46	ROL	absolute	3
$2F	47		not used	
$30	48	BMI	relative	2
$31	49	AND	(indirect),Y	2
$32	50		not used	
$33	51		not used	
$34	52		not used	
$35	53	AND	zero page,X	2
$36	54	ROL	zero page,X	2
$37	55		not used	
$38	56	SEC	implied	1
$39	57	AND	absolute,Y	3
$3A	58		not used	
$3B	59		not used	
$3C	60		not used	
$3D	61	AND	absolute,X	3
$3E	62	ROL	absolute,X	3
$3F	63		not used	
$40	64	RTI	implied	1
$41	65	EOR	(indirect,X)	2
$42	66		not used	
$43	67		not used	
$44	68		not used	
$45	69	EOR	zero page	2
$46	70	LSR	zero page	2
$47	71		not used	
$48	72	PHA	zero page	2
$49	73	EOR	immediate	2
$4A	74	LSR	implied	1
$4B	75		not used	
$4C	76	JMP	absolute	3
$4D	77	EOR	absolute	3
$4E	78	LSR	absolute	3
$4F	79		not used	
$50	80	BVC	relative	2

Table 4-2 (cont.)

Op Code Hex	Dec	Mnemonic	Addressing Mode	Number of Bytes
$51	81	EOR	(indirect),Y	2
$52	82		not used	
$53	83		not used	
$54	84		not used	
$55	85	EOR	zero page,X	2
$56	86	LSR	zero page,X	2
$57	87		not used	
$58	88	CLI	implied	1
$59	89	EOR	absolute,Y	3
$5A	90		not used	
$5B	91		not used	
$5C	92		not used	
$5D	93	EOR	absolute,X	3
$5E	94	LSR	absolute,X	3
$5F	95		not used	
$60	96	RTS	implied	1
$61	97	ADC	(indirect,X)	2
$62	98		not used	
$63	99		not used	
$64	100		not used	
$65	101	ADC	zero page	2
$66	102	ROR	zero page	2
$67	103		not used	
$68	104	PLA	implied	1
$69	105	ADC	immediate	2
$6A	106	ROR	accumulator	1
$6B	107		not used	
$6C	108	JMP	(indirect)	3
$6D	109	ADC	absolute	3
$6E	110	ROR	absolute	3
$6F	111		not used	
$70	112	BVS	relative	2
$71	113	ADC	(indirect),Y	2
$72	114		not used	
$73	115		not used	
$74	116		not used	
$75	117	ADC	zero page,X	2
$76	118	ROR	zero page,X	2
$77	119		not used	
$78	120	SEI	implied	1
$79	121	ADC	absolute,Y	3
$7A	122		not used	
$7B	123		not used	
$7C	124		not used	
$7D	125	ADC	absolute,X	3
$7E	126	ROR	absolute,X	3
$7F	127		not used	
$80	128	BCS	relative	2
$81	129	STA	(indirect,X)	2
$82	130		not used	
$83	131		not used	

Table 4-2 (cont.)

Op Code Hex	Dec	Mnemonic	Addressing Mode	Number of Bytes
$84	132	STY	zero page	2
$85	133	STA	zero page	2
$86	134	STX	zero page	2
$87	135		not used	
$88	136	DEY	implied	1
$89	137		not used	
$8A	138	TXA	implied	1
$8B	139		not used	
$8C	140	STY	absolute	3
$8D	141	STA	absolute	3
$8E	142	STX	absolute	3
$8F	143		not used	
$90	144	BCC	relative	2
$91	145	STA	(indirect),Y	2
$92	146		not used	
$93	147		not used	
$94	148	STY	zero page,X	2
$95	149	STA	zero page,X	2
$96	150	STX	zero page,X	2
$97	151		not used	
$98	152	TYA	implied	1
$99	153	STA	absolute,Y	3
$9A	154	TXS	implied	1
$9B	155		not used	
$9C	156		not used	
$9D	157	STA	absolute,X	3
$9E	158		not used	
$9F	159		not used	
$A0	160	LDY	immediate	2
$A1	161	LDA	(indirect,X)	2
$A2	162	LDX	immediate	2
$A3	163		not used	
$A4	164	LDY	zero page	2
$A5	165	LDA	zero page	2
$A6	166	LDX	zero page	2
$A7	167		not used	
$A8	168	TAY	implied	1
$A9	169	LDA	immediate	2
$AA	170	TAX	implied	1
$AB	171		not used	
$AC	172	LDY	absolute	3
$AD	173	LDA	absolute	3
$AE	174	LDX	absolute	3
$AF	175		not used	
$B0	176	BCS	relative	2
$B1	177	LDA	(indirect),Y	2
$B2	178		not used	
$B3	179		not used	
$B4	180	LDY	zero page,X	2
$B5	181	LDA	zero page,X	2
$B6	182	LDX	zero page,X	2

Table 4-2 (cont.)

Op Code Hex	Op Code Dec	Mnemonic	Addressing Mode	Number of Bytes
$B7	183		not used	
$B8	184	CLV	implied	1
$B9	185	LDA	absolute,Y	3
$BA	186	TSX	implied	1
$BB	187		not used	
$BC	188	LDY	absolute,X	3
$BD	189	LDA	absolute,X	3
$BE	190	LDX	absolute,Y	3
$BF	191		not used	
$C0	192	CPY	immediate	2
$C1	193	CMP	(indirect,X)	2
$C2	194		not used	
$C3	195		not used	
$C4	196	CPY	zero page	2
$C5	197	CMP	zero page	2
$C6	198	DEC	zero page	2
$C7	199		not used	
$C8	200	INY	implied	1
$C9	201	CMP	immediate	2
$CA	202	DEX	implied	1
$CB	203		not used	
$CC	204	CPY	absolute	3
$CD	205	CMP	absolute	3
$CE	206	DEC	absolute	3
$CF	207		not used	
$D0	208	BNE	relative	2
$D1	209	CMP	(indirect),Y	2
$D2	210		not used	
$D3	211		not used	
$D4	212		not used	
$D5	213	CMP	zero page,X	2
$D6	214	DEC	zero page,X	2
$D7	215		not used	
$D8	216	CLD	implied	1
$D9	217	CMP	absolute,Y	3
$DA	218		not used	
$DB	219		not used	
$DC	220		not used	
$DD	221	CMP	absolute,X	3
$DE	222	DEC	absolute,X	3
$DF	223		not used	
$E0	224	CPX	immediate	2
$E1	225	SBC	(indirect,X)	2
$E2	226		not used	
$E3	227		not used	
$E4	228	CPX	zero page	2
$E5	229	SBC	zero page	2
$E6	230	INC	zero page	2
$E7	231		not used	
$E8	232	INX	implied	1
$E9	233	SBC	immediate	2

Table 4-2 (cont.)

Op Code Hex	Dec	Mnemonic	Addressing Mode	Number of Bytes
$EA	234	NOP	implied	1
$EB	235		not used	
$EC	236	CPX	absolute	3
$ED	237	SBC	absolute	3
$EE	238	INC	absolute	3
$EF	239		not used	
$F0	240	BEQ	relative	2
$F1	241	SBC	(indirect),Y	2
$F2	242		not used	
$F3	243		not used	
$F4	244		not used	
$F5	245	SBC	zero page,X	2
$F6	246	INC	zero page,X	2
$F7	247		not used	
$F8	248	SED	implied	1
$F9	249	SBC	absolute,Y	3
$FA	250		not used	
$FB	251		not used	
$FC	252		not used	
$FD	253	SBC	absolute,X	3
$FE	254	INC	absolute,X	3
$FF	255		not used	

Figure 4-1 shows the organization of registers within the 8502 microprocessor, including flag-bit details of the processor status register, P.

The 8502 Instruction Set

The remainder of this chapter is devoted to a detailed version of the 8502 instruction set. The material is arranged in alphabetical order by instruction-set mnemonics. Asterisks shown under the heading *Status Register (P)* indicate the flag bits affected by the operation:

P bit 7 = N—negative-sign flag

P bit 6 = V—overflow flag

P bit 5—not used

P bit 4—break flag

P bit 3 = D—decimal flag

P bit 2 = I—interrupt disable flag

P bit 1 = Z—zero flag

P bit 0—not used

Fig. 4-1 Organization of the main working registers within the 8502 microprocessor

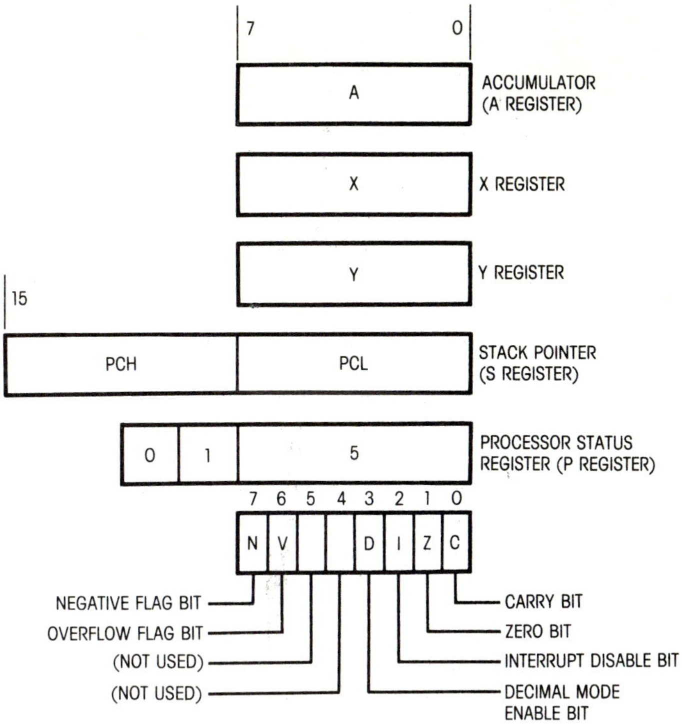

ADC Add memory to accumulator with carry.

Operation: Sum the contents of memory, accumulator, and C. Place result in accumulator.

Status Register (P)

N	V	D	I	Z	C
*	*	—	—	*	*

Addressing Mode	Assembly Language Format	Hex Op Code	Dec Op Code	No. Bytes
(indirect,X)	ADC (Oper,X)	$61	97	2
zero page	ADC Oper	$65	101	2
immediate	ADC #Oper	$69	105	2
absolute	ADC Oper	$6D	109	3
(indirect),Y	ADC (Oper),Y	$71	113	2
zero page,X	ADC Oper,X	$75	117	2
absolute,Y	ADC Oper,Y	$79	121	3
absolute,X	ADC Oper,X	$7D	125	3

AND Logically AND memory with accumulator.

Operation: Logically AND the content of the accumulator with that of memory. Result to accumulator.

Status Register (P)

N	V		D	I	Z	C
*	—	—	—	—	*	—

Addressing Mode	Assembly Language Format	Hex Op Code	Dec Op Code	No. Bytes
(indirect,X)	AND (Oper,X)	$21	33	2
zero page	AND Oper	$25	37	2
immediate	AND #Oper	$29	41	2
absolute	AND Oper	$2D	45	3
(indirect),Y	AND (Oper),Y	$31	49	2
zero page,X	AND Oper,X	$35	53	2
absolute,Y	AND Oper,Y	$39	57	3
absolute,X	AND Oper,X	$3D	61	3

ASL Arithmetic shift left.

Operation: Shift the content of memory or accumulator one bit to the left, with the high-order bit going to C. Shift a zero bit into the low-order bit location.

Status Register (P)

N	V		D	I	Z	C
*	—	—	—	—	*	*

Addressing Mode	Assembly Language Format	Hex Op Code	Dec Op Code	No. Bytes
zero page	ASL Oper	$06	6	2
accumulator	ASL	$0A	10	1
absolute	ASL Oper	$0E	14	3
zero page,X	ASL Oper,X	$16	22	2
absolute,X	ASL Oper,X	$1E	30	3

BCC Branch on carry clear.

Operation: Branch if C = 0.

BCC *(cont.)*

Status Register (P)

N V D I Z C

— — — — — —

Addressing Mode	Assembly Language Format	Hex Op Code	Dec Op Code	No. Bytes
relative	BCC	$90	144	2

BCS Branch on carry set.

Operation: Branch if C = 1.

Status Register (P)

N V D I Z C

— — — — — —

Addressing Mode	Assembly Language Format	Hex Op Code	Dec Op Code	No. Bytes
relative	BCS	$B0	176	2

BEQ Branch if equal.

Operation: Branch if Z = 1.

Status Register (P)

N V D I Z C

— — — — — —

Addressing Mode	Assembly Language Format	Hex Op Code	Dec Op Code	No. Bytes
relative	BEQ	$F0	240	2

BIT Test bits in accumulator with bits in memory.

Operation: Logically AND the content of memory with the accumulator, result of bit 7 to N and bit 6 to V. Set Z = 1 if bytes in accumulator and memory are identical.

NOTE: The operation does not affect the content of the accumulator or memory location.

BIT *(cont.)*

		Status Register (P)		
		N V D I Z C		
		M7 M6 __ __ * __		
Addressing Mode	Assembly Language Format	Hex Op Code	Dec Op Code	No. Bytes
zero page	BIT Oper	$24	36	2
absolute	BIT Oper	$2C	44	3

BMI Branch on result minus.

Operation: Branch if N = 1.

		Status Register (P)		
		N V D I Z C		
		__ __ __ __ __ __		
Addressing Mode	Assembly Language Format	Hex Op Code	Dec Op Code	No. Bytes
relative	BMI	$30	48	2

BNE Branch if not equal.

Operation: Branch if Z = 0.

		Status Register (P)		
		N V D I Z C		
		__ __ __ __ __ __		
Addressing Mode	Assembly Language Format	Hex Op Code	Dec Op Code	No. Bytes
relative	BNE	$D0	208	2

BPL Branch if result plus.

Operation: Branch if N = 0.

		Status Register (P)		
		N V D I Z C		
		__ __ __ __ __ __		
Addressing Mode	Assembly Language Format	Hex Op Code	Dec Op Code	No. Bytes
relative	BPL	$10	16	2

BRA Branch.

Operation: Unconditional branch.

Status Register (P)

N	V		D	I	Z	C
—	—		—	—	—	—

Addressing Mode	Assembly Language Format	Hex Op Code	Dec Op Code	No. Bytes
relative	BRA	$80	128	2

BRK Break.

Operation: Forced break. Place next address on the stack—high-order byte followed by low-order byte. Set I = 1.

Status Register (P)

N	V		D	I	Z	C
—	—		—	1	—	—

Addressing Mode	Assembly Language Format	Hex Op Code	Dec Op Code	No. Bytes
implied	BRK	$00	0	1

BVC Branch on overflow clear.

Operation: Branch if V = 0.

Status Register (P)

N	V		D	I	Z	C
—	—		—	—	—	—

Addressing Mode	Assembly Language Format	Hex Op Code	Dec Op Code	No. Bytes
relative	BVC	$50	80	2

BVS Branch on overflow set.

Operation: Branch if V = 1.

BVS *(cont.)*

Status Register (P)

N	V		D	I	Z	C
—	—		—	—	—	—

Addressing Mode	Assembly Language Format	Hex Op Code	Dec Op Code	No. Bytes
relative	BVS	$70	112	2

CLC Clear carry bit.

Operation: Set C = 0.

Status Register (P)

N	V		D	I	Z	C
—	—		—	—	—	0

Addressing Mode	Assembly Language Format	Hex Op Code	Dec Op Code	No. Bytes
implied	CLC	$18	24	1

CLD Clear decimal mode.

Operation: Set D = 0.

Status Register (P)

N	V		D	I	Z	C
—	—		0	—	—	—

Addressing Mode	Assembly Language Format	Hex Op Code	Dec Op Code	No. Bytes
implied	CLD	$D8	216	1

CLI Clear interrupt.

Operation: Set I = 0.

Status Register (P)

N	V		D	I	Z	C
—	—		—	0	—	—

Addressing Mode	Assembly Language Format	Hex Op Code	Dec Op Code	No. Bytes
implied	CLI	$58	88	1

CLV Clear overflow bit.

Operation: Set V = 0.

Status Register (P)

N	V	D	I	Z	C
—	0	—	—	—	—

Addressing Mode	Assembly Language Format	Hex Op Code	Dec Op Code	No. Bytes
implied	CLV	$B8	184	1

CMP Compare memory and accumulator.

Operation: Compare the content of memory and accumulator. Adjust status bits accordingly.

Status Register (P)

N	V	D	I	Z	C
*	—	—	—	*	*

Addressing Mode	Assembly Language Format	Hex Op Code	Dec Op Code	No. Bytes
(indirect,X)	CMP (Oper,X)	$C1	193	2
zero page	CMP Oper	$C5	197	2
immediate	CMP #Oper	$C9	201	2
absolute	CMP Oper	$CD	205	3
(indirect),Y	CMP (Oper),Y	$D1	209	2
zero page,X	CMP Oper,X	$D5	213	2
absolute,Y	CMP Oper,Y	$D9	217	3
absolute,X	CMP Oper,X	$DD	221	3

CPX Compare memory and X register.

Operation: Compare the content of memory and X register. Adjust status bits accordingly.

Status Register (P)

N	V	D	I	Z	C
*	—	—	—	*	*

Addressing Mode	Assembly Language Format	Hex Op Code	Dec Op Code	No. Bytes
immediate	CPX #Oper	$E0	224	2
zero page	CPX Oper	$E4	228	2
absolute	CPX Oper	$EC	236	3

CPY Compare memory and Y register.

Operation: Compare the content of memory and Y register. Adjust the status bits accordingly.

Status Register (P)

N	V		D	I	Z	C
*	—		—	—	*	*

Addressing Mode	Assembly Language Format	Hex Op Code	Dec Op Code	No. Bytes
immediate	CPY #Oper	$C0	192	2
zero page	CPY Oper	$C4	196	2
absolute	CPY Oper	$CC	204	3

DEC Decrement the content of memory by one.

Operation: Decrement the content of memory by one. Adjust N and Z bits accordingly.

Status Register (P)

N	V		D	I	Z	C
*	—		—	—	*	—

Addressing Mode	Assembly Language Format	Hex Op Code	Dec Op Code	No. Bytes
zero page	DEC Oper	$C6	198	2
absolute	DEC Oper	$CE	206	3
zero page,X	DEC Oper,X	$D6	214	2
absolute,X	DEC Oper,X	$DE	222	3

DEX Decrement the X register.

Operation: Decrement the content of the X register. Adjust N and Z bits accordingly.

Status Register (P)

N	V		D	I	Z	C
*	—		—	—	*	—

Addressing Mode	Assembly Language Format	Hex Op Code	Dec Op Code	No. Bytes
implied	DEX	$CA	202	1

DEY Decrement the Y register.

Operation: Decrement the contents of the Y register. Adjust N and Z bits accordingly.

Status Register (P)

N	V	D	I	Z	C
*	—	—	—	*	—

Addressing Mode	Assembly Language Format	Hex Op Code	Dec Op Code	No. Bytes
implied	DEY	$88	136	1

EOR EXCLUSIVE-OR memory with accumulator.

Operation: Logically EXCLUSIVE-OR the content of memory and accumulator. Result to accumulator. Adjust N and Z bits accordingly.

Status Register (P)

N	V	D	I	Z	C
*	—	—	—	*	—

Addressing Mode	Assembly Language Format	Hex Op Code	Dec Op Code	No. Bytes
(indirect,X)	EOR (Oper,X)	$41	65	2
zero page	EOR Oper	$45	69	2
immediate	EOR #Oper	$49	73	2
absolute	EOR Oper	$4D	77	3
(indirect),Y	EOR (Oper),Y	$51	81	2
zero page,X	EOR Oper,X	$55	85	2
absolute,Y	EOR Oper,Y	$59	89	3
absolute,X	EOR Oper,X	$5D	93	3

INC Increment memory.

Operation: Increment memory by one. Adjust the N and Z bits accordingly.

Status Register (P)

N	V	D	I	Z	C
*	—	—	—	*	—

Addressing Mode	Assembly Language Format	Hex Op Code	Dec Op Code	No. Bytes
zero page	INC Oper	$E6	230	2

INC *(cont.)*

Status Register (P)

N	V	D	I	Z	C
*	—	—	—	*	—

Addressing Mode	Assembly Language Format	Hex Op Code	Dec Op Code	No. Bytes
absolute	INC Oper	$EE	238	3
zero page,X	INC Oper,X	$F6	246	2
absolute,X	INC Oper,X	$FE	254	3

INX Increment the X register.

Operation: Increment the X register by one. Adjust the N and Z bits accordingly.

Status Register (P)

N	V	D	I	Z	C
*	—	—	—	*	—

Addressing Mode	Assembly Language Format	Hex Op Code	Dec Op Code	No. Bytes
implied	INX	$E8	232	1

INY Increment the Y register.

Operation: Increment the Y register by 1. Adjust the N and Z bits accordingly.

Status Register (P)

N	V	D	I	Z	C
*	—	—	—	*	—

Addressing Mode	Assembly Language Format	Hex Op Code	Dec Op Code	No. Bytes
implied	INY	$C8	200	1

JMP Jump unconditionally.

Operation: Jump unconditionally to new address. Low byte of memory to PCL and high byte to PCH.

JMP *(cont.)*

Status Register (P)

N	V	D	I	Z	C
—	—	—	—	—	—

Addressing Mode	Assembly Language Format	Hex Op Code	Dec Op Code	No. Bytes
absolute	JMP Oper	$4C	76	3
(indirect)	JMP (Oper)	$6C	108	3

JSR Jump and save return.

Operation: Jump to new address and save the return (next address). Return address to stack. Jump address to program counter.

Status Register (P)

N	V	D	I	Z	C
—	—	—	—	—	—

Addressing Mode	Assembly Language Format	Hex Op Code	Dec Op Code	No. Bytes
absolute	JSR Oper	$20	32	3

LDA Load accumulator with memory.

Operation: Load the content of memory to the accumulator. Adjust the N and Z bits accordingly.

Status Register (P)

N	V	D	I	Z	C
*	—	—	—	*	—

Addressing Mode	Assembly Language Format	Hex Op Code	Dec Op Code	No. Bytes
(indirect,X)	LDA (Oper,X)	$A1	161	2
zero page	LDA Oper	$A5	165	2
immediate	LDA #Oper	$A9	169	2
absolute	LDA Oper	$AD	173	3
(indirect),Y	LDA (Oper),Y	$B1	177	2
zero page,X	LDA Oper,X	$B5	181	2
absolute,Y	LDA Oper,Y	$B9	185	3
absolute,X	LDA Oper,X	$BD	189	3

LDX Load X register from memory.

Operation: Load the content of memory to register X. Adjust the N and Z bits accordingly.

Status Register (P)

N	V	D	I	Z	C
*	—	—	—	*	—

Addressing Mode	Assembly Language Format	Hex Op Code	Dec Op Code	No. Bytes
immediate	LDX #Oper	$A2	162	2
zero page	LDX Oper	$A6	166	2
absolute	LDX Oper	$AE	174	3
zero page,X	LDX Oper,X	$B6	182	2
absolute,Y	LDX Oper,Y	$BE	190	3

LDY Load Y register with memory.

Operation: Load the content of memory to the Y register. Adjust the N and Z bits accordingly.

Status Register (P)

N	V	D	I	Z	C
*	—	—	—	*	—

Addressing Mode	Assembly Language Format	Hex Op Code	Dec Op Code	No. Bytes
immediate	LDY #Oper	$A0	160	2
zero page	LDY Oper	$A4	164	2
absolute	LDY Oper	$AC	172	3
zero page,X	LDY Oper,X	$B4	180	2
absolute,X	LDY Oper,X	$BC	188	3

LSR Logical shift-right one bit.

Operation: Shift the content of memory or accumulator one bit to the right, with the low-order bit going to C. Shift a zero bit into the high-order bit location.

LSR *(cont.)*

Status Register (P)

N	V	D	I	Z	C
0	—	—	—	*	*

Addressing Mode	Assembly Language Format	Hex Op Code	Dec Op Code	No. Bytes
zero page	LSR Oper	$46	70	2
accumulator	LSR	$4A	74	1
absolute	LSR Oper	$4E	78	3
zero page,X	LSR Oper,X	$56	86	2
absolute,X	LSR Oper,X	$5E	94	3

NOP No operation.

Operation: No effect.

Status Register (P)

N	V	D	I	Z	C
—	—	—	—	—	—

Addressing Mode	Assembly Language Format	Hex Op Code	Dec Op Code	No. Bytes
implied	NOP	$EA	234	1

ORA OR memory with accumulator.

Operation: Logically OR the content of memory and accumulator. Place result in the accumulator and adjust N and Z bits accordingly.

Status Register (P)

N	V	D	I	Z	C
*	—	—	—	*	—

Addressing Mode	Assembly Language Format	Hex Op Code	Dec Op Code	No. Bytes
(indirect,X)	ORA (Oper,X)	$01	1	2
zero page	ORA Oper	$05	5	2
immediate	ORA #Oper	$09	9	2
absolute	ORA Oper	$0D	13	3
(indirect),Y	ORA (Oper),Y	$11	17	2
zero page,X	ORA Oper,X	$15	21	2
absolute,Y	ORA Oper,Y	$19	25	3
absolute,X	ORA Oper,X	$1D	29	3

PHA Push accumulator onto stack.

Operation: Push the content of the accumulator onto the current stack.

Status Register (P)

N	V		D	I	Z	C
—	—		—	—	—	—

Addressing Mode	Assembly Language Format	Hex Op Code	Dec Op Code	No. Bytes
zero page	PHA Oper	$48	72	2

PHP Push status register onto stack.

Operation: Push the content of the status register (P) onto the current stack.

Status Register (P)

N	V		D	I	Z	C
—	—		—	—	—	—

Addressing Mode	Assembly Language Format	Hex Op Code	Dec Op Code	No. Bytes
implied	PHP	$08	8	1

PLA Pull accumulator from stack.

Operation: Pull the top byte from the current stack and place it into the accumulator. Adjust the N and Z bits accordingly.

Status Register (P)

N	V		D	I	Z	C
*	—		—	—	*	—

Addressing Mode	Assembly Language Format	Hex Op Code	Dec Op Code	No. Bytes
implied	PLA	$68	104	1

PLP Pull P register from the stack.

Operation: Pull the top byte from the current stack and load it to the status register (P).

PLP *(cont.)*

Status Register (P)

N	V	D	I	Z	C
*	*	*	*	*	*

Addressing Mode	Assembly Language Format	Hex Op Code	Dec Op Code	No. Bytes
implied	PLP	$28	40	1

ROL Rotate left.

Operation: Rotate memory or accumulator one bit to the left through the C bit.

Status Register (P)

N	V	D	I	Z	C
*	—	—	—	*	*

Addressing Mode	Assembly Language Format	Hex Op Code	Dec Op Code	No. Bytes
zero page	ROL Oper	$26	38	2
accumulator	ROL	$2A	42	1
absolute	ROL Oper	$2E	46	3
zero page,X	ROL Oper,X	$36	54	2
absolute,X	ROL Oper,X	$3E	62	3

ROR Rotate right.

Operation: Rotate memory or accumulator one bit to the right through the C bit.

Status Register (P)

N	V	D	I	Z	C
*	—	—	—	*	*

Addressing Mode	Assembly Language Format	Hex Op Code	Dec Op Code	No. Bytes
zero page	ROR Oper	$66	102	2
accumulator	ROR	$6A	106	1
absolute	ROR Oper	$6E	110	3
zero page,X	ROR Oper,X	$76	118	2
absolute,X	ROR Oper,X	$7E	126	3

RTI Return from interrupt.

Operation: Return from interrupt by pulling the status register and program counter from the current stack.

Status Register (P)

N	V	D	I	Z	C
*	*	*	*	*	*

Addressing Mode	Assembly Language Format	Hex Op Code	Dec Op Code	No. Bytes
implied	RTI	$40	64	1

RTS Return from subroutine.

Operation: Return from a subroutine by pulling the program counter bytes from the stack.

Status Register (P)

N	V	D	I	Z	C
—	—	—	—	—	—

Addressing Mode	Assembly Language Format	Hex Op Code	Dec Op Code	No. Bytes
implied	RTS	$60	96	1

SBC Subtract with carry as borrow bit.

Operation: Subtract the content of memory from accumulator, subtract inverted C bit from the result, and place the result in the accumulator.

Status Register (P)

N	V	D	I	Z	C
*	*	—	—	*	*

Addressing Mode	Assembly Language Format	Hex Op Code	Dec Op Code	No. Bytes
(indirect,X)	SBC (Oper,X)	$E1	225	2
zero page	SBC Oper	$E5	229	2
immediate	SBC #Oper	$E9	233	2
absolute	SBC Oper	$ED	237	3
(indirect),Y	SBC (Oper),Y	$F1	241	2
zero page,X	SBC Oper,X	$F5	245	2
absolute,Y	SBC Oper,Y	$F9	249	3
absolute,X	SBC Oper,X	$FD	253	3

SEC Set carry bit.

Operation: Set C = 1.

Status Register (P)

N	V		D	I	Z	C
—	—		—	—	—	1

Addressing Mode	Assembly Language Format	Hex Op Code	Dec Op Code	No. Bytes
implied	SEC	$38	56	1

SED Set decimal mode.

Operation: Set D = 1.

Status Register (P)

N	V		D	I	Z	C
—	—		1	—	—	—

Addressing Mode	Assembly Language Format	Hex Op Code	Dec Op Code	No. Bytes
implied	SED	$F8	248	1

SEI Set interrupt disable.

Operation: Set I = 1.

Status Register (P)

N	V		D	I	Z	C
—	—		—	1	—	—

Addressing Mode	Assembly Language Format	Hex Op Code	Dec Op Code	No. Bytes
implied	SEI	$78	120	1

STA Store accumulator to memory.

Operation: Store the content of the accumulator to memory.

STA *(cont.)*

Status Register (P)

N V D I Z C

— — — — — —

Addressing Mode	Assembly Language Format	Hex Op Code	Dec Op Code	No. Bytes
(indirect,X)	STA (Oper,X)	$81	129	2
zero page	STA Oper	$85	133	2
absolute	STA Oper	$8D	141	3
(indirect),Y	STA (Oper),Y	$91	145	2
zero page,X	STA Oper,X	$95	149	2
absolute,Y	STA Oper,Y	$99	153	3
absolute,X	STA Oper,X	$9D	157	3

STX Store register X to memory.

Operation: Store the content of the X register to memory.

Status Register (P)

N V D I Z C

— — — — — —

Addressing Mode	Assembly Language Format	Hex Op Code	Dec Op Code	No. Bytes
zero page	STX Oper	$86	134	2
absolute	STX Oper	$8E	142	3
zero page,X	STX Oper,X	$96	150	2

STY Store register Y to memory.

Operation: Store the content of register Y to memory.

Status Register (P)

N V D I Z C

— — — — — —

Addressing Mode	Assembly Language Format	Hex Op Code	Dec Op Code	No. Bytes
zero page	STY Oper	$84	132	2
absolute	STY Oper	$8C	140	3
zero page,X	STY Oper,X	$94	148	2

TAX Transfer accumulator to register X.

Operation: Transfer the content of the accumulator to register X.

Status Register (P)

N	V		D	I	Z	C
*	_		_	_	*	_

Addressing Mode	Assembly Language Format	Hex Op Code	Dec Op Code	No. Bytes
implied	TAX	$AA	170	1

TAY Transfer accumulator to register Y.

Operation: Transfer the content of the accumulator to register Y.

Status Register (P)

N	V		D	I	Z	C
*	_		_	_	*	_

Addressing Mode	Assembly Language Format	Hex Op Code	Dec Op Code	No. Bytes
implied	TAY	$A8	168	1

TSX Transfer the stack pointer to register X.

Operation: Transfer the content of the stack pointer to register X.

Status Register (P)

N	V		D	I	Z	C
*	_		_	_	*	_

Addressing Mode	Assembly Language Format	Hex Op Code	Dec Op Code	No. Bytes
implied	TSX	$BA	186	1

TXA Transfer register X to accumulator.

Operation: Transfer the content of register X to the accumulator.

TXA *(cont.)*

Status Register (P)

N	V		D	I	Z	C
*	—		—	—	*	—

Addressing Mode	Assembly Language Format	Hex Op Code	Dec Op Code	No. Bytes
implied	TXA	$8A	138	1

TXS Transfer register X to the current stack pointer.

Operation: Transfer the content of the X register to the stack pointer.

Status Register (P)

N	V		D	I	Z	C
—	—		—	—	—	—

Addressing Mode	Assembly Language Format	Hex Op Code	Dec Op Code	No. Bytes
implied	TXS	$9A	154	1

TYA Transfer register Y to accumulator.

Operation: Transfer the content of the Y register to the accumulator. Adjust the N and Z bits accordingly.

Status Register (P)

N	V		D	I	Z	C
*	—		—	—	*	—

Addressing Mode	Assembly Language Format	Hex Op Code	Dec Op Code	No. Bytes
implied	TYA	$98	152	1

5

Introduction to CP/M Procedures

CP/M (Control Program for Microcomputers) is a relatively simple, highly successful control scheme. It is not an integral part of the Commodore 128 as BASIC is. The CP/M system has to be loaded into the computer from the CP/M SYSTEM DISK. Once the system is in place, however, a user gets the impression of working with an entirely different computer system.

The system is provided for one simple reason: there are thousands of pieces of good software already available for CP/M systems. Given the right circumstances, CP/M software written for one kind of computer can be readily adapted for use on other kinds of computers—provided the computer can run machine code written for Z80 and 8080 microprocessors. The Commodore 128 is built around an entirely different kind of microprocessor, the 8502. This poses no real difficulty when you consider that the system includes a Z80 microprocessor for running CP/M programming.

CP/M is a topic worthy of a book of its own, and it is impossible to fit a definitive introduction into a book of this scope. Therefore, the discussions in this chapter are limited to a summary of special features that should give Commodore 128 users good reason to pursue the subject in greater depth.

Bringing Up CP/M on the Commodore 128

The CP/M operating system has to be loaded into the Commodore 128 from the CP/M System Disk. The disk is auto-booting, so it can be loaded and run by turning on the computer, doing a Reset operation, or entering the BOOT command. The system is ready for use when the A> prompt symbols appear on the screen.

CP/M software is written for the 80-column screen display. If your system is set up for 80-column text, make sure the 40/80 DISPLAY switch is latched down when you boot the CP/M disk.

You can run CP/M on a 40-column screen but you can see only 40 of the 80 columns at a time. Scroll the display to the left and right by holding down the CONTROL key and pressing the gray left- and right-arrow keys.

You can return to C128 mode by removing the CP/M disk from the disk drive and operating the Reset pushbutton.

Help for Beginners

Commodore 128 users, especially those who are not fully acquainted with CP/M ought to spend an evening or two exploring the extensive HELP feature. It describes the main features of the system and provides a few helpful examples.

Bring up CP/M as described above and respond to the A> prompt by entering HELP. That brings up the list of help topics shown in Figure 5-1 and puts the system into the help mode. You know you are in the help mode when the prompt message looks like this:

```
HELP>
```

Respond to the prompt by typing one of the topic names. When you are ready to leave the help mode, press the RETURN key.

Fig. 5-1 List of topics available under the HELP mode

C128_CP/M	COMMANDS	CNTRLCHARS	COPYSYS
DIR	DUMP	ED	ERASE
GET	HELP	HEXCOM	INITDIR
LINK	MAC	PATCH	PIP (COPY)
RMAC	SAVE	SET	SETDEF
SUBMIT	TYPE	USER	XREF
DATE	DEVICE		
FILESPEC	GENCOM		
KEYFIG	LIB		
PUT	RENAME		
SHOW	SID		

The first topic in the list offers a general view of CP/M for the Commodore 128. You can access this information by responding to the HELP> prompt:

C128_CP/M

> *NOTE:* The Commodore 128 keyboard does not include the underline character that is often used in CP/M names. That character is printed to the screen in the CP/M mode, however, when you press the *white, left-arrow key.*

Specifying the HELP topic, C128__CP/M, lists further subtopics. You can access any of the subtopics by typing a period followed by the name of the subtopic. If you want to see information about COMMAND__LINE, follow the HELP> prompt with this:

.COMMAND__LINE

The explanation on the screen is complete, but because it represents the end of a sequence of topics and subtopics, it shows the HELP> prompt without reference to entering a period followed by a subtopic name.

As long as the system remains in the HELP mode, you can get to any topic and subtopic in this general fashion:

topic,subtopic

If you want to view VIRTUAL__DISK subtopic under C128__CP/M, answer the HELP> prompt with:

C128__CP/M,VIRTUAL__DISK

You are wise to begin your computerized study of CP/M for the Commodore 128 by reviewing the notational conventions used on the HELP screens. Use the following command to display that summary:

COMMANDS,CONVENTIONS

The following paragraphs list all help commands and the kinds of information they offer. The commands, as shown here, assume the system is displaying the HELP> prompt.

Help Mode Command: **C128__CP/M**

A brief introduction to CP/M as implemented on the Commodore 128.

Help Mode Command: **C128__CP/M,COMMAND__LINE**

A description of the application of the two white CRSR keys.

Help Mode Command: **C128__CP/M,DISK__STATUS**

A description of the meaning of the disk-status report located in the lower-right corner of the screen.

Help Mode Command: **C128__CP/M,KEYBRD__DEFS**

A general description of how CP/M utilizes the SHIFT, CONTROL, and COMMODORE keys.

Help Mode Command: **C128_CP/M,KEYBRD_DEFS, ALPHNUM_KEYS**

A description of the function of the alphanumeric keys and the numeric keys on the calculator keypad.

Help Mode Command: **HELP C128_CP/M,KEYBRD_DEFS, ARROW_KEYS**

A description of the system's use of the four gray arrow keys.

Help Mode Command: **C128_CP/M,KEYBRD_DEFS, EXTRA_KEYS**

A description of the functions of the British pound-sign, white up-arrow, and other control keys.

Help Mode Command: **C128_CP/M,RT_SHFT_FNCT**

A summary of procedures for redefining the functions assigned to keys.

Help Mode Command: **C128_CP/M,RT_SHFT_FNCT, MODE_TOGGLE**

A description of the ALT key and ways to change screen attributes.

Help Mode Command: **C128_CP/M,RT_SHFT_FNCT, STRING_EDIT**

Instructions on how to redefine the application of keys in terms of string expressions.

Help Mode Command: **C128_CP/M,RT_SHFT_FNCT, HEX_EDIT**

Instructions on how to edit the hexadecimal value assigned to a key.

Help Mode Command: **C128_CP/M,SPECIAL_FNCT**

A description of the default functions assigned to the NO SCROLL, gray left- and right-arrow, ENTER, and RUN/STOP keys.

Help Mode Command: **C128_CP/M,VIRTUAL_DISK**

A description of the virtual disk drive, drive E.

Help Mode Command: **C128_CP/M,MFM_FORMATS**

A description of the disk formats supported by the system.

Help Mode Command: **CNTRLCHARS**

A complete listing of CONTROL-*key* editing functions.

Summary of CP/M Commands

Commands for CP/M can be classified as built-in and transient. The technical difference is that the built-in commands are loaded into RAM along with the CP/M operating system. Transient commands are loaded from disk and run only when needed. The practical difference is that you can execute the built-in commands without having the main CP/M disk in the disk drive. That is not the case for transient commands.

First-time users also ought to be aware of the fact that the CP/M System Disk supplied with the Commodore 128 has programming on both sides. It is not a double-sided disk in the technical sense, however. The two sides are entirely separate and use separate directories.

Thus, when you make a backup copy on the 1571 disk drive, you should be prepared to copy files from both sides—to copy all the files from one side, flip the disk, and copy the files from the other. Figure 5-2 shows the two directories. The appropriate copying procedures are described in the closing sections of this chapter.

Fig. 5-2 Directory listings for sides 1 and 2 of the master CP/M disk

Side 1—

CPM+.SYS	KEYFIG.HLP
CCP.COM	FORMAT.COM
HELP.COM	PIP.COM
HELP.HLP	DIR.COM
KEYFIG.COM	COPYSYS.COM

Side 2—

DATE.COM	PATCH.COM
DATEC.ASM	PIP.COM
DATEC.RSX	PUT.COM
DEVICE.COM	RENAME.COM
DIR.COM	SAVE.COM
DIRLBL.RSX	SET.COM
DUMP.COM	SETDEF.COM
ED.COM	SHOW.COM
ERASE.COM	SUBMIT.COM
GENCOM.COM	TYPE.COM
GET.COM	
INITDIR.COM	

COPYSYS The COPYSYS command copies system files to a new disk. Although the command is not implemented on the CP/M system disk supplied with the Commodore 128, procedures are available for emulating it.

Help Mode Command: **COPYSYS**

DIR The DIR command displays the content of the disk directory. The extent of the display depends on the nature of options that might be used with it.

Command Type: **DIR** is a built-in command.
DIR with options is a transient command.

Help Mode Commands: **DIR**
DIR,BUILT-IN
DIR,BUILT-IN,EXAMPLES
DIR,WITHOPTIONS
DIR,WITHOPTIONS,OPTIONS
DIR,WITHOPTIONS,EXAMPLES

DUMP The DUMP command displays the ASCII coding for a specified file.

Command Type: Transient.

Help Mode Command: **DUMP**

ED The ED command invokes a simple line editor that is intended for generating source files for 8080A coding.

Command Type: Transient.

Help Mode Commands: **ED**
ED,COMMANDS
ED,EXAMPLES

ERASE The ERASE command deletes a specified file from a disk directory.

Command Type: Transient.

Help Mode Commands: **ERASE**
ERASE,OPTION
ERASE,EXAMPLES

GET The GET command shifts the input from the console (keyboard) to a specified disk file. It is the complement of the PUT command.

Command Type: Transient.

Help Mode Commands: GET
GET,OPTIONS
GET,EXAMPLES

HELP The HELP command invokes the system's help mode of operation.

Help Mode Command: HELP

HEXCOM The HEXCOM command converts a hexadecimal (binary) file to a COM (Command) file for execution under CP/M.

Help Mode Command: HEXCOM

INITDIR The INITDIR command initializes an existing file for date time stamping.

Help Mode Command: INITDIR

LINK The LINK command links (concatenates) one binary file to the end of another. The command is not included on the basic CP/M disk.

Help Mode Commands: LINK
LINK,OPTIONS
LINK,EXAMPLES

MAC The MAC command assembles 8080A/Z80 source-code, ASM, files to executable machine code. The command is not included on the basic CP/M disk.

Help Mode Commands: MAC
MAC,OPTIONS
MAC,EXAMPLES

PATCH The PATCH command displays or installs a patch number to a specified system or command file.

Help Mode Commands: PATCH

PIP The PIP command copies a file from a specified source to a specified destination. This command is often used for copying disk files.

Help Mode Commands: PIP
PIP,OPTIONS
PIP,EXAMPLES

RMAC The RMAC command converts a source file into a relocatable REL file that can be linked to COM files. The command is not included on the basic CP/M disk.

Help Mode Commands: RMAC
RMAC,OPTIONS
RMAC,EXAMPLE

SAVE The SAVE command saves a specified block of memory to disk.

Help Mode Commands: SAVE,EXAMPLE

SET The SET command sets a number of different disk parameters.

Command Type: Transient.

Help Mode Commands: SET
SET,LABEL
SET,LABEL,EXAMPLES
SET,PASSWORDS
SET,PASSWORDS,MODES
SET,ATTRIBUTES
SET,ATTRIBUTES,EXAMPLES
SET,DEFAULT
SET,TIME-STAMPS
SET,TIME-STAMPS,OPTIONS
SET,TIME-STAMPS,EXAMPLES
SET,DRIVES

SETDEF The SETDEF command displays or defines disk drives for search order under loading or SUBMIT operations.

Command Type: Transient.

Help Mode Commands: SETDEF
SETDEF,EXAMPLES

SUBMIT The SUBMIT command executes a specified CP/M batch (executive) file.

Command Type: Transient.

Help Mode Commands: SUBMIT
SUBMIT,SUBFILE
SUBMIT,EXECUTE
SUBMIT,PROFILE.SUB

TYPE The TYPE command displays or types the contents of an ASCII file.

Command Type: Built-in for screen display.
Transient for multiple files and printer.

Help Mode Commands: TYPE
TYPE,EXAMPLES

USER The USER command sets the user number for disk-file access.

Command Type: Built-in.

Help Mode Commands: USER
USER,EXAMPLES

XREF The XREF command provides a summary of variables used in assembly programming. The command is not available on the basic CP/M disk.

Help Mode Command: XREF

DATE The DATE command is used for setting and displaying the calendar clock built into the CP/M system.

Command Type: Transient.

Help Mode Commands: DATE
DATE,EXAMPLES

DEVICE The DEVICE command is the primary mechanism for setting device parameters, such as screen size and RS-232-C baud rate.

Command Type: Transient.

Help Mode Commands: DEVICE
DEVICE,OPTIONS
DEVICE,EXAMPLES
DEVICE,C128_DEVICES

FILESPEC FILESPEC is a non-executable text file that describes the procedure for specifying files in the appropriate CP/M format.

Help Mode Command: FILESPEC

GENCOM The GENCOM commands creates a COM file with RSX files. It is not included on the basic CP/M disk.

Help Mode Commands: GENCOM
GENCOM,OPTIONS
GENCOM,EXAMPLES

KEYFIG The KEYFIG command makes possible the redefinition of the function of any key on the keyboard.

Command Type: Transient.

Help Mode Commands: KEYFIG
KEYFIG,EDITING_KEYS
KEYFIG,EDITING_KEYS,EDIT_COLORS
KEYFIG,EDITING_KEYS,EDIT_HEX
KEYFIG,EDITING_KEYS,EDIT_SPECIAL
KEYFIG,EDITING_KEYS,EDIT_STRINGS
KEYFIG,FINISHING_UP
KEYFIG,FOR_EXPERTS
KEYFIG,KEY_VALUES
KEYFIG,LOG/PHY_CLRS
KEYFIG,SELECT_A_KEY
KEYFIG,SETTING_UP
KEYFIG,SETTING_UP,WHAT_TO_DO

LIB The library command creates library files for REL files. It is not included on the basic CP/M disk.

Help Mode Commands: LIB
LIB,OPTIONS
LIB,MODIFIERS
LIB,EXAMPLES

PUT The PUT command directs printer or output operations to a specified device. It is the complement of the GET command.

Command Type: Transient.

Help Mode Commands: PUT
PUT,OPTIONS
PUT,EXAMPLES

SHOW The SHOW command displays the current disk-status information.

Command Type: Transient.

Help Mode Commands: SHOW
SHOW,EXAMPLES

SID The SID command invokes the symbolic debugger for 8080A/Z80 programming. It is not included as part of the basic CP/M disk.

Help Mode Commands: SID,COMMANDS
SID,EXAMPLES
SID,UTILITIES

Making a Backup Copy of the CP/M System Disk

It is always a good idea to make copies of important master disks, including the CP/M System Disk. The copying operation must be done while operating in the CP/M mode. Of course, you will need a fresh, double-sided disk as well as the CP/M master disk.

The general procedure is to format the new disk, then use a version of the PIP command that instructs the system to copy all files. The actual mechanical procedure depends on whether you are using a single- or double-drive system.

Using a Single-Drive System

The procedure for making a backup copy of the CP/M master disk refers to virtual disk Drive E. No such disk drive exists, but the system "thinks" it does. For all practical purposes, Drive A and Drive E are the same.

1. Bring up the CP/M operating system.
2. When the A> prompt appears, enter the FORMAT command.
3. Use the gray up- and down-arrow keys to select the *C128 double sided* format option and press the RETURN key.
4. When prompted to do so, replace the CP/M master disk with the new disk to be formatted and type $.
5. When you are eventually asked whether you want to format another disk, respond by pressing the N key. This step completes the formatting procedure for the new disk.
6. Replace the newly formatted disk with the CP/M master disk and enter this command:

   ```
   PIP E:=A:*.*
   ```

Through the remainder of the backup procedure, the master CP/M disk being copied is called Disk A. The new disk is called Disk E. Prompting messages at the bottom of the screen tell you when to swap disks. Make the swaps as directed and press the RETURN key when ready.

When copying is done for the first side of the CP/M master disk, flip it over and repeat the procedure from Step 6.

Using a Two-Drive System

The procedure for making a backup copy of the CP/M master disk refers to Drives A and B. These are simply alternative names for Drives 0 and 1.

1. Bring up the CP/M operating system with the CP/M master disk in Drive A and the new disk in Drive B.
2. When the A> prompt appears, enter this command:

    FORMAT B:

3. Use the gray up- and down-arrow keys to select the *C128 double sided* format option and press the RETURN key.
4. When prompted to do so, replace the CP/M master disk with the new disk to be formatted and type $.
5. When you are eventually asked whether you want to format another disk, respond by pressing the N key. This step completes the formatting procedure for the new disk.
6. Begin the copying procedure by entering this command:

    PIP B:=A:*.*

When copying is done for the first side of the CP/M master disk, flip it over and repeat the procedure from Step 6.

6

Text Screen Procedures

The most conspicuous parts of the Commodore 128 system are the keyboard and video screen. Indeed, they should be the most conspicuous because they are the primary links between the user and the system's internal workings.

Most of what you put into the system enters via the keyboard, and most of what comes out of the system is displayed on the video screen. Except when executing a purely graphics routine, the computer communicates with you in a text format—with symbols, code words, numerals, and printed messages. Understanding the essential features and limitations of available text screen operations is thus vital to the preparation of meaningful and high-quality programs for the Commodore 128.

Preliminary Considerations

The text features of the Commodore 128 personal computer are quite dynamic and extensive. Given the broad scope of text-screen procedures, it is appropriate to introduce various features of the topic before attempting to explain them in detail. Bear in mind that the discussions assume you are using all-text screens or portions of split (text-graphics) screens devoted to text operations.

Column Formats

The text screens for the Commodore 128 are most often specified as 40-column or 80-column screens. The 40-column format is available through the composite-video output, whereas the 80-column screen is visible only through the RGB output.

The 40-Column Text Screen Format

Unless you specify otherwise, the Commodore 128 brings up its normal 40-column text screen format. This screen allows up to 40 characters per line and uses 25 lines per screen. This adds up to a maximum of 1000 character locations. Of course, you can print fewer than 40 characters per line and use fewer than 25 lines of text—those are simply the maximum figures.

The 40-column screen is the most frequently used text screen. The characters reproduce quite well on a standard TV screen and look even better on a wideband monitor. Figure 6-1 shows the 40-column text screen and indicates the locations of its 1000 possible character locations. The numerals at the top of the drawing indicate the *column* number for each line of text. The numerals along the side indicate the line or *(row)* numbers.

Notice the column and row labels. Both begin with 0 in the upper-left corner of the screen. The column numbering goes from left

Fig. 6-1 Column-row organization of 40-column text screen

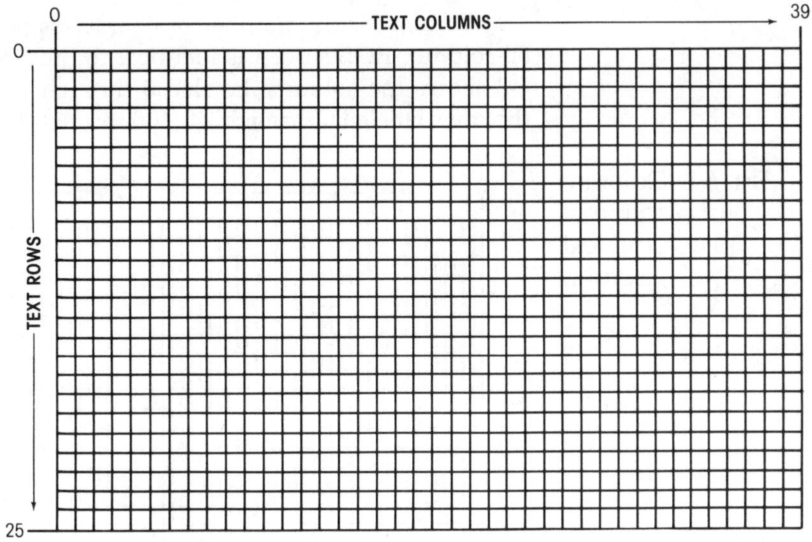

to right, using numerals 0 through 39 or hexadecimal $00 through $27. The numbering for the rows runs from top to bottom and from 0 through 24 ($00 through $18).

Thus, the character location in the extreme upper-left corner of the screen is located at column 0, row 0. A character located very near the middle of the screen is at column 19, row 12.

Virtually all 40-column text presentations use this column-row format in some way. However, as described in this chapter, you can reduce the size of the screen area to create a smaller text window.

The 80-Column Text Screen Format

The Commodore 128 system also has an 80-column screen—two of them, actually. One kind of 80-column screen uses characters that have the same height, but half the width, of the 40-column characters. That 80-column format is the most commonly used version and is available only through the RGB video output. The second 80-column format uses characters that are the same size as those used for the 40-column screens, but the software makes possible scrolling the text horizontally so that complete lines can be viewed through composite-video connections. This format is generally used when running 80-column CP/M programs through 40-column, composite-video hardware. Avoid writing programs that use the 80-column format unless you are sure that potential users will be working with an RGB display.

The RGB 80-column screen has room for twice as many characters as its 40-column, composite-video counterpart. An RGB screen uses the same number of lines as the composite-video screen, though: 25 of them. Therefore, the 80-column screen can display up to 2000 characters at any given time.

Except for the number of characters per row, the layout of the 80-column, RGB screen is identical to the 40-column version. Figure 6-2 shows the columns labeled 0 through 79 ($00 through $4F), and the rows labeled 0 through 24 ($00 through $18).

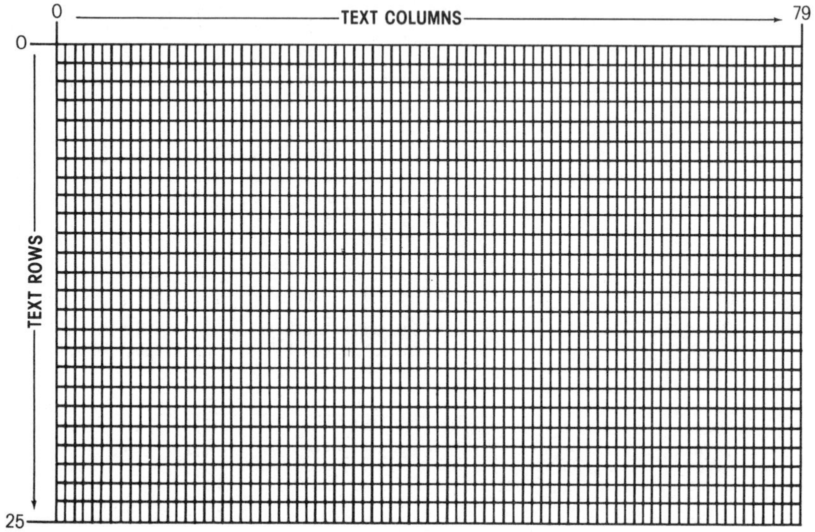

Fig. 6-2 Column-row organization of 80-column text screen

The character location in the upper-left corner can be specified as column 0, row 0—the same labeling format that applies to the 40-column screen. The extreme lower-right corner of the 80-column screen, however, is at column 79, row 24.

Alternative Text Window Configurations

The default text window is the largest possible text-screen area. Generally speaking, the default text window files all of the area within the screen's border area. You can reduce the size of the text window, which does not change the size of the characters but rather the size of the screen area where normal printing and text-scrolling operations take place.

Using appropriate techniques, you can print important text in one part of the screen, limit the size of the text window, and restrict subsequent printing operations to a different area of the screen.

Text Printing Techniques

BASIC programs most often print text characters to the screen by executing PRINT statements, although you can achieve the same result by POKEing character data directly to selected video RAM. Machine-language programs generally print text to the screen through the

Kernal routine, CHROUT. The character to be printed is loaded into the accumulator of the 8502, and the Kernal is called immediately after that. The routine supports the standard text features, including automatic advancement to the next column location, scrolling, and a host of cursor- and screen-related control operations.

Text Character Sets

The Commodore 128 features a ROM-based character set of 256 characters—upper- and lowercase letters of the alphabet, numerals 0 through 9, standard punctuation marks, a handful of mathematical symbols, and a family of graphic-like characters. Only 128 different characters, however, are plotted as *normal* characters and 128 as *reverse* characters. All characters are plotted with two color attributes, a *foreground* color and a *background* color. The normal characters appear in the designated foreground color against the designated background color. Reverse characters, on the other hand, are plotted in the background color against the foreground color.

The 40- and 80-column screens support all 256 characters but handle them in different ways. The 80-column screen is better in that it can display any combination of all the characters at one time. The 40-column screen cannot do so.

As far as 40-column displays are concerned, two different character sets exist. One is commonly called the *uppercase/graphics* set. It is the system's default character set that prints all alphabetical characters in their uppercase format and supports all the special graphics characters. The second 40-column character set, the *uppercase/lowercase* set, prints both upper- and lowercase characters but supports few graphics characters. A 40-column screen displays characters from one set or the other but never both at the same time.

Text Cursor and Screen Control Procedures

Text printing operations normally take place in a systematic column-by-column, row-by-row fashion. You can, however, defeat the usual course of printing events and print a character at any valid column-row location on the screen.

The cursor normally keeps track of where the next character is to be printed on the screen. The cursor location is marked on the screen when running in the immediate (programming) mode. The cursor symbol appears as a flashing solid rectangle in the current character color.

The cursor symbol is invisible through most operations where the system is executing a program. In such instances, the cursor appears on the screen only while certain keyboard-input operations are being executed.

BASIC's PRINT statements, along with Kernal routines such as CHROUT, control cursor operations automatically. PRINTing certain code numbers prints nothing to the screen, but rather performs cursor-related operations, such as upward and downward linefeeds, homing the cursor, clearing portions of the screen, changing character colors, and so on.

Such operations keep track of the cursor location in designated RAM registers. Some of those registers portray the cursor position in a column-row format, whereas others reflect the same information in terms of video RAM addresses.

In any case, you can set and determine the current cursor location at any time. The Commodore 128, in other words, includes provisions for gaining complete software control over cursor-related text operations.

Text Screens and Video RAM

You can POKE or load text-character data directly to video RAM addresses. There is little justification for resorting to this more cumbersome technique under normal text-screen conditions. But POKEing does open the door for more sophisticated procedures that call for using multiple screens of text and loading text data directly from a disk file.

The closing sections of this chapter describe the nature of video RAM and the kinds of character data that can be loaded directly to it. Those sections shed light on some key principles that are difficult to implement in any other fashion.

Switching Column Formats

Unless directed otherwise, turning on or resetting the Commodore 128 brings up the 40-column text format with the uppercase/graphics character set, which is the system's default screen. This discussion deals with techniques for changing column formats, both from the keyboard and through programmed operations.

> *NOTE:* Procedures referring to the 80-column text screen have no practical meaning if your system does not include an RGB monitor and the proper RGB cabling to the Commodore 128 console. Data for the 80-column display is found only at the RGB connector, never at the composite-video or RF connector.

The presence of the 40/80 DISPLAY switch on the keyboard provides a straightforward means for switching between the 40- and 80-column text screens. The computer normally tests that switch only under three circumstances:

1. When you turn on the computer
2. When you momentarily depress the Reset pushbutton
3. When you press RUN/STOP-RESTORE

If the 40/80 DISPLAY is in its up unlatched position, executing one of the three operations instructs the system to use the 40-column screen. If the switch is latched down, any of those operations sets up the 80-column screen format. Unless you are using some custom software to direct otherwise (a technique described subsequently in this section), the 40/80 DISPLAY switch cannot be used to change the column format without resorting to one of the three initialization routines.

Switching Column Formats from the Keyboard

The procedures described in the previous paragraphs cite one kind of approach to switching column formats. They are drastic procedures, however, because they restore many other default screen attributes, and situations exist where that is quite inconvenient.

The preferred way to switch column formats from the keyboard is by pressing ESC/X—press the ESC key, release it, then press the X key. This operation toggles the screen format: If the system is using the 40-column format, ESC/X changes it to the 80-column format, and vice versa.

An alternative procedure assumes that the F1 function key is using its default function, GRAPHIC, and that the system is currently running in BASIC. BASIC supports six graphics modes numbered 0 through 5. GRAPHIC 0 happens to be the normal 40-column text screen and GRAPHIC 5 is the 80-column screen.

Pressing the F1 function key should make the system print GRAPHIC on the screen. Respond by pressing the 0 key to set the 40-column screen or the 5 key to set the 80-column format. Follow that keystroke with a RETURN.

Of course, typing and entering GRAPHIC0 or GRAPHIC4 works equally well.

The ESC/X procedure is preferred because it works under all C128 operating conditions—under BASIC as well as in the machine language monitor.

Switching Column Formats from BASIC Programming

The procedures for switching between the 40- and 80-column screens described here override the setting of the 40/80 DISPLAY switch. For most practical purposes, the setting is not relevant.

Using the GRAPHIC Statement

The most direct procedure for setting a desired column format from BASIC programming is through the GRAPHIC statement:

Use GRAPHIC 0 to set the 40-column format.
Use GRAPHIC 5 to set the 80-column format.

If you want to set the new column format and clear the new screen as well, follow the GRAPHIC statement with a SCNCLR or take advantage of the screen-clearing option for the GRAPHIC statement:

Use GRAPHIC 0,1 to set and clear the 40-column screen.
Use GRAPHIC 5,1 to set and clear the 80-column screen.

PRINTing the ESC/X Function

You can use the toggling effect of the ESC/X keyboard operation to change column formats. The general idea is to PRINT a string composed of ASCII characters for ESC and X:

```
PRINT CHR$(27)+CHR$(88)
```

or

```
PRINT CHR$(27)+"X"
```

Both examples take advantage of the fact that ASCII code 27 is the ESCape code. The first example follows it with the ASCII code for the X character, whereas the second prints it as a string character.

Using the 40/80COL Register and SWAP Kernal

The system's zero-page RAM includes a register that flags the use of the 40- or 80-column screen format. The following summary shows both the decimal and hexadecimal values most relevant for using this register.

40/80COL A zero-page register that flags the use of a 40- or 80-column text screen.

Decimal address: **215**
Hexadecimal address: **$D7**

Values:

$00 (0) = 40-column format
$80 (128) = 80-column format

Writing the appropriate values to this register sets the corresponding screen format, and reading the values determines the current format.

Having access to the 40/80COL register suggests the following procedures for switching screen formats from BASIC programming:

Use POKE 215,0 to set the 40-column screen.
Use POKE 215,128 to set the 80-column screen.

That register, incidentally, provides a convenient means for determining the current column format:

If PEEK(215)=0, the system is using the 40-column screen.
If PEEK(215)>0, the system is using the 80-column screen.

The Kernal includes a routine that toggles (swaps) the column format in much the same way as the ESC/X operation. This routine is located at $FF5F (65375) and can be implemented from BASIC in this simple fashion:

```
SYS 65375
```

Switching Column Formats from Machine Language Programming

The zero-page 40/80COL register at $D7 is critical for executing the simplest column-format routines in machine language programming. The data in this register flags the screen format: $00 for a 40-column screen and $80 for the 80-column screen.

Use this procedure to set the 80-column screen:

```
LDA #$00
STA $D7
```

and this one to set the 40-column text format:

```
LDA #$80
STA $D7
```

Of course, you can use an LDA $D7 instruction to fetch the current column status to register A.

The SWAP routine in the Kernal provides a simple procedure for switching the current column format. The entry-point address is $FF5F and can be accessed from a machine language program this way:

```
JSR $FF5F
```

Polling the 40/80 DISPLAY Switch

The Commodore 128 looks at the status of the 40/80 DISPLAY switch only when running an initialization routine—when the user turns on the computer, does a Reset operation, or executes a RUN/STOP-RESTORE keystroke. You can write some programming instructions for checking the status of this switch and responding accordingly.

The 40/80 DISPLAY switch status is carried as bit 7 of $D505 (54533). That bit is set (equal to 1) when the switch is unlatched for the 40-column mode and cleared (equal to 0) when the switch is latched down for the 80-column mode.

Reading the 40/80 DISPLAY switch status from BASIC programming is a matter of executing this sort of PEEK function:

```
PEEK(54533) AND 128
```

If this function returns a value of 0, the switch is latched down (80 column). Otherwise, this function returns a value of 128 to show that the switch is in its unlatched position (40 column).

That is a read-only operation. It has no effect on the current column format. You must apply one of the column-format operations to take advantage of the information you find there.

Suppose that you want to check the 40/80 DISPLAY switch and adjust the column format accordingly. Consider this approach:

```
10 SS=PEEK(54533) AND 128
20 IF SS=0 THEN POKE 215,128
30 IF SS=128 THEN POKE 215,0
```

Line 10—Check the status of the 40/80 DISPLAY switch.

Line 20—If it is DOWN, set the 80-column format.

Line 30—If it is UP, set the 40-column format.

The program in Listing 6-1 suggests a machine language implementation of the same procedure.

Switching Character Sets

The Commodore 128 can print characters from one of two different character sets at a given time. As described in this section, you can switch easily between the two.

Listing 6-1

```
        LDA #$00        ;ASSUME SET 40-COL
        BIT $D505       ;LOOK AT THE SWITCH
        BMI DOIT        ;USE 40-COL IF UP
        LDA#$80         ;ELSE SET FOR 80-COL
DOIT    STA $D7         ;SET THE SCREEN
        RTS
```

The main difference between the sets is that the uppercase/lowercase set includes upper- and lowercase letters of the alphabet, whereas the uppercase/graphics set includes only uppercase letters of the alphabet. Both share the same punctuation marks and numerals.

Switching character sets always means that subsequent characters will be plotted to the screen from the current set—at least until the sets are switched again. When working with the 80-column screen, switching character sets does not affect characters previously plotted on the screen. On a 40-column screen, however, switching character sets changes all previously printed characters as well as those to be printed after the switch takes place.

The uppercase/graphics character set is the system's default set. Unless directed by keyboard operations or some programming, the system remains in that mode of operation.

Switching Character Sets from the Keyboard

The preferred way to switch column formats from the keyboard is by pressing SHIFT-C= (holding down one of the SHIFT keys while pressing the Commodore key [C=]). This operation toggles the character set: if the system is using the uppercase/graphics set, SHIFT-C= changes to the uppercase/lowercase set, and vice versa.

The following CONTROL-key operations offer additional features:

CONTROL-N: Set the uppercase/lowercase character set
CONTROL-K: Disable further character-set changes
CONTROL-L: Enable character-set changes

Pressing CONTROL-N (holding down the CONTROL key while pressing the N key) sets the uppercase/lowercase character set. No corresponding CONTROL keystroke exists for returning to the uppercase/graphics set, which has to be done by toggling the set with SHIFT-C=.

If you find that the business of switching character sets is causing some difficulties, lock out the change—freeze the current character set—by pressing CONTROL-K. Having done that, you can restore the normal character-set changing feature by pressing CONTROL-L.

Switching Character Sets from BASIC Programming

A small group of ASCII control codes offers the most direct procedure for setting the desired character set from BASIC programming. Using the following codes in PRINT CHR$ statements implements the character-set functions:

PRINT CHR$(14): Set uppercase/lowercase character set.
PRINT CHR$(142): Set uppercase/graphics character set.
PRINT CHR$(11): Disable subsequent character-set changes.
PRINT CHR$(12): Enable subsequent character-set changes.

Suppose that you've written a program which requires the user to INPUT some information from the keyboard, and you want to make absolutely certain that the information is entered in uppercase format. As a programmer, you have no way of knowing in advance which character set the user will be using at the moment. The example in Listing 6-2 forces the issue:

Line 10—Clear the screen and home the cursor.

Line 20—Set the uppercase/graphics character set and disable any further change.

Lines 30 and 40—Get information from the keyboard.

Lines 50 and 60—Print the information.

Line 70—Release the lock on character-set changes.

Listing 6-2

```
10 SCNCLR
20 PRINT CHR$(142);CHR$(11)
30 INPUT "YOUR FIRST NAME";F1$
40 INPUT "YOUR SURNAME";F2$
50 SCNCLR
60 FOR K=0 TO 9:PRINT F1$SPC(1)F2$:NEXT K
70 PRINT CHR$(12)
```

There are two registers that have some relevance to the current character-set selection and locking out character-set changes. A zero-page flag register, MODE, determines whether the user can change character sets.

MODE A zero-page flag register that enables/disables subsequent character-set changes.

Hexadecimal address: **$F7**
Decimal address: **247**

Values:

$00 (0) = Enable character-set change
$80 (128) = Disable character-set change

Writing the appropriate values to this register sets the status of the character-set change, and reading the values determines the current status.

Use POKE 247,0 to allow character-set changes.
Use POKE 247,128 to lock out subsequent attempts to switch character sets.

PEEKing to 247 returns the current status of the MODE register.

You can use a second register for setting the character set or determining which character set is being used, but the results are reliable only if the system is using its built-in character set. Assuming that the system is indeed using its own character set, bit 1 in the register at $0A2C (2604) is cleared to zero when using the uppercase/graphics character set and set to 1 when using the uppercase/lowercase set:

If PEEK(2604) AND 2=0, the system is using the uppercase/graphics character set.
If PEEK(2604) AND 2=2, the system is using the uppercase/lowercase character set.

If you want to change character sets, you can POKE the appropriate values to that register. The character set will change without regard to the enable/disable status of the set-change register.

To set the uppercase/graphics character set:

```
POKE 2604,PEEK(2604) AND 253
```

and the uppercase/lowercase character set:

```
POKE 2604,PEEK(2604) AND 253 OR 2
```

Machine Language Procedures for Changing Character Sets

The simplest machine language procedures for working with character-set changes amount to little more than machine language versions of the BASIC PRINT CHR$ statement.

Setting the uppercase/graphics character set

```
LDA #$8E
JSR $FFD2
```

is equivalent to

```
PRINT CHR$(142)
```

Setting the uppercase/lowercase character set

```
LDA #$0E
JSR $FFD2
```

is equivalent to

```
PRINT CHR$(14)
```

Disabling character-set changes

```
LDA #$0B
JSR $FFD2
```

is equivalent to

```
PRINT CHR$(11)
```

Enabling character-set changes

```
LDA #$12
JSR $FFD2
```

is equivalent to

```
PRINT CHR$(12)
```

Provided the system is using its standard ROM-based character set, machine language routines referring to bit 1 in register $0A2C can switch character sets without regard to the locking feature of the MODE register. The following routine sets the uppercase/graphics character set:

```
LDA $0A2C
AND #$FD
STA $0A2C
```

This one sets the uppercase/lowercase character set:

```
LDA $0A2C
ORA #$02
STA $0A2C
```

Determining the current character set configuration is a matter of executing a BIT $F7. This instruction clears the Z flag to 0 if the character-set change is enabled or sets the Z flag to 1 if the feature is disabled.

Setting the Normal/Inverse Character Format

All characters are plotted with two different color attributes: the *foreground* and *background* colors. The character is plotted with one of those colors, and the remaining area allocated for that character is plotted with the other color. The two colors are usually different, (otherwise the character is not visible on the screen).

The default relationship between foreground and background colors is one where the character is printed in the foreground color and the remaining area uses the background color. The default foreground color is light green and the background is dark gray. Thus, the screen tends to show light-colored characters on a darker-colored background.

You can reverse the standard foreground/background format and plot subsequent characters in their *reverse* mode. In that case, the character is plotted with the background color, and the remaining space uses the foreground color. The reverse mode is frequently used for highlighting portions of text on the screen.

Switching Normal/Reverse Characters from the Keyboard

The preferred procedure for setting normal and reverse characters from the keyboard involves a couple of simple keystrokes:

CONTROL-9 or CONTROL-R: Enable reverse mode
CONTROL-0: Disable reverse mode

Pressing a CONTROL-9 or CONTROL-R enables the reverse mode so that subsequent characters are printed in that mode. The mode remains in force until you press the RETURN key or CONTROL-0.

This is the preferred keyboard procedure because it works equally well in BASIC and the machine language monitor.

Programming Normal/Reverse Characters in BASIC

The simplest BASIC statements for enabling and disabling the reverse-character mode apply the PRINT CHR$ emulations of the direct-keyboard procedures.

PRINT CHR$(18): Enable the reverse-character mode.
PRINT CHR$(146): Disable the reverse-character mode.

The example in Listing 6-3 directly implements those control codes. This program prints THIS IS GOING TO BE A GREAT DAY! with GREAT highlighted in reverse-mode characters. Program line 30 first enables the reverse mode, prints GREAT, then disables the reverse mode.

Listing 6-3

```
10 SCNCLR
20 PRINT "THIS IS GOING TO BE A ";
30 PRINT CHR$(18)"GREAT"CHR$(146);
40 PRINT "DAY!"
```

Quote-mode techniques simplify the programming somewhat as shown in Listing 6-4.

Listing 6-4

```
10 SCNCLR
20 PRINT "THIS IS GOING TO BE A{space}{RvsOn}GREAT{RvsOff}
{space}DAY!"
```

An alternative procedure refers to the reverse/normal flag register, RVS, at zero-page address $F3 (243). This register is cleared to zero when the system is to print normal characters, and the register is set to a value greater than zero when printing reverse characters.

RVS A zero-page flag register that determines whether characters are printed in the normal or reverse format.

Hexadecimal address: $F3
Decimal address: 243

Values:

$00 (0): Disable reverse format
>zero: Enable reverse format

Use POKE 243,0 to disable reverse characters.
Use POKE 243,128 to enable reverse characters.
Use PEEK(243) to determine the current status:

PEEK(243) = 0—normal
PEEK(243) > 0—reverse

The routine in Listing 6-5 uses these POKEs and PEEKs to flash a message on the screen. Program line 40 is responsible for switching the normal/reverse format every time it is executed.

Listing 6-5

```
10 SCNCLR
20 DO WHILE K$=""
30 PRINT CHR$(19);
40 IF PEEK(243)=0 THEN POKE 243,128:ELSE POKE 243,128
50 PRINT "STRIKE ANY KEY TO STOP THIS . . .";
60 GET K$
70 LOOP
```

Machine Language Programming for Normal/Reverse Characters

The machine language procedures for working with reverse and normal character sets rely on the RVS register described in the previous section of this chapter. Fetching the data from RVS at $F3 sets the Z flag to 1 if the system is currently using the normal character set. Otherwise, fetching the data clears the Z flag to 0.

Storing $00 to RVS disables the reverse mode, and storing $80 to that register enables the reverse mode.

Setting Screen and Character Colors

The three principal color attributes for the text screens are the foreground, background, and border colors. The background color is the overall color of the "blank" portion of the screen. The border color is the color of the area surrounding the actual working portion of the screen.

The background and foreground colors work together to define the appearance of characters on the screen. In the normal character mode, characters are plotted with the foreground color, and the space surrounding them uses the overall background color. Conversely, when the reverse character mode is used, the characters are plotted with the background color and surrounded by the designated foreground colors.

The extended color mode adds a fourth color to the text screen—an additional background color for text characters.

Tables 6-1 and 6-2 show the colors available for text-screen applications. The only difference between the two tables is found in the Code column. The codes in Table 6-1 run from 1 through 16 and generally apply to BASIC's color-setting statements. The codes in Table 6-2 run from 0 through 15 and apply to direct-register procedures—POKEing and machine language operations.

Table 6-1
Colors and Codes Using 1-through-16 Format

Code	40-Column Color	80-Column Color
1	Black	Black
2	White	White
3	Red	Dark Red
4	Cyan	Light Cyan
5	Purple	Light Purple
6	Green	Green
7	Blue	Blue
8	Yellow	Light Yellow
9	Orange	Dark Purple
10	Brown	Dark Yellow
11	Light Red	Light Red
12	Dark Gray	Dark Cyan
13	Medium Gray	Medium Gray
14	Light Green	Light Green
15	Light Blue	Light Blue
16	Light Gray	Light Gray

Table 6-2
Colors and Codes Using 0-through-15 Format

Code		40-Column Color	80-Column Color
Hex	Dec		
$00	0	Black	Black
$01	1	White	White
$02	2	Red	Dark Red
$03	3	Cyan	Light Cyan
$04	4	Purple	Light Purple
$05	5	Green	Green
$06	6	Blue	Blue
$07	7	Yellow	Light Yellow
$08	8	Orange	Dark Purple
$09	9	Brown	Dark Yellow
$0A	10	Light Red	Light Red
$0B	11	Dark Gray	Dark Cyan
$0C	12	Medium Gray	Medium Gray
$0D	13	Light Green	Light Green
$0E	14	Light Blue	Light Blue
$0F	15	Light Gray	Light Gray

Setting the Border Color

There are two ways to go about setting the border color—the color of the area surrounding the working portion of the screen. One procedure uses

BASIC's COLOR statement and the other loads a color code directly to the border-color register in the video interface controller (VIC).

The general form of the COLOR statement is:

COLOR *srce,colr*

where *srce* is the source (screen attribute), and *colr* is a code number representing the desired color. For the sake of setting the border color, *srce* is set to 4. The *colr* code is selected from Table 6-1. Thus, the statement looks like this:

COLOR 4,*colr*

where *colr* is a value between 1 and 16 (Table 6-1).

The default border color is light green. Therefore, restoring that attribute is a matter of executing:

COLOR 4,14

The statement can be executed directly from the keyboard or within BASIC programming.

The four lower-order bits in the VIC register at $D020 (53280) carry the current border color as represented by the codes in Table 6-2—0 through 15. The presence of this register suggests an alternative procedure for setting the border color from BASIC:

POKE 53280,*colr*

where *colr* is a code number, 0 through 15. The default light-green border can thus be set by:

POKE 53280,13

The border-color register at $D020 provides the most convenient means for setting the border color from machine language routines. The general idea is to load the hexadecimal color code (see Table 6-2) to register A, then store it to $D020. The following sequence of instructions sets a white border color:

```
LDA #$01
STA $D020
```

The VIC's border-color register can also be used for determining the current border color code. When reading the content of that register, remember that the four higher-order bits are not relevant. The following BASIC statement returns the current border color in the 0-through-15 format:

```
PEEK(53280) AND 15
```

Use the following assembly language routine to fetch the current border color to register A:

```
LDA $D020
AND #$0F
```

Setting the Background Color

The expression *background color* is used in a couple of different ways in the context of text screen colors. Generally *background color* refers to the color used for blank portions of the screen, and that is the sense of the term as used in this discussion. The subject of the extended color mode defines *background color* in a slightly different fashion.

The default background color is dark gray. As with the border color, the default can be changed by using BASIC's COLOR statement or by writing appropriate values to a background-color register in the VIC.

Two COLOR statements exist for setting background colors: one for the 40-column screen and another for the 80-column screen. Both use color codes, *colr*, in the 1-through-16 format (See Table 6-1).

For the 40-column screen, use:

COLOR 0,*colr*

For the 80-column screen, use:

COLOR 6,*colr*

The statement can be executed directly from the keyboard or within BASIC programming.

The four lower-order bits in the VIC register at $D021 (53281) carry the current border color in the 0-through-15 format (see Table 6-2). This suggests an alternative procedure for setting the background color from BASIC:

POKE 53281,*colr*

where *colr* is a code number, 0 through 15. The default dark-gray background can thus be set by:

```
POKE 53281,11
```

Setting the background color from a machine language routine is a matter of loading the hexadecimal version of the desired color code to $D021. The next example sets a yellow background color:

```
LDA #$07
STA $D021
```

The VIC's background-color register can also be used for determining the current background color. The four higher-order bits are not relevant and, in fact, often take on unpredictable values. Exclude them from the reading.

Use this type of BASIC statement for determining the current background color in the 0-through-15 format:

```
PEEK(53281) AND 15
```

Use the following kind of assembly language routine to fetch the current border color to register A:

```
LDA $D021
AND #$0F
```

Setting the Character Colors

The color attributes of a text character are defined in terms of its foreground and background colors. Unless the system is operating in the reverse mode, the characters are plotted with the foreground color.

Setting Foreground Colors from the Keyboard

Character colors can be changed directly from the keyboard and specified in quote-mode statements according to the keystrokes summarized in Table 6-3. The change is immediate and applies to characters subsequently printed on the screen.

Using the ASCII Color-Control Codes

The Commodore 128 sets aside 16 ASCII codes for setting the foreground color for text characters. The codes and corresponding colors, shown in Table 6-4, can be implemented from both BASIC and machine language programming.

The procedure for using these ASCII codes from BASIC is to specify the desired decimal value in a PRINT CHR$ statement:

PRINT CHR$(*colr*)

Table 6-3
Keystrokes for Changing Character Foreground Colors

Key Operation	40-Column Foreground	80-Column Foreground
CONTROL-1	Black	Black
CONTROL-2	White	White
CONTROL-3	Red	Dark Red
CONTROL-4	Cyan	Light Cyan
CONTROL-5	Purple	Light Purple
CONTROL-6	Green	Green
CONTROL-7	Blue	Blue
CONTROL-8	Yellow	Light Yellow
C=-1	Orange	Dark Purple
C=-2	Brown	Dark Yellow
C=-3	Light Red	Light Red
C=-4	Dark Gray	Dark Cyan
C=-5	Medium Gray	Medium Gray
C=-6	Light Green	Light Green
C=-7	Light Blue	Light Blue
C=-8	Light Gray	Light Gray

Table 6-4
Keystrokes for Changing Character Foreground Colors

Code		40-Column Foreground	80-Column Foreground
Hex	Dec		
$90	144	Black	Black
$05	5	White	White
$1C	28	Red	Dark Red
$9F	159	Cyan	Light Cyan
$9C	156	Purple	Light Purple
$1E	30	Green	Green
$1F	31	Blue	Blue
$9E	158	Yellow	Light Yellow
$81	129	Orange	Dark Purple
$95	149	Brown	Dark Yellow
$96	150	Light Red	Light Red
$97	151	Dark Gray	Dark Cyan
$98	152	Medium Gray	Medium Gray
$99	153	Light Green	Light Green
$9A	154	Light Blue	Light Blue
$9B	155	Light Gray	Light Gray

where *colr* is a decimal value from Table 6-4. The following procedure sets a white foreground color for text characters:

```
PRINT CHR$(5)
```

This one restores the normal light-green character color:

```
PRINT CHR$(153)
```

Implementing the same procedure from machine language programming is a matter of loading the hexadecimal version of the desired foreground color to register A and calling the CHROUT Kernal routine at $FFD2. The following routine sets light-blue characters:

```
LDA #$9A
JSR $FFD2
```

Using BASIC's COLOR Statement

A version of BASIC's color statement can be used for setting character colors for the 40- and 80-column screens. The general form is:

COLOR 5,*colr*

where *colr* is a 1-through-16 color code (see Table 6-1). The statement can be executed directly from the keyboard or within BASIC programming.

Using the COLOR Register

The four lower-order bits in the zero-page register at $F1 (241) carry the current character color in the 0-through-15 format (see Table 6-2). This suggests an alternative procedure for setting the character color from BASIC:

POKE 241,*colr*

where *colr* is a code number, 0 through 15.

The general procedure for setting the character color from a machine language routine involves loading the hexadecimal version of the desired color code to $F1. For example:

```
LDA #$07
STA $F1
```

sets the screen for printing yellow text characters.

The COLOR register also can be used for determining the current character color. The four higher-order bits are not relevant and, in fact, often take on unpredictable values. Exclude them from the reading.

Use this type of BASIC statement for determining the current background color in the 0-through-15 format:

```
PEEK(241) AND 15
```

Use the following assembly language routine to fetch the current character color to register A:

```
LDA $F1
AND #$0F
```

Using Extended Character Colors

The background color used for printing characters to the screen is normally the same color as the overall screen background color. This situation can be altered, however, making it possible to print characters against a field that has a third color.

Suppose that you are using a dark gray background but want to plot yellow characters on a red field. This cannot be done in the normal character mode. All you can produce is yellow characters on a gray background or gray characters on a yellow field (reverse-mode).

The third color can be added but only at the expense of the full range of text and graphics characters. The extended color mode limits the character set to the first 64 characters shown in Table 6-5. Most programmers find the smaller family of characters adequate for most extended-color operations.

Although just 64 characters are available, they can be handled in four different ways:

1. As normal (reverse-off) non-shifted characters
2. As normal shifted characters
3. As reverse non-shifted characters
4. As reverse shifted characters

When the extended-color mode is enabled, the system uses background colors from Background Color registers 0 through 3, respectively.

Switching Between the Extended and Non-Extended Modes

The Commodore 128 normally runs the non-extended color mode, thereby making all text/graphics characters readily available. This can be changed by altering the status of bit 6 in the VIC control register at $D011 (53265). Setting this bit to 1 enables the extended-color mode, and clearing it to 0 restores the normal non-extended color mode.

Setting the extended-color mode from BASIC is thus a matter of executing this sort of POKE statement:

Table 6-5 Text Characters that Can Be Printed in Extended-Color Mode

Uppercase/ Graphics	Uppercase/ Lowercase	Uppercase/ Graphics	Uppercase/ Lowercase
@	@	space	space
A	a	!	!
B	b	"	"
C	c	#	#
D	d	$	$
E	e	%	%
F	f	&	&
G	g	'	'
H	h	(	(
I	i	)	)
J	j	*	*
K	k	+	+
L	l	,	,
M	m	−	−
N	n	.	.
O	o	/	/
P	p	0	0
Q	q	1	1
R	r	2	2
S	s	3	3
T	t	4	4
U	u	5	5
V	v	6	6
W	w	7	7
X	x	8	8
Y	y	9	9
Z	z	:	:
[	[	;	;
£	£	<	<
]	]	=	=
↑	↑	>	>
←	←	?	?

```
POKE 53265,PEEK(53265) OR 64
```

Unless you have changed the content of Background Color 2, you immediately notice that the blinking cursor is red rather than the current character color.

Returning to the non-extended color mode calls for clearing bit 6 to 0:

```
POKE 53265,PEEK(53265) AND 191
```

You can determine the status of the extended-color mode by PEEKing into that register and ANDing the value with 64 to isolate bit 6:

```
PEEK(53265) AND 64
```

This function returns a value of 0 if the extended-color mode is disabled and a value of 64 if it is enabled.

Machine language implementations of the procedures are straightforward translations of the BASIC versions.

Set the extended-color mode:

```
LDA $D011
ORA #$40
STA $D011
```

Turn off the extended-color mode:

```
LDA $D011
AND #$BF
STA $D011
```

Fetch the status to register A:

```
LDA $D011
AND #$BF
```

The latter example sets the Z flag to 1 if the extended-color mode is disabled. Otherwise, it clears the Z flag to 0.

Specifying and Using Extended Text Colors

Once the extended-color mode is enabled, as described previously, character background colors are taken from four different VIC registers. The selection of registers depends on whether the character is specified as shifted or non-shifted and whether it is using the normal or reverse format.

Background Color 0 $D021 (53281)

The four lower-order bits in this register always hold the color code for the overall screen background. When the extended-color mode is not enabled, this register specifies the background color for all characters.

When the extended-color mode is enabled, this register supplies the background for characters that are printed in a non-shifted, normal format.

Background Color 1 $D022 (53282)

When the extended-color mode is enabled, the four lower-order bits in this register supply the background for characters printed in a shifted normal format.

Background Color 2 $D023 (53283)

When the extended-color mode is enabled, the four lower-order bits in this register supply the background for characters printed in a non-shifted reverse format.

Background Color 3 $D024 (53284)

When the extended-color mode is enabled, the four lower-order bits in this register supply the background for characters printed in a shifted reverse format.

Using Cursor Control Features

BASIC includes several cursor-positioning statements. The system offers a Kernal routine for fixing the cursor position. Zero-page RAM has two registers devoted to the current cursor position.

BASIC's CHAR Statement

The CHAR statement represents an especially powerful cursor and text-control operation. In its simplest form, the statement looks like this:

CHAR,*col*,*row*

where *col* is the desired column location and *row* is the desired row (line) location.

The upper-left corner of the text window is located at column 0, row 0. Thus, the following statement emulates the action of a HOME operation:

```
CHAR,0,0
```

If you are using a full 40-column screen, the following version of the CHAR statement sets the text cursor in the lower-right corner:

```
CHAR,39,24
```

The next example clears the screen, sets the text cursor to column 10, row 4, and prints HELLO from that position:

```
10 SCNCLR
20 CHAR,10,4
30 PRINT "HELLO"
```

The CHAR statement, however, can be extended to specify the string to be printed from the designated cursor location. The general form of that extended version looks like this:

CHAR,*col*,*row*[,*string*]

where *string* is an optional string variable, expression, or constant. Printing HELLO from cursor location 10,4 (as demonstrated previously) can be done this way:

CHAR,10,4,"HELLO"

Use another enhancement of the CHAR statement to specify whether the designated string is printed in normal or reverse. The general form is:

CHAR,*col*,*row*[,*string*][,*invflg*]

where *invflg* is omitted or set to zero for normal text printing or to 1 for inverse printing.

> ***NOTE:*** The optional *invflg* parameter in the CHAR statement applies only to the *string* included in that statement. Attempting to use the *invflg* feature without specifying a *string* parameter results in error conditions.

A final enhancement of the CHAR statement applies only when printing text on a multicolor bit-map screen. Assuming that multicolors 1 and 2 have been established with earlier programming, a *colrsrce* parameter can be used to determine the source of colors for *string* in a CHAR statement.

The Kernal's PLOT Routine

The Kernal includes a PLOT routine that makes it quite simple to set or determine the current cursor location from machine-language programs.

PLOT A Kernal routine that sets or reads the column-row location of the text cursor.

Entry address: $FFF0

Set or read:

Set the carry flag to fix a new cursor location. Clear the carry flag to read the current cursor location.

Registers:

The Y register is associated with the column location. The X register is associated with the row location.

The general procedure for using PLOT to set the cursor position is:

1. Execute CLC to clear the carry flag.
2. Load the desired column number to the Y register.
3. Load the desired row number to the X register.
4. Execute JSR $FFF0 to run the PLOT routine.

The example in Listing 6-6 sets the cursor to row 4, column 10.

Listing 6-6

```
CLC                 ;CLEAR THE CARRY FLAG
LDY #$0A            ;COLUMN NUMBER TO REGISTER Y
LDX #$04            ;ROW NUMBER TO REGISTER X
JSR $FFF0           ;CALL PLOT
```

Use this general procedure to return the current column and row location to registers Y and X, respectively:

1. Execute SEC to set the carry flag.
2. Execute JSR $FFF0 to fetch the cursor location.
4. Read the column number from register Y.
5. Read the row number from register X.

For example:

```
SEC                 ;SET THE CARRY FLAG
JSR $FFF0           ;CALL PLOT
```

Setting Alternative Text Windows

The *text window* is that portion of the screen that accepts characters as they are directed to the screen by the current screen-printing mechanism. The normal text windows are the full-screen versions illustrated in Figures 6-1 and 6-2. You can, however, limit the text window to any rectangular portion of the screen.

The Commodore 128 offers a number of techniques for specifying and establishing custom text windows: simple keystrokes, POKEs from BASIC, a BASIC statement dedicated to the operation and machine-language operations.

Once a custom window is established, most text-printing and cursor-control operations take place within it. Doing a CLR/HOME keystroke, for example, clears only that portion of the screen set aside for the text window and homes the cursor to the upper-left corner of that window. Automatic text-scrolling applies only to material printed within the custom window.

Understand that BASIC's most popular cursor-positioning statement, CHAR, uses the upper-left corner of the custom text window as its 0,0 reference point. No matter where the custom window is located with respect to the upper-left corner of the screen, executing a CHAR,0,0 command sets the cursor to the upper-left corner of the custom window. The range of allowable column-row values that can be used with the CHAR statement is also limited to the size of the custom text window. If the window is just 20 columns wide, attempting to execute a CHAR,30,0 statement returns an **?ILLEGAL QUANTITY** error message.

Although you can work only within one custom text window at any given moment, you can specify multiple text windows and work with them individually.

Setting Text Windows through BASIC's WINDOW Statement

BASIC's WINDOW statement provides a convenient means for configuring text windows from within BASIC programming. The general form of the statement is:

WINDOW *topcol,toprow,botcol,botrow*[,*clf*]

where *topcol* and *toprow* represent the column-row location of the upper-left corner of the window, and *botcol* and *botrow* represent the location of the lower-right corner. These parameters are always specified in respect to the default full-screen window, so the allowable ranges of the column parameters, *topcol* and *botcol,* are 0-39 for a 40-column screen and 0-79 for an 80-column screen. The range of values for the row parameters, *toprow* and *botrow,* is 0-24.

You can use optional parameter, *clf,* for automatically clearing the custom text window the moment it is specified. Setting *clf* to a value of 1 invokes the custom window-clearing feature. Setting *clf* to 0, or omitting it from the statement, establishes the new window without clearing any text from it.

The same statement can be used for restoring the default full-screen text window. This is a matter of specifying the default parameters. For the 40-column screen:

```
WINDOW 0,0,39,24
```

and for the 80-column screen:

```
WINDOW 0,0,79,24
```

Add the *clf* parameter and set it to 1 if you want to clear the entire screen.

The routine in Listing 6-7 demonstrates the use of the WINDOW statement.

Listing 6-7

```
10 SCNCLR                     :REM -- CLEAR FULL SCREEN
20 REM           -- FILL FULL SCREEN WITH TEXT --
30 FOR L=0 TO 24
40 PRINT "**** THIS IS A WINDOW DEMONSTRATION ****"
50 NEXT L
60 REM           -- SET AND CLEAR A WINDOW --
70 WINDOW 11,5,31,15,1
80 REM           -- WORK WITHIN THE WINDOW --
90 CHAR,3,4:PRINT "THIS IS IN THE"
100 CHAR,7,5:PRINT "WINDOW"
110 REM          -- DELAY AND RESTORE DEFAULT SCREEN --
120 FOR T=1 TO 2500:NEXT T
130 WINDOW 0,0,39,24,1
```

Setting Text Windows with ESCape Codes

The Commodore 128 uses a pair of ESCape-key operations for setting the upper-left and lower-right bounds of custom text windows. They are two-step operations that require setting the text cursor to the desired corner—upper-left or lower-right—then executing the appropriate ESCape sequence. The general procedure goes something like this:

1. Use any appropriate means to set the text cursor to the upper-left corner of the desired custom window.
2. Use an appropriate technique for executing an ESC-T command to fix the upper-left corner of the window at the current cursor location.
3. Use any appropriate means to set the text cursor to the lower-right corner of the desired custom window.
4. Use an appropriate technique for executing an ESC-B command to fix the upper-left corner of the window at the current cursor location.

In the context of this ESCape technique, restoring the default full-screen window is a matter of executing two HOME operations in succession.

Keyboard Procedures

Use the following procedure to set a custom window from the keyboard:

1. Use the cursor-control keys to position the cursor at the upper-left corner of the desired window area.
2. Do an ESC-T key operation (press the ESC key, followed by the T key).
3. Use the cursor-control keys to position the cursor at the lower-right corner of the desired window area.
4. Press ESC-B.

Restore the default full-screen text window by pressing the HOME key twice in succession.

BASIC Procedures

ESCape operations can be executed from BASIC statements by PRINTing the ASCII equivalent of the ESC character followed by the character to be associated with ESC. The ASCII code for the ESC key is decimal 27, so an ESC-T operation looks like this:

```
PRINT CHR$(27);"T"
```

An ESC-T operation sets the upper-left corner of a custom window to the current cursor position, so this statement does the job.

Doing the equivalent of ESC-B sets the lower-right corner of a text window at the current cursor position:

```
PRINT CHR$(27);"B"
```

The following BASIC routine sets a text window with the upper-left corner at 10,5 and the lower-right at 20,10:

```
10 CHAR,10,5
20 PRINT CHR$(27);"T"
30 CHAR,20,10
40 PRINT CHR$(27);"B"
```

The ASCII code for a HOME-key operation is 19, so you can PRINT it twice in succession to return to the default screen:

```
PRINT CHR$(19);CHR$(19)
```

Machine Language Procedures

You can implement ESC-T and ESC-B procedure for setting custom text windows from a machine language routine by loading and printing the ESCape character followed by the ASCII equivalent of character T or B. As described earlier, the text cursor position should be set to the upper-left position before running the ESC-T routine and to the lower-right before running ESC-B.

The example in Listing 6-8 is based on this general sequence of operations:

1. Clear the screen and home the cursor by using the CHROUT Kernal to print ASCII 147 (keyboard equivalent of CLR/HOME).
2. Set the upper-left cursor position by using the PLOT Kernal.
3. Set the upper-left window position by using the CHROUT Kernal to print ASCII 27 followed by the ASCII for T (equivalent of ESC-T).
4. Set the lower-right cursor position by using the PLOT Kernal.
5. Set the lower-right window position by using the CHROUT Kernal to print ASCII 27 followed by the ASCII for B (equivalent of ESC-B).

Listing 6-8

```
                ;CLEAR THE SCREEN AND HOME THE CURSOR
LDA#$93         ;CHR$(147) TO REGISTER A
JSR $FFD2       ;PRINT IT
                ;SET THE CURSOR TO ROW 4, COL 18
LDX#$04
LDY#$0A
CLC
JSR $FFF0       ;SET WITH PLOT
                ;EXECUTE ESC-T
LDA#$1B         ;ESC CHARACTER TO REGISTER A
JSR $FFD2       ;PRINT IT
LDA#$54         ;T CHARACTER TO REGISTER A
JSR $FFD2       ;PRINT IT
                ;SET THE CURSOR TO ROW 18, COL 20
LDX#$12
LDY#$14
CLC
JSR $FFF0       ;SET WITH PLOT
                ;EXECUTE ESC-B
LDA#$1B         ;ESC CHARACTER TO REGISTER A
JSR $FFD2       ;PRINT IT
LDA#$42         ;B CHARACTER TO REGISTER A
JSR $FFD2       ;PRINT IT
```

The routine for restoring the default full-screen window uses a machine language equivalent of two HOME operations in succession—loading the HOME character to register A and calling CHROUT twice:

```
                      ;RESTORE DEFAULT WINDOW
LDA#$13               ;HOME TO REGISTER A
JSR $FFD2             ;PRINT IT ONCE
JSR $FFD2             ;PRINT IT AGAIN
```

Setting Text Windows through Window Registers

A set of four registers in zero-page memory contains information regarding the configuration of the current text window. You can determine current window configuration by reading the data from those registers, and you can set the window configuration by writing appropriate data to them.

WINDBOT A zero-page register that contains the row number of the bottom line of the current text window.

Decimal address = 228
Hexadecimal address = $E4

Default value = $18 (24)
Allowable ranges of values = $00 through $18 (0 through 24)

WINDTOP A zero-page register that contains the row number of the top line of the current text window.

Decimal address = 229
Hexadecimal address = $E5

Default value = $0 (0)
Allowable ranges of values = $00 through $17 (0 through 23)

WINDLEFT A zero-page register that contains the column number of the left side of the current text window.

Decimal address = 230
Hexadecimal address = $E6

Default value = $0 (0)
Allowable ranges of values = 40-column screen: $00 through $26 (0 through 38),

80-column screen: $00 through $4E (0 through 78)

WINDRIGT A zero-page register that contains the column number of the right side of the current text window.

Decimal address = 231
Hexadecimal address = $E7

Default values = 40-column screen: $27 (39), 80-column screen: $4F (79)
Allowable ranges of values = 40-column screen: $01 through $27 (1 through 39), 80-column screen: $01 through $4F (0 through 79)

BASIC Programming for Window Registers

Setting text windows by POKEing data directly to the text-window registers is a fairly straightforward procedure. However, you must conclude the sequence with a statement that places the text cursor within the new next window.

The example in Listing 6-9 sets up a text window with these specifications: top at row 4, bottom at row 12, left edge at column 10, and right edge at column 30. The PRINT CHR$(147) statement homes the cursor within the newly defined text window and clears that area of the screen.

Listing 6-9

```
10 POKE 229,4           :REM--ROW 4 TO WINDTOP
20 POKE 228,12          :REM--ROW 12 TO WINDBOT
30 POKE 230,10          :REM--COL 10 TO WINDLEFT
40 POKE 231,30          :REM--COL 30 TO WINDRIGT
50 PRINT CHR$(147)      :REM--HOME AND CLEAR
```

The default screen can be restored by POKEing the default values to the window registers or, as suggested in preceding discussion, by PRINTing CHR$(19) two times in succession.

Assembly Programming for Window Registers

Setting a custom text window from assembly language programming is a simple matter of loading the window parameters to the appropriate window registers and setting the cursor within the new window area. The routine in Listing 6-10 establishes the same text window demonstrated in the previous BASIC program.

Restore the default window by applying the routine with the default window parameters or by printing the HOME character, through CHROUT, two times in succession.

Listing 6-10

```
LDA #$04        ;ROW 4
STA $E5;        TO WINDTOP
LDA #$0C        ;ROW 12
STA $E4         ;TO WINDBOT
LDA #$0A        ;COL 10
STA $E6         ;TO WINDLEFT
LDA #$1E        ;COL 30
STA $E7         ;TO WINDRIGT
LDA #$93        ;CLEAR AND HOME
JSR $FFD2
```

Using the Screen-Editing Features

The growing demand for more sophisticated and higher-speed text presentations makes necessary the consideration of the application of special screen-editing features. Most of the features described in this section have been used for editing operations—directly from the keyboard—on virtually all Commodore personal computer products.

Given the proper level of programming thought and planning, the same screen-editing techniques can be implemented from BASIC and machine-language programs: changing the cursor position, deleting or erasing selected portions of text, and changing the text-scrolling parameters. The purpose of this section is to describe these features in the context of programming tools.

Cursor-Motion Operations

The cursor-positioning procedures previously described in this chapter use absolute column row addressing. BASIC's CHAR statement, for example, sets the cursor to specified locations on the screen, and so does the PLOT Kernal.

With the notable exception of the HOME operation, the cursor-motion operations described below use relative addressing—the cursor is moved to a position *relative* to its current position. The actual column-row designation is not relevant.

HOME Set the cursor to the upper-left corner of the current text window. Leave any text unchanged.

Key operation = SHIFT-HOME
BASIC routine = PRINT CHR$(19)
Assembly routine = LDA #$13
JSR $FFD2

LF Linefeed, move the cursor down one line. Leave the text unchanged.

Key operation = LINEFEED
BASIC routine = PRINT CHR$(10);
Assembly routine = LDA #$0A
JSR $FFD2

LF2 Move the cursor down one line. Leave the text unchanged.

Key operation = Method 1: CRSR down
Method 2: down-arrow key
Method 3: CONTROL/Q
BASIC routine = PRINT CHR$(17);
Assembly routine = LDA #$11
JSR $FFD2

LFCR Execute a linefeed/carriage-return operation. Leave the text unchanged.

Key operation = RETURN
BASIC routine = Method 1: PRINT
Method 2: PRINT CHR$(13);
Assembly routine = LDA #$0D
JSR $FDD2

UP Move the cursor up one line. Leave the text unchanged.

Key operation = Method 1: SHIFT/CRSR up
Method 2: up-arrow key
BASIC routine = PRINT CHR$(145);
Assembly routine = LDA #$91
JSR $FFD2

ADV Move the cursor right one column. Leave the text unchanged.

Key operation = Method 1: CRSR right
Method 2: right-arrow key
Method 3: CONTROL/]
BASIC routine = PRINT CHR$(29);
Assembly routine = LDA #$1D
JSR $FFD2

CREOL Move the cursor to the end of the current line. Leave the text unchanged.

Key operation = ESC-K
BASIC routine = PRINT CHR$(27);CHR$(75)
Assembly routine = LDA #$1B

```
JSR $FFD2
LDA #$4B
JSR $FFD2
```

BS Move the cursor left one column. Leave the text unchanged.

Key operation = Method 1: SHIFT/CRSR left
Method 2: left-arrow key
BASIC routine = PRINT CHR$(157);
Assembly routine = LDA #$9D
JSR $FFD2

CRBOL Move the cursor to the beginning of the current line. Leave the text unchanged.

Key operation = ESC-J
BASIC routine = PRINT CHR$(27);CHR$(74);
Assembly routine = LDA #$1B
JSR $FFD2
LDA #$4A
JSR $FFD2

Text-Scrolling Operations

The text screen normally uses an automatic up-scrolling feature. That is, attempting to print text below the lowest line in the window causes the entire screen to shift upward one line. The new material then appears on the bottom line and what was the top line of text is no longer visible.

The text-scrolling operations described in this section make it possible to change the normal, automatic-scrolling feature. You can up- or down-scroll the entire window and even disable the scrolling feature altogether.

The techniques are especially helpful when working with interactive multiple-window displays.

DSCRL Disable automatic text scrolling.

Key operation = ESC-M
BASIC routine = PRINT CHR$(27);CHR$(77);
Assembly routine = LDA #$1B
JSR $FFD2
LDA #$4D
JSR $FFD2

ESCRL Enable automatic text scrolling.

Key operation = ESC-L
BASIC routine = PRINT CHR$(27);CHR$(76);
Assembly routine = LDA #$1B
JSR $FFD2
LDA #$4C
JSR $FFD2

SCRL Scroll entire text screen up one line. Leave the cursor location unchanged. The top line of text is lost.

Key operation = ESC-V
BASIC routine = PRINT CHR$(27);CHR$(86);
Assembly routine = LDA #$1B
JSR $FFD2
LDA #$56
JSR $FFD2

SCRLD Scroll entire text screen down one line. Leave the cursor location unchanged. The bottom line of text is lost.

Key operation = ESC-W
BASIC routine = PRINT CHR$(27);CHR$(87);
Assembly routine = LDA #$1B
JSR $FFD2
LDA #$57
JSR $FFD2

Text-Erasing Operations

The ability to delete one or more selected characters from the screen is not only a handy editing feature, but also a powerful, interactive text-handling feature.

HOME/CLR Set the cursor to the upper-left corner of the current text window. Clear all text from the window.

Key operation = HOME
BASIC routine = PRINT CHR$(147)
Assembly routine = LDA #$93
JSR $FFD2

EREOL Erase from the current cursor location to the end of the current line. Leave the cursor location unchanged.

Key operation = ESC-Q
BASIC routine = PRINT CHR$(27);CHR$(81);

Assembly routine = LDA #$1B
JSR $FFD2
LDA #$51
JSR $FFD2

ERBOL Erase from the current cursor location to the beginning of the current line. Leave the cursor location unchanged.

Key operation = ESC-P
BASIC routine = PRINT CHR$(27);CHR$(80);
Assembly routine = LDA #$1B
JSR $FFD2
LDA #$80
JSR $FFD2

EREOP Erase from the current cursor location to the end of the text window. Leave the cursor location unchanged.

Key operation = ESC-@
BASIC routine = PRINT CHR$(27);CHR$(64);
Assembly routine = LDA #$1B
JSR $FFD2
LDA #$40
JSR $FFD2

DCHAR Delete the character to the left of the current cursor column. Move the cursor and all text to the end of the line one space to the left.

Key operation = Method 1: DEL
Method 2: CONTROL/T
BASIC routine = PRINT CHR$(20);
Assembly routine = LDA #$14
JSR $FFD2

DLINE Delete the entire current line of text. Set the cursor to the beginning of that line. Scroll all lower text up one line.

Key operation = ESC-D
BASIC routine = PRINT CHR$(27);CHR$(68);
Assembly routine = LDA #$1B
JSR $FFD2
LDA #$44
JSR $FFD2

ILINE Insert an entire blank at the current cursor row. Set the cursor to the beginning of that line. Scroll all lower text down one line.

Key operation = ESC-I
BASIC routine = PRINT CHR$(27);CHR$(73);
Assembly routine =

```
LDA #$1B
JSR $FFD2
LDA #$49
```

ICHAR Insert a space at the current cursor location. Move the cursor and remaining text one column to the right.

Key operation = INST
BASIC routine = PRINT CHR$(148);
Assembly routine =

```
LDA #$94
JSR $FFD2
```

Printing Text from Machine Language Programs

Figure 6-3 shows the complete family of ROM-based characters that can be printed to the screen. Two sets of characters are available: one for the uppercase/graphics mode and another for the uppercase/lowercase mode. Notice that some of the character locations do not represent actual characters, but rather control functions. A good many CHR$ and CHROUT functions cited in this chapter take advantage of the code numbers associated with these control operations.

Fig. 6-3 Screen characters and functions and their codes

Dec	Hex	Uppercase/Graphics	Uppercase/Lowercase
0	$00	—	
1	$01	—	
2	$02	underline on (80-col only)	
3	$03	white	
4	$04	—	
5	$05	—	
6	$06	—	
7	$07	bell	
8	$08	—	
9	$09	tab	
10	$0A	—	
11	$0B	disable SHIFT-C=	
12	$0C	enable SHIFT-C=	
13	$0D	RETURN	
14	$0E	set lowercase	
15	$0F	enable flash (80-col only)	

Fig. 6-3 (cont.)

Dec	Hex	Uppercase/Graphics	Uppercase/Lowercase
16	$10	—	
17	$11	cursor down	
18	$12	set reverse	
19	$13	home	
20	$14	delete	
21	$15	—	
22	$16	—	
23	$17	—	
24	$18	set/clear tab stops	
25	$19	—	
26	$1A	—	
27	$1B	ESCape	
28	$1C	red	
29	$1D	cursor right	
30	$1E	green	
31	$1F	blue	
32	$20	space	
33	$21	!	!
34	$22	"	"
35	$23	#	#
36	$24	$	$
37	$25	%	%
38	$26	&	&
39	$27	'	'
40	$28	(	(
41	$29	)	)
42	$2A	*	*
43	$2B	+	+
44	$2C	,	,
45	$2D	-	-
46	$2E	.	.
47	$2F	/	/
48	$30	0	0
49	$31	1	1
50	$32	2	2
51	$33	3	3

Fig. 6-3 (cont.)

Dec	Hex	Uppercase/Graphics	Uppercase/Lowercase
52	$34	4	4
53	$35	5	5
54	$36	6	6
55	$37	7	7
56	$38	8	8
57	$39	9	9
58	$3A	:	:
59	$3B	;	;
60	$3C	<	<
61	$3D	=	=
62	$3E	>	>
63	$3F	?	?
64	$40	@	@
65	$41	A	a
66	$42	B	b
67	$43	C	c
68	$44	D	d
69	$45	E	e
70	$46	F	f
71	$47	G	g
72	$48	H	h
73	$49	I	i
74	$4A	J	j
75	$4B	K	k
76	$4C	L	l
77	$4D	M	m
78	$4E	N	n
79	$4F	O	o
80	$50	P	p
81	$51	Q	q
82	$52	R	r
83	$53	S	s
84	$54	T	t
85	$55	U	u
86	$56	V	v
87	$57	W	w

Fig. 6-3 (cont.)

Dec	Hex	Uppercase/Graphics	Uppercase/Lowercase
88	$58	X	x
89	$59	Y	y
90	$5A	Z	z
91	$5B	[	[
92	$5C	£	£
93	$5D	]	]
94	$5E	↑	↑
95	$5F	←	←
96	$60		
97	$61		A
98	$62		B
99	$63		C
100	$64		D
101	$65		E
102	$66		F
103	$67		G
104	$68		H
105	$69		I
106	$6A		J
107	$6B		K
108	$6C		L
109	$6D		M
110	$6E		N
111	$6F		O
112	$70		P
113	$71		Q
114	$72		R
115	$73		S
116	$74		T
117	$75		U
118	$76		V
119	$77		W
120	$78		X
121	$79		Y
122	$7A		Z
123	$7B		

Fig. 6-3 (cont.)

Dec	Hex	Uppercase/Graphics	Uppercase/Lowercase
124	$7C		
125	$7D		
126	$7E		
127	$7F		
128	$80	—	
129	$81	orange (40-col)/purple (80-col)	
130	$82	underline off (80-col only)	
131	$83	—	
132	$84	—	
133	$85	reserved for F1	
134	$86	reserved for F3	
135	$87	reserved for F5	
136	$88	reserved for F7	
137	$89	reserved for F2	
138	$8A	reserved for F4	
139	$8B	reserved for F6	
140	$8C	reserved for F8	
141	$8D	SHIFT-RETURN	
142	$8E	set uppercase	
143	$8F	flash off (80-col only)	
144	$90	black	
145	$91	cursor up	
146	$92	reverse off	
147	$93	clear screen	
148	$94	insert	
149	$95	brown (40-col)/dark yellow (80-col)	
150	$96	light red	
151	$97	dark gray (40-col)/dark cyan (80-col)	
152	$98	medium gray	
153	$99	light green	
154	$9A	light blue	
155	$9B	light gray	
156	$9C	purple	
157	$9D	cursor left	
158	$9E	yellow	
159	$9F	cyan	

Fig. 6-3 (cont.)

Dec	Hex	Uppercase/Graphics	Uppercase/Lowercase
160	$A0	SHIFT-space	
161	$A1		
162	$A2		
163	$A3		
164	$A4		
165	$A5		
166	$A6		
167	$A7		
168	$A8		
169	$A9		
170	$AA		
171	$AB		
172	$AC		
173	$AD		
174	$AE		
175	$AF		
176	$B0		
177	$B1		
178	$B2		
179	$B3		
180	$B4		
181	$B5		
182	$B6		
183	$B7		
184	$B8		
185	$B9		
186	$BA		
187	$BB		
188	$BC		
189	$BD		
190	$BE		
191	$BF		
192	$C0		
193	$C3		A
194	$C4		B
195	$C3		C

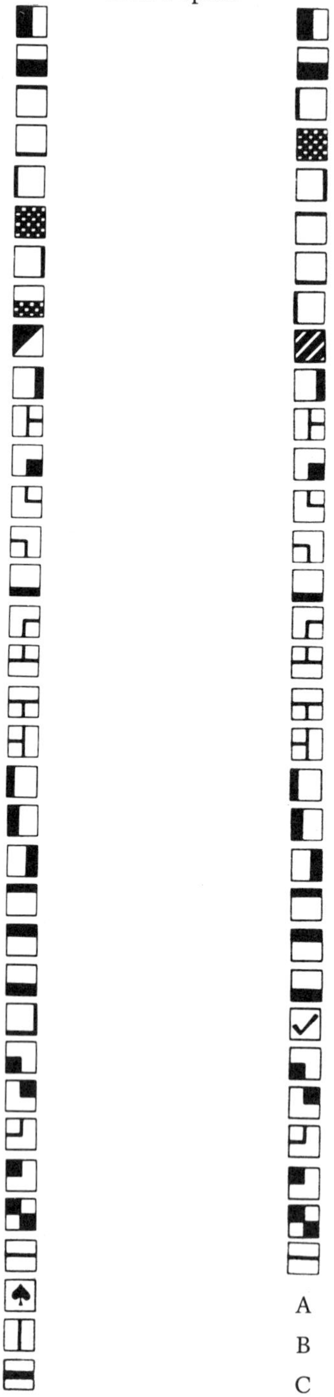

Fig. 6-3 (cont.)

Dec	Hex	Uppercase/Graphics	Uppercase/Lowercase
196	$C4		D
197	$C5		E
198	$C6		F
199	$C7		G
200	$C8		H
201	$C9		I
202	$CA		J
203	$CB		K
204	$CC		L
205	$CD		M
206	$CE		N
207	$CF		O
208	$D0		P
209	$D1		Q
210	$D2		R
211	$D3		S
212	$D4		T
213	$D5		U
214	$D6		V
215	$D7		W
216	$D8		X
217	$D9		Y
218	$DA		Z
219	$DB		
220	$DC		
221	$DD		
222	$DE		
223	$DF		
224	$E0	SHIFT-space	
225	$E1		
226	$E2		
227	$E3		
228	$E4		
229	$E5		
230	$E6		
231	$E7		

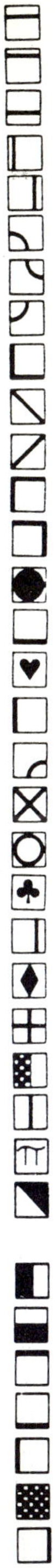

Fig. 6-3 (cont.)

Dec	Hex	Uppercase/Graphics	Uppercase/Lowercase
232	$E8		
233	$E9		
234	$EA		
235	$EB		
236	$EC		
237	$ED		
238	$EE		
239	$EF		
240	$F0		
241	$F1		
242	$F2		
243	$F3		
244	$F4		
245	$F5		
246	$F6		
247	$F7		
248	$F8		
249	$F9		
250	$FA		✓
251	$FB		
252	$FC		
253	$FD		
254	$FE		
255	$FF		

The simplest way to print characters to the screen in BASIC is by using PRINT *string* statements, where *string* is any combination of keyboard characters. You may find helpful, however, substituting PRINT CHR$(*n*) statements, where *n* is the decimal code number for a character or control operation.

Writing the machine-language versions of programs that print characters to the screen is not quite so easy. The printing operation is quite simple. The difficult part is specifying the characters to be printed.

The CHROUT Kernal routine at $FFD2 is the most-used character-printing routine for machine language programs. All you need do is load the desired character code into register A and do a JSR $FFD2. CHROUT takes care of printing the character and advancing the text cursor to the next column location on the screen.

Listing 6-11 represents a workable, but rather primitive, application of CHROUT. The routine begins by printing $93 to clear the screen and home the cursor. Then it prints the message, HELLO, one character at a time.

Listing 6-11

```
LDA #$93        ;HOME AND CLEAR CODE
JSR $FFD2       ;PRINT IT
LDA #$48        ;H
JSR $FFD2       ;PRINT IT
LDA #$45        ;E
JSR $FFD2       ;PRINT IT
LDA #$4C        ;L
JSR $FFD2       ;PRINT IT
JSR $FFD2       ;PRINT IT AGAIN
LDA #$4F        ;O
JSR $FFD2       ;PRINT IT
RTS
```

A more elegant example, and a technique frequently used in the operating system, is one that places the character codes together in a known block of RAM. The idea is to use some incrementing and indexing operations to load the characters into register A. The example in Listing 6-12 prints the HELLO string in that fashion.

Listing 6-12

```
>F0D00 48 45 4C 4C 4F 00                    HELLO.

        LDX #$00        ;SET INDEX TO ZERO
NEXT    LDA $0D00,X     ;FETCH A CHARACTER
        BEQ END         ;IF $00, THEN END
        JSR $FFD2       ;ELSE PRINT IT
        INX             ;INCREMENT THE INDEX
        BNE NEXT        ;AND FETCH NEXT
END     RTS
```

The Kernal for the Commodore 128 includes a routine specifically intended for printing long strings—up to 255 characters. This Kernal is accessed by doing a JSR to $FF7D. The unique feature of the routine is that the screen characters to be printed immediately follow the JSR instruction. The series of characters must end with $00, and the next instruction must immediately follow it.

The following example uses the technique to print HELLO:

```
>F0C00 20 7D FF 48 45 4C 4C 4F
>F0C08 00 60
```

The first three bytes represent the instruction, JSR $FF7D. The next five bytes are the character codes for HELLO, and the byte at $0C08 is the end-of-string marker. The final byte is an RTS instruction.

Working with the Character Sets

Figure 6-4 illustrates the first half of the built-in character set for the Commodore 128 computer. Each character has a code number assigned to it—one of decimal values 0 through 127. When the system is instructed to print an *S* character to the screen, it searches the character set for character number 19 and uses the bit-mapped data at that place in ROM.

Fig. 6-4 Character-set codes for ROM-based character sets

Dec	Hex	Uppercase/Graphics	Uppercase/Lowercase
0	$00	@	@
1	$01	A	a
2	$02	B	b
3	$03	C	c
4	$04	D	d
5	$05	E	e
6	$06	F	f
7	$07	G	g
8	$08	H	h
9	$09	I	i
10	$0A	J	j
11	$0B	K	k
12	$0C	L	l
13	$0D	M	m
14	$0E	N	n
15	$0F	O	o
16	$10	P	p
17	$11	Q	q
18	$12	R	r
19	$13	S	s
20	$14	T	t
21	$15	U	u
22	$16	V	v
23	$17	W	w
24	$18	X	x

Fig. 6-4 (cont.)

Dec	Hex	Uppercase/Graphics	Uppercase/Lowercase
25	$19	Y	y
26	$1A	Z	z
27	$1B	[	[
28	$1C	£	£
29	$1D	]	]
30	$1E	↑	↑
31	$1F	←	←
32	$20	space	
33	$21	!	!
34	$22	"	"
35	$23	#	#
36	$24	$	$
37	$25	%	%
38	$26	&	&
39	$27	'	'
40	$28	(	(
41	$29	)	)
42	$2A	*	*
43	$2B	+	+
44	$2C	,	,
45	$2D	-	-
46	$2E	.	.
47	$2F	/	/
48	$30	0	0
49	$31	1	1
50	$32	2	2
51	$33	3	3
52	$34	4	4
53	$35	5	5
54	$36	6	6
55	$37	7	7
56	$38	8	8
57	$39	9	9
58	$3A	:	:
59	$3B	;	;
60	$3C	<	<

Fig. 6-4 (cont.)

Dec	Hex	Uppercase/Graphics	Uppercase/Lowercase
61	$3D	=	=
62	$3E	>	>
63	$3F	?	?
64	$40		
65	$41		A
66	$42		B
67	$43		C
68	$44		D
69	$45		E
70	$46		F
71	$47		G
72	$48		H
73	$49		I
74	$4A		J
75	$4B		K
76	$4C		L
77	$4D		M
78	$4E		N
79	$4F		Q
80	$50		P
81	$51		Q
82	$52		R
83	$53		S
84	$54		T
85	$55		U
86	$56		V
87	$57		W
88	$58		X
89	$59		Y
90	$5A		Z
91	$5B		
92	$5C		
93	$5D		
94	$5E		
95	$5F		
96	$60	SHIFT-space	

Fig. 6-4 (cont.)

Dec	Hex	Uppercase/Graphics	Uppercase/Lowercase
97	$61		
98	$62		
99	$63		
100	$64		
101	$65		
102	$66		
103	$67		
104	$68		
105	$69		
106	$6A		
107	$6B		
108	$6C		
109	$6D		
110	$6E		
111	$6F		
112	$70		
113	$71		
114	$72		
115	$73		
116	$74		
117	$75		
118	$76		
119	$77		
120	$78		
121	$79		
122	$7A		
123	$7B		
124	$7C		
125	$7D		
126	$7E		
127	$7F		

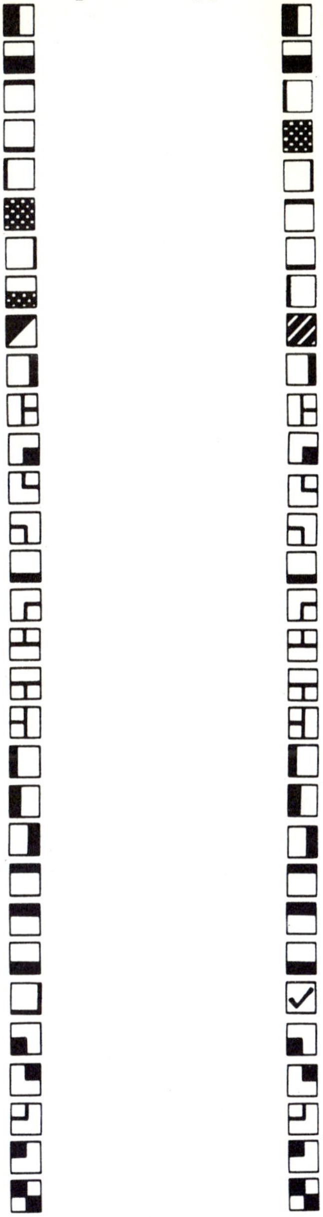

The second half of the character set uses the same characters in the same order but specifies them in the reverse format. The codes for the reverse versions are equal to the normal versions plus 128. Thus, the system searches for character number 38 when it is to print a normal ampersand but looks for character 38+128 (166) to print the reverse version.

The 40-column version of the character set is located in Bank-14 ROM at $D000 through $DFFF (53248–57343), and is organized as shown in Figure 6-5.

Fig. 6-5 Organization of standard character set in Bank-14 ROM

Normal Uppercase/Graphics Set (1024 bytes)

Address range: **$D000–$D3FF (53248–54271)**

Reverse Uppercase/Graphics Set (1024 bytes)

Address range: **$D400–$D7FF (54272–55295)**

Normal Uppercase/Lowercase Set (1024 bytes)

Address range: **$D800–$DBFF (55296–56319)**

Reverse Uppercase/Lowercase Set (1024 bytes)

Address range: **$DC00–DFFF (56320–57343)**

NOTE: The address ranges are in Bank 14 rather than BASIC's usual Bank 15 or the machine-language monitor's default Bank 0.

The 40- and 80-column screens use the same character set but in different ways. For all practical purposes, the 40-column screen uses the characters directly as they are portrayed in Bank-14 ROM. When invoking the 80-column mode, the system copies that character set into a special 80-column RAM area where it is reformatted and used.

The master character set—the one built into Bank-14 ROM—is composed of 512 character definitions. Each character is defined by eight consecutive bytes of data. The bits in each byte are set to 1 to indicate a plotted portion of the character and cleared to 0 to indicate a portion that is not to be plotted. Table 6-6 illustrates the idea for the first two characters: @ and A. Replace the 1s with a white color and the 0s with a dark color, and you can clearly see the character that the data represent.

Table 6-6 Bank-14 Addresses and Data that Define Two Different Characters in Character Set

(A) Normal @ Character

Address	Data (Hex)	Data (Binary)
ED000	3C	00111100
ED001	66	01100110
ED002	6E	01101110
ED003	6E	01101110
ED004	60	01100000
ED005	62	01100010
ED006	3C	00111100
ED007	00	00000000

Table 6-6 (cont.) *(B) Normal A Character*

Address	Data	
	Hex	Binary
ED008	18	00011000
ED009	3C	00111100
ED00A	66	01100110
ED00B	7E	01111110
ED00C	66	01100110
ED00D	66	01100110
ED00E	66	01100110
ED00F	00	00000000

The character sets contain 512 characters. Each uses 8 bytes, so the sets occupy 4096 consecutive ROM addresses. You can explore that character set from the monitor, beginning with this command:

MED000

You can see that each character ends with a $00 byte. This leaves one blank scan line between consecutive rows of characters on the screen.

The 80-column character set uses the same general character codes but each character uses 16 bytes of data in the special 80-column chip. The first 8 bits are identical to those of the corresponding 40-column character, and the last 8 are simply filled with zeros. The 80-column character set is not directly accessible for inspection or alteration, although it can be reached through techniques described in the closing section of this chapter.

The 40-column character set is normally defined from Bank-14 ROM, but it can be relocated and read directly from Bank-15 RAM. The primary justification for reading the set is to provide a means for modifying the characters or reorganizing the character set to suit special needs.

In principle, a RAM-based character set can begin at an address determined by multiplying integers 0 through 15 times 1024. The principle isn't quite that versatile in practice, though.

The first consideration is trading off the limited number of addresses where a RAM-based character set can begin against the size of the desired character set. Table 6-7 shows possible starting addresses but does not take into account how much RAM is required for the character definitions.

One important consideration is that no part of a character-set definition should spill into the block of RAM between $1000 and $1FFF (4096–8191). This is the system's virtual character-set area, and it cannot read RAM-based characters from that block. This area is thus omitted from the table.

Table 6-7
Starting Addresses for RAM-Based Character Sets and Corresponding Nibble Values to Be Loaded to $0A2C

Nibble		Starting Addresses	
Hex	Dec	Hex	Dec
$2	2	$0800	2048
$3	3	$0C00	3072
$8	8	$2000	8192
$9	9	$2400	9216
$A	10	$2800	10240
$B	11	$2C00	11264
$C	12	$3000	12288
$D	13	$3400	13312
$E	14	$3800	14336
$F	15	$3C00	15360

Zero-page RAM is omitted because it is dedicated to too many internal operations. The block beginning at $0400 is normally used for screen RAM, so character definitions should not be placed there, either.

A 1K character set can be moved to $0C00 as long as the RS-232-C and sprite-definition buffers that normally occupy that block are not needed.

All things considered, the prime working area for RAM-based character sets begins at $2000 (8192). If you plan to use the character set in conjunction with BASIC programming, make sure that the bottom of BASIC memory is moved up out of the area. Because a RAM character set overlays the bit-map RAM, it is difficult to use the characters and bit-mapped graphics at the same time.

Two registers are involved in the procedure for defining a RAM-based character set: $D9 (217) and $0A2C (2604). Setting bit 2 of $D9 instructs the system to use a RAM-based character set. Clearing this bit to 0 restores the normal ROM-based character functions. The four lower-order bits of $0A2C point to the starting address of the character set. The default value is 4, but it can be set to any of the nibble values shown in Table 6-7.

The following procedure describes how to relocate the ROM-based character set in a general fashion.

1. Make sure the starting address for BASIC is above the highest address used by the character set.
2. Transfer the desired block of character definitions from Bank-14 ROM to Bank-15 RAM.
3. Set the flag bit for reading characters from RAM instead of ROM:

   Set bit 2 of $D9 (217) to 1

4. Set the four lower-order bits of $0A2C (2604) to point to the starting address of the RAM-based character set, using the nibble values in Table 6-7.

The BASIC program in Listing 6-13 transfers the normal uppercase/lowercase characters to RAM address $2000 (8192).

Line 10—Move the start of BASIC to $4000.

Line 20—Set BASIC for fast operation. Executing this statement doubles the operating speed but blanks the screen.

Lines 30–60—Transfer the character set:

> **Line 40**—Get a character from Bank-14 ROM.
>
> **Line 50**—POKE it to Bank-15 RAM.

Line 70—Slow down the operating speed to turn on the text screen.

Line 80—Set the read-from-RAM flag.

Line 90—Point to the start of the character set. The value 8 is the nibble required for pointing to address 8192.

Listing 6-13

```
10 GRAPHIC 2:GRAPHIC 0
20 FAST
30 FOR K=0 TO 1023
40 BANK 14:C=PEEK(55296+K)
50 BANK 15:POKE 8192+K,C
60 NEXT K
70 SLOW
80 POKE 217,4
90 POKE 2604,PEEK(2604) AND 240 OR 8
```

The transfer requires several seconds, but once it is done, the system operates only from the normal uppercase/lowercase character set. Attempting to print other character sets yields garbage.

The character set is readily available for bit-mapped modifications—any sort of character you wish to design into the 8-bit format illustrated in Table 6-6.

Operating the Reset pushbutton returns the system to the ROM-based character set. A programmed routine simply requires clearing bit 2 of $D9 (217) to zero and setting the lower four bits in $0A2C (2604) to 4:

```
POKE 217,0
POKE 2604,PEEK(2604) AND 240 OR 4
```

The relatively long delay required for making the initial transfer from ROM to RAM can be eliminated from future programming by saving the RAM-based version as a binary file. This file can then be loaded much faster at any later time.

Suppose that you do BSAVE the RAM-based character set as NEWCHARS. This reduces the setup procedure to this form:

```
10 GRAPHIC 2:GRAPHIC 0
20 BLOAD "NEWCHARS"
30 POKE 217,4
40 POKE 2604,PEEK(2604) AND 240 OR 8
```

Line 10—Make sure BASIC is set up to $4000.

Line 20—Load the character set.

Line 30—Fetch characters from RAM.

Line 40—Point to the start of the character set.

Working Directly with Screen Data

The video scheme for the Commodore 128 is fully memory mapped. That is, a one-for-one correspondence exists between a given character location on the screen and a particular address in the screen RAM area. Knowing how each address is mapped to a position on the screen makes possible the plotting of characters by writing them directly to the appropriate RAM addresses. The procedure for writing directly to 40-column text screens is relatively simple. Unfortunately, as described in the closing section of this chapter, writing to the 80-column screen is rather tedious and indirect.

The Commodore 128 offers a selection of powerful text-plotting routines that eliminate the need for writing characters directly to screen RAM. However, there are a couple of good reasons why you should consider writing directly. Perhaps the best reason is that it offers insight into how and why the video system functions the way it does. Furthermore, having command of this kind of knowledge makes it possible to design software that performs at a higher standard of excellence than might be possible otherwise. Finally, a good understanding of the direct-writing procedures leads to an understanding of using multiple pages of text information.

Writing Directly to Default Screen RAM

Table 6-8 is a memory map of the default screen RAM area. Each line on the screen uses 40 consecutive RAM address locations. The left-to-right progression of column locations corresponds to increasing RAM addresses. The first line, line 0, uses consecutive screen RAM addresses $0400 through $0427 (1024–1063).

The second line begins where the first ends. The progression continues through the final column location on line 24—RAM address $07E7 (2023).

Table 6-8 Starting and Ending Addresses for Each Line of Default Screen RAM Area

Line	Address Range	
	Hex	Dec
0	$0400-$0427	1024-1063
1	$0428-$044F	1064-1103
2	$0450-$0477	1104-1143
3	$0478-$049F	1144-1183
4	$04A0-$04C7	1184-1223
5	$04C8-$04EF	1224-1263
6	$04F0-$0517	1264-1303
7	$0518-$053F	1304-1343
8	$0540-$0567	1344-1383
9	$0568-$058F	1384-1423
10	$0590-$05B7	1424-1463
11	$05B8-$05DF	1464-1503
12	$05E0-$0607	1504-1543
13	$0608-$062F	1544-1583
14	$0630-$0657	1584-1623
15	$0658-$067F	1624-1663
16	$0680-$06A7	1664-1703
17	$06A8-$06CF	1704-1743
18	$06D0-$06F7	1744-1783
19	$06F8-$071F	1784-1823
20	$0720-$0747	1824-1863
21	$0748-$076F	1864-1903
22	$0770-$0797	1904-1943
23	$0798-$07BF	1944-1983
24	$07C0-$07E7	1984-2023

The data to be written to these RAM locations are the character-set codes shown in Figure 6-4. Thus, this command prints an at (@) sign in the upper-left corner of the screen:

```
POKE 1024,0
```

and this one prints the same character in the extreme lower-right corner:

```
POKE 2023,0
```

The BASIC program in Listing 6-14 directly writes all 255 characters from the current character set to screen RAM. The version in Listing 6-15 does the same job in a machine language format. Both programs write the sequence of character codes to a corresponding sequence of screen RAM addresses.

Listing 6-14

```
10 SCNCLR
20 FOR K=0 TO 255
30 POKE 1024+K,K
40 NEXT K
50 CHAR,0,20
```

Listing 6-15

```
        LDX #$00      ;ZERO THE INDEX POINTER
AGAIN   TXA           ;COPY TO REGISTER A
        STA $0400,X   ;PLOT TO SCREEN RAM
        INX           ;INCREMENT THE COUNT
        BNE AGAIN     ;IF NOT DONE, DO NEXT CHAR
        RTS
```

Reading Character Data from Screen RAM

Just as you can write data directly to a specified location on the screen, so you can read character codes directly from screen RAM.

The notion of reading the data at one point or another on screen RAM has little practical application. The idea is more often used for doing screen dumps—transferring a screen full of text to another block of RAM or to a serial output device.

The example in Listing 6-16 transfers all 1000 bytes of screen data to a different block of RAM, which begins at $2000 (8192). For the sake of demonstration, the routines erase the original screen as the transfer takes place. The routine ends by restoring the original screen—from the block at $2000 to the screen.

Line 10—Move BASIC up to $4000.

Line 20—Clear the screen and home the cursor.

Line 30—Fill the screen with some STUFF.

Lines 40–70—Transfer the screen to a RAM block beginning at 8192:

> **Line 50**—Load to RAM block from screen RAM.
>
> **Line 60**—Write a space to screen RAM.

Lines 80–100—Transfer data back to screen RAM.

Writing Directly to Color RAM

When you work directly with screen RAM, the address determines where the character is plotted, and the data written to that address determines which character is plotted there. Commodore text offers one more special feature color.

Listing 6-16

```
10 GRAPHIC 2:GRAPHIC 0
20 SCNCLR
30 FOR K=1 TO 166:PRINT "STUFF ";:NEXT K
40 FOR K=0 TO 999
50 POKE 8192+K,PEEK(1024+K)
60 POKE 1024+K,32
70 NEXT K
80 FOR K=0 TO 99
90 POKE 1024+K,PEEK(8192+K)
100 NEXT K
```

The color of a character plotted on the screen is determined by writing color codes, $00–$0F (0–15), to addresses representing each of the 1000 character locations. Text color RAM is located in a block of Bank-15 RAM that begins at $DB00 (55296). Table 6-9 shows the starting and ending addresses for each line of text in color RAM.

Table 6-9 Starting and Ending Addresses for Each Line of Text Color RAM Area

Line	Address Range	
	Hex	Dec
0	$D800-$D827	55296-55335
1	$D828-$D84F	55336-55375
2	$D850-$D877	55376-55415
3	$D878-$D89F	55416-55455
4	$D8A0-$D8C7	55456-55495
5	$D8C8-$D8EF	55496-55535
6	$D8F0-$D917	55536-55575
7	$D918-$D93F	55576-55615
8	$D940-$D967	55616-55655
9	$D968-$D98F	55656-55695
10	$D990-$D9B7	55696-55735
11	$D9B8-$D9DF	55736-55775
12	$D9E0-$DA07	55776-55815
13	$DA08-$DA2F	55816-55855
14	$DA30-$DA57	55856-55895
15	$DA58-$DA7F	55896-55935
16	$DA80-$DAA7	55936-55975
17	$DAA8-$DACF	55976-56015
18	$DAD0-$DAF7	56016-56055
19	$DAF8-$DB1F	56056-56095
20	$DB20-$DB47	56096-56135
21	$DB48-$DB6F	56136-56175
22	$DB70-$DB97	56176-56215
23	$DB98-$DBBF	56216-56255
24	$DBC0-$DBE7	56256-56295

The color data written to those color RAM locations is the same as that shown in Table 6-2. Thus, this statement prepares the way for printing a red character in the extreme upper-left corner of the screen:

```
POKE 55196,2
```

This version sets up the color RAM for printing a dark blue character in the lower-right corner of the screen:

```
POKE 56295,6
```

You can read the color assigned to a location in color RAM also. Bear in mind, however, that only the four lower-order bits are significant. The four higher-order bits take on unpredictable and meaningless values.

When PEEKing or doing a machine-language reading operation from color RAM, you must mask off the four higher-order bits to get the color values normally associated with the text screen.

The following example returns the color value, 0 through 15, assigned to color RAM location 55296:

```
PRINT PEEK(55296) AND 15
```

Using Alternative Screen Ram Locations

The lower RAM area between $0400 and $07FF (1024–2047) is reserved for 40-column screen RAM. You can, however, link the video display to a few other RAM locations. The primary justification for such a procedure is to have a couple of text screens "hidden" in the background and ready for immediate presentation.

You can, for instance, show one screen while preparing the text for a couple of others. Then you can flip around through those alternative screens, displaying full screens of text much more rapidly than is possible with normal screen-printing operations.

Alternative 40-column video screens can begin only at decimal addresses that are multiples of 1024. The highest possible multiple is 15.

This has to do with the fact that the upper four bytes of a register at $0A2C (2604) hold a value that indicates the starting address of 40-column screen RAM. The system always deals with that value by multiplying it by 1024.

The default value in the upper nibble of $0A2C is 1, so it follows that the default screen RAM begins at 1024*1, or 1024. Having access to 15 other values in that nibble, it is possible to relocate the screen to 15 other locations.

Table 6-10 indicates all possible locations for the 40-column screen RAM and the corresponding values that are written to the upper nibble of $0A2C. Some of those locations should not be used, however, and others ought to be used with special care.

Table 6-10 Address Blocks for Possible Alternative Screen RAM Locations

Nibble		Range of Addresses	
Hex	Dec	Hex	Dec
$1	16	$0400-$07FF	1024-2047
$2	32	$0800-$0BFF	2048-3071
$3	48	$0C00-$0FFF	3072-4095
$8	128	$2000-$23FF	8192-215
$9	144	$2400-$27FF	9216-10239
$A	160	$2800-$2BFF	10240-11263
$B	176	$2C00-$2FFF	11264-12287
$C	192	$3000-$33FF	12288-13311
$D	208	$3400-$37FF	13312-14335
$E	224	$3800-$3BFF	14336-15359
$F	240	$3C00-$3FFF	15360-16383

The RAM block beginning at $0000 should not be used for screen RAM because it is always reserved for other important operations. The block beginning at $0400, on the other hand, can be used at any time because it is the system's default location for screen RAM.

The general procedure for displaying an alternative RAM location looks like this:

1. Determine the value to be written to the upper nibble of $0A2C.
2. Fetch the current value of $0A2C.
3. Set the four upper bits to the desired value.
4. Write the result back to $0A2C.

The following BASIC statement moves the screen RAM to 3072:

```
POKE 2604,PEEK(2604) AND 15 OR 48
```

When using BASIC in conjunction with an alternative block of screen RAM that begins at $2000 (8192) or above, make sure that the lowest address for BASIC is moved up to $4000 (16284). This is accomplished rather easily by making the system think you want to use bit-mapped graphics. Here is one way to go about doing that:

```
GRAPHIC 2:GRAPHIC 0
```

The first statement allocates bit-mapped RAM, and the second restores the 40-column text format. In the process, the lowest address used by BASIC is set up to $4000.

Unfortunately the most efficient way to write characters to an alternative block of screen RAM is by writing their codes directly to that area. A preceding section in this chapter describes the procedure for writing characters directly to the default block of screen RAM. The same principles apply here.

Table 6-11 shows index values that point to the starting and ending address for each line of an alternative block of screen RAM. Determining the actual value is a matter of adding the desired index value to the starting address of the block of screen RAM.

Table 6-11 Indexes for Starting and Ending Addresses for Each Line of an Alternative Screen RAM Location

Line	Address Range Hex	Dec
0	$0000-$0027	0-39
1	$0028-$004F	40-79
2	$0050-$0077	80-119
3	$0078-$009F	120-159
4	$00A0-$00C7	160-199
5	$00C8-$00EF	200-239
6	$00F0-$0117	240-279
7	$0118-$013F	280-319
8	$0140-$0167	320-359
9	$0168-$018F	360-399
10	$0190-$01B7	400-439
11	$01B8-$01DF	440-479
12	$01E0-$0207	480-519
13	$0208-$022F	520-559
14	$0230-$0257	560-599
15	$0258-$027F	600-639
16	$0280-$02A7	640-679
17	$02A8-$02CF	680-719
18	$02D0-$02F7	720-759
19	$02F8-$031F	760-799
20	$0320-$0347	800-839
21	$0348-$036F	840-879
22	$0370-$0397	880-919
23	$0398-$03BF	920-959
24	$03C0-$03E7	960-999

Color RAM, described in the previous section of this chapter, cannot be relocated. The one-for-one correspondence between color and screen RAM remains in effect, even when using an alternative block of screen RAM.

Writing Directly to the 80-Column Screen

The VIC chip has been an integral part of the Commodore line of personal computers for a long time. And it is a vital part of the Commodore 128—for 40-column text, bit-mapped graphics, and sprite animation. The 80-column feature, however, is handled by an entirely different device.

The 80-column chip handles its own logic and has 16K of RAM that is not part of the system's overall memory configuration. This chip is the only avenue for dealing directly with the 80-column character set, screen RAM, and color RAM.

Two 80-column chip registers are open to the outside world. One is located at Bank-15 address $D600 and the other is at $D601. There are 37 other registers, but they are not directly accessible from any of the usual memory banks. Rather, they are accessed through those two special address locations.

The control register, at $D600, accepts register numbers. Every 80-column chip operation begins by writing a particular register number to that address. When the register is thus specified, data can be written or read from the specified register through the data register at $D601.

Figure 6-6 shows the three major areas of RAM—built into the 80-column chip—that are most useful for 80-column screen applications. Table 6-12 is the memory map of the screen area, showing the first and last address for each line. Table 6-13 shows the organization of the 80-column color RAM.

Fig. 6-6 The three major areas of RAM built into the 80-column chip

$0000-$07CF: 80-column screen RAM
$0800-$0FCF: 80-column color RAM
$2000-$3FFF: Character-definition RAM

Table 6-12 Memory Map of 80-Column Chip's Screen RAM, Showing Addresses of First and Last Columns in Each Row

Line	Address Range	
	Hex	Dec
0	$0000-$004F	0–79
1	$0050-$009F	80–159
2	$00A0-$00EF	160–239
3	$00F0-$013F	240–319
4	$0140-$018F	320–399
5	$0190-$01DF	400–479
6	$01E0-$022F	480–559
7	$0230-$027F	560–639
8	$0280-$02CF	640–719
9	$02D0-$031F	720–799
10	$0320-$036F	800–879

Table 6-12 (cont.)

Line	Address Range	
	Hex	Dec
11	$0370 - $03BF	880-959
12	$03C0 - $040F	960-1039
13	$0410 - $045F	1040-1119
14	$0460 - $04AF	1120-1199
15	$04B0 - $04FF	1200-1279
16	$0500 - $054F	1280-1359
17	$0550 - $059F	1360-1439
18	$05A0 - $05EF	1440-1519
19	$05F0 - $063F	1520-1599
20	$0640 - $068F	1600-1679
21	$0690 - $06DF	1680-1759
22	$06E0 - $072F	1760-1839
23	$0730 - $077F	1840-1919
24	$0780 - $07CF	1920-1999

Table 6-13
Memory Map of 80-Column Chip's Color RAM, Showing Addresses of First and Last Columns in Each Row

Line	Address Range	
	Hex	Dec
0	$0800 - $084F	2048-2127
1	$0850 - $089F	2128-2207
2	$08A0- $08EF	2208-2287
3	$08F0 - $093F	2288-2367
4	$0940 - $098F	2368-2447
5	$0990 - $09DF	2448-2527
6	$09E0 - $0A2F	2528-2607
7	$0A30- $0A7F	2608-2687
8	$0A80- $0ACF	2688-2767
9	$0AD0 - $0B1F	2768-2847
10	$0B20- $0B6F	2848-2927
11	$0B70- $0BBF	2928-3007
12	$0BC0- $0C0F	3008-3087
13	$0C10- $0C5F	3088-3167
14	$0C60- $0CAF	3168-3247
15	$0CB0- $0CFF	3248-3327
16	$0D00 - $0D4F	3328-3407
17	$0D50- $0D9F	3408-3487
18	$0DA0 - $0DEF	3488-3567
19	$0DF0 - $0E3F	3568-3647
20	$0E40 - $0E8F	3648-3727
21	$0E90 - $0EDF	3728-3807
22	$0EE0- $0F2F	3808-3887
23	$0F30 - $0F7F	3888-3967
24	$0F80 - $0FCF	3968-4047

Writing data directly to the 80-column screen requires the use of three registers designated $12, $23, and $1F. These three provide full access to the chip's built-in 16K of RAM—which includes screen, color, and character RAM. The MSB of the address goes to register $12, the LSB goes to $13, and the character data goes to register $1F.

The general procedure for working with the available RAM in the 80-column chip looks like this:

1. Write register $12 to the control register at $D600.
2. Write the MSB of the address to the data register at $D601.
3. Write register $13 to the control register at $D600.
4. Write the LSB of the address to the data register at $D601.
5. Write register $1F to the control register at $D600.
6. Write the desired character code to the data register at $D601 (or read the current character data from it).

The example in Listing 6-17 is a direct implementation of the procedure. It prints an uppercase X character at the beginning of the second line of the 80-column screen—character code $18 at address $0050.

Listing 6-17

```
LDA  #$12;   REGISTER $12
STA  $D600   ;TO THE CONTROL REGISTER
LDA  #$00    ;MSB OF ADDRESS
STA  $D601   ;TO DATA REGISTER
LDA  #$13    ;REGISTER $13
STA  $D600   ;TO THE CONTROL REGISTER
LDA  #$50    ;LSB OF ADDRESS
STA  $D601   ;TO DATA REGISTER
LDA  #$1F    ;REGISTER $1F
STA  $D600   ;TO THE CONTROL REGISTER
LDA  #$18    ;X CODE
STA  $D601   ;TO DATA REGISTER
```

This approach to dealing with the 80-column screen would obviously lead to very lengthy programs for doing very little useful work. A better approach would be to prepare a subroutine that writes specified data to the control and data registers. Call the routine shown in Listing 6-18 after loading the character data to register A, the MSB of the address to register X, and the LSB of the address to register Y.

The routine in Listing 6-19 uses the 80-column plotting routine to plot a blue X at the first column in the second row on the screen.

The 80-column character set exists only in the 80-column chip's RAM area. The characters are the same as those used for 40-column text operations. In fact, invoking the 80-column screen automatically

Listing 6-18

```
F0D00  PHA          ;SAVE REG. A
F0D01  LDA #$12     ;SPECIFY REG. $12
F0D03  JSR $0D1B    ;WRITE TO CONTROL REG.
F0D06  STX $D601    ;MSB TO DATA REG.
F0D09  LDA #$13     ;SPECIFY REG. $13
F0D0B  JSR $0D1B    ;WRITE TO CONTROL REG.
F0D0E  STY $D601    ;LSB TO DATA REG.
F0D11  LDA #$1F     ;SPECIFY REG. $1F
F0D13  JSR $0D1B    ;WRITE TO CONTROL REG.
F0D16  PLA          ;GET CHAR. BYTE
F0D17  STA $D601    ;CHAR. TO DATA REG.
F0D1A  RTS
F0D1B  STA $D600    ;WRITE TO CONTROL REG.
F0D1E  BIT $D600    ;AND WAIT FOR HIGH
F0D21  BPL $0D1E    ;BIT TO BE SET
F0D23  RTS
```

Listing 6-19

```
LDA  #$18    ;X CHARACTER
LDX  #$00    ;MSB OF SCREEN ADDR
LDY  #$50    ;LSB OF SCREEN ADDR
JSR  $0D00   ;PLOT IT
LDA  #$02    ;BLUE COLOR
LDX  #$08    ;MSB OF COLOR ADDR
LDY  #$50    ;LSB OF COLOR ADDR
JSR  $0D00   ;SET THE COLOR
```

calls an initialization routine that copies the 40-column character set into the appropriate block in the 80-column chip.

> *NOTE:* The 80-column character set is not available until the 80-column mode is initialized at least once.

The 80-column character set uses the same general character codes, but each code uses 16 bytes of data in the special 80-column chip. The first eight bits are identical to those of the corresponding 40-column character, and the last eight are simply filled with zeros.

7

Bit-Mapped Graphics Procedures

In those instances where the keyboard graphics characters do not offer adequate resolution or flexibility for a desired graphics presentation, the Commodore 128's bit-mapped graphics screens become an attractive alternative. Although the 40- and 80-column screens offer 900 and 1800 graphics locations, respectively, bit-mapped screens offer up to 64,000 different plotting locations. With the bit-mapped graphics screens, you can plot figures with much finer detail than is possible with the text screens and the graphics characters available from the character sets.

You must pay a price for the higher-resolution, bit-mapped graphics—the amount of RAM devoted to it. But considering the amount of RAM available with the Commodore 128, the price is small indeed.

The graphics environment for the Commodore 128 is fully accessible through BASIC 7.0 statements and functions. For that reason, most of the information in this chapter is presented from a BASIC point of view.

The discussions, however, eventually turn to the principles involved in working directly to the bit-mapped graphics screens—first through POKE and PEEK statements, then from machine language routines.

Bit-Mapped Screen Formats

High-resolution, or bit-mapped, graphics for the Commodore 128 feature two different kinds of screens. One screen, called the *standard screen,* allows you to plot text and figures from two different color sources: foreground and background. The second, the *multicolor* screen, provides a choice of four different color sources: foreground, background, multicolor 1, and multicolor 2.

In either screen, the colors assigned to the sources can be changed during the course of a plotting operation, thus making it possible to portray all 16 standard colors on the high-resolution screens. The multicolor mode provides better color resolution, but that advantage has a price: half as many horizontal plotting locations.

Figures 7-1 and 7-2 show the organization of two kinds of standard, bit-mapped screens. The first shows a full screen of graphics. The entire screen, with the exception of the border area, is devoted to graphics operations. Note that the 320 horizontal locations are labeled 0 through 219 and the 200 vertical locations are labeled 0 through 119. Dots, lines, and curves of all kinds can be plotted within this X-Y area.

The standard bit-mapped screen in Figure 7-2 allows lines of 40-column text to show through at the bottom. The same number of horizontal graphics locations are used as for the full-screen version, but only 160 vertical locations, numbered 0 through 159, are available.

The reason for leaving a 40-column text area at the bottom of

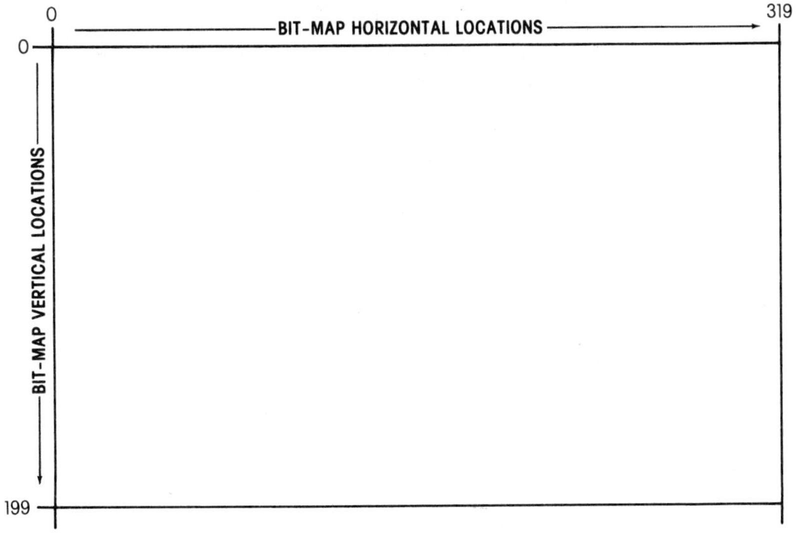

Fig. 7-1 Organization of the standard bit-mapped graphics screen

the screen is to make it simpler to print meaningful text. You can print text characters in the graphics portion of the standard bit-mapped screen, but only through BASIC's CHAR statement. Prompting messages that might be associated with INPUT statements, for example, can be printed only in the text portion of a split screen.

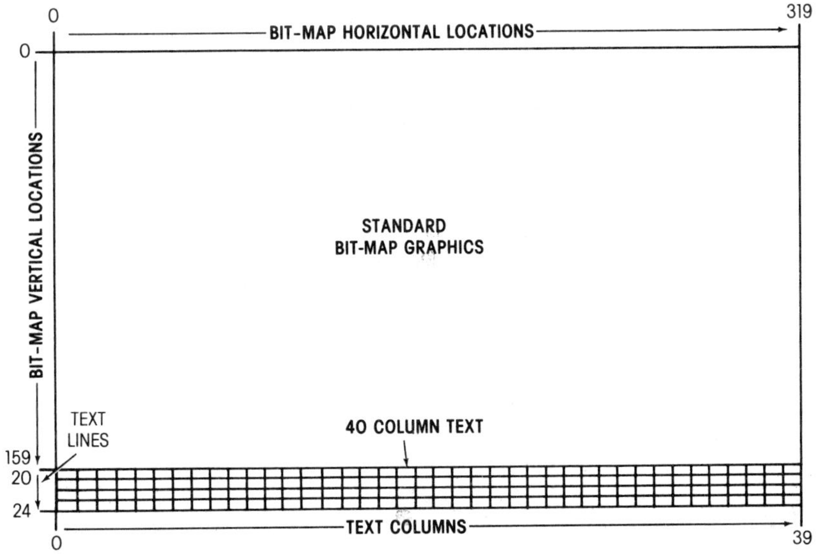

Fig. 7-2 Organization of the standard, split bit-mapped graphics screen

The color sources of particular interest to the standard bit-mapped screens include those for the usual 40-column background and border colors. In addition, there is a source for a foreground color. The foreground color is the one used for plotting points to the graphics area of the screen, including text that is printed with the CHAR statement. The character color source is meaningful, too, but only for the split-screen version. The standard character color source determines the color of any text printed in the 40-column text portion of the split screen.

Figures 7-3 and 7-4 show the layout of full- and split-screen versions for two multicolor screens. In both instances, the 160 horizontal locations are labeled 0 through 159. The full-screen version uses 200 vertical locations, whereas the split-screen version uses just 160.

Fig. 7-3 Organization of the multicolor bit-mapped graphics screen

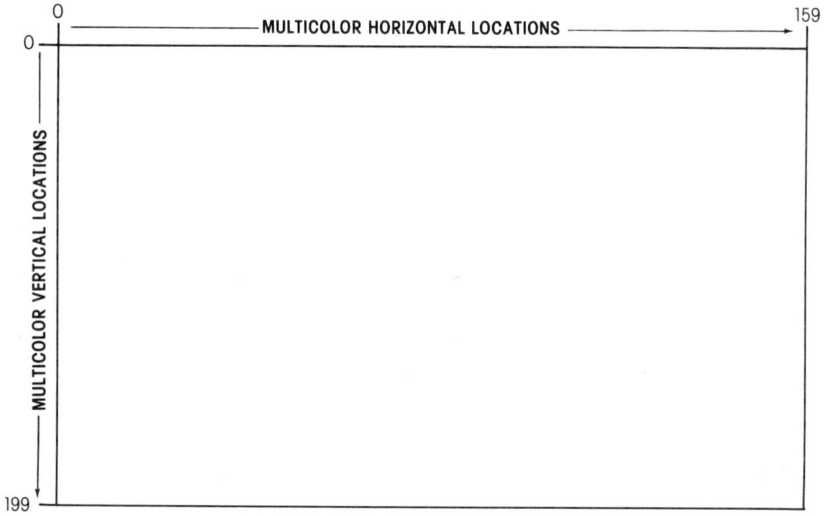

Fig. 7-4 Organization of the multicolor, split bit-mapped graphics screen

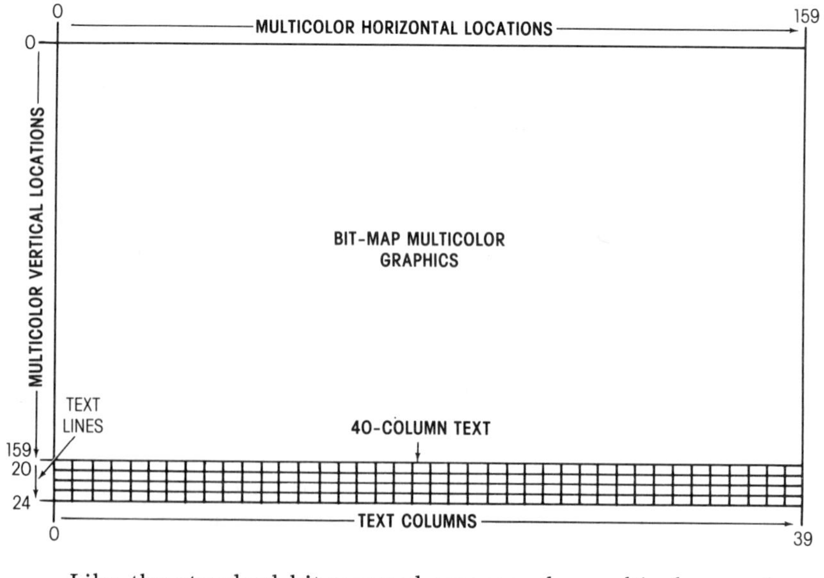

Like the standard bit-mapped screens, the multicolor versions

use color sources for the border, background, foreground, and 40-column characters in the text portion of the split screen. Dots, lines, and curves can be plotted from the foreground and background color sources, but they also can be plotted from the multicolor-1 and multicolor-2 sources. Although the computer allows you to specify text characters in the graphics portion of multicolor screens, the lack of horizontal resolution makes them difficult to read.

Setting the Screen Formats with the GRAPHIC Statement

BASIC's GRAPHIC statement provides the simplest means for moving from one screen format to another. The simplest form of the statement is

GRAPHIC *fmat*

where *fmat* is a value between 0 and 5 that indicates the desired screen format. Table 7-1 summarizes these values and their meanings.

Table 7-1
Summary of *fmat* Values for Setting Screen Formats with GRAPHIC *fmat*

fmat	**Screen Format**
0	40-column text
1	Standard, full-screen, bit-mapped graphics
2	Standard, split-screen, bit-mapped graphics
3	Multicolor, full-screen, bit-mapped graphics
4	Multicolor, split-screen, bit-mapped graphics
5	80-column text

Setting up the standard split-screen format is a matter of executing this sort of statement:

GRAPHIC 4

Of course, you can return to the 40-column text screen by doing a GRAPHIC 0 command.

Incidentally, programming errors that occur while you use one of the bit-mapped screens automatically return you to the 40-column text format. Doing a RUN/STOP-RESTORE also restores the current text screen and sets all the default screen colors.

A useful extension of the GRAPHIC statement has this general form:

GRAPHIC *fmat,clrf*

where *clrf* is a screen-clearing flag. If this term is set to 0 or omitted altogether the statement goes to the designated screen format without clearing the screen. Set *clrf* to 1, however, and the system clears the screen the instant it is set up.

Thus, the GRAPHIC statement not only sets one of the six possible screens but offers the option of automatically clearing the screen it establishes.

A final extension of the GRAPHIC statement lets you adjust the number of lines of 40-column text that appear at the bottom of the split screens—GRAPHIC 2 and GRAPHIC 4. The statement, extended to include that option, looks like this:

```
GRAPHIC fmat,clrf,twind
```

where *twind* indicates the number of 40-column text lines to be devoted to bit-mapped graphics—0 through 25. The following example sets up the GRAPHIC 2 format, leaving just two lines for text at the bottom of the screen:

```
GRAPHIC 2,,23
```

Setting the Graphics Colors with BASIC's COLOR Statement

BASIC's graphics-drawing operations always use colors previously assigned to sets of color sources. All the graphics screens have color sources set aside for the border, background, and foreground colors, for example. You can assign any combination of colors to these sources, but you must bear in mind that the BASIC GRAPHICs statements described in this chapter refer directly to the color sources and not to the color codes.

The general form of a COLOR assignment statement looks like this:

```
COLOR srce,colr
```

where *srce* is a color-source code, 0 through 6, and *colr* is a code number for one of the 16 standard colors, 1 through 16. The statement literally says: "Assign color *colr* to source *srce*." Table 7-2 summarizes both the sources and colors that are used with BASIC's COLOR statement.

The following routine sets the colors relevant to a standard split screen:

```
10 COLOR 0,15
20 COLOR 1,8
30 COLOR 4,6
40 COLOR 5,2
50 GRAPHIC 2,1
```

Line 10—Set background to black.

Line 20—Set foreground to yellow.

Line 30—Set border to green.

Line 40—Set character color to white.

Line 50—Set and clear the standard, split bit-mapped screen.

Table 7-2 Summary of Values for BASIC's COLOR Statement

(A) Color-Source Codes for the srce *Term*

srce	Color Source
0	40-column background
1	Graphics foreground
2	Multicolor foreground 1
3	Multicolor foreground 2
4	40-column border
5	Character color
6	80-column background

(B) Color Codes for the colr *Term*

colr	Color
1	Black
2	White
3	Red
4	Cyan
5	Purple
6	Green
7	Blue
8	Yellow
9	Orange
10	Brown
11	Pink
12	Dark Gray
13	Medium Gray
14	Light Green
15	Light Blue
16	Light Gray

Plotting Text Characters to a Bit-Mapped Screen

The configuration of the standard 40-column character set lines up perfectly with the organization of the standard bit-mapped screens. The standard text and graphics characters thus can be plotted in the graphics area of the standard screens.

The plotting statement for that sort of task has this general form:

CHAR *srce,col,row,string*

The *srce* term specifies the desired color source. The only sources that you can cite for the CHAR statement and a standard bit-mapped screen are 0 and 1—background and foreground colors, respectively.

The *col* and *row* terms specify the screen coordinate of the plotting operation. CHAR uses the usual 40-column text format: 40 columns (0 through 39) and 25 rows (0 through 24).

The *string* term represents any string constant, variable, or function to be printed to the screen. String constants, of course, must be enclosed in quotation marks.

The routine shown in Listing 7-1 sets up a standard bit-mapped screen and prints HELLO near the middle of it. Pressing any key ends the program and returns you to the 40-column text screen:

Line 10—Set background to light blue.

Line 20—Set foreground to yellow.

Line 30—Set border to green.

Line 40—Set and clear the standard, full, bit-mapped screen.

Line 50—Use the foreground color to print HELLO at text coordinate 17,20.

Line 60—Wait for any keystroke.

Line 70—Restore the background color to dark gray.

Line 80—Restore the border color to light green.

Line 90—Set and clear the 40-column text screen.

Line 100—List the program.

Listing 7-1

```
10 COLOR 0,15
20 COLOR 1,8
30 COLOR 4,6
40 GRAPHIC 1,1
50 CHAR 1,17,12,"HELLO"
60 GETKEY K$
70 COLOR 0,12
80 COLOR 4,14
90 GRAPHIC 0,1
100 LIST
```

The CHAR statement can be extended to include a term that reverses the color format of the string:

CHAR *srce,col,row,string,invflg*

This statement normally prints the string such that the characters appear in the foreground color against a field fixed by the current background color. This is also the case when the optional *invflg* term is set to 0. However, setting the *invflg* to 1 reverses the format: The characters are printed in the background color against a field specified by the current foreground color.

Plotting Figures on the Graphics Screens

Commodore BASIC 7.0 includes a powerful set of statements and functions for working with the bit-mapped screens. The following discussions describe those features with enough detail to help you understand how they can be used. The great variety of procedures and combinations of procedures makes it virtually impossible to do much more in a book of this scope.

In these discussions, the following definitions apply: A *pixel* is defined as the smallest dot that can be plotted to the screen, and the *pixel cursor* is an imaginary mechanism that points to the position where the next pixel is to be plotted.

Working with the Position of the Pixel Cursor

BASIC's LOCATE statement fixes the position of the pixel cursor on the standard and multicolor graphics. The general form of the statement is

LOCATE *x,y*

where *x* and *y* indicate the horizontal and vertical components of the desired pixel location. These arguments can be expressed as numeric constants, variables, or expressions, but in any case, the values should conform to the X-Y formats illustrated in Figures 7-1 through 7-4.

> ***NOTE:*** The LOCATE statement fixes the position of the pixel cursor. This statement does not plot anything to the screen.

The *x* and *y* terms in the LOCATE statement also can be expressed as absolute or relative terms. Absolute terms indicate the actual screen locations and are specified by using unsigned integer values.

Using relative terms makes it possible to reLOCATE the pixel cursor to a position relative to its current position. Relative terms are specified by affixing + and − signs. A + sign preceding the *x* term indicates relative displacement to the right, and a − sign indicates relative motion to the left. With regard to the *y* term, preceding it with a + sign displaces the pixel cursor downward, and using a − sign displaces it upward.

The following example uses absolute coordinates to set the pixel cursor to the middle of the standard, full-screen graphics environment:

```
LOCATE 159,99
```

The next example uses relative coordinates to move (relative to the current position) the pixel cursor 10 locations to the right and 22 toward the top of the screen:

```
LOCATE +10, -22
```

Absolute and relative terms can be combined within the same LOCATE statement. For example:

```
LOCATE 100,+40
```

This example sets the horizontal position of the pixel cursor to 100, and moves it 40 locations downward from its present vertical location.

> *NOTE:* Negative relative terms for the Y axis do not function as described here on the earlier models of the Commodore 128. In fact, the term interrupts the program and brings up an **ILLEGAL QUANTITY ERROR.**

Using relative coordinates makes it rather easy for you to lose track of the actual (absolute) position of the pixel cursor. That position can be determined at any time by means of the RDOT function where:

RDOT(0) returns the horizontal component of the current pixel-cursor location
RDOT(1) returns the vertical component of the current pixel-cursor location

Plotting Points and Straight Lines

The DRAW statement is the most flexible of all graphics-plotting statements. It can be used for plotting individual points, straight lines, and any combination of straight lines.

The simplest form of the DRAW statement is

```
DRAW
```

This version plots a pixel at the current pixel-cursor location, using the most recently specified color source.

The next version includes a term that defines the desired color source:

DRAW *srce*

where *srce* is one of the color-source codes in Table 7-2A. The source values relevant for the standard bit-mapped screen are 0 and 1. Multicolor screens can DRAW with colors from sources 0, 1, 2, and 3.

You can use the LOCATE statement to set the position of the pixel cursor just prior to using the DRAW statement. A more convenient procedure, however, takes advantage of the fact that the DRAW statement can be extended to include the coordinate of the point:

DRAW *srce,x1,y1*

where *x1* and *y1* are the horizontal and vertical components of the desired plotting location. So the following statement fixes the location at 100,100 and plots a dot from the foreground source:

```
DRAW 1,100,100
```

In instances where you want to omit the *srce* term, but specify the location, the statement must include the comma that normally separates the *srce* term from the coordinate. For example:

```
DRAW,120,40
```

The example uses the most recently specified color source to plot a point at absolute coordinate 120,40. If you omitted the leading comma, BASIC would attempt to interpret 120 as a color source and ultimately return an **?ILLEGAL QUANTITY** error.

Because the DRAW statement can be used for plotting a point of color at any location on the graphics screen, you can fit it into a loop (a FOR. . .NEXT loop, for example) to draw a straight line between any two points. However, it is far easier to take advantage of yet another extension of the DRAW statement:

DRAW *srce,x1,y1* TO *x2,y2*

where *x1* and *y1* is the coordinate of the starting point, and *x2* and *y2* is the coordinate of the ending point. Consider this example:

```
DRAW 1,10,80 TO 120,8
```

This one uses the color from the foreground source to plot a straight line from coordinate 10,80 to coordinate 120,8.

> ***NOTE:*** At the conclusion of a DRAW. . .TO. . . statement, the pixel cursor is located at the position of the final point.

The DRAW statement has provisions for adding one line to the end of the original line without having to resort to another DRAW statement. The routine in Listing 7-2 plots a triangle, changes the foreground color, then plots a four-sided figure:

Line 10—Set foreground color to yellow.

Line 20—Set and clear the standard split screen.

Line 30—Draw a triangle starting from coordinate 80,10, then to 130,90, then to 20,90, and finally back to the starting point at 80,10.

Line 40—Change the foreground color to red.

Line 50—Draw a four-sided figure beginning at coordinate 160,50 and eventually ending at that same point.

Listing 7-2

```
10 COLOR 1,8
20 GRAPHIC 2,1
30 DRAW 1,80,10 TO 130,90 TO 20,90 TO 80,10
40 COLOR 1,3
50 DRAW 1,160,50 TO 210,50 TO 280,150 TO 130,150 TO 160,50
```

> *HINT:* Use source 0 (background color) to delete a figure from the screen. First DRAW it from an appropriate color source, then when you are ready to delete it, DRAW it again from the background color source.

The DRAW statement supports relative coordinate components as well as absolute coordinates. See the discussion of this topic for the LOCATE statement. Bear in mind, however, that earlier models do not support −y relative values.

Using the BOX Statement

Although you can draw rectangular figures with the DRAW statement, the need to draw them is so commonly encountered in Commodore graphics programs that the engineers decided to include a special statement for this purpose. The BOX statement automatically draws rectangles based on the coordinates for just two points—any pair of diagonal corners.

The general form of the BOX statement is

BOX *srce,x1,y1,x2,y2*

where *srce* is the color source to be used for the plotting operation, and the remainder of the terms represent the X and Y components of a pair of opposite corners:

x1,y1 = the coordinate of one corner of the box
x2,y2 = the coordinate of the opposing corner of the box

The following example uses the foreground color to plot a box having an upper-left corner at coordinate 100,100 and lower-right coordinate at 120,120:

```
BOX 1,100,100,120,120
```

> ***NOTE:*** At the conclusion of a BOX statement, the pixel cursor is located at the *x2,y2* corner.

The *srce* term can be omitted from the BOX statement. When this is the case, the system plots the box with the color assigned to the last-used *srce* term. The comma separating the *srce* term from the *x1,y1* coordinate must be included in either case.

The *x2,y2* coordinate also can be omitted from the BOX statement. In this instance, the corner is fixed at the pixel-cursor location in effect prior to executing the statement.

Consider the following routine:

```
10 BOX 1,100,100,120,120
20 BOX,10,10
```

Line 10 in this example uses the color assigned to the foreground source to plot a box having its upper-left corner at 100,100 and the lower-right at 120,120. Bearing in mind that the pixel cursor is left at the lower-right coordinate—at 120,120—the statement in program line 20 plots a box (using the same color) that has its upper-left corner at 10,10 and lower-right at 120,120. The pixel cursor is left at 120,120 at the end of the routine.

BOX can be extended to include a term that rotates the rectangle a specified number of degrees about its center. That version looks like this:

BOX *srce,x1,y1,x2,y2,ang*

where *ang* is a positive integer. The direction is always clockwise, and 360 degrees is the same as 0 degrees. So in instances where you might want to rotate the box in the counterclockwise direction, say

−45 degrees, you must actually specify a clockwise rotation of 360 − 45, or 335 degrees.

Taking advantage of the rotation feature does not change the location of the pixel cursor—it remains at the *x2,y2* coordinate specified in the BOX statement.

Having thus used the BOX statement to plot a rectangular figure, and possibly rotating it, you can fill it with the same color used for drawing it. This is a matter of appending the statement with an additional term, *paintflg:*

BOX *srce,x1,y1,x2,y2,ang,paintflg*

where setting *paintflg* to 1 fills the box with the current color, and setting it to 0 (or omitting it) does not fill the figure.

If you do not wish to specify an angle of rotation, but want to set *paintflg* to 1, you must use the same number of commas. For instance:

```
BOX,10,10,50,50,,1
```

This example uses the last-used source of color and fills the specified box with no rotation effect.

Using The CIRCLE Statement

Whereas the BOX statement plots simple rectangles, the CIRCLE statement can be used for plotting just about anything else. As its name implies, it can plot circles, but it also plots ellipses, arcs, and even regular polygons.

The general form of the CIRCLE statement is

CIRCLE *srce,x,y,xr*

where *srce* is the color source for the plotting operation and the remaining terms are defined in this fashion:

x,y = the coordinate of the center of the circle
xr = the radius of the circle in the horizontal dimension

The following example uses the foreground color to plot a "circle" that is centered on coordinate 100,100 and has a radius in the X direction of 20 units:

```
CIRCLE 1,100,100,20
```

The fact that the horizontal and vertical scaling are not the same on the graphics screens means that the CIRCLE statement, as described thus far, plots ellipses instead of circles. The figures are elongated in the vertical direction.

One way to compensate for this sort of distortion is by extending the statement to include a *yr* parameter and setting ratios between *xr* and *yr* in this fashion:

When using the standard bit-mapped screens: ***yr*** **= 0.75*** ***xr***
When using the multicolor screens: ***yr*** **= 1.5*** ***xr***

The extended version of the CIRCLE statement looks like this:

CIRCLE ***srce,x,y,xr,yr***

where *xr* and *yr* are the maximum horizontal and vertical radii.

This statement plots a good circle on a standard graphics screen:

```
CIRCLE 1,100,100,20,15
```

and this version does the job on a multicolor screen:

```
CIRCLE 1,100,100,20,30
```

> ***NOTE:*** When *yr* is not specified, the system assigns it a value that is equal to *xr*.

The CIRCLE statement, as described thus far, generates ellipses, including circles when the ratios of *xr* and *yr* are properly adjusted. The next extension of the statement makes possible the limitation of the drawing to arcs (portions of the ellipse). The general idea is to specify a starting angle and an ending angle as reckoned in degrees in the clockwise direction from the upper maximum-vertical point on the figure. Here is the CIRCLE statement extended to include terms for the starting and ending angles:

CIRCLE ***srce,x,y,xr,yr,strtang,endang***

where *strtang* is the starting angle of the arc and *endang* is the ending angle.

This version of the CIRCLE statement plots an arc between the 45-degree and 135-degree portions of an ellipse:

```
CIRCLE 1,100,100,50,,45,135
```

The default value for *startang* is 0 degrees, and the default value of *endang* is 360 degrees. Setting *startang* to 270 and omitting the *endang* parameter draws an arc between 270 and 360 degrees.

The eighth optional CIRCLE parameter establishes an angle of rotation, in the counterclockwise direction, of the ellipse or arc specified by the preceding parameters. The angle-of-rotation parameter, *ang*, is specified in degrees:

CIRCLE *srce,x,y,xr,yr,strtang,endang,ang*

Although the following statement plots an ellipse that is elongated in the horizontal direction:

```
CIRCLE 1,100,100,50,10
```

this version rotates it 30 degrees in the clockwise direction:

```
CIRCLE 1,100,100,50,10,,,30
```

In instances where you want to rotate the ellipse or arc (little is to be gained by rotating a circle) in the counterclockwise direction, you must specify a clockwise rotation of 360–ANG, where ANG is the desired amount of angular rotation in the counterclockwise direction.

The final extension of the CIRCLE command specifies the number of degrees between successive points plotted on the ellipse. The default value is two degrees. Specifying a lesser number of degrees between points doesn't change the appearance very much, and it takes longer to plot the figure. Increasing the number of degrees between points creates coarse figures that take on the appearance of polygons.

CIRCLE *srce,x,y,xr,yr,strtang,endang,ang,inxcr*

where *incr* is the number of degrees between successive points on the figure. Setting *inc* to 120, for example, plots a simple three-sided figure—a triangle:

```
CIRCLE 1,100,100,50,20,,,,120
```

This one plots the ellipse into a hexagon:

```
CIRCLE 1,100,100,50,37,,,,72
```

Incidentally, the string of four successive commas in these examples specifies default values for items 6, 7, and 8 in the CIRCLE command: *strtang* = 0, *endang* = 360, and *ang* = 0.

> ***NOTE:*** Any CIRCLE statement leaves the pixel cursor at the last-plotted point on the figure.

Using the PAINT Statement

The BOX statement includes a "paint" flag. When this flag is set to 1, the system automatically fills the box with the same color used for drawing its outline. The CIRCLE statement, however, does not offer that feature. But BASIC's PAINT statement makes possible the filling of a circle or ellipse with a color from the same source used for plotting the outline of the figure.

In fact, the PAINT statement makes possible the filling of any sort of closed figure, including those drawn by means of DRAW statements.

The general form of the PAINT statement is

PAINT *srce,x,y*

where *srce* is the color source for the PAINT color and *x,y* is the coordinate of any point within the figure to be filled.

The following routine plots an ellipse and fills it with the same color:

```
10 COLOR 0,2:COLOR 1,8
20 GRAPHIC 2,1
30 CIRCLE 1,200,100,50
40 PAINT,200,100
```

Line 10—Set background to white and foreground to yellow.

Line 20—Set the standard, split screen.

Line 30—Plot a yellow ellipse.

Line 40—Fill it with the same color, yellow.

The coordinate that you specify for a PAINT statement must be *within* the figure and the figure must be completely closed. Specifying a PAINT coordinate outside the figure paints the area outside the screen. If the figure has any gaps, the paint "leaks" through the hole to the outside area.

The PAINT statement has an extension that is useful in the multicolor mode. That form of the statement looks like this:

PAINT *srce,x,y,mode*

where *mode* is a flag value (0 or 1) that determines the sort of color which marks the boundary of the painting operation. If *mode* is set to 0, the painting uses the *srce* color as a boundary. Setting *mode* to 1 instructs the PAINT statement to paint to a border of any non-background color.

Rescaling the Screen

Figure 7-1 shows that the standard bit-mapped screen uses a 320 x 200 coordinate system, and Figure 7-3 shows that the multicolor version uses a 160 x 200 format. This is only the system's default scaling, however. The scaling of these coordinates can be changed to suit particular needs (such as copying the graphics data from a program written for a computer that uses a different high-resolution scaling scheme).

Changing the scaling of the coordinate systems does not change the number of points that can be plotted. It simply shrinks or stretches the measuring stick.

The general form of the SCALE statement is

SCALE *sflg,xmax,ymax*

The *sflg* term turns the scaling operation on or off. Setting it to 0 turns off the scaling effect and restores the normal 320 x 200 and 160 x 200 screens. In that case, the remaining terms are not relevant and can be omitted.

Thus, turning off the scaling effect is a matter of executing this statement:

```
SCALE 0
```

Setting *sflg* to 1 enables the scaling effect, and the values assigned to *xmax* and *ymax* become relevant. Consider the following example:

```
SCALE 1,1000,1000
```

This changes the scaling of the screen so that plotting operations which use X-Y coordinates can handle values up to 999 in both dimensions.

The following example scales the screen to 1000,1000 and draws a horizontal line half the distance across the screen:

```
10 COLOR 0,1:COLOR 1,2
20 GRAPHIC 2,1
30 SCALE 1,1000,1000
40 DRAW 1,0,500 TO 500,500
50 SCALE 0
```

The allowable range of scaling values for the standard bit-mapped screens are

ymax = 320 through 32767
xmax = 320 through 32767

And if you execute a SCALE 1 statement:

xmax = 1023
ymax = 1023

The range of scaling values for the multicolor screen is a bit different:

ymax = 160 through 32767
xmax = 160 through 32767

Executing SCALE 1 for the multicolor screen:

ymax = 511
xmax = 511

Saving and Reloading Bit-Mapped Shapes

The plotting statements described in the previous section of this chapter are capable of drawing virtually any sort of figure. The drawing process, however, can take some time, particularly in the case of complex or large, painted figures. This becomes troublesome in instances where you want to plot the figure a number of different times.

The procedures described here do not eliminate the need for plotting a figure in the usual fashion one time. Once it is plotted, though, you can make a copy that can be duplicated any number of times at a much more rapid rate.

Two BASIC statements are involved in the procedure: SSHAPE and GSHAPE. Assuming that you have plotted a figure on the screen in the usual fashion, the SSHAPE command lets you assign a rectangular area of the bit-mapped screen to a string variable. Of course, this rectangular area should include the figure of interest to you.

Having thus saved the figure—a rectangular area that includes the figure—you can plot it at any later time by specifying the coordinate of the upper-left corner in a GSHAPE command.

The general form of the figure-saving statement, SSHAPE, is

SSHAPE *strvar,x1,y1,x2,y2*

where

> ***strvar*** = any valid string variable name
> ***x1,y1*** = coordinate of the upper-left corner of the rectangular area to be saved
> ***x2,y2*** = coordinate of the lower-right corner of the rectangular area to be saved

Consider this example:

```
SSHAPE F1$,20,40,60,100
```

which defines a rectangular area having its upper-left corner at coordinate 20,40 and lower-right at 60,100. The information is saved as variable F1$.

You can omit the *x2,y2* coordinate from the statement, in which case, the current position of the pixel cursor defines the second corner of the graphics area being saved.

A BASIC string variable can handle no more than 255 bytes, so there is a limit on the size of the rectangular area that can be assigned to a string. Two equations are available for determining the number of bytes in an SSHAPE field. The choice depends on whether the figure is taken from a standard bit-map screen or a multicolor screen.

For a standard bit-mapped screen:

```
L=INT((ABS(x1 - x2)+1)/4+.99)*(ABS(y1 - y2) + 1)+4
```

And for a multicolor screen:

```
L=INT((ABS(x1 - x2)+1)/8+.99)*(ABS(y1 - y2) + 1)+4
```

In both instances:

> **L** = number of bytes (must be less than 255)
> **x1** = X component of the upper-left coordinate of the SSHAPE area
> **x2** = X component of the lower-right coordinate of the SSHAPE area
> **y1** = Y component of the upper-left coordinate of the SSHAPE area
> **y2** = X component of the lower-right coordinate of the SSHAPE area

However, a more straightforward procedure is available for determining the number of bytes in an SSHAPEd area: Execute the SSHAPE command for the desired area, then apply the LEN(*strvar*) function for its string variable name. If the result is larger than 255, you have to reduce the size of the area or divide it between different string variables.

The SSHAPE statement is virtually worthless without some means for plotting the shapes back to the screen. The GSHAPE statement serves this function:

GSHAPE *strvar,x,y*

where *strvar* is a string variable that has had a shape assigned to it, and *x,y* is the screen coordinate where the upper-left corner of the shape is to appear.

The following example illustrates the application of the SSHAPE and GSHAPE statements:

```
10 COLOR 1,8
20 GRAPHIC 2,1
30 DRAW 1,0,0 TO 20,0 TO 20,20 TO 0,0
40 SSHAPE F$,0,0,20,20
50 GSHAPE F$,100,100
```

Line 10—Set foreground color to yellow.

Line 20—Set and clear the standard split-screen graphics mode.

Line 30—Plot a triangle in the upper-left corner of the screen.

Line 40—Use SSHAPE to assign that figure to F$.

Line 50—Use GSHAPE to copy the figure to a different place on the screen—its upper-left corner at coordinate 100,100.

The GSHAPE statement can be extended to include a *mode* term:

GSHAPE *strvar,x,y,mode*

where *mode* is an integer value between 0 and 4.

Mode 0 is the default mode. It is the one used when the mode term is omitted from the statement. It plots the figure exactly as prescribed, regardless of the nature of graphics information that might occupy the same segment of the screen.

Mode 1 plots the figure in an inverse form. Points turned on in the original version are turned off, and those specified as turned off are turned on. In a manner of speaking, this mode plots a negative image of the original figure. It does the job without regard for any other graphics information that might be on the same part of the screen.

Mode 2 technically performs a logical OR operation between the figure being plotted to the screen and any other graphic information in the same area. It enables you to overlay unlike figures, allowing segments of previously plotted figures to be exposed around the edges of more recent plots.

Mode 3 performs a logical AND operation between two or more figures plotted in the same area. The result is a graphic that represents only the area the figures have in common.

Mode 4 performs an exclusive-OR operation between two or more figures that occupy the same portion of the screen. The areas that the figures have in common are changed to the current background color.

Setting Graphics Screens from Machine Language Routines

BASIC's bit-mapped plotting statements are so versatile that there is little reason to consider using POKEs to control graphics operations and set up the screens. If you are using BASIC at all, you might as well use it all the way through a graphics routine. The presentations through the end of this chapter deal mainly with the graphics environment from a machine language point of view. References to decimal values are for the benefit of programmers who might want to write hybrid programs—those using combinations of BASIC and machine language routines.

Allocating RAM for Bit-Mapped Graphics

System initialization routines set $1C00 as the starting address for BASIC operations. Unfortunately, this is also the starting address for two blocks of RAM set aside for bit-mapped graphics color and screen RAM. If you have any intention of using bit-mapped graphics in conjunction with BASIC programming, the lower address used by BASIC has to be moved beyond the bit-mapped graphics area—to $4000 or higher.

When the computer is first turned on, you will find that the content of MEMBOT register $2E is set to $1C. That value, used together with the LSB of the value at $2D, shows that BASIC programming begins at address $1C01. Use a GRAPHIC statement to set up one of the bit-mapped screens, however, and you will find the values in MEMBOT indicate the start of BASIC programming at $4001. This value remains in effect even after executing a GRAPHIC 0 to leave the bit-mapped mode.

The point is that executing a GRAPHIC statement for one of the bit-mapped screens automatically moves the start of BASIC programming out of the bit-mapped graphics RAM area. It remains in that condition until you execute a GRAPHIC CLR statement.

If you are using a hybrid program—a combination of BASIC and machine language routines—you might as well move BASIC out of the bit-map block of RAM by doing something such as this:

```
GRAPHIC 1:GRAPHIC 0
```

The first statement establishes the standard, full screen of bit-mapped graphics, but more important, it sets the pointers for BASIC programming out of the bit-map RAM area. The second statement simply returns the system to the text mode.

Setting the Graphics Modes

A zero-page register at $D8 (216) controls the screen mode at any given moment. Loading the appropriate values to that register sets the desired screen mode, and reading the content of the register returns a value that indicates the current screen mode.

GRAPHIC register

Address: **$D8 (216)**
Data:

$00 (0) = 40-column text
$20 (32) = Standard, full bit-mapped screen
$60 (96) = Standard, split bit-mapped screen
$A0 (160) = Multicolor, full bit-mapped screen
$E0 (224) = Multicolor, split bit-mapped screen

Thus, setting the equivalent of the GRAPHIC 2 mode is a matter of storing $60 to zero-page register $D8. For example:

```
LDA #$60
STA $D8
```

To return to 40-column text:

```
LDA #$00
STA $D8
```

Clearing the Graphics Screen

Storing values directly to the GRAPHIC register at $D8 certainly sets up the specified screen format but does not clear the graphics portion of the new screen. The machine language routine in Listing 7-3 does that job for you.

The basic idea is to clear two blocks of RAM. The first block is the bit-map color RAM located between $1C00 and $1FFF. The data in these addresses is set to the background color assigned to $D021 in the VIC. The second block is the bit-mapped screen RAM located between $2000 and $3FFF. The routine plots spaces to that 8K block.

Using the routine, called GRCLR, is a matter of loading the desired background color code to $D021, then doing a JSR to the entry point for GRCLR.

Listing 7-3

```
        LDA #$00        ;LSB OF COLOR BASE ADDRESS
        STA $FA         ;TO ZERO-PAGE $FA
        LDA #$1C        ;MSB OF COLOR BASE ADDRESS
        STA $FB         ;TO ZERO-PAGE $FB
NEXT2   LDA $D021       ;GET CURRENT BKGND COLOR
        AND #$0F        ;MASK LOWER NIBBLE
        LDY #$00        ;INITIALIZE POINTER
NEXT1   STA ($FA),Y     ;SET COLOR
        INY             ;INCREMENT THE POINTER
        BNE NEXT1       ;IF NOT END OF PAGE THEN AGAIN
        INC $FB         ;INCR. MSB OF BASE ADDRESS
        LDA #$20        ;IS IT DONE?
        CMP $FB         ;
        BNE NEXT2       ;IF NOT, DO NEXT PAGE
        STA $FB         ;MSB OF SCREEN BASE ADDR
NEXT4   LDA #$00        ;ZERO TO CLEAR SCREEN
        TAY             ;INITIALIZE POINTER
NEXT3   STA ($FA),Y     ;CLEAR THE BYTE
        INY             ;INCREMENT THE POINTER
        BNE NEXT3       ;IF NOT END OF PAGE THEN AGAIN
        INC $FB         ;INCR. MSB OF BASE ADDRESS
        LDA #$40        ;IS IT DONE?
        CMP $FB         ;
        BNE NEXT4       ;IF NOT, DO NEXT PAGE
        RTS             ;
```

Setting Alternative Screen Sizes

Recall that the GRAPHIC statement can be extended to include a specification for the number of text lines to appear on split screens. This also can be set by loading an appropriate value to register $0A34.

The decimal value to be loaded to that register is determined by this equation:

$$val = 48 + 8 * tline$$

where *val* is the decimal value to be loaded to $0A34, and *tline* is the line number for the uppermost line of text (0 through 25).

The following example sets the standard split bit-mapped screen, but begins the text area at line 22:

```
LDA #$60     ;BYTE FOR GRAPHIC 2
STA $D8      ;SET THE SCREEN
LDA #$E0     ;BYTE FOR TEXT LINE 22
STA $0A34    ;SET IT
```

The routine should call GRCLR in Listing 7-3 if you also want to clear the graphics portion of the screen.

Working Directly with the Standard Bit-Mapped Screens

Like the text screens, the bit-mapped screens use two separate blocks for RAM for distinctly different purposes. One block of RAM determines the patterns of dots that are to appear on the screen, and the other determines their color. You must know how to work with both of those blocks to do any meaningful graphics from machine-language programming.

Writing Directly to Standard Bit-Map RAM

The bit-mapped screen is located in an 8K block of Bank-0 RAM, $2000 through $3FFF (8192–16383). Figure 7-1 shows that the screen is organized into 320 horizontal and 200 vertical locations. This figures out to be 64,000 different locations. Being able to access one of 64,000 locations within an 8,000 byte block of RAM obviously calls for some understanding of how all those locations are organized within a relatively small amount of address space.

One important clue to how this is accomplished is the fact that each bit in a screen byte represents one dot location on the screen. Eight bits are in each byte, so using 8,000 bytes provides 64,000 dot locations.

The first address in the bit-mapped screen RAM holds eight bits that correspond to the first sequence of eight dots on the screen. Doing a POKE 8192,255 while the system is in one of the standard bit-mapped modes (GRAPHIC 1 or GRAPHIC 2) does indeed plot a short horizontal line in the upper-left corner of the screen.

Unfortunately for programmers who want to write directly to the bit-mapped screens, POKEing to the next address location, 8193, does not plot a second line that begins where the previous one ends. Rather, it plots a line directly below the first one. Although one might think that the following example would plot a long horizontal line across the top of the screen, it actually plots a block in the upper-left corner that measures eight dots in the horizontal direction and eight lines in the vertical direction.

```
10 FOR K=0 TO 7
20 POKE 8192+K,255
30 NEXT K
```

Figure 7-5 illustrates the situation. The first eight bytes in bit-mapped screen RAM correspond to eight rows of dots. The first byte points to the uppermost row, and the last byte points to the lowest row. The screen is thus divided into fields of eight bytes each. Because each byte represents a left-to-right sequence of dots (0=off, 1=on), each field is composed of a rectangular array of 64 dot locations.

Perhaps it is no surprise that the bit-mapped screen is organized into 1000 fields—40 columns and 25 rows. It is the same format used for the 40-column text screen. The fields are arranged in a systematic, left-to-right, top-to-bottom fashion.

The following example sets and clears the standard, split version of the bit-mapped screen, then draws a thin straight line along the second graphics line on the screen. It is tantamount to executing BASIC's DRAW,0,1 TO 319,1. It actually turns on all eight bits in the second byte in all of the fields along the top of the screen.

```
10 GRAPHIC 2,1
20 FOR K=0 TO 8*39 STEP 8
30 POKE 8193+K,255
40 NEXT K
```

The X-Y format used with BASIC's plotting statements makes quite easy the specification of any one of the 64,000 dot locations. The task is not quite so easy when you write directly to the bit-mapped screen. The general procedure begins by determining which field is to be used, then which one of its eight bytes is relevant, and finally the bit within that byte. Some mathematical techniques can be of great help, however.

Assuming that you are thinking in terms of BASICS's X-Y format, the coordinate of the corresponding bit-map field can be reckoned this way:

COL=INT(X/8)
ROW=INT(Y/8)

where X is the bit-map horizontal location, Y is the vertical location, and ROW and COL are the row and column locations of the field.

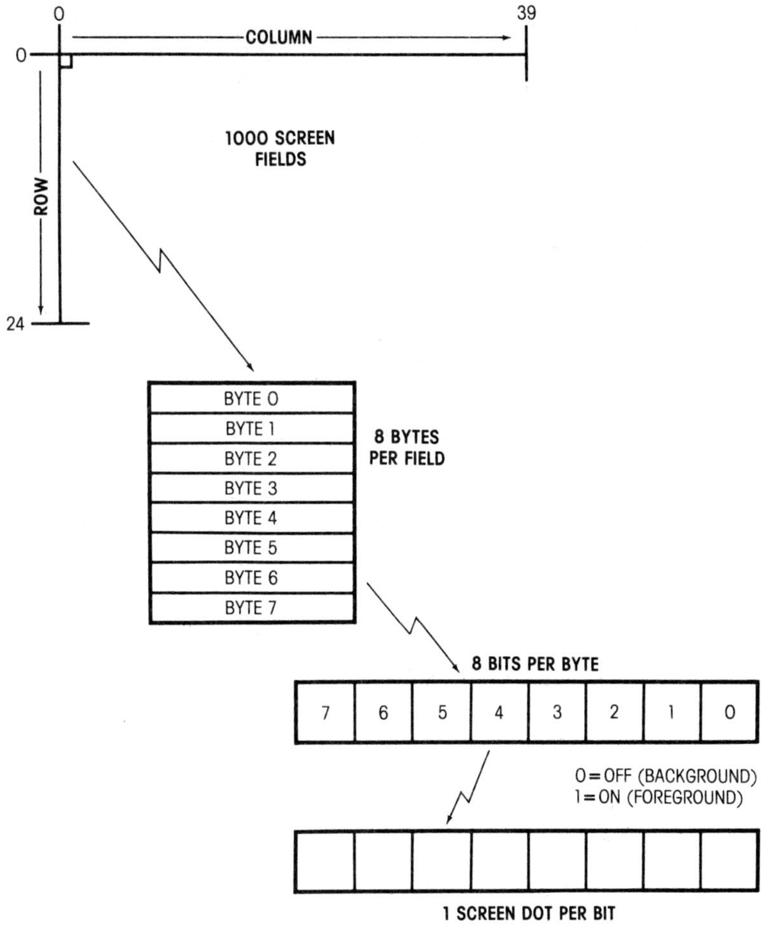

Fig. 7-5 Organization of lines, fields, and bytes for standard bit-mapped screen RAM

If you are planning to plot a dot at bit-map coordinate 120,42:

COL = INT(120/8) = 15
ROW = INT(42/8) = 5

The dot will be somewhere in the field located at column 15, row 5.

The next step is to determine the byte within the field is found by this sort of relation:

BYTE = Y AND 7

The example cites Y = 42:

BYTE = 42 AND 7 = 2

It is now established that the point is located somewhere within byte 2 of the field at column 15, row 5.

Having thus established the location of the field and the byte within it, you have sufficient information for determining the RAM address of that byte. That is done this way:

ADDR=BASE+8*COL+320*ROW+BYTE

where BASE is the starting address of the screen block (8192 in this case) and COL, ROW, and BYTE are the values determined in the previous steps. If BASE = 8192, COL = 15, ROW = 5, and BYTE = 2, then ADDR = 9914.

The final step is to determine which one of the eight bits in the data byte is to be turned on (set to 1). The following Boolean relation takes care of that situation:

BIT = 7 – (X AND 7)

If X = 120, then BIT = 7. So bit 7 should be set to 1, and the others to zero. The decimal value of such a byte is 128.

Putting the information together, you can see that these two statements do the same job:

```
DRAW,120,42
POKE 9914,128
```

Considering all the calculations required for determining the POKE address, you can understand why most programmers let the computer do the work—usually as a subroutine. All the calculations for determining the bit-mapped screen address come down to this:

ADDR=8192+8*(INT(X/8))+320*(INT(Y/8))+(Y AND 7)

where X and Y represent the coordinate of the point in the usual bit-mapped format (Figures 7-1 and 7-2).

Carrying the procedure to its ultimate conclusion, you can plot a point anywhere on the bit-mapped screen with this sort of statement:

```
POKE 8192+8*(INT(X/8))+320*(INT(Y/8))+(Y AND 7),7 – (X AND 7)
```

Table 7-3 summarizes the starting and ending addresses for each eight-line band across the standard bit-mapped screen.

Writing Directly to the Standard Bit-Map Color RAM

The standard bit-map screen provides a way to address 64K dot locations within an 8K block of RAM. Bytes of data sent to those locations

Table 7-3 Range of Addresses for Each Eight-Line Segment of the Standard Bit-Mapped Screen RAM

Line	Address Range	
	Dec	Hex
0	8192-8511	$2000 -$213F
1	8512-8831	$2140 -$227F
2	8832-9151	$2280 -$23BF
3	9152-9471	$23C0 -$24FF
4	9472-9791	$2500 -$263F
5	9792-10111	$2640 -$277F
6	10112-10431	$2780 -$28BF
7	10432-10751	$28C0 -$29FF
8	10752-11071	$2A00 -$2B3F
9	11072-11391	$2B40 -$2C7F
10	11392-11711	$2C80 -$2DBF
11	11712-12031	$2DC0-$2EFF
12	12032-12351	$2F00 -$303F
13	12352-12671	$3040 -$317F
14	12672-12991	$3180 -$32BF
15	12992-13311	$32C0 -$33FF
16	13312-13631	$3400 -$353F
17	13632-13951	$3540 -$367F
18	13952-14271	$3680 -$37BF
19	14272-14591	$37C0 -$38FF
20	14592-14911	$3900 -$3A3F
21	14912-15231	$3A40 -$3B7F
22	15232-15551	$3B80 -$3CBF
23	15552-15871	$3CC0-$3DFF
24	15872-16191	$3E00 -$3F3F

Column base address = Line start address + (8*column number)

determine the on/off pattern of dots, when a 0 bit turns the point off and a 1 bit turns it on. The screen RAM contains no information regarding the colors of the dots. That is the job of the bit-map color RAM.

One might suppose that the color RAM for the standard bit-map screen would be the same size as the corresponding screen RAM. This is indeed true for the 40- and 80-column text screens but not for a bit-map screen.

Color RAM for the standard bit-map screen occupies only 1K of RAM—one-eighth the amount of RAM allocated for screen RAM. Obviously, no provisions exist for setting the color of individual dots on the standard bit-mapped screen. Rather, the colors are set for groups of dots, and therein lies the shortcoming of standard bit-map graphics.

Bit-map color RAM is organized according to the *fields* of bytes in screen RAM. Recall that the standard bit-map RAM is organized into fields: 40 in the horizontal direction and 25 in the vertical direction. Each field contains eight consecutive bytes of data, and each byte contains eight bits. What is more important is the fact that color RAM is also organized in a 40-by-25 format—one addressable color location for each field on the screen.

This leads to the conclusion that the group of 64 dots in each screen-RAM field must use the same foreground and background colors as specified by the corresponding color-RAM location. Colors can be different from one screen field to another, but no more than two different colors can be in a given field: the background and foreground colors.

Bit-map color RAM occupies the block of memory from $1C00 through $1FE7 (7168–8167). Figure 7-6 shows the general column-row layout with regard to screen fields, and Table 7-4 shows the starting and ending addresses for each line of bit-map color RAM.

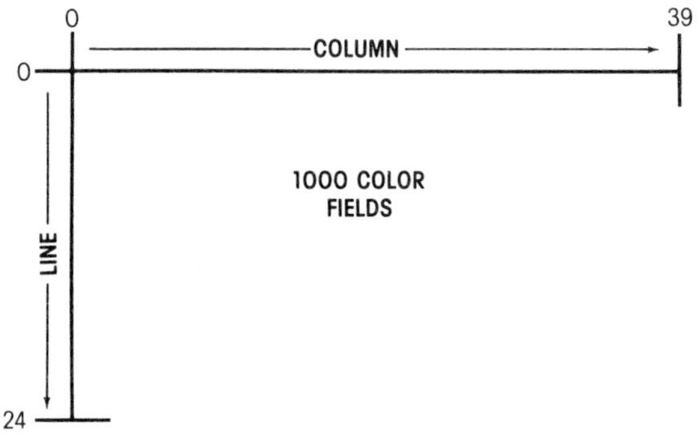

Fig. 7-6 Column-row organization of fields for bit-map color RAM

Table 7-4 Starting and Ending Addresses for Each Line of Fields in Bit-Map Color RAM

Line	Address Range	
	Dec	Hex
0	7168–7207	$1C00 – $1C27
1	7208–7247	$1C28 – $1C4F
2	7248–7287	$1C50 – $1C77
3	7288–7327	$1C78 – $1C9F
4	7328–7367	$1CA0 – $1CC7
5	7368–7407	$1CC8 – $1CEF
6	7408–7447	$1CF0 – $1D17
7	7448–7487	$1D18 – $1D3F
8	7488–7527	$1D40 – $1D67
9	7528–7567	$1D68 – $1D8F
10	7568–7607	$1D90 – $1DB7
11	7608–7647	$1DB8 – $1DDF
12	7648–7687	$1DE0 – $1E07

Table 7-4 (cont.)

Line	Address Range	
	Dec	Hex
13	7688-7727	$1E08 -$1E2F
14	7728-7767	$1E30 -$1E57
15	7768-7807	$1E58 -$1E7F
16	7808-7847	$1E80 -$1EA7
17	7848-7887	$1EA8 -$1ECF
18	7888-7927	$1ED0 -$1EF7
19	7928-7967	$1EF8 -$1F1F
20	7968-8007	$1F20 -$1F47
21	8008-8047	$1F48 -$1F6F
22	8048-8087	$1F70 -$1F97
23	8088-8127	$1F98 -$1FBF
24	8128-8167	$1FC0 -$1FE7

Each byte in standard bit-map color RAM is divided into two equal nibbles. As indicated in Figure 7-7, the four higher-order bytes determine the foreground color and the four lower-order bytes fix the background color. Table 7-5 shows the values associated with each color that can be assigned to nibbles of color RAM.

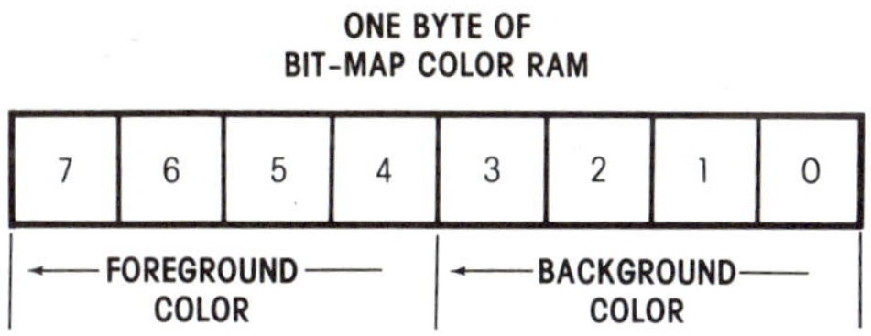

Fig. 7-7 Organization of nibbles in a byte of data for the standard bit-map color RAM

Table 7-5 Color Codes that Can Be Assigned to Foreground and Background Nibbles in Standard Bit-Map Color RAM

Code		Color
Dec	Hex	
0	0	Black
1	1	White
2	2	Red
3	3	Cyan
4	4	Purple
5	5	Green
6	6	Blue
7	7	Yellow
8	8	Orange
9	9	Brown
10	A	Pink
11	B	Dark Gray

Table 7-5 (cont.)

Code		Color
Dec	Hex	
12	C	Medium Gray
13	D	Light Green
14	E	Light Blue
15	F	Light Gray

The routine in Listing 7-4 bit maps a small green square within a white field in the upper-left corner of the screen.

Listing 7-4

```
LDA #$60     ;SPECIFY GRAPHIC 2
STA $D8      ;SET THE SCREEN
LDA #$51     ;SPECIFY GREEN ON WHITE
STA $1C00    ;SET IT TO COLOR RAM
LDA #$00     ;SPECIFY 00000000
STA $2000    ;FIELD 0,0 BYTE 0
STA $2001    ;FIELD 0,0 BYTE 1
STA $2006    ;FIELD 0,0 BYTE 6
STA $2007    ;FIELD 0,0 BYTE 7
LDA #$3C     ;SPECIFY 00111100
STA $2002    ;FIELD 0,0 BYTE 2
STA $2005    ;FIELD 0,0 BYTE 5
LDA #$24     ;SPECIFY 00100100
STA $2003    ;FIELD 0,0 BYTE 3
STA $2004    ;FIELD 0,0 BYTE 4
```

Working Directly with the Multicolor Bit-Map Screen

The multicolor bit-map screen uses the same blocks of screen and color RAM as does the standard graphics screen. However, the multicolor bit-map mode works in an entirely different fashion.

Recall that the standard bit-map screen uses just two color sources: foreground and background. Thus, you can specify the desired color source with a single bit. When the bit is set to 0, the system plots the background color. When the bit is set to 1, the system plots the foreground color.

The multicolor mode has access to four different color sources. This means it is necessary to use two bits to specify the source. Each pixel on the multicolor screen requires two bits to specify its color and consequently maps as two successive dot locations on the screen. This accounts for the fact that half as many horizontal locations are on a multicolor screen as on a standard bit-mapped screen.

Figure 7-8 shows the organization of the screen RAM for multicolor bit-mapped graphics. It is divided into 1000 screen fields—40 in the horizontal direction and 25 in the vertical direction. Each field is composed of eight consecutive bytes of data, and each byte is divided into eight bits. To this point, the organization is no different from the standard bit-mapped screen as shown in Figure 7-5.

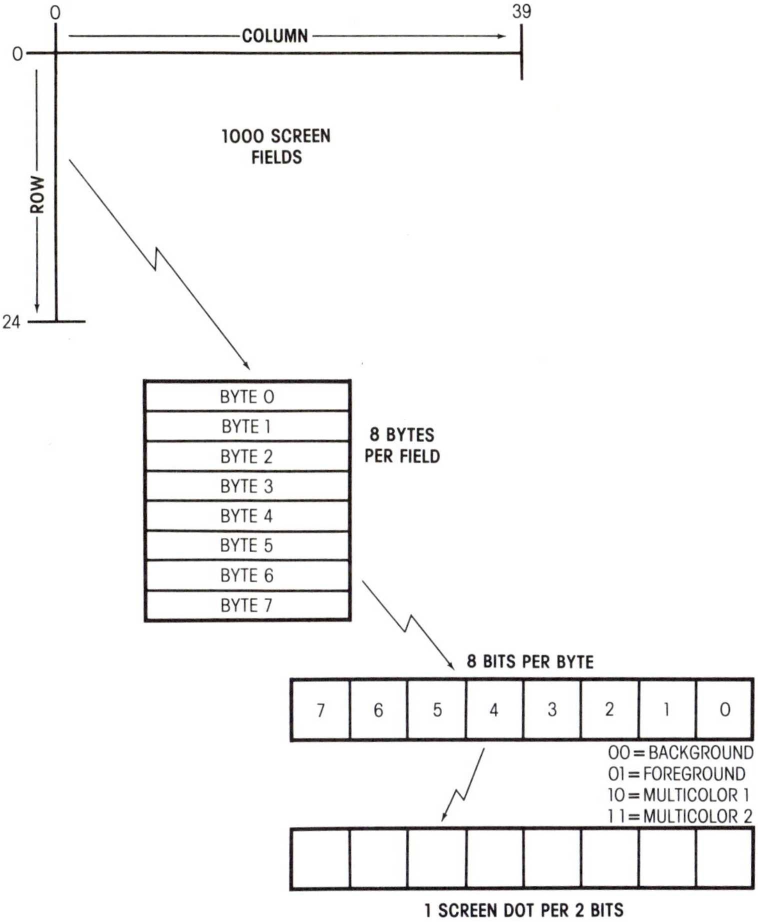

Fig. 7-8 Organization of lines, fields, and bytes for the multicolor bit-map screen RAM

The difference is in the way the bits are mapped to the screen. The standard bit-mapped screen plots one pixel for each bit. The multicolor screen plots one pixel for every two bits.

A multicolor bit-mapped figure is thus composed of pairs of bits that specify the desired color source, where:

00 = Background color
01 = Four higher-order bits of color RAM (foreground)

10 = Four lower-order bits of color RAM (multicolor 1)
11 = Color memory (multicolor 2)

Notice that the bit-map color RAM plays a part in specifying colors for the multicolor mode. Each byte specifies the color for two different sources, where the upper nibble holds the color code for screen bit-pair 01 (foreground color) and the lower nibble holds the color for bit-pair 10 (multicolor 1).

Figure 7-9 shows the bit plan for a simple multicolor figure. Listing 7-5 uses the data to plot the figure in the upper-left corner of the GRAPHIC 4 screen.

Fig. 7-9 Bit plan for a simple multicolor figure

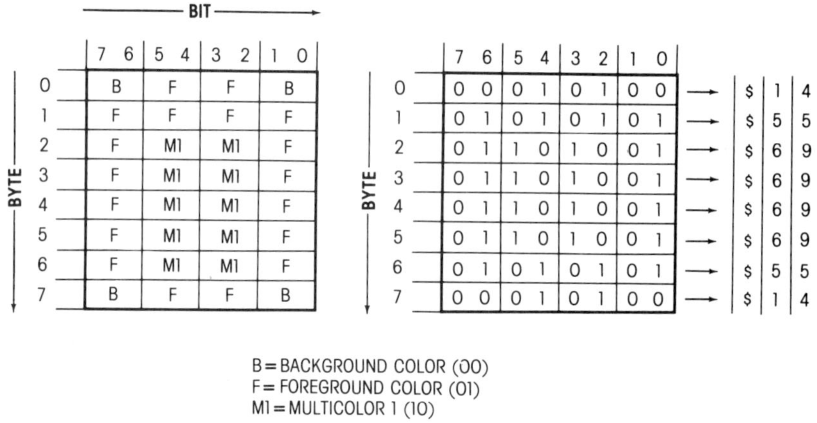

Listing 7-5

```
LDA #$0E      ;SPECIFY GRAPHIC 4
STA $D8       ;SET THE SCREEN
LDA #$0B      ;SPECIFY DARK GRAY BKGND
STA $D021     ;SET IT
LDA #$16      ;WHITE/BLUE NIBBLES
STA $1C00     ;SET IT TO COLOR RAM
STA #$141     ;SPECIFY 00/01/01/00
STA $2000     ;FIELD 0,0 BYTE 0
STA $2007     ;FIELD 0,0 BYTE 7
LDA #$55      ;SPECIFY 01/01/01/01
STA $2001     ;FIELD 0,0 BYTE 1
STA $2006     ;FIELD 0,0 BYTE 6
LDA #$69      ;SPECIFY 01/10/10/01
STA $2003     ;FIELD 0,0 BYTE 3
STA $2004     ;FIELD 0,0 BYTE 4
STA $2005     ;FIELD 0,0 BYTE 5
```

8

Sprite Animation Procedures

A lexicographer would define a *sprite* as a disembodied being—a ghost—having elfish or impish qualities. Although the term is technically meaningless in the context of animation procedures for the Commodore personal computers, it does convey a sense of the matter. Sprites are relatively small but colorful and active images.

Creating Sprite Figures

Three general techniques are available for generating new sprite figures. The most straightforward technique takes advantage of BASIC's built-in SPRDEF routine. SPRDEF is executed from the keyboard as though it were a BASIC command, but it is actually a separate operating mode with its own commands and procedures.

SPRDEF allows on-screen, freehand development of a sprite. The technique requires little previous planning, it shows exactly what the sprite will look like on the screen, and it does not require any bit manipulations and number-system conversions. It is a handy technique for all levels of Commodore users and an invaluable aid for those who have no skill with binary and hexadecimal number systems.

The SPRDEF technique leaves its sprites in the sprite-definition tables.

An alternative sprite-generating technique takes advantage of BASIC's bit-map drawing procedures described in the previous chapter. The technique begins with the application of statements such as LOCATE, DRAW, BOX, CIRCLE, and PAINT to develop the desired image within an area that is 24 pixels wide and 21 tall. The next step is to use the shape-saving command, SSHAPE, to assign the shape to a string variable. The final step—one unique to generating sprites—is to copy the figure to a sprite-table area with the SPRSAVE command.

The remaining alternative is the most cumbersome because it requires a great deal of planning and manipulation of binary/hexadecimal data. The idea is to load the bit-map data for a sprite figure directly into the sprite tables.

Using the Sprite-Definition Routine, SPRDEF

SPRDEF is a BASIC command that invokes a self-contained operating mode which makes rather easy the development of new sprite figures. This operating mode is invoked from the BASIC interpreter by entering the SPRDEF command.

Executing SPRDEF sets up a completely different sort of operating environment. A working area is blocked off in the upper-left portion of the screen, an area on the right side of the screen that shows the actual sprite as you develop it and a prompting message asking SPRITE NUMBER?

Respond to this message by pressing a numeric key that indicates the desired sprite number you want assigned to the new sprite.

After you indicate the sprite number, the screen shows the sprite currently assigned that number. If no sprites have been previously assigned to that sprite number, you will see a meaningless arrangement of horizontal bars. Clear the working area by pressing SHIFT-CLR/HOME.

The cross in the upper-left corner of the working area is the drawing cursor. Use the cursor arrow keys to move it anywhere within the working area.

Plot the figure with the foreground color by pressing the 2 key. Erase portions by pressing the 1 key. The figure as it appears in the working area is many times larger than the actual sprite will be. But you can see it portrayed with its actual size on the right side of the screen.

There are a number of other useful keyboard controls that you can use in the SPRDEF mode. They are summarized in the latter part of this discussion. What is most important is knowing how to set up the SPRDEF mode, plot a figure, and save it as a sprite. The previous paragraphs outline the procedures for setting up the SPRDEF mode and plotting a figure.

The figure that you develop with SPRDEF is not actually entered into the system as a legitimate sprite until you do an unusual key operation: SHIFT-RETURN—hold down one of the SHIFT keys and press RETURN.

Pressing SHIFT-RETURN loads the figure into the sprite definition area you specified in response to the original SPRITE NUMBER query. From there, you can plot another sprite by indicating a different sprite number or leave the SPRDEF mode by pressing the RETURN key once again.

CLR key Erase the work and home the cursor within the work area.

HOME key Home the cursor within the work area.

1 key Plot the background color at the current cursor location. Erase a pixel.

2 key Plot the foreground color at the current cursor location (both standard and multicolor graphics mode).

3 key Plot multicolor 1 color at the current cursor location (or foreground color if in the standard graphics mode).

4 key Plot multicolor 2 color at the current cursor location (or foreground color if in the standard graphics mode).

CRSR keys and arrow keys Move the cursor the designated direction within the work area.

C key or F1 key Copy a designated sprite to the work area. A prompting message requests COPY FROM? Respond by pressing a numeric key (1 through 8) indicating the sprite to be copied to the work area.

M key or F8 key Change between standard and multicolor sprite mode. SPRDEF begins with the standard sprite mode, as indicated by a single + cursor. Striking the M or F8 key then switches to the multicolor sprite mode that uses the ++ cursor.

A key or F2 key Enable/disable automatic cursor motion. When this feature is enabled, pressing a plotting key (1 through 4) plots the color and advances the cursor one pixel location to the right. When it is disabled, the cursor does not advance and is moved only by means of the CRSR and arrow keys. SPRDEF begins with the automatic cursor-advance feature enabled.

RETURN key or F6 key Set the cursor to the beginning of the next line.

SHIFT-RETURN Transfer the figure to the sprite definition area and prepare to define another sprite.

SHIFT-RETURN followed by RETURN Transfer the figure to the sprite definition area and return to BASIC.

RUN/STOP followed by RETURN Abort the operation and return to the BASIC interpreter.

A sprite generated by SPRDEF carries your specified color sources with it, but not the colors. Thus, areas that you plot as foreground and background colors go with the sprite with those color-source definitions. Sprite manipulation statements include terms for assigning desired colors to the various color sources.

Tinkering with SPRDEF is the best way to learn your way around.

Creating Sprites with Graphics Statements

Any of the bit-map drawing procedures described in the previous chapter can be used for generating sprite figures. The only real limitation is the size of the figure. Using standard bit-mapped graphics with no scaling, the area measures 24 pixels in the horizontal direction and 21 in the vertical. Multicolor figures must fit within a 12 x 21 pixel area.

The general procedure is to plot the figure by any available means, then use the SSHAPE statement to convert it to a string format. Once a figure is saved in this fashion, it can be plotted anywhere else on the screen by means of the GSHAPE statement. This is all described in Chapter 7.

For the sake of generating a sprite, however, the next step is to transfer the string version of the figure to the sprite definition area of RAM. That can be done with this form of the SPRSAV statement:

SPRSAV *string,num*

where *string* is the string variable specified for the figure in the SSHAPE statement and *num* is the sprite number. The example in Listing 8-1 plots and paints a circle on the GRAPHIC 2 screen, saves it as F$, then uses the SPRSAVE statement to convert it to sprite 1. Having accomplished that, the figure is ready to be treated as a sprite.

Listing 8-1

```
10 GRAPHIC 2,1
20 CIRCLE 1,10,10,10,8
30 PAINT 1,10,10
40 SSHAPE F$,0,0,20,20
50 SPRSAV F$,1
60 GRAPHIC 0,1
```

The overall procedure can also be used in conjunction with the SPRDEF routine. You can, for example, use the usual bit-map drawing procedures to generate larger portions of a figure, define it as a sprite, then use the SPRDEF routine to add the finishing touches.

Using the SPRSAV Statement

The SPRSAV statement offers several options for transferring sprite data from one place to another and, indeed, from one form to another. This is a move statement that virtually copies from a graphic source to a graphic destination.

Suppose that you have defined a sprite for the definition set aside for sprite 1. You can use one form of the SPRSAV statement to copy that sprite to another area. The general form of such a statement is:

SPRSAV *sprsrce,sprdest*

where *sprsrce* is the sprite number to be moved and *sprdest* is the destination sprite number. Copying a sprite 1 to sprite 6 is a matter of executing this statement:

SPRSAV 1,6

Descriptions of the SSHAPE statement in Chapter 7 demonstrate how you can assign a graphics figure to a string variable (and subsequently use GSHAPE statements to plot that figure anywhere else on the screen). The SPRSAV statement represents a vital link between SSHAPE/GSHAPE and sprite procedures. The only restriction is that the SSHAPEd figures are no more than 24 standard bit-map-dot wide in the horizontal direction and 21 bits long in the vertical direction.

The following version of the SPRSAV statement copies an SSHAPEd string version of a figure to a designated sprite-definition area:

SPRSAV *string,num*

where *string* represents the string version of a figure that has been defined by an SSHAPE statement and *num* is the sprite number (1–8) that the figure is to have.

If you've used SSHAPE to define a figure as F$ and you now want to redefine it as sprite 2, this statement does the job:

SPRSAV F$,2

Once this statement is executed, the figure originally generated as F$ is not ready for use as sprite 2.

Conversely, a sprite can be redefined as a string that then can be used with GSHAPE statements to plot it anywhere on the screen as a bit-mapped figure. The general form of the conversion statement is:

SPRSAV *num,string*

where *num* is the sprite to be converted to a string definition and *string* is the string variable name.

Saving and Reloading Sprites

Sprites are saved on disk as binary files. Following discussions in this chapter deal with the organization of ROM where the sprites reside. However it is necessary to outline the idea so that you can save them properly.

The general form of the BSAVE statement for saving sprites looks like this:

BSAVE "*sprname*",P*strtaddr* TO P*endaddr*

where *sprname* is the disk file name you want to assign the sprite and *strtaddr* and *endaddr* are the first and last addresses of the desired sprite definition area. Table 8-1 shows the range of addresses for each sprite definition area, so if you want to save sprite 1 as FACE, you can do this:

```
BSAVE "FACE",P3584 TO P3647
```

To save both sprites 1 and 2 as FACES:

```
BSAVE "FACES",P3584 TO P3711
```

To save the data for all eight sprite-definition areas as GAME10:

```
BSAVE "GAME10",P3584 TO P4095
```

Table 8-1 Summary of Starting and Ending Addresses for the Sprite Definition RAM Area

Sprite	Address Range	
	Hex	Dec
Sprite 1	$0E00 - $0E3F	3584-3647
Sprite 2	$0E40 - $0E7F	3648-3711
Sprite 3	$0E80 - $0EBF	3712-3775
Sprite 4	$0EC0 - $0EFF	3776-3839
Sprite 5	$0F00 - $0F3F	3840-3903
Sprite 6	$0F40 - $0F7F	3904-3967
Sprite 7	$0F80 - $0FBF	3968-4031
Sprite 8	$0FC0 - $0FFF	4032-4095

Saving sprites on disk for future use is a simple matter of BSAVEing the block of RAM that is set aside for them. And recalling them again from disk is just as simple: BLOAD them according to the file names originally assigned to them. The following example loads a set of sprites originally saved as GAME10:

```
BLOAD "GAME10"
```

Once you have thus loaded some sprite definitions, either directly from the keyboard or through some BASIC programming, they are in place and ready for use.

Specifying, Positioning, and Moving Sprites

The mere definition of a sprite does not automatically place it at a desired position on the screen. You also need to define how and where you want the sprite to appear. If you are using multicolor sprites, assign colors to multicolor sources 1 and 2.

Two BASIC statements, SPRITE and MOVESPR, are adequate for defining standard sprites. The SPRCOLOR statement is necessary for assigning colors to the two multicolor sources when using multicolor sprites.

Specifying Sprite Parameters with the SPRITE Statement

The SPRITE statement is rather lengthy and does not allow any optional terms. That fact is a good indication of the statement's overall importance. The general form is:

SPRITE *num,flg,colr,pri,xexp,yexp,mode*

where:

num = Sprite number (1 through 8)
flg = On/off flag

0 = Turn off the sprite
1 = Turn on the sprite

colr = Sprite foreground color (1 through 15)
pri = Sprite priority

0 = Sprite moves in front of other objects
1 = Sprite moves behind other objects

xexp = Horizontal 2X expansion on/off

0 = Normal horizontal dimension
1 = 2X expansion in horizontal dimension

yexp = Vertical 2X expansion on/off

0 = Normal vertical dimension
1 = 2X expansion in vertical dimension

mode = Screen mode flag

0 = standard sprite
2 = multicolor sprite

The first term, *num,* specifies the sprite being defined by the remainder of the terms. It must be a numeric constant, variable, or expression in the range of 1 through 8.

The *flg* term determines whether the sprite is to be turned on or off. Setting the *flg* term to 1 turns it on. Setting it to 0 turns it off. For all practical purposes, turning off a sprite takes it completely out of action—out of the picture, so to speak.

The *colr* term fixes the foreground color for that particular sprite. That and the overall background color are the only two colors available for standard sprites.

Table 8-2 summarizes the colors and *colr* values for your convenience.

Table 8-2
Summary of Colors for the *colr* Term in BASIC'S SPRITE Statement

colr	COLOR
1	Black
2	White
3	Red
4	Cyan
5	Purple
6	Green
7	Blue
8	Yellow
9	Orange
10	Brown
11	Pink
12	Dark Gray
13	Medium Gray
14	Light Green
15	Light Blue
16	Light Gray

The fact that you are using a sprite generally implies you are planning to work with a dynamic sort of screen presentation. Objects might be moving about on the screen, and the question is whether a given sprite is to move behind or in front of other objects plotted in the same screen area. That is the purpose of the *pri* (priority) term in the SPRITE statement.

If you want the current sprite—the one you are defining with the SPRITE statement—to move in front of other objects on the screen, set the *pri* term to 0. Set it to 1, and the sprite moves behind other objects.

Sprites can be expanded to twice their normal dimensions. You have the choice of expanding them in the horizontal dimension, the vertical dimension, or both. Setting the *xexp* term to 1 expands the sprite in the horizontal dimension, and setting *yexp* to 1 expands it in the vertical direction. Setting the terms to 0 restores the normal dimension.

Incidentally, sprite expansion takes place with respect to the upper-left point of the sprite definition area.

Finally, the *mode* term determines whether the sprite is defined as a standard or multicolor sprite. Setting *mode* to 0 establishes a standard high-resolution sprite. Setting it to 1 establishes it as a multicolor sprite.

Setting Sprite Positions with MOVESPR

Turning on a sprite with the SPRITE statement fixes the position of the sprite at the location last specified for it. The last-specified position is not likely to be the most desirable one. The MOVSPR statement takes care of that situation.

The simplest form of the MOVSPR statement looks like this:

MOVSPR *num,xpos,ypos*

where *num* is the sprite number (1 through 8), and *xpos* and *ypos* represent the coordinate of the desired screen position—the position of the upper-left corner of the sprite definition area.

Sprites are handled separately from all other kinds of text and graphics information on the Commodore 128. Therefore, you should not be surprised that sprites use their own screen format. Figure 8-1 shows the organization of the sprite screen. The 512 horizontal locations are labeled 0 through 511, and the 256 vertical locations are labeled 0 through 255.

Fig. 8-1 Organization of the sprite screen

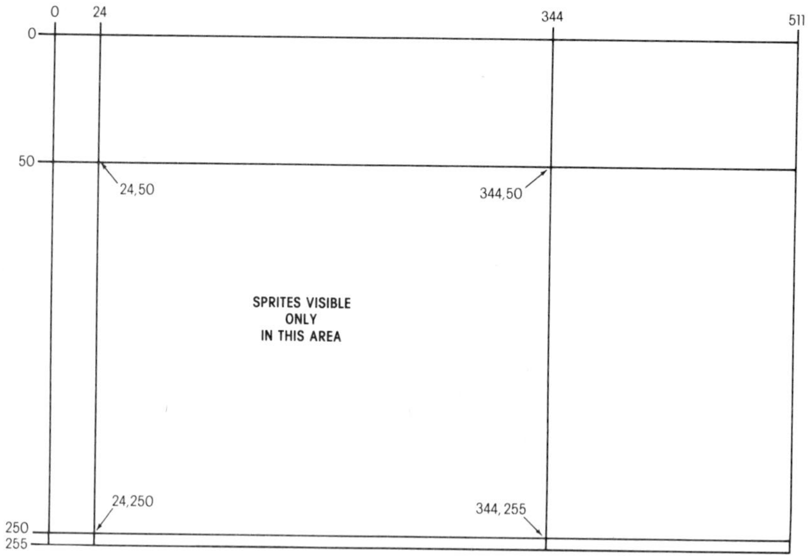

Unlike any of the other screen formats, the sprite screen includes the border area. Thus, sprites are not visible throughout the entire coordinate system. Rather, they are visible in an area marked by horizontal locations 24 through 344 and vertical locations 50 through 250.

Fix a sprite at coordinate 0,0 for example, and you won't be able to see it. It is indeed located in the extreme upper-left corner of the screen but hidden behind the border. Set the position as shown in the next example, though, and you will see the sprite in the upper-left corner of the actual viewing area.

```
MOVSPR 1,24,50
```

The MOVSPR statement also supports relative positioning terms. Plus or minus signs inserted in front of *xpos* and *ypos* terms instruct the system to interpret them as relative values. An expression such as −4,+2 moves the sprite four units to the left and two downward from the present position.

Assuming that you have a definition for sprite 1, the following example fixes its position on the screen, then plots it as a dark blue standard sprite:

```
10 MOVSPR 1,100,90
20 SPRITE 1,1,7,1,0,0,0
```

Somewhat akin to the notion of positioning a sprite by using relative coordinates is that of specifying a distance and angle of motion. That form of the MOVSPR statement uses a semicolon to separate the distance angle terms:

MOVSPR *num,dist;ang*

where *num* is the sprite number, *dist* is the distance to be moved, and *ang* is the angle. The angle is conveniently expressed in degrees (0 through 360), and positive angles refer to a clockwise direction.

Finally, you can set a sprite into continuous motion with a single MOVSPR statement. That form of the statement looks like this:

MOVSPR *num,ang #speed*

where *num* is the sprite number, *ang* is the angle of motion on the screen, and *speed* is the speed of motion. The *ang* term is expressed in degrees relative to the screen's coordinate system and in the clockwise direction. Thus an *ang* of 45 moves the sprite upward and to the right. The *speed* term can be any numeric constant, variable, or expression between 0 and 15, where 15 is the fastest possible speed.

The demonstration program in Listing 8-2 illustrates the sprite procedures described thus far and, incidentally, the incredible animation power available with the Commodore 128 computer.

Lines 10–60—Define a shape.

Line 10—Set and clear the GRAPHIC 2 screen.
Line 20—Plot a circle.

Line 30—Paint the circle.
Line 40—Save it as F$.
Line 50—Copy the shape to sprite 1.
Line 60—Set and clear the 40-column text screen.

Line 70—Copy sprite 1 as sprites 2 through 8.

Line 80—Turn on sprites 1 through 8 with different colors.

Line 90—Set sprite 1 at 0,60 and move it 90 degrees with a speed of 10.

Line 100—Set sprite 2 at 0,90 and move it 270 degrees with a speed of 10.

Line 110—Set sprite 3 at 0,120 and move it 90 degrees with a speed of 5.

Line 120—Set sprite 4 into motion at 45 degrees and with a speed of 5.

Line 130—Set sprite 5 into motion at 245 degrees and with a speed of 15.

Line 150—Set sprite 6 at 100,100 and move it 0 degrees with a speed of 1.

Line 160—Set sprite 7 at 300,100 and move it 180 degrees with a speed of 10.

Line 170—Set sprite 8 into motion at 80 degrees with a speed of 10.

Listing 8-2

```
10 GRAPHIC 2,1
20 CIRCLE 1,10,10,10,8
30 PAINT 1,10,10
40 SSHAPE F$,0,0,20,20
50 SPRSAV F$,1
60 GRAPHIC 0,1
70 FOR K=2 TO 8:SPRSAV 1,K:NEXT
80 FOR K=1 TO 8:SPRITE K,1,K+1,1,0,0,0:NEXT
90 MOVSPR 1,0,60:MOVSPR 1,90 #10
100 MOVSPR 2,0,90:MOVSPR 2,270 #10
110 MOVSPR 3,0,120:MOVSPR 3,90 #5
120 MOVSPR 4,45 #5
130 MOVSPR 5,245 #15
140 MOVSPR 6,100,100:MOVSPR 6,0 #1
150 MOVSPR 7,300,100:MOVSPR 7,180 #10
160 MOVSPR 8,80 #10
```

Setting Colors for Multicolor Sprites

Use the COLOR 0,*colr* statement to set the background color for sprite graphics and the *colr* term in the SPRITE statement to set the foreground color. Multicolor sprites use two additional colors, those from multicolor 1 and multicolor 2. The statement most appropriate for assigning colors to those sources is:

SPRCOLOR *mcolr1,mcolr2*

where *mcolr1* is the code for a color (1 through 16) to be assigned to multicolor 1, and *mcolr2* is the code for the color to be assigned to multicolor 2.

Whereas the *color* term in the SPRITE statement assigns foreground colors to individual sprites, the SPRCOLOR specifications affect the multicolor components of all sprites that use them.

The following example sets a light blue background, yellow for multicolor 1 and red for multicolor 2:

```
10 COLOR 0,15
20 SPRCOLOR 8,3
```

Detecting Sprite Collisions

Through the evolution of video arcade games and personal computers, Commodore has retained its sprite environment as a truly useful and attractive feature. Part of that arcade-style environment calls for a mechanism that detects contact between two or more objects on the screen.

Commodore's BASIC 7.0 deals with sprite contact situations with a pair of statements, COLLISION and BUMP. Generally speaking, both respond to a contact between sprites or between sprites and other objects on the screen. The statements respond in different ways, though, and they are thus used in different ways.

Using the COLLISION Statement

The COLLISION statement is an interrupt statement that is executed only when a type of contact specified by you takes place. When such a contact takes place, the computer completes the execution of the current statement and goes to a subroutine specified by the COLLISION statement. In effect, it executes its own GOSUB. After executing the subroutine, the system resumes normal program operations from where it left off.

The general form of the COLLISION statement is:

COLLISION *type,lineno*

where *type* is a collision type code (1-3) and *lineno* is the first BASIC line number of the collision-handling subroutine. Codes for the *type* term are:

type = 1: Sprite-to-sprite collision
type = 2: Sprite-to-text/graphic collision
type = 3: Light pen cursor contact

Consider this COLLISION statement:

COLLISION 1,1000

This literally says: When two sprites collide, finish the current statement and GOSUB to program line 1000.

The programming cannot handle more than one collision-handling routine at a time. That means you should never include a second COLLISION statement within a collision subroutine. If you ever need to change the line number for a COLLISION statement during the execution of a program, first turn off the previous COLLISION. Turning off a COLLISION is a matter of executing the statement without a *lineno* term:

COLLISION *type*

So COLLISION *type,lineno* enables a collision interrupt, and COLLISION *type* disables it.

COLLISION statements are not intended for use with the sprite auto-motion feature—the sort of action put into effect by MOVSPR *num,ang #speed*. The problem is that the VIC chip has full control of sprite motion in that case, and because it operates so much faster than the BASIC interpreter, COLLISION cannot do its job until some time after the actual collision occurs, often too late to be of any use. Thus, the COLLISION statement is most effective when you are moving sprites one step at a time under the control of BASIC programming, rather than under the control of the VIC chip.

You must remember that the RENUMBER command does not adjust the line-number specification in a COLLISION statement. RENUMBER can, however, adjust the line numbers for the collision-handling routine. After doing a RENUMBER, you must determine the starting line number for the collision-handling subroutine and edit the COLLISION statement accordingly.

> ***IMPORTANT:*** The RENUMBER command can change the line numbers assigned to a collision-handling subroutine, but it does not alter the *lineno* term in COLLISION statements accordingly. You must make the adjustment yourself.

Using the BUMP Function

The BUMP function returns a value that indicates the exact collision status as reckoned from the start of the program or the last reference to BUMP. In a manner of speaking, BUMP accumulates a history of contact situations between sprites and between sprites and other objects on the screen.

The general form of the BUMP statement is:

```
BUMP(n)
```

where *n* is equal to 1 or 2. BUMP(1) returns the status of sprite-to-sprite collisions, and BUMP(2) returns the status of sprite-to-text/graphic collisions. Referring to either one of them automatically resets its value to 0.

BUMP is a function that does not stand alone. It must be used in a complete statement such as:

```
IF BUMP(2)=4 THEN PRINT "OUCH"
```

That tells the system to print "OUCH" if sprite 3 runs into another kind of object while other sprites are not in a contact situation.

If you are acquainted with binary-to-decimal number conversions, you can understand easily the values returned by the BUMP functions. Regarding the value returned by BUMP as an eight-bit binary number:

A sprite-1 collision sets bit 0
A sprite-2 collision sets bit 1
A sprite-3 collision sets bit 2
A sprite-4 collision sets bit 3
A sprite-5 collision sets bit 4
A sprite-6 collision sets bit 5
A sprite-7 collision sets bit 6
A sprite-8 collision sets bit 7

Table 8-3 summarizes the values returned by the BUMP functions according to the sprites involved. The table is valid for both BUMP(1) and BUMP(2), but the interpretations are different. When using BUMP(1), for example, a value of 3 indicates a collision between sprite 1 and sprite 2. When using BUMP(2), however, a value of 2 indicates that sprites 1 and 2 have both bumped into other kinds of objects.

Table 8-3 Summary of All Possible Combinations of Sprite Collisions and Values Returned by BUMP Functions

(In Sprite Columns, 0 Indicates No Collision and 1 Indicates Collision)

Sprite(s) Involved								BUMP Value	
8	7	6	5	4	3	2	1	Dec	Hex
0	0	0	0	0	0	0	0	0	$00
0	0	0	0	0	0	0	1	1	$01
0	0	0	0	0	0	1	0	2	$02
0	0	0	0	0	0	1	1	3	$03
0	0	0	0	0	1	0	0	4	$04
0	0	0	0	0	1	0	1	5	$05
0	0	0	0	0	1	1	0	6	$06
0	0	0	0	0	1	1	1	7	$07
0	0	0	0	1	0	0	0	8	$08
0	0	0	0	1	0	0	1	9	$09
0	0	0	0	1	0	1	0	10	$0A
0	0	0	0	1	0	1	1	11	$0B
0	0	0	0	1	1	0	0	12	$0C
0	0	0	0	1	1	0	1	13	$0D
0	0	0	0	1	1	1	0	14	$0E
0	0	0	0	1	1	1	1	15	$0F
0	0	0	1	0	0	0	0	16	$10
0	0	0	1	0	0	0	1	17	$11
0	0	0	1	0	0	1	0	18	$12
0	0	0	1	0	0	1	1	19	$13
0	0	0	1	0	1	0	0	20	$14
0	0	0	1	0	1	0	1	21	$15
0	0	0	1	0	1	1	0	22	$16
0	0	0	1	0	1	1	1	23	$17
0	0	0	1	1	0	0	0	24	$18
0	0	0	1	1	0	0	1	25	$19
0	0	0	1	1	0	1	0	26	$1A
0	0	0	1	1	0	1	1	27	$1B
0	0	0	1	1	1	0	0	28	$1C
0	0	0	1	1	1	0	1	29	$1D
0	0	0	1	1	1	1	0	30	$1E
0	0	0	1	1	1	1	1	31	$1F
0	0	1	0	0	0	0	0	32	$20
0	0	1	0	0	0	0	1	33	$21
0	0	1	0	0	0	1	0	34	$22
0	0	1	0	0	0	1	1	35	$23
0	0	1	0	0	1	0	0	36	$24
0	0	1	0	0	1	0	1	37	$25
0	0	1	0	0	1	1	0	38	$26
0	0	1	0	0	1	1	1	39	$27
0	0	1	0	1	0	0	0	40	$28
0	0	1	0	1	0	0	1	41	$29
0	0	1	0	1	0	1	0	42	$2A
0	0	1	0	1	0	1	1	43	$2B
0	0	1	0	1	1	0	0	44	$2C
0	0	1	0	1	1	0	1	45	$2D
0	0	1	0	1	1	1	0	46	$2E
0	0	1	0	1	1	1	1	47	$2F
0	0	1	1	0	0	0	0	48	$30
0	0	1	1	0	0	0	1	49	$31
0	0	1	1	0	0	1	0	50	$32

Table 8-3 (cont.)

Sprite(s) Involved								BUMP Value	
8	7	6	5	4	3	2	1	Dec	Hex
0	0	1	1	0	0	1	1	51	$33
0	0	1	1	0	1	0	0	52	$34
0	0	1	1	0	1	0	1	53	$35
0	0	1	1	0	1	1	0	54	$36
0	0	1	1	0	1	1	1	55	$37
0	0	1	1	1	0	0	0	56	$38
0	0	1	1	1	0	0	1	57	$39
0	0	1	1	1	0	1	0	58	$3A
0	0	1	1	1	0	1	1	59	$3B
0	0	1	1	1	1	0	0	60	$3C
0	0	1	1	1	1	0	1	61	$3D
0	0	1	1	1	1	1	0	62	$3E
0	0	1	1	1	1	1	1	63	$3F
0	1	0	0	0	0	0	0	64	$40
0	1	0	0	0	0	0	1	65	$41
0	1	0	0	0	0	1	0	66	$42
0	1	0	0	0	0	1	1	67	$43
0	1	0	0	0	1	0	0	68	$44
0	1	0	0	0	1	0	1	69	$45
0	1	0	0	0	1	1	0	70	$46
0	1	0	0	0	1	1	1	71	$47
0	1	0	0	1	0	0	0	72	$48
0	1	0	0	1	0	0	1	73	$49
0	1	0	0	1	0	1	0	74	$4A
0	1	0	0	1	0	1	1	75	$4B
0	1	0	0	1	1	0	0	76	$4C
0	1	0	0	1	1	0	1	77	$4D
0	1	0	0	1	1	1	0	78	$4E
0	1	0	0	1	1	1	1	79	$4F
0	1	0	1	0	0	0	0	80	$50
0	1	0	1	0	0	0	1	81	$51
0	1	0	1	0	0	1	0	82	$52
0	1	0	1	0	0	1	1	83	$53
0	1	0	1	0	1	0	0	84	$54
0	1	0	1	0	1	0	1	85	$55
0	1	0	1	0	1	1	0	86	$56
0	1	0	1	0	1	1	1	87	$57
0	1	0	1	1	0	0	0	88	$58
0	1	0	1	1	0	0	1	89	$59
0	1	0	1	1	0	1	0	90	$5A
0	1	0	1	1	0	1	1	91	$5B
0	1	0	1	1	1	0	0	92	$5C
0	1	0	1	1	1	0	1	93	$5D
0	1	0	1	1	1	1	0	94	$5E
0	1	0	1	1	1	1	1	95	$5F
0	1	1	0	0	0	0	0	96	$60
0	1	1	0	0	0	0	1	97	$61
0	1	1	0	0	0	1	0	98	$62
0	1	1	0	0	0	1	1	99	$63
0	1	1	0	0	1	0	0	100	$64
0	1	1	0	0	1	0	1	101	$65

Table 8-3 (cont.)

Sprite(s) Involved								BUMP Value	
8	7	6	5	4	3	2	1	Dec	Hex
0	1	1	0	0	1	1	0	102	$66
0	1	1	0	0	1	1	1	103	$67
0	1	1	0	1	0	0	0	104	$68
0	1	1	0	1	0	0	1	105	$69
0	1	1	0	1	0	1	0	106	$6A
0	1	1	0	1	0	1	1	107	$6B
0	1	1	0	1	1	0	0	108	$6C
0	1	1	0	1	1	0	1	109	$6D
0	1	1	0	1	1	1	0	110	$6E
0	1	1	0	1	1	1	1	111	$6F
0	1	1	1	0	0	0	0	112	$70
0	1	1	1	0	0	0	1	113	$71
0	1	1	1	0	0	1	0	114	$72
0	1	1	1	0	0	1	1	115	$73
0	1	1	1	0	1	0	0	116	$74
0	1	1	1	0	1	0	1	117	$75
0	1	1	1	0	1	1	0	118	$76
0	1	1	1	0	1	1	1	119	$77
0	1	1	1	1	0	0	0	120	$78
0	1	1	1	1	0	0	1	121	$79
0	1	1	1	1	0	1	0	122	$7A
0	1	1	1	1	0	1	1	123	$7B
0	1	1	1	1	1	0	0	124	$7C
0	1	1	1	1	1	0	1	125	$7D
0	1	1	1	1	1	1	0	126	$7E
0	1	1	1	1	1	1	1	127	$7F
1	0	0	0	0	0	0	0	128	$80
1	0	0	0	0	0	0	1	129	$81
1	0	0	0	0	0	1	0	130	$82
1	0	0	0	0	0	1	1	131	$83
1	0	0	0	0	1	0	0	132	$84
1	0	0	0	0	1	0	1	133	$85
1	0	0	0	0	1	1	0	134	$86
1	0	0	0	0	1	1	1	135	$87
1	0	0	0	1	0	0	0	136	$88
1	0	0	0	1	0	0	1	137	$89
1	0	0	0	1	0	1	0	138	$8A
1	0	0	0	1	0	1	1	139	$8B
1	0	0	0	1	1	0	0	140	$8C
1	0	0	0	1	1	0	1	141	$8D
1	0	0	0	1	1	1	0	142	$8E
1	0	0	0	1	1	1	1	143	$8F
1	0	0	1	0	0	0	0	144	$90
1	0	0	1	0	0	0	1	145	$91
1	0	0	1	0	0	1	0	146	$92
1	0	0	1	0	0	1	1	147	$93
1	0	0	1	0	1	0	0	148	$94
1	0	0	1	0	1	0	1	149	$95
1	0	0	1	0	1	1	0	150	$96
1	0	0	1	0	1	1	1	151	$97
1	0	0	1	1	0	0	0	152	$98

Table 8-3 (cont.)

Sprite(s) Involved								BUMP Value	
8	7	6	5	4	3	2	1	Dec	Hex
1	0	0	1	1	0	0	1	153	$99
1	0	0	1	1	0	1	0	154	$9A
1	0	0	1	1	0	1	1	155	$9B
1	0	0	1	1	1	0	0	156	$9C
1	0	0	1	1	1	0	1	157	$9D
1	0	0	1	1	1	1	0	158	$9E
1	0	0	1	1	1	1	1	159	$9F
1	0	1	0	0	0	0	0	160	$A0
1	0	1	0	0	0	0	1	161	$A1
1	0	1	0	0	0	1	0	162	$A2
1	0	1	0	0	0	1	1	163	$A3
1	0	1	0	0	1	0	0	164	$A4
1	0	1	0	0	1	0	1	165	$A5
1	0	1	0	0	1	1	0	166	$A6
1	0	1	0	0	1	1	1	167	$A7
1	0	1	0	1	0	0	0	168	$A8
1	0	1	0	1	0	0	1	169	$A9
1	0	1	0	1	0	1	0	170	$AA
1	0	1	0	1	0	1	1	171	$AB
1	0	1	0	1	1	0	0	172	$AC
1	0	1	0	1	1	0	1	173	$AD
1	0	1	0	1	1	1	0	174	$AE
1	0	1	0	1	1	1	1	175	$AF
1	0	1	1	0	0	0	0	176	$B0
1	0	1	1	0	0	0	1	177	$B1
1	0	1	1	0	0	1	0	178	$B2
1	0	1	1	0	0	1	1	179	$B3
1	0	1	1	0	1	0	0	180	$B4
1	0	1	1	0	1	0	1	181	$B5
1	0	1	1	0	1	1	0	182	$B6
1	0	1	1	0	1	1	1	183	$B7
1	0	1	1	1	0	0	0	184	$B8
1	0	1	1	1	0	0	1	185	$B9
1	0	1	1	1	0	1	0	186	$BA
1	0	1	1	1	0	1	1	187	$BB
1	0	1	1	1	1	0	0	188	$BC
1	0	1	1	1	1	0	1	189	$BD
1	0	1	1	1	1	1	0	190	$BE
1	0	1	1	1	1	1	1	191	$BF
1	1	0	0	0	0	0	0	192	$C0
1	1	0	0	0	0	0	1	193	$C1
1	1	0	0	0	0	1	0	194	$C2
1	1	0	0	0	0	1	1	195	$C3
1	1	0	0	0	1	0	0	196	$C4
1	1	0	0	0	1	0	1	197	$C5
1	1	0	0	0	1	1	0	198	$C6
1	1	0	0	0	1	1	1	199	$C7
1	1	0	0	1	0	0	0	200	$C8
1	1	0	0	1	0	0	1	201	$C9
1	1	0	0	1	0	1	0	202	$CA
1	1	0	0	1	0	1	1	203	$CB

Table 8-3 (cont.)

Sprite(s) Involved								BUMP Value	
8	7	6	5	4	3	2	1	Dec	Hex
1	1	0	0	1	1	0	0	204	$CC
1	1	0	0	1	1	0	1	205	$CD
1	1	0	0	1	1	1	0	206	$CE
1	1	0	0	1	1	1	1	207	$CF
1	1	0	1	0	0	0	0	208	$D0
1	1	0	1	0	0	0	1	209	$D1
1	1	0	1	0	0	1	0	210	$D2
1	1	0	1	0	0	1	1	211	$D3
1	1	0	1	0	1	0	0	212	$D4
1	1	0	1	0	1	0	1	213	$D5
1	1	0	1	0	1	1	0	214	$D6
1	1	0	1	0	1	1	1	215	$D7
1	1	0	1	1	0	0	0	216	$D8
1	1	0	1	1	0	0	1	217	$D9
1	1	0	1	1	0	1	0	218	$DA
1	1	0	1	1	0	1	1	219	$DB
1	1	0	1	1	1	0	0	220	$DC
1	1	0	1	1	1	0	1	221	$DD
1	1	0	1	1	1	1	0	222	$DE
1	1	0	1	1	1	1	1	223	$DF
1	1	1	0	0	0	0	0	224	$E0
1	1	1	0	0	0	0	1	225	$E1
1	1	1	0	0	0	1	0	226	$E2
1	1	1	0	0	0	1	1	227	$E3
1	1	1	0	0	1	0	0	228	$E4
1	1	1	0	0	1	0	1	229	$E5
1	1	1	0	0	1	1	0	230	$E6
1	1	1	0	0	1	1	1	231	$E7
1	1	1	0	1	0	0	0	232	$E8
1	1	1	0	1	0	0	1	233	$E9
1	1	1	0	1	0	1	0	234	$EA
1	1	1	0	1	0	1	1	235	$EB
1	1	1	0	1	1	0	0	236	$EC
1	1	1	0	1	1	0	1	237	$ED
1	1	1	0	1	1	1	0	238	$EE
1	1	1	0	1	1	1	1	239	$EF
1	1	1	1	0	0	0	0	240	$F0
1	1	1	1	0	0	0	1	241	$F1
1	1	1	1	0	0	1	0	242	$F2
1	1	1	1	0	0	1	1	243	$F3
1	1	1	1	0	1	0	0	244	$F4
1	1	1	1	0	1	0	1	245	$F5
1	1	1	1	0	1	1	0	246	$F6
1	1	1	1	0	1	1	1	247	$F7
1	1	1	1	1	0	0	0	248	$F8
1	1	1	1	1	0	0	1	249	$F9
1	1	1	1	1	0	1	0	250	$FA
1	1	1	1	1	0	1	1	251	$FB
1	1	1	1	1	1	0	0	252	$FC
1	1	1	1	1	1	0	1	253	$FD
1	1	1	1	1	1	1	0	254	$FE
1	1	1	1	1	1	1	1	255	$FF

Sprites and Machine Language Routines

Seven basic parameters need to be considered when setting up a sprite. Those parameters translate into a set of seven programming steps:

1. Enable/disable a specified sprite.
2. Set the foreground color for a specified sprite.
3. Select standard or multicolor for a specified sprite.
4. Set multicolor 1 and multicolor 2 if multicolor sprites are used.
5. Set the priority for a specified sprite.
6. Set the X and Y expansion for a specified sprite.
7. Set the position of a specified sprite.

The Commodore 128 has registers specifically reserved for such operations. Programmers acquainted with 6502/8502 machine-language procedures should find the operations rather straightforward.

Enabling and Disabling Sprites

Any combination of sprites can be enabled and disabled at a single address location: $D015 (53269). Eight different sprites and eight bits in the byte of data are at that address—one bit for each sprite.

Sprite Enable Writing to this register enables/disables the sprite display mode. Reading from the register returns a value that indicates the sprite-display status.

Address: **$D015 (53269)**
Data: **0** = Disable the sprite
1 = Enable the sprite

Bit 0 = Sprite 1
Bit 1 = Sprite 2
Bit 2 = Sprite 3
Bit 3 = Sprite 4
Bit 4 = Sprite 5
Bit 5 = Sprite 6
Bit 6 = Sprite 7
Bit 7 = Sprite 8

Loading a value of $01 to $D015 enables sprite 1. Loading a value of $03 enables sprites 1 and 2. Loading a value of $FF enables all sprites, and a value of $00 turns them all off. Bits cleared to zero turns off the corresponding sprite, and bits set to 1 turns them on.

Setting Sprite Colors

For the purposes of machine language programming, border and background colors are determined by the color codes written to $D020 (53280) and $D021 (53281), respectively. The color codes use the $00-through-$0F format shown in Table 8-4.

Table 8-4
Summary of Codes and Colors for Sprite Color Registers

Hex	Dec	Color
$00	0	Black
$01	1	White
$02	2	Red
$03	3	Cyan
$04	4	Purple
$05	5	Green
$06	6	Blue
$07	7	Yellow
$08	8	Orange
$09	9	Brown
$0A	10	Pink
$0B	11	Dark Gray
$0C	12	Medium Gray
$0D	13	Light Green
$0E	14	Light Blue
$0F	15	Light Gray

The foreground colors for the eight individual sprites are in the four lower-order bytes of a set of VIC registers, $D027 through $D02E.

Sprite Foreground Colors Writing color values, $00 through $0F (0–15), to these registers sets the foreground color for the corresponding sprites. Reading four lower-order bits of data from the registers returns the foreground color value.

$D027 (53287) = Sprite 1 foreground color
$D028 (53288) = Sprite 2 foreground color
$D029 (53289) = Sprite 3 foreground color
$D02A (53290) = Sprite 4 foreground color
$D02B (53291) = Sprite 5 foreground color
$D02C (3292) = Sprite 6 foreground color
$D02D(53293) = Sprite 7 foreground color
$D02E (53294) = Sprite 8 foreground color

The example in Listing 8-3 turns on sprites 1 and 2 and assigns white to sprite 1 and blue to sprite 2.

Listing 8-3

```
LDA #$03        ;SPECIFY SPRITES 1 AND 2
STA $DO15       ;TURN THEM ON
LDA #$01        ;WHITE COLOR
STA $DO27       ;TO SPRITE 1 FOREGND
LDA #$06        ;BLUE COLOR
STA $D028       ;TO SPRITE 2 FOREGND
```

Sprites are normally set for the standard high-resolution color format, but they can be changed to the multicolor format through a mode register at $D01C. Each bit in that register sets the color mode for one of the eight sprites. Bit 0 represents sprite 1, bit 1 represents sprite 2, and so on. The highest-order bit, bit 7, represents sprite 8.

Setting any of those bits to 1 enables the multicolor mode for the corresponding sprites. Clearing them to zero disables the multicolor mode. Writing $40 to multicolor mode register, for example, sets sprite 7 for the multicolor mode and the remainder for the standard color mode. Writing $FF sets them all for multicolor operation, and $00 restores all sprites to the standard color mode.

Sprite Multicolor Enable Writing to this register enables/disables the sprite multicolor mode. Reading from the register returns a value that indicates the sprite multicolor status.

Address: **$D01C (53276)**
Data: **0** = Disable multicolor mode
1 = Enable multicolor mode

Bit 0 = Sprite 1
Bit 1 = Sprite 2
Bit 2 = Sprite 3
Bit 3 = Sprite 4
Bit 4 = Sprite 5
Bit 5 = Sprite 6
Bit 6 = Sprite 7
Bit 7 = Sprite 8

If indeed you are enabling any sprites for the multicolor mode, you must also specify the colors. Colors for multicolor sprites cannot be specified individually. Whatever color you use for multicolor 1 for one sprite has to apply to any other multicolor sprite.

Two different sprite multicolor registers exist—one for multicolor 1 and a second for multicolor 2.

Multicolor Sprite Registers Writing color values, $00 through $0F (0–15), to these registers sets the multicolor 1 and multicolor 2 for all sprites that use them. Reading four lower-order bits of data from the registers returns the current multicolor assignments.

$D025 (53285) = Sprite multicolor 1
$D026 (53286) = Sprite multicolor 2

The example in Listing 8-4 enables sprites 1, 2, and 3. It assigns foreground colors green, red, and blue, respectively, then it enables sprites 1 and 3 for the multicolor mode, assigning white for multicolor 1 and yellow for multicolor 2.

Listing 8-4

```
LDA #$07        ;SPECIFY SPRITES 1,2,3
STA $D015       ;TURN THEM ON
LDA #$05        ;GREEN COLOR
STA $D027       ;TO SPRITE 1 FOREGND
LDA #$02        ;RED COLOR
STA $D028       ;TO SPRITE 2 FOREGND
LDA #$06        ;BLUE COLOR
STA $D029       ;TO SPRITE 3 FOREGND
LDA #$05        ;SPECIFY SPRITES 1,3
STA $D01C       ;SET MULTICOLOR MODE
LDA #$01        ;WHITE COLOR
STA $D025       ;TO MULTICOLOR 1
LDA #$07        ;YELLOW COLOR
STA $D026       ;TO MULTICOLOR 2
```

Setting Sprite Priorities

Sprite priority flags, 0 or 1, determine whether a given sprite moves behind or in front of other graphics figures on the screen. The flag for each sprite is contained in a single data byte located at address $D01B. Clearing a bit to 0 causes the corresponding sprite to move in front of other kinds of objects on the screen, whereas setting the bit to 1 causes the sprite to move behind other objects.

Sprite Priority Writing to this register sets the priority flag for each of the eight sprites. Reading from the register returns a value that indicates the current priority status.

Address: $D01B (53275)
Data: 0 = Sprite moves in front of graphics
1 = Sprite moves behind graphics

Bit 0 = Sprite 1
Bit 1 = Sprite 2
Bit 2 = Sprite 3
Bit 3 = Sprite 4
Bit 4 = Sprite 5
Bit 5 = Sprite 6

Bit 6 = Sprite 7
Bit 7 = Sprite 8

Enabling/Disabling the 2X Expansion Feature

Sprites can be expanded twofold in the horizontal dimension, vertical dimension, or both dimensions. Two VIC registers handle this job—one for enabling/disabling the 2X feature in the horizontal dimension and another for the vertical dimension.

In both instances, bits 0 through 7 correspond to sprites 1 through 8. Setting a bit value to 1 enables the 2X expansion. Clearing it to 0 restores the normal dimension.

Sprite Expansion Registers Writing to these registers enables/disables the 2X sprite-expansion feature. Reading from the registers returns values that indicate the current expansion status:

Addresses: Horizontal expansion = $D01D (53277)
Vertical expansion = $D017 (53271)
Data: 0 = Normal dimension
1 = 2X expansion

Bit 0 = Sprite 1
Bit 1 = Sprite 2
Bit 2 = Sprite 3
Bit 3 = Sprite 4
Bit 4 = Sprite 5
Bit 5 = Sprite 6
Bit 6 = Sprite 7
Bit 7 = Sprite 8

The portion of a machine language routine shown in Listing 8-5 sets sprite 1 for 2X expansion in the horizontal dimension, sprite 2 for 2X expansion in the vertical dimension, and sprite 3 for 2X expansion in both dimensions.

Listing 8-5

```
LDA #$05        ;SPECIFY SPRITES 1,3
STA $D01D       ;SET 2X HOR. EXPANSION
LDA #$06        ;SPECIFY SPRITES 2,3
STA $D017       ;SET 2X VERT. EXPANSION
```

Setting Sprite Positions

Sprites are positioned according to their own coordinate system. That coordinate system features 512 horizontal locations and 256 vertical locations. A single eight-bit register is capable of dealing with the 256 different vertical locations. Indeed, one register is set aside for setting the vertical location of each of the eight sprites.

However a single eight-bit register cannot handle the 512 different horizontal locations. That task requires nine bits. The Commodore 128 handles the situation in an efficient manner. First, eight eight-bit registers determine, in part, the horizontal location of each sprite. One additional register allocates one bit for each of the sprites—the ninth bit needed in each case.

Therefore, a total of 17 registers are allocated for sprite positions. Eight vertical-position registers are available; one for each sprite. Eight horizontal-position registers handle the lower eight bits, one register for each sprite. Finally, a single eight-bit register handles the high-order, horizontal-position bit for each of the sprites.

A sprite's position on the screen is determined by the value in its vertical-position register ($00–$FF), the value in its own horizontal-position register ($00–$FF), plus a single bit in the special high-order, horizontal-position register (binary 0 or 1).

Table 8-5 summarizes the position registers for each of the eight sprites. The addresses are actually "shadows" of the same VIC registers from $D000 through $D010. The operating system updates the registers every 1/60th of a second, and most programmers prefer to work with the RAM versions shown in the table.

Table 8-5
Summary of Position Registers for Eight Sprites

Sprite	High Bit of X Position	LSB of X Position	Y Position
1	Bit 0 of $11E6 (4582)	$11D6 (53248)	$11D7 (53249)
2	Bit 1 of $11E6 (4582)	$11D8 (4568)	$11D9 (4569)
3	Bit 2 of $11E6 (4582)	$11DA (4570)	$11DB (4571)
4	Bit 3 of $11E6 (4582)	$11DC (4572)	$11DD (4573)
5	Bit 4 of $11E6 (4582)	$11DE (4574)	$11DF (4575)
6	Bit 5 of $11E6 (4582)	$11E0 (4576)	$11E1 (4577)
7	Bit 6 of $11E6 (4582)	$11E2 (4578)	$11E3 (4579)
8	Bit 7 of $11E6 (4582)	$11E4 (4580)	$11E5 (4581)

As long as you can position a specified sprite anywhere on the screen, you can move it from place to place. Because a single register is adequate for vertical positioning, machine language routines for moving sprites in that direction are rather straightforward. The example in Listing 8-6 assumes that you already have defined sprite 1. This routine turns on that sprite, assigns to it a yellow color, and moves it upward on the screen at a rate determined by the values assigned to registers X and Y. You can make the sprite move downward by changing DEC $11D7 to read INC $11D7.

Listing 8-6

```
        LDA #$01      ;SPECIFY SPRITE 1
        STA $D015     ;TURN IT ON
        LDA #$07      ;SPECIFY YELLOW
        STA $D027     ;SET SPRITE 1 FGND COLOR
        LDA #$00      ;SPECIFY X HIGH BIT TO 0
        STA $11E6     ;SET X HIGH BIT TO 0
        LDA #$A0      ;SPECIFY X POS $0A
        STA $11D6     ;SET LSB OF X POS FOR SPRITE 1
        LDA #$00      ;SPECIFY Y POS 0
        STA $11D7     ;SET Y POS OF SPRITE 1
DOIT    LDX #$08      ;KILL SOME TIME
TIME2   LDY #$FF
TIME1   DEY
        BNE TIME1
        DEX
        BNE TIME2
        DEC $11D7     ;MOVE SPRITE 1 UP
        CLC
        BCC DOIT      ;AND REPEAT
```

The program runs in an endless loop, so you should end it by doing a RUN/STOP-RESTORE operation.

Moving sprites horizontally is just a bit trickier because you have to work with the appropriate 9th bit in $11E6. The general idea is to increment or decrement the horizontal-position register containing the four lower-order bits, then invert the sign of the ninth bit when the count passes through. The problem is that the lower-order byte and the ninth bit cannot be changed at the same instant, so if you are working directly with those registers, an image of the sprite sometimes appears at location 255 when it is actually supposed to be at 0.

The most satisfactory solution is to write the movement routine into an IRQ interrupt handler of your own. The sprite features were designed to be handled in that fashion anyway. Setting up an interrupt handler for sprite motion requires two different routines. The first redirects the system's normal interrupt handler and defines the quality of the motion. The second puts the motion into effect.

Listing 8-7 first changes the IRQ handler's starting address to $0D0C. That portion of the routine begins by doing an SEI to disable the normal interrupt action, and ends by reestablishing it with a CLI. The remainder of the routine sets sprite 1 into motion in the horizontal direction, from left to right, two pixels at a time—ADC #$02. The EOR #$01 takes care of switching the ninth bit of sprite 1's horizontal position at the appropriate time.

The routine ends by doing a direct jump to the starting address of the system's normal IRQ handler.

Listing 8-7

```
0D00 SEI              ;SET INTERRUPT DISABLE
0D01 LDA #$0C         ;LSB OF NEW IRQ
0D00 SEI              ;SET INTERRUPT DISABLE
0D01 LDA #$0C         ;LSB OF NEW IRQ
0D03 STA $0314        ;TO IRQ VECTOR
0D06 LDA #$0D         ;MSB OF NEW IRQ
0D08 STA $0315        ;TO IRQ VECTOR
0D0B CLI              ;CLEAR INTERRUPT DISABLE
0D0C LDA $11D6        ;GET LSB OF SPRITE 1 X POS
0D0F CLC              ;CLEAR THE CARRY FLAG
0D10 ADC #$02         ;ADD DISPLACEMENT
0D12 STA $11D6        ;SET NEW LSB OF SPRITE 1 X POS
0D15 BCC $0D1F        ;IF NO CARRY THEN BRANCH TO END
0D17 LDA $11E6        ;GET 9TH BIT FOR ALL SPRITES
0D1A EOR #$01         ;SWITCH BIT FOR SPRITE 1
0D1C STA $11E6        ;SET NEW 9TH BIT
0D1F JMP $FA65        ;JUMP TO NORMAL IRQ OPS
```

Once you enter and run this routine, it remains in place until you do something that executes the system's initialization routines—doing a Reset pushbutton operation, for instance.

Getting some horizontal motion for sprite 1 is then a simple matter of turning it on, specifying a Y position and, if desired, an initial X position. Executing such a routine begins the action immediately. You do not need to run the interrupt handler.

Assuming that you have run the routine in Listing 8-7, the following abbreviated routine sets sprite 1 into motion:

```
LDA #$01     ;SPECIFY SPRITE 1
STA $D015    ;TURN IT ON
LDA #$BA     ;SPECIFY Y POSITION
STA $11D7    ;SET SPRITE 1 Y POSITION
RTS
```

The speed of horizontal motion can be changed by modifying the value assigned to the ADC statement in Listing 8-7. The figure can be stopped by changing the statement to read ADC #$00. The larger the value, the faster the motion.

You can likewise change the direction of horizontal motion by changing the ADC statement to an SBC statement. Changing it to read SBC #$02, for example, moves the sprite two pixels at a time in the right-to-left direction.

Working with the Bump Registers

The BASIC functions, BUMP(1) and BUMP(2), refer directly to a pair of VIC registers. The only real difference between reading the registers in BASIC and from a machine language program is that the latter does not automatically clear the content to zero.

BUMP Registers Reading data from these registers indicates the collision status of sprites and other objects on the screen. The format is the same as indicated in Table 8-3.

Addresses:
$D01E (53278) = Sprite-to-sprite collisions
$D01F (53279) = Sprite-to-text/graphic collisions

Unfortunately for the casual programmer, the VIC chip updates the bump registers only during the vertical-retrace IRQ interval. Unless the sprite-motion programming is included in a custom interrupt routine, fast-moving sprites are likely to pass through one another before the VIC has a chance to respond.

Programmers who are unwilling to tackle interrupt programming—including bump sensing in a routine such as the one shown in Listing 8-7—usually end up sensing collisions by comparing the actual coordinates of the objects on the screen.

9

Sound and Music Procedures

The Commodore 128 uses a special built-in device called the SID (sound interface device) to generate a wide variety of tones and tonal qualities. BASIC 7.0 includes a number of flexible SID control statements that make possible the creation of special sound effects and that play musical compositions with as many as three voices at once. These BASIC statements require no special understanding of the SID and its control registers.

Machine language programmers will find the SID and its registers to be a truly flexible and dynamic sound synthesizer. For one who is able to compose IRQ interrupt routines, the sounds can be executed without reference to other on-going programming.

In short, the SID is a powerful sound-musical device, that, alas, has far more practical potential than can be illustrated in a book of this type. This chapter has enough information to get a BASIC programmer started on the right foot and to suggest that the possibilities for a machine language programmer are limited only by patience and imagination.

Preliminary Considerations

Amplitude, volume, and loudness: terms that mean much the same thing and are often used interchangeably. No matter what you choose to call volume-level specification, it is a vital quality of sound synthesis, and SID operations are meaningless without it.

The amplitude (volume or loudness) of sounds is normally measured in units of *bels* or, more commonly, *decibels.* The SID chip does not recognize those units of measurement, however. It operates on the basis of simple integer values—the larger the value, the louder the sound. In most instances, a volume specification of 0 indicates no volume, and 15 indicates maximum volume.

The frequency of a sound is a second important quality. As with amplitude, SID operations are generally meaningless without a frequency specification.

Frequency is normally measured in units of *Hertz* (cycles per second). The human ear can generally detect frequencies in the range of 5Hz to 15,000Hz—assuming, of course, the frequencies are generated with sufficient amplitude. The SID chip, however, accepts frequency parameters that allow a much smaller range of values: 1Hz to about 4,000Hz. As described later in this discussion, SID waveforms can include complex combinations of other frequencies that exceed the upper limit of human hearing and, indeed, the sound-reproducing qualities of most loudspeakers used with a Commodore 128 system.

The SID chip does not recognize frequency specifications in units of Hertz. It works on the basis of integer values in the range of 0 through 65535, where 0 is the lowest possible frequency and 65535 is the highest.

Returning to the subject of sound amplitude, the SID chip offers more than simple amplitude adjustment. You can specify an amplitude envelope—a dynamic combination of amplitude changes that create a wide range of sound qualities.

Figure 9-1 illustrates the main features of a sound envelope: attack interval, peak volume, decay interval, sustain level, and release interval. All can be controlled by BASIC programming or setting certain combinations of integer values to the SID registers.

Fig. 9-1 Elements of a sound envelope

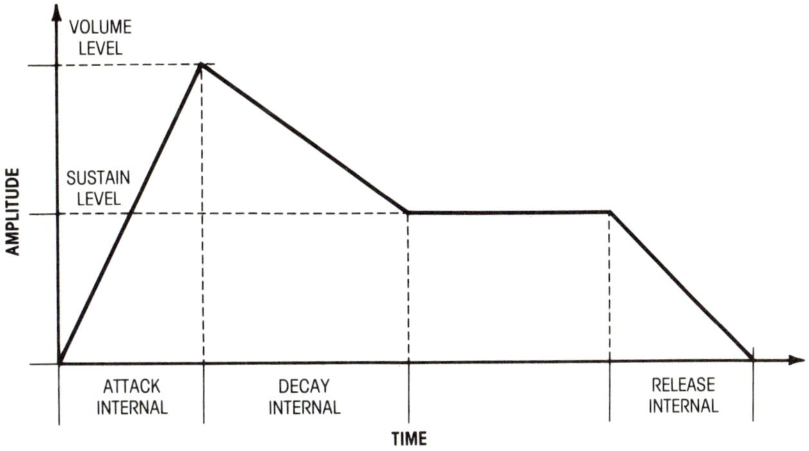

The attack interval sets the time required from the onset of a sound to the point where the waveform reaches a peak amplitude. Having thus reached a peak amplitude, the decay interval determines the time required for decreasing the amplitude to the sustain level. The release interval determines the time required for diminishing the amplitude from the sustain level to zero.

You can choose from the four different kinds of sound waveforms illustrated in Figure 9-2. The sawtooth waveform produces the purest tone. The sawtooth waveform has a raspier quality but tends to be more forceful. The pulse waveform is a compromise between the triangular and sawtooth sounds, and the system includes provisions for adjusting the relative width of the rectangular pulse. The noise waveform generates a specified frequency but is accompanied with a great deal of noise (static).

The SID also offers techniques for tailoring the output volume as a function of frequency. An ideal audio system is capable of reproducing the entire range of frequencies at a fixed volume level. However, situations occur where you want to emphasize certain bands of frequencies and diminish others. That is the purpose of the filtering techniques available as options.

Figure 9-3 shows the three kinds of filtering available with the Commodore 128 sound scheme. A low-pass filter is one that empha-

Fig. 9-2 The four kinds of waveforms available from SID

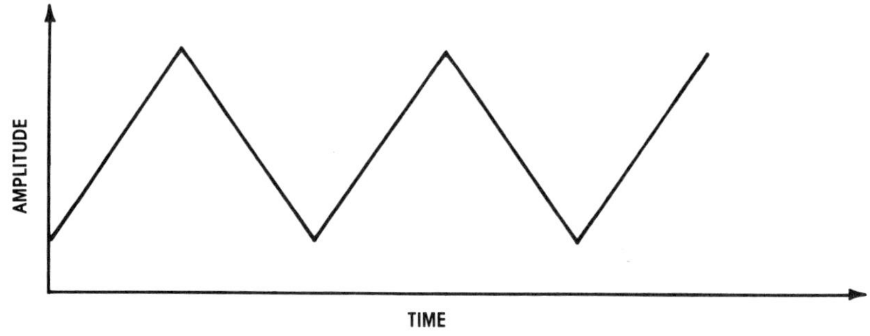

(A) Triangle waveform.

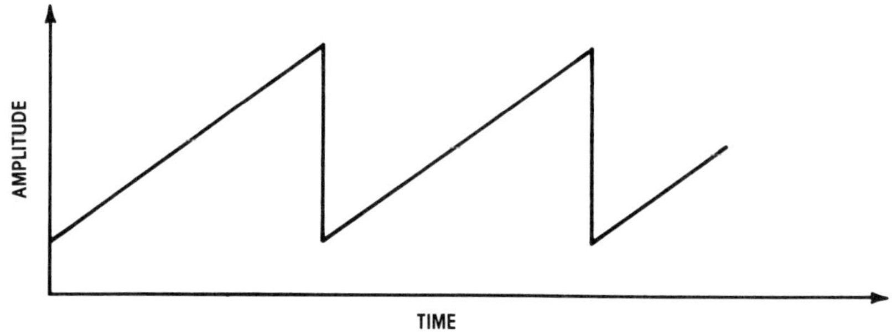

(B) Sawtooth waveform.

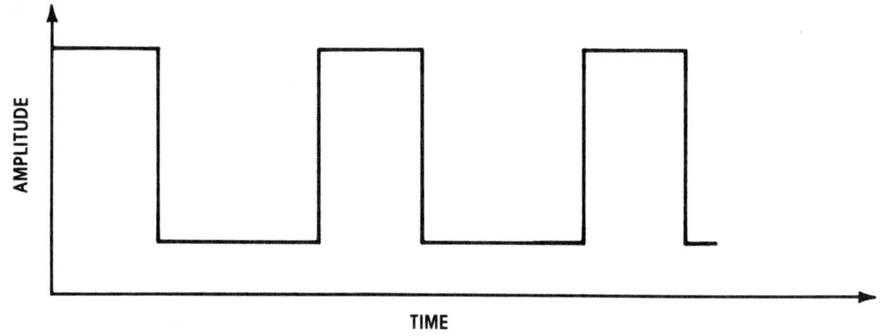

(C) Variable pulse waveform.

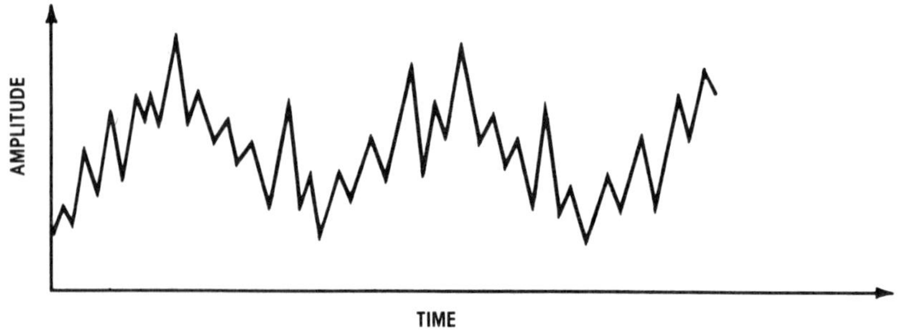

(D) Noise waveform.

sizes the lower frequencies and diminishes the higher frequencies. A high-pass filter, on the other hand, emphasizes the higher frequencies and cuts the volume level for the lower ones. The band-pass filter emphasizes a range of frequencies and diminishes the frequencies above and below.

Fig. 9-3 SID filtering effects

(A) Low-pass filter *(B) High-pass filter*

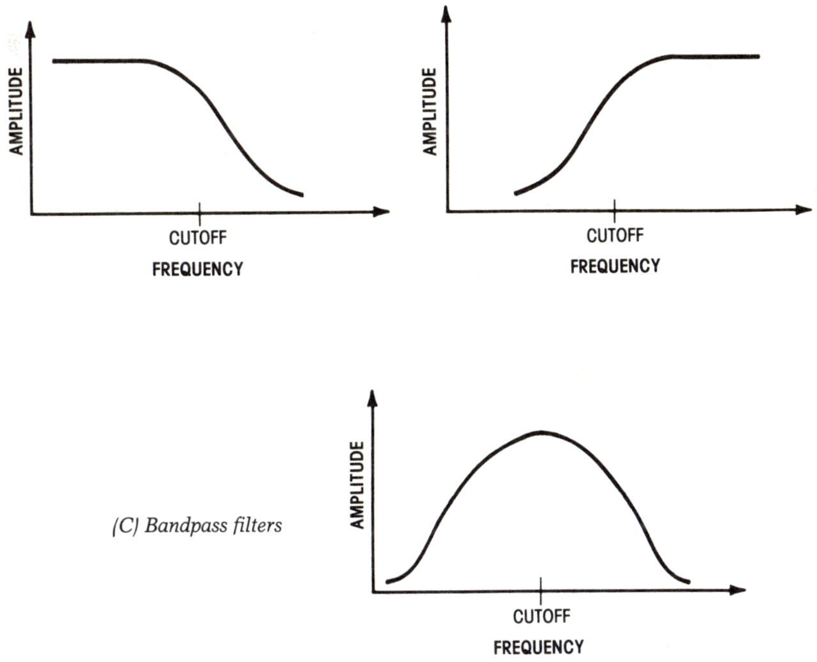

(C) Bandpass filters

When using the filtering features, remember that your system's audio amplifier and loudspeaker most likely reproduce higher frequencies better than lower ones. The system has an inherent high-pass quality.

Using BASIC'S VOL and SOUND Statements

BASIC's VOL and SOUND statements are tools for producing the most elementary sorts of sounds and musical tones. The VOL statement sets the maximum volume level for all voices, and SOUND specifies a voice, frequency, and duration of sound.

The general form of the VOL statement is:

```
VOL n
```

where *n* is a numeric value or expression proportional to the amplitude of the sound, 0 through 15. Assigning a value of 0 to the VOL statement produces no amplitude. Larger values of *n*, through 15, produce louder sounds.

However, the VOL statement does not define a sound. The SOUND statement does that job. The SOUND statement can use a number of optional parameters, but all versions must begin with this general form:

SOUND *voice,freq,dur*

where the parameters are defined as:

voice = voice channel to be used (1 through 3)
freq = numeric value representing desired frequency (0 through 65535)
dur = duration of sound (0 through 32767)

Table 9-1 shows some values for the *freq* parameter as they apply to notes on a 12-octave musical scale. In practice, *freq* values less than 128 sound more like clicking sounds than musical notes.

Table 9-1 Notes Produced by Selection of *freq* Values Assigned to Sound Statement

Octave	Note	*freq* Value	Octave	Note	*freq* Value
0	C	19	2	C	76
0	C#	20	2	C#	81
0	D	21	2	D	86
0	D#	23	2	D#	91
0	E	24	2	E	96
0	F	25	2	F	102
0	F#	27	2	F#	108
0	G	29	2	G	114
0	G#	30	2	G#	121
0	A	32	2	A	128
0	A#	34	2	A#	136
0	B	36	2	B	144
1	C	38	3	C	152
1	C#	40	3	C#	161
1	D	43	3	D	171
1	D#	45	3	D#	181
1	E	48	3	E	192
1	F	51	3	F	203
1	F#	54	3	F#	215
1	G	57	3	G	228
1	G#	60	3	G#	242
1	A	64	3	A	256
1	A#	68	3	A#	271
1	B	72	3	B	288

Table 9-1 (cont.)

Octave	Note	*freq* Value
4	C	305
4	C#	323
4	D	342
4	D#	363
4	E	384
4	F	407
4	F#	431
4	G	457
4	G#	484
4	A	512
4	A#	543
4	B	575
5	C	610
5	C#	646
5	D	684
5	D#	725
5	E	768
5	F	813
5	F#	862
5	G	913
5	G#	968
5	A	1025
5	A#	1086
5	B	1151
6	C	1219
6	C#	1291
6	D	1368
6	D#	1450
6	E	1537
6	F	1627
6	F#	1724
6	G	1827
6	G#	1935
6	A	2050
6	A#	2172
6	B	2301
7	C	2439
7	C#	2582
7	D	2737
7	D#	2900
7	E	3073
7	F	3254
7	F#	3448
7	G	3653
7	G#	3870
7	A	4099
7	A#	4343
7	B	4602
8	C	4877
8	C#	5165
8	D	5474
8	D#	5800
8	E	6146
8	F	6508
8	F#	6895
8	G	7306
8	G#	7740
8	A	8198
8	A#	8686
8	B	9204
9	C	9754
9	C#	10329
9	D	10947
9	D#	11600
9	E	12292
9	F	13015
9	F#	13790
9	G	14612
9	G#	15480
9	A	16396
9	A#	17372
9	B	18408
10	C	19508
10	C#	20658
10	D	21894
10	D#	23200
10	E	24584
10	F	26030
10	F#	27580
10	G	29224
10	G#	30960
10	A	32792
10	A#	34744
10	B	36816
11	C	39016
11	C#	41316
11	D	43788
11	D#	46400
11	E	49168
11	F	52060
11	F#	55160
11	G	58448
11	G#	61920

The duration parameter, *dur*, sets the length of time the tone is heard. Each unit of *dur* represents 1/60 of a second. So setting *dur* to 60 generates a tone for precisely one second. Setting it to the maximum value, 32767, the tone lasts about nine minutes.

The following example uses the SOUND command to generate a middle-C tone for one second and through voice 1:

```
SOUND 1,4877,60
```

The SOUND statement sets up the SID chip. The moment SOUND is executed, the system goes to the next statement in the program. The program in Listing 9-1 uses all three voices and coordinates their activity to create a special musical effect. The final line in the program silences all three voices at the same time by setting their SOUND parameters to 0.

Listing 9-1

```
10 VOL 4
20 SOUND 1,4877,280
30 FOR T=1 TO 250:NEXT T
40 SOUND 2,6146,280
50 FOR T=1 TO 250:NEXT T
60 SOUND 3,7306,280
70 FOR T=1 TO 500;NEXT T
80 FOR K=1 TO 3:SOUND K,0,0:NEXT K
```

> ***NOTE:*** Use the SOUND statement to turn off sounds. Turning sounds on and off with the VOL statement often creates an unwanted popping sound.

The *voice,freq,dur* parameters must be used with the SOUND statement. However, some useful options are available. Consider this extended version:

SOUND *voice,freq,dur,dir,fmin,sstep*

The three additional parameters specify tone-sweeping effects:

dir = direction of sweep

- 0 = up
- 1 = down
- 2 = up and down

fmin = the lower frequency the sweep (0 through 65535)

sstep = the frequency interval between each sweep tone (0 through 32767)

All three sweep parameters interact with one another as well as the three main parameters. The *dir* parameter sets the direction of sweep but has no meaning unless the statement also specifies a pair of end-point frequencies. In that regard, the *freq* parameter sets the upper limit frequency limit and *fmin* sets the lower.

The sweeping effect does not take place, however, until *sstep* is set to some value other than 0. The larger the value assigned to *sstep*, the greater the interval between successive steps in sweeping frequency. Given the limits, *fmin* and *freq*, the *sstep* parameter actually determines how long it takes to sweep between the two extremes.

The following example generates a wailing tone by oscillating between frequency values 30000 and 40000 in steps of 200:

```
SOUND 1,4000,240,2,3000,200
```

Another parameter provides the opportunity to select the waveform of the sound:

SOUND *voice,freq,dur,dir,fmin,sstep,wfrm*

where *wfrm* is an integer between 0 and 3 that indicates the waveform to be used:

0 = triangle
1 = sawtooth
2 = variable pulse
3 = noise

The default value of *wfrm* is 0—the triangular waveform. Setting it to 1 changes the waveform to a sawtooth shape, and 3 adds random noise to it. Option 2, the variable pulse, is not meaningful without setting a pulse width as described subsequently in this section.

In instances where you want to change the waveform but the frequency-sweep parameters are not relevant, the statement has to take this general form:

SOUND *voice,freq,dur,,,,wfrm*

This version omits the actual sweep parameters but includes the commas that would otherwise separate them.

The final option for the SOUND statement is a pulse-width specification. This has no meaning unless the statement specifies the variable-pulse waveform, and the following general form reflects that fact:

```
SOUND voice,freq,dur,dir,fmin,sstep,2,pw
```

The pulse-width parameter, *pw*, sets the duration of pulses when operating in the variable-pulse mode. The range of values is 0 through 4095. Unless specified otherwise, *pw* is set to 2048. Compare the sounds generated by the next two versions of the SOUND statement:

```
SOUND 1,4000,250,,,,2,2048
SOUND 1,4000,250,,,,2,1000
```

The SOUND statement is certainly well designed for creating all sorts of sound effects. It can also be used for generating musical scenarios, but the programming procedure can be difficult and time consuming. BASIC 7.0 offers a far more convenient means for working with musical scenarios effectively—the PLAY, TEMPO, and ENVELOPE statements described in the next section of this chapter.

Using Basic's Play and Tempo Statements

BASIC's PLAY, TEMP, and ENVELOPE statements are specifically designed for programmers who want to play musical compositions. A programmer who knows how to read musical scores and understands a bit about BASIC's musical statements can program virtually any composition into the system. The only real compromise is that the Commodore 128 can handle only three voices at one time.

The general form of the PLAY statement is quite simple:

```
PLAY string
```

where *string* is a string constant, variable, or function that indicates what is to be PLAYed. The simplicity of the general form of the statement belies its flexibility. The *string* term carries the burden of the work.

The *string* term is composed of a series of letters of the alphabet and a few special symbols. Each character has a well-defined meaning. Programming a musical composition is largely a matter of assigning characters to one or more string statements.

Selecting the Notes to Be Played

Notes to be played are indicated by letters A through G. The following example plays a one-octave scale:

```
PLAY "C D E F G A B"
```

Spaces between the letters are optional and are often used only to separate portions of a score.

Sharps and flats can be indicated by preceding the letter with a # or $, respectively. To play C-sharp, for example, indicate #C in the string. B-flat is indicated by $B. The next example plays a one-octave chromatic scale:

```
10 A$="C #C D $E E F #F G $A A $B B"
20 PLAY A$
```

The range of notes can be extended by including code that indicates one of seven octaves. The general form of the code is O*n*, where *n* is the desired octave (0 through 6). The lower the octave value, the lower the notes. Once the octave is included in the PLAY string, it remains in effect until changed.

Including an O0 in the string places all subsequent notes in the lowest octave. The default octave is O4. The next example plays a single-octave chromatic scale, but the octave is lower than the one used in the previous example:

```
10 A$="O1 C #C D $E E F #F G $A A $B B"
20 PLAY A$
```

The following example plays the entire chromatic scale for the system. Notice you can work with the PLAY strings to extend the basic musical effects.

```
10 A$="C #C D $E E F #F G $A A $B B"
20 FOR K=0 TO 6
30 B$="O"+STR$(K)
40 PLAY B$+A$
50 NEXT K
```

Selecting the Duration of Notes and Rests

The duration of a given note can be specified as whole (W), half (H), quarter (Q), eighth (I), sixteenth (S), and dotted (.). The letters precede the note they affect. Once specified, the durations remain in effect until changed.

A whole C-sharp is thus specified as W#C, and a dotted-sixteenth A is shown as .SA.

Rests are specified with an R character. The duration of the rest can be set the same way as the duration of playable notes. QR, for example, indicates a quarter-note rest.

Use the TEMPO statement to set the overall tempo of a composition. This statement must be executed prior to the PLAY statements that are to use it, and the specification remains in effect until changed by another TEMPO.

The general form of the TEMPO statement is:

TEMPO *n*

where *n* is an integer between 0 and 255. The larger the value of *n*, the faster the tempo. The default value is 8.

Setting Volume Levels

The overall volume level can be set with a separate VOL statement. PLAY strings should have some means for changing the loudness from one part of a composition to another. The volume can thus be adjusted within a PLAY string by means of a U*n* code, where *n* is a volume level between 0 and 8.

Selecting the Sound Quality (Envelope)

A T*n* code is used within a PLAY string to specify the tonal quality, where *n* is an integer between 0 and 9, inclusively. Unless you change the tone envelopes as described subsequently, the T*n* code produces tones that sound much like the instruments shown here:

T0 = Piano
T1 = Accordion
T2 = Calliope
T3 = Drum
T4 = Flute
T5 = Guitar
T6 = Harpsichord
T7 = Organ
T8 = Trumpet
T9 = Xylophone

The next example illustrates a drum selection that uses the U term to achieve some accent effects:

```
10 PLAY "T3O4"
20 PLAY "U8IESRU4SESEU8IESRIE.IRO6IESRIE"
```

Selecting Voices

The SID chip is capable of producing up to three different sounds at one time. Those sounds are defined in terms of voices and specified by a V*n* code in the PLAY strings. Including a V1 within a PLAY string refers subsequent codes to voice 1. The situation can be changed by specifying a different voice, V2 or V3.

The following example uses the three voices to generate a simple harmony:

```
10 PLAY "V1T8O4WC"
20 PLAY "V2T8QRO4.HE"
30 PLAY "V3T8QRO4HG"
```

Line 10—Set voice 1 for a trumpet sound, set octave 4, and begin playing a whole-note C.

Line 20—Set voice 2 for a trumpet sound, do a quarter rest, set octave 4, and play a dotted-half E.

Line 30—Set voice 3 for a trumpet sound, do a quarter rest, set octave 4, and play a half-note G.

Holding Things Together with the M Code

As you begin writing musical programs that use more complex combinations of multiple voices, you sometimes sense an occasional, slight timing discrepancy. A bit of fine tuning of note duration and rests usually clears up the problem or reduces it to a point where it is not noticeable.

The timing problem becomes more apparent when using PLAY strings within program loops—within FOR. . .NEXT loops, for example. The example in Listing 9-2 illustrates the problem.

Line 10—Set the tempo

Line 20—Define piano sounds for all three voices

Line 30—Define the first measure

Line 40—Define the second measure

Line 50—Play the first measure three times in succession

Line 60—Play the second measure

Listing 9-2

```
10 TEMPO 20
20 PLAY "V1T0 V2T0 V2T0
30 M$(1)="V1O2WC V2O3HE V303QCQE V2O3HE V3O3QGO4QC
40 M$(2)="V1O2WC V2O3HE V3O3QGQE V2O3HE V3O3HC
50 FOR K=1 TO 3:PLAY M$(1):NEXT K
60 PLAY M$(2)
```

The timing discrepancy for M$(1) becomes quite apparent the third time it is executed in the FOR. . .NEXT loop. The three voices run out of synchronization and spoil the musical effect.

The cure is simple: End each measure with an M code. That code holds up execution of the program until all three voices reach the end of the measure. Add an M to the end of line 30, and you will notice that the composition no longer runs out of synchronization.

Figure 9-4 summarizes all the codes for PLAY statements.

Fig. 9-4 Summary of codes that can be used in the string portion of a PLAY statement

V*n*—Voice selection: n = 1-2
T*n*—Tone envelope: n = 0-9

0—Piano
1—Accordion
2—Calliope
3—Drum
4—Flute
5—Guitar
6—Harpsichord
7—Organ
8—Trumpet
9—Xylophone

U*n*—Volume: n = 0-8
O*n*—Octave: n = 0-6
A, B, C, D, E, F, G—Notes

#—Sharp
$—Flat
W—Whole note
H—Half note
I—Eighth note
S—Sixteenth note
.—(Period) dotted note

R—Rest
M—Wait for all voices to catch up
X*n*—Filter control: n = 0 for Off
n = 1 for On

Using the Envelope Statement

The T*n* code in a PLAY statement specifies which one of ten sounds is to be used for a given musical scenario. The character of those tones is fixed in terms of attack and decay intervals, sustain volume level, release interval, waveform shape and, if variable pulses are used, in terms of the pulse width as well.

As long as you are satisfied with the standard family of sounds, you don't need to change them. But when you want to modify one of the tones or invent new ones, BASIC 7.0 provides the means through its ENVELOPE statement.

The general form of the ENVELOPE statement is

ENVELOPE ***n,atk,dcy,sus,rel,wfrm,pw***

n = Envelope number (0-9)

atk = Attack duration (0–15)
dcy = Decay duration (0–15)
sus = Sustain volume level
rel = Release duration (0–15)
wfrm = Waveform (0–4):

0 = Triangle
1 = Sawtooth
2 = Pulse
3 = Noise
4 = Ring

pw = Pulse width (0–4095)

Table 9-2 shows the values that the Commodore 128 assigns to the ten envelopes.

Table 9-2 Table of Parameters Initially Assigned to ENVELOPES 0 through 9

			Envelope Parameters				Sound
n	*atk*	*dcy*	*sus*	*rel*	*wfrm*	*pw*	
0	0	9	0	0	2	1536	Piano
1	12	0	12	0	1		Accordion
2	0	0	15	0	0		Calliope
3	0	5	5	0	3		Drum
4	9	4	4	0	0		Flute
5	0	9	2	1	1		Guitar
6	0	9	9	0	2	512	Harpsichord
7	0	9	9	0	2	2048	Organ
8	8	9	4	1	2	512	Trumpet
9	0	9	0	0	0		Xylophone

When you select the pulse waveform, you must also specify a value that represents the percent of time the waveform is "high." That is the role of the *pw* term. Table 9-3 summarizes the values of *pw* required for "high" times in steps of 5 percent.

Table 9-3 Summary of Pulse Widths in Steps of Five Percent and *pw* Values for ENVELOPE Statement

Pulse Width (percent)	*pw* Value
0	0
5	205
10	410
15	614
20	819
25	1024
30	1229
35	1433
40	1638
45	1843

Table 9-3 (cont.)

Pulse Width (percent)	*pw* Value
50	2048
55	2252
60	2457
65	2662
70	2867
75	3071
80	3276
85	3481
90	3686
95	3890
100	4095

Using the Filter Statement

The FILTER statement allows you to set one of the three filtering formats shown in Figure 9-3. The general form of the statement is

FILTER *cof,lof,bpf,hpf,rel*

cof = The cutoff frequency (0 through 2047)
lof = Low-pass filter flag (0=off, 1=on)
bpf = Band-pass filter flag (0=off, 1=on)
hpf = High-pass filter flag (0=off, 1=on)
rel = Resonance level (0 through 15)

The cutoff frequency sets the critical point for specifying where the filtering begins or ends. The larger the value, the higher the cutoff frequency.

The next three terms in the FILTER statement—*lof, bpf* and *hpf*—determine which one of the filtering effects are applied. The values to be assigned are either 0 or 1. Combinations of more than one selected filter produce the corresponding filtering effects.

The *rel* term fixes the sharpness of the filtering effect. The larger the value, the sharper and more pronounced the filtering effect becomes.

Once you have specified a FILTER statement, it can be fit into a PLAY string by including an X1 command. In the PLAY string, X1 turns on the filtering for the current voice and X0 turns it off.

> ***HINT:*** Include an X0 code in the initial PLAY strings for all voices. This is one way to make sure that previous FILTER settings do not affect the new musical scenario.

Working Directly with the SID Registers

Although BASIC offers some fine avenues for developing sound and musical programs, the SID registers offer a bit more potential and far more flexibility. Of course, working directly with the SID registers is a more abstract procedure. Then, too, no built-in provisions exist for setting the overall duration of a tone—it has to be gated on with one kind of operation and gated off with another. A time delay routine is usually inserted between the turn-on and turn-off operations.

The SID registers of particular importance to sound procedures occupy a block of I/O from $D400 through $D418. These registers include bytes and bits for setting all the sound parameters available from BASIC in a less direct fashion.

Many of the registers serve more than one purpose. Often they are divided into two groups of four bits (nibbles). The higher-order nibble is composed of the four higher-order bits (bits 4 through 7), and the lower-order nibble is defined in terms of the four lower-order bits (bits 0 through 3).

Setting Frequencies

Each of the three voices uses pairs of registers for setting the desired frequency—LSB followed by MSB. The larger the values written to those registers, the higher the frequency.

Voice 1 frequency:	**$D400 and $D401 (54272 and 54273)**
Voice 2 frequency:	**$D407 and $D408 (54279 and 54280)**
Voice 3 frequency:	**$D40E and $D40F (54286 and 54287)**

Using two registers means that the range of frequency values is $0000 through $FFFF (0 through 65535). Just remember that the lower-order byte goes to the first of the two registers and the higher-order byte goes to the second. Thus, a frequency specification of $2906 for voice 1 is specified by loading $06 to $D400 and $29 to $D401.

Setting Overall Volume

The four lower-order bits at address $D418 (54296) determine the maximum volume level for all three voices. The range of values for that nibble is $0 through $F (0–15). The larger the value, the higher the volume.

The volume level is usually set just prior to initiating a sound scenario.

The four higher-order bits of the volume register are used for setting some filter options. If you are using those filter options, include them in the data that specifies the overall volume level. When the filter options are not relevant, you only need write the desired volume level to $D418 with values between $00 and $0F.

Setting Attack and Decay Intervals

Each voice has a register dedicated to its own attack and decay interval. The registers are divided into two equal parts, the higher-order nibble handles values for the attack interval and the lower-order nibble handles the decay interval.

Voice 1 Attack/Decay: **$D405 (54277)**
Voice 1 Attack/Decay: **$D40C (54284)**
Voice 1 Attack/Decay: **$D413 (54291)**

Percussive sounds, such as those of bells, drums, and pianos, use very short attack intervals and relatively long decay intervals. Selecting an attack interval of $1 and a decay interval of $9 produces such a sound. It is assembled in the attack/decay register this way: $19—attack nibble followed by the decay nibble.

Setting Sustain Level and Release Interval

Each voice uses a single register for setting the sustain volume level and release level. In each case, the upper nibble sets the sustain level and the lower nibble sets the release interval.

Voice 1 Sustain/Release: **$D406 (54278)**
Voice 2 Sustain/Release: **$D40D (54285)**
Voice 3 Sustain/Release: **$D414 (54292)**

Setting a sustain level of $2 and a release interval of $4 is a matter of loading the register with $24—sustain level followed by the desired release interval.

Using Waveform/Gate Registers

Each voice has a multiple-purpose register that serves at least two different, but critical, purposes. Setting one of the four higher-order bits determines the nature of the sound waveform: random noise, pulsed, sawtooth, or triangular. The lowest-order bit—0—is the gate bit for the voice. Loading the data to the register with bit 0 set to 1 initiates the attack. Loading the data with bit 0 cleared to zero initiates the release cycle. In short, bit 0 in these registers gates the voices on and off.

Voice 1 Waveform/Gate: **$D404 (54276)**
Voice 2 Waveform/Gate: **$D40B (54283)**
Voice 3 Waveform/Gate: **$D412 (54290)**

One, and only one, of the four bytes in the higher-order nibble must set to 1:

Setting bit 7 to 1 specifies a noise waveform.
Setting bit 6 to 1 specifies a pulse waveform.
Setting bit 5 to 1 specifies a sawtooth waveform.
Setting bit 4 to 1 specifies a triangular waveform.

Just four values are possible for the higher-order, waveform-selecting nibble: $1, $2, $4 or $8.

Bearing in mind that bit 0 gates a sound on and off, writing $11 to $D404 initiates the voice-1 sound with a triangular waveform, and writing $10 begins the release cycle for the same voice and waveform.

Bits 1, 2, and 3 of these registers are used for specifying special functions between two voices. These ring and synchronization features are described subsequently.

Planning and Executing Simple Sounds

Programmers tend to use a certain sequence of data-writing operations for machine-language sound routines. The sequence is based on a few important facts. First, a chance always exists that a previous SID program has left some of the registers set in unwanted states, so begin a routine in some fashion that ensures no leftover settings are in effect.

Second, changing the overall volume level at $D418 often causes a popping sound if any of the voices is gated on. Thus, write the desired volume level to that address prior to gating on any of the voices. This is one of the first things to be done.

Third, a voice should not be gated on—the attack interval should not be initiated—until all parameters for the voice have been defined. Gating the voice on before setting all the parameters generally creates silence.

The following suggested procedure deals only with the parameters described thus far in this chapter.

1. Clear all SID registers to zero—write $00 to the SID registers, $D400 through $D418.
2. Set the overall volume level—write the volume level to the lower-order nibble of $D418.
3. Set the frequency for the voice—write the LSB and MSB to the pair of frequency registers for the voice.
4. Set the attack/decay parameters—write to the attack/decay register for the voice.

5. Set the sustain/release parameters—write to the sustain/release register for the voice.
6. Set the waveform and initiate the sound—write to the waveform/gate register for the voice with bit 0 set to 1.
7. Time the operation—do a time delay or some other program routines.
8. Gate off the sound—write to the waveform/gate register for the voice with bit 0 cleared to 0.

A couple of ways are available for implementing the preceding general procedure. One is to load-immediate the data and write it directly to the SID registers. That is the technique illustrated in Listing 9-3.

Listing 9-3

```
        LDY #$18        ;CLEAR SID REGISTERS
        LDA #$00
NEXT1   STA $D400,Y
        BPL NEXT1
        LDA #$0F        ;SPECIFY MAX VOLUME
        STA $D018       ;SET SID VOLUME
        LDA #$00        ;SPECIFY LSB OF FREQUENCY
        STA $D400       ;SET LSB OF V1 FREQUENCY
        LDA #$CA        ;SPECIFY MSB OF FREQUENCY
        STA $D401       ;SET MSB OF V1 FREQUENCY
        LDA #$0A        ;SPEC. 0 ATTACK, $A DECAY
        STA $D405       ;SET V1 ATTACK/DECAY
        LDA #$00        ;SPEC. 0 SUSTAIN, 0 RELEASE
        STA $D406       ;SET V1 SUSTAIN/RELEASE
        LDA #$21        ;SPEC. TRIANGLE, GATE ON
        STA $D404       ;SET V1 WAVEFORM/GATE
        LDA #$04        ;KILL SOME TIME
        STA $FA
NEXT 4  LDX #$FF
NEXT 3  LDY #$FF
NEXT 2  DEY
        BNE NEXT2
        DEX
        BNE NEXT3
        DEC $FA
        BNE NEXT4
        LDA #$00        ;SPEC. GATE OFF
        STA $D404       ;GATE OFF V1
        RTS
```

An alternative technique is less direct but offers far more flexibility. The idea is to build a table of values to be written to the SID registers. Then when the time is right, transfer them to the SID. The example in Listing 9-4 uses this procedure.

Listing 9-4

```
0D00  00  CA  00  00  20  0A  00  00
0D08  00  00  00  00  00  00  00  00
0D10  00  00  00  00  00  00  00  00
0D18  0F

            LDY #$18          ;SET INDEX
NEXT1       LDA $0D00,Y       ;GET A DATA BYTE
            STA $D400,Y       ;SET TO SID
            DEY               ;DECREMENT INDEX
            BPL NEXT1         ;NEXT IF NOT DONE
            LDA $0D04         ;GET WAVE/GATE BYTE
            ORA #$01          ;SET GATE BIT
            STA $D404         ;GATE ON VOICE 1
            JSR DELAY         ;DO TIME DELAY
            LDA $0D04         ;GET WAVE/GATE BYTE
            AND #$FE          ;CLEAR THE GATE BIT
            STA $D404         ;GATE OFF VOICE 1
            RTS               ;END THE ROUTINE

DELAY       LDA #$04          ;SPEC. HIGH BYTE OF DELAY
            STA $FA           ;USE REGISTER $FA
NEXT4       LDX #$FF          ;SET MID BYTE OF DELAY
NEXT3       LDY #$FF          ;SET LOW BYTE OF DELAY
NEXT2       DEY               ;DECREMENT LOW BYTE
            BNE NEXT2         ;IF NOT DONE, DO AGAIN
            DEX               ;DECREMENT MID BYTE
            BNE NEXT3         ;DO LOW BYTE AGAIN
            DEC $FA           ;DECREMENT HIGH BYTE
            BNE NEXT4         ;DO MID AND LOW AGAIN
            RTS               ;RETURN TO MAIN ROUTINE
```

The listing shows a block of RAM organized in the same sequence as the SID registers. The first two bytes, $0D00 and $0D01, are the LSB and MSB of the frequency for voice 1. The byte at $0D04 indicates the waveform selection for voice 1, $0D05 is the attack/decay selection and $0D06 is the sustain/release selection for voice 1. The sound is percussive in nature, so the attack is set to 0, the decay to $A, the sustain level to 0 and the release interval to 0. The volume nibble in $D018 is set for maximum loudness.

Having thus defined the sound (indeed, the entire SID format) in a block of RAM, the next part of the listing controls the presentation.

Listing 9-5 demonstrates the flexibility of the approach in an example that uses all three voices.

Listing 9-5

```
0D00  00  04  00  00  20  00  F0  00
0D08  08  00  00  20  00  F0  00  0C
0D10  00  00  20  00  F0  00  00  00
0D18  0F

        LDY #$18          ;SET INDEX
NEXT1   LDA $0D00,Y       ;GET A DATA BYTE
        STA $D400,Y       ;SET TO SID
        DEY               ;DECREMENT INDEX
        BPL NEXT1         ;NEXT IF NOT DONE
        LDA $0D04         ;GET V2 WAVE/GATE BYTE
        ORA #$01          ;SET GATE BIT
        STA $D404         ;GATE ON VOICE 1
        LDA #$01          ;SET DELAY
        JSR DELAY         ;DO TIME DELAY
        LDA $0D0B         ;GET V2 WAVE/GATE BYTE
        ORA #$01          ;SET GATE BIT
        STA $D40B         ;GATE ON VOICE 2
        LDA #$01          ;SET DELAY
        JSR DELAY         ;DO TIME DELAY
        LDA $0D12         ;GET V3 WAVE/GATE BYTE
        ORA #$01          ;SET GATE BIT
        STA $D412         ;GATE ON VOICE 3
        LDA #$08          ;SET DELAY
        JSR DELAY         ;DO TIME DELAY
        LDA #$00
        STA $D404         ;GATE OFF VOICE 1
        STA $D40B         ;GATE OFF VOICE 2
        STA $D412         ;GATE OFF VOICE 3
        RTS               ;END THE ROUTINE

DELAY   STA $FA           ;USE REGISTER $FA
NEXT4   LDX #$FF          ;SET MID BYTE OF DELAY
NEXT3   LDY #$FF          ;SET LOW BYTE OF DELAY
NEXT2   DEY               ;DECREMENT LOW BYTE
        BNE NEXT2         ;IF NOT DONE, DO AGAIN
        DEX               ;DECREMENT MID BYTE
        BNE NEXT3         ;DO LOW BYTE AGAIN
        DEC $FA           ;DECREMENT HIGH BYTE
        BNE NEXT4         ;DO MID AND LOW AGAIN
        RTS               ;RETURN TO MAIN ROUTINE
```

Using the Pulse Waveform Controls

Selecting the pulse-waveform option in the waveform/gate register for the SID voices makes it mandatory to set a corresponding pulse width. The pulse width is written to two consecutive registers allocated for the purpose. The lower-order byte goes to the first register and the higher-order to the second register. The range of values is $0000 through $0FFF, so only the lower-order nibble in the second register is used.

The pulse-width registers for the three voices are located at the following SID addresses:

Voice 1 pulse width: **$D402 and $D403 (54274 and 54275)**
Voice 2 pulse width: **$D409 and $D40A (54281 and 54282)**
Voice 3 pulse width: **$D410 and $D411 (54288 and 54289)**

Table 9-4 summarizes the range of pulse widths in steps of five percent and shows the hexadecimal values to be written to the pulse registers.

Table 9-4 Summary of Pulse Widths in Steps of Five Percent and Corresponding Values to Be Written to Pulse-Width Registers

Pulse Width (percent)	Register Values
0	$0000
5	$00CD
10	$019A
15	$0266
20	$0333
25	$0400
30	$04CD
35	$0599
40	$0666
45	$0733
50	$0800
55	$08CC
60	$0999
65	$0A66
70	$0B33
75	$0BFF
80	$0CCC
85	$0D99
90	$0E66
95	$0F32
100	$0FFF

If you want a 75-percent pulse waveform for voice 1, load $FF to $D402, $0B to $D402, and initiate the sound by writing $41 to $D404.

Working with SOUND Enhancement Registers

Three other SID enhancements are ring modulation, synchronization and filtering. Ring modulation produces a vibrato effect, the synchronization feature logically ANDs the waveforms from two oscillators, and the filtering enhances certain frequencies and diminishes others.

Like every other SID operation, these enhanced features are implemented by writing bytes, nibbles, and bits to certain locations.

Using Ring Modulation

Ring modulation mixes the oscillator of one voice with the output waveform of another so one affects the amplitude of the other. The most popular combination modulates a main tone with a low frequency from another voice—it produces a vibrato effect. Other combinations produce other kinds of interesting effects.

The SID has provisions for three different ring-modulation formats:

Modulate voice 1 with oscillator 3.
Modulate voice 2 with oscillator 1.
Modulate voice 3 with oscillator 2.

The format is established by setting a single bit in one of three registers—bit 2 in the three waveform/gate registers. Setting the bit to 1 invokes the modulation format, and clearing it to 0 turns this format off.

To modulate voice 1 with oscillator 3, set bit 2 in $D404 (54276).
To modulate voice 2 with oscillator 1, set bit 2 in $D40B (54283).
To modulate voice 3 with oscillator 1, set bit 2 in $D412 (54290).

Voice 1 in Listing 9-6 generates a relatively high-pitched pinging sound with a triangular waveform. No attack interval is included, but a decay interval drops the volume to a 0 sustain level. The byte at $0D04 not only indicates the use of a triangular waveform, but ring modulation with oscillator 3 as well.

Voice 3 might appear to have some unworkable waveform parameters—no waveform specification, no attack, decay, sustain, or release. Voice 3, in fact, is not to be heard. A frequency is specified and the oscillator is turned on. This is all that is necessary for modulating voice 1.

Using Oscillator Synchronization

Very little difference exists between the way the SID uses the oscillator synchronization feature and ring modulation. In fact, the sounds are often quite similar. The sound from a synchronized oscillator generally has a more obvious fluttering quality and can generate frequencies that are different from the two oscillators involved in the procedure.

The system has provisions for three different synchronization formats:

Synchronize oscillator 1 with oscillator 3.
Synchronize oscillator 2 with oscillator 1.
Synchronize oscillator 3 with oscillator 2.

Listing 9-6

```
0D00  00  80  00  00  14  0A  00  00
0D08  00  00  00  00  00  00  F0  00
0D10  00  00  00  00  00  00  00  00
0D18  0F

        LDY #$18         ;SET INDEX
NEXT1   LDA $0D00,Y      ;GET A DATA BYTE
        STA $D400,Y      ;SET TO SID
        DEY              ;DECREMENT INDEX
        BPL NEXT1        ;NEXT IF NOT DONE
        LDA $0D04        ;GET V2 WAVE/GATE BYTE
        ORA #$01         ;SET GATE BIT
        STA $D404        ;GATE ON VOICE 1
        LDA $0D12        ;GET V3 WAVE/GATE BYTE
        ORA #$01         ;SET GATE BIT
        STA $D412        ;GATE ON VOICE 3
        LDA #$04         ;SET DELAY
        JSR DELAY        ;DO TIME DELAY
        LDA #$00
        STA $D404        ;GATE OFF VOICE 1
        STA $D412        ;GATE OFF VOICE 3
        RTS              ;END THE ROUTINE

DELAY   STA $FA          ;USE REGISTER $FA
NEXT4   LDX #$FF         ;SET MID BYTE OF DELAY
NEXT3   LDY #$FF         ;SET LOW BYTE OF DELAY
NEXT2   DEY              ;DECREMENT LOW BYTE
        BNE NEXT2        ;IF NOT DONE, DO AGAIN
        DEX              ;DECREMENT MID BYTE
        BNE NEXT3        ;DO LOW BYTE AGAIN
        DEC $FA          ;DECREMENT HIGH BYTE
        BNE NEXT4        ;DO MID AND LOW AGAIN
        RTS              ;RETURN TO MAIN ROUTINE
```

The format is established by setting a single bit in one of three waveform/gate registers. Setting the bit to 1 invokes the modulation format, and clearing it to 0 turns the format off.

To synchronize 1 with 3, set bit 1 in $D404 (54276).
To synchronize 2 with 1, set bit 1 in $D40B (54283).
To synchronize 3 with 1, set bit 1 in $D412 (54290).

Using the Filtering Features

Ideally, sounds that are produced with no filtering yield the same amplitude through the entire range of frequencies. This is hardly the case, considering the poor low-frequency characteristics of the loudspeakers and the audio amplifiers. Using some of the filtering features of the SID can go a long way toward compensating for some of the lack of good high fidelity. The primary purpose of the filtering features, however, is to produce special effects with volume levels as functions of oscillator frequency.

Figure 9-3 illustrates the three kinds of filtering directly available. The general procedure for using the filter feature is:

1. Specify the cutoff frequency, $0000 to $FF08 (0–65288).
2. Specify the resonance level, $0 to $F (1–15).
3. Specify one or more kinds of filtering, low-pass, high-pass, and bandpass.
4. Gate the filtering on for one or more voices.

The procedure is implemented by writing to registers allocated for the purpose.

Cutoff frequency: Low-order value; bits 0, 1, and 2 of $D415 (54293)
High-order byte: $D416 (54294)
Resonance level: Bits 4–7 of $D417 (54295)
External filter flag: Bit 3 of $D417 (45295); 0=off, 1=on
Voice 3 filter flag: Bit 2 of $D417 (45295); 0=off, 1=on
Voice 2 filter flag: Bit 1 of $D417 (45295); 0=off, 1=on
Voice 1 filter flag: Bit 0 of $D417 (45295); 0=off, 1=on
High-pass filter flag: Bit 6 of $D418 (54296); 0=off, 1=on
Bandpass filter flag: Bit 5 of $D418 (54296); 0=off, 1=on
Low-pass filter flag: Bit 4 of $D418 (54296); 0=off, 1=on

Summary of SID Sound Registers

The following is a complete summary of SID sound registers.

VOICE 1 Frequency Registers Writing to these registers fixes the output frequency of voice 1. The larger the value, the higher the frequency.

Addresses: $D400 (54272) = LSB of voice-1 frequency
$D401 (54273) = MSB of voice-1 frequency

Data: $00–$FF (0–255) for both registers.
Total range = $0000–$FFFF (0–65535)

VOICE 1 Pulse Width Registers Writing to these registers sets the pulse width when the pulse waveform mode is enabled. The larger the values, the longer the duty cycle of the waveform.

Addresses: $D402 (54274) = LSB of pulse waveform
$D403 (54275) = MSB of pulse waveform

Data: LSB = $00-$FF (0-255)
MSB = $00-$0F (0-15)

Overall range = $0000-$0FFF (0-4095)

NOTE: Bits 4-7 of $D403 are not used.

VOICE 1 Control Register Writing to this register sets the character of the tonal quality of the waveform and starts the attack and decay cycles. The register is entirely bit mapped.

Address: $D404 (54276)

Data: 0 = disable
1 = enable

Bit 7: Random noise
Bit 6: Pulse waveform
Bit 5: Sawtooth waveform
Bit 4: Triangular waveform
Bit 3: Oscillator test bit
Bit 2: Ring modulate 1 with 3
Bit 1: Synchronize 1 with 3
Bit 0: Start attack/sustain, decay gate

1 = start attack/sustain
0 = start decay

VOICE 1 Envelope Generator 1 Writing to this register sets the attack and decay interval.

Address: $D405 (54277)

Data: Bits 4-7 = Attack duration
Bits 0-3 = Decay duration

VOICE 1 Envelope Generator 2 Writing to this register sets the sustain volume level and release interval.

Address: $D406 (54278)

Data: Bits 4–7 = Sustain volume level
Bits 0–3 = Release duration

VOICE 2 Frequency Registers Writing to these registers fixes the output frequency of voice 2. The larger the value, the higher the frequency.

Addresses: $D407 (54279) = LSB of voice-2 frequency
$D408 (54280) = MSB of voice-2 frequency

Data: $00–$FF (0–255) for both registers.
Total range = $0000–$FFFF (0–65535)

VOICE 2 Pulse Width Registers Writing to these registers sets the pulse width when the pulse waveform mode is enabled. The larger the values, the longer the duty cycle of the waveform.

Addresses: $D409 (54281) = LSB of pulse waveform
$D40A (54282) = MSB of pulse waveform

Data: LSB = $00–$FF (0–255)
MSB = $00–$0F (0–15)

Overall range = $0000–$0FFF (0–4095)

NOTE: Bits 4–7 of $D40A are not used.

VOICE 2 Control Register Writing to this register sets the character of the tonal quality of the waveform and starts the attack and decay cycles. The register is entirely bit mapped.

Address: $D40B (54283)

Data: 0 = disable
1 = enable

Bit 7 = Random noise
Bit 6 = Pulse waveform
Bit 5 = Sawtooth waveform
Bit 4 = Triangular waveform
Bit 3 = Oscillator on/off
0 = on
1 = off
Bit 2 = Ring modulate 2 with 1
Bit 1 = Synchronize 2 with 1
Bit 0 = Start attack/sustain, decay gate

1 = start attack/sustain
0 = start decay

VOICE 2 Envelope Generator 1 Writing to this register sets the attack and decay interval.

Address: $D40C (54284)

Data: Bits 4–7 = Attack duration
Bits 0–3 = Decay duration

VOICE 2 Envelope Generator 2 Writing to this register sets the sustain volume level and release interval.

Address: $D40D (54285)

Data: Bits 4–7 = Sustain volume level
Bits 0–3 = Release duration

VOICE 3 Frequency Registers Writing to these registers fixes the output frequency of voice 3. The larger the value, the higher the frequency.

Addresses: $D40E (54286) = LSB of voice-3 frequency
$D40F (54287) = MSB of voice-3 frequency

Data: $00–$FF (0–255) for both registers.
Total range = $0000–$FFFF (0–65535)

VOICE 3 Pulse Width Registers Writing to these registers sets the pulse width when the pulse waveform mode is enabled. The larger the values, the longer the duty cycle of the waveform.

Addresses: D410 (54288) = LSB of pulse waveform
$D411 (54289) = MSB of pulse waveform

Data: LSB = $00–$FF (0–255)
MSB = $00–$0F (0–15)

Overall range = $0000–$0FFF (0–4095)

NOTE: Bits 4–7 of $D411 are not used.

VOICE 3 Control Register Writing to this register sets the character of the waveform's tonal quality and starts the attack and decay cycles. The register is entirely bit mapped.

Address: **$D412 (54290)**

Data: 0 = disable
1 = enable

Bit 7 = Random noise
Bit 6 = Pulse waveform
Bit 5 = Sawtooth waveform
Bit 4 = Triangular waveform
Bit 3 = Oscillator test bit
Bit 2 = Ring modulate 3 with 2
Bit 1 = Synchronize 3 with 2
Bit 0 = Start attack/sustain, decay gate

1 = start attack/sustain
0 = start decay

VOICE 3 Envelope Generator 1 Writing to this register sets the attack and decay interval.

Address: **$D413 (54291)**

Data: Bits 4–7 = Attack duration
Bits 0–3 = Decay duration

VOICE 3 Envelope Generator 2 Writing to this register sets the sustain volume level and release interval.

Address: **$D414 (54292)**

Data: Bits 4–7 = Sustain volume level
Bits 0–3 = Release duration

OVERALL VOLUME Writing to the four lower-order bytes in this register sets the peak volume level for all voices.

Address: **$D418 (54296)**

Data: Bits 0–3
$00 (0)—minimum volume
0F (15)—maximum volume

NOTE: The four higher-order bits are used for setting filtering modes. Unless you are using the filtering features, the range of values is $00 through $0F (0–15).

10

Keyboard Procedures

The Commodore 128 keyboard assembly not only provides an avenue for entering data and programs into the system, but can also serve as an elaborate, multiple-switch assembly for controlling the execution of programs. Most keys have prescribed dedicated applications when the system is running in BASIC, the monitor, or CP/M: getting text to the screen and setting up commands of all kinds. In a very real sense, the keyboard is the user's primary input link with the computer system. It is in fact the system's default input device, device number 0.

The keyboard is part of a very flexible, but basically simple, scheme. You can do plenty of good programming without knowing much about the inner workings of the keyboard system. However, knowing a bit about how it works and how the operating systems use it goes a long way toward preparing even better programs.

Keyboard Scanning Operations

The keyboard scheme for the Commodore 128 is based on the 11 x 8 keyboard matrix illustrated in Figure 10-1. Any one of the keys shown on the diagram can be specified in terms of the column-row coordinate.

The Kernal's SCNKEY routine scans that matrix to determine whether a key is pressed at the moment. If so, this routine determines its matrix coordinate according to values in CIA #1, registers $DC00 and $DC01. SCNKEY is an integral part of the system's normal IRQ interrupt handler, so the operation automatically takes place 60 times a second.

Unless you are prepared to write your own interrupt-handler, there is little point in trying to deal directly with the keyboard matrix and the CIA registers. It is far simpler and more convenient to allow the normal IRQ handler to do its job and work with the SFDX register at zero-page $D4 (212).

The SFDX register is organized according to the diagram in Figure 10-2. The row value from the keyboard matrix occupies bits 0 through 2, whereas the column value occupies bits 3 through 7.

The H key, for example, is located at row 5, column 3 in the keyboard matrix. Therefore, if you happen to be pressing the H key, SCNKEY returns a binary 101 (decimal 5) for the row component and binary 00011 (decimal 3) for the column component. The operation thus loads binary 00011101 to the SFDX register. The hexadecimal and decimal versions of that value are $1D and 29, respectively. And that value is readily accessible from the SFDX register.

When no key is pressed, SCNKEY is ultimately responsible for loading $58 (88) to SFDX.

Figure 10-3 shows the hexadecimal and decimal values found in SFDX as the result of pressing most of the keys included in the keyboard matrix assembly. You can confirm the information in the figure

Fig. 10-1 Column-row keyboard matrix for the Commodore 128. Keys that do not appear on this diagram are handled in a different manner

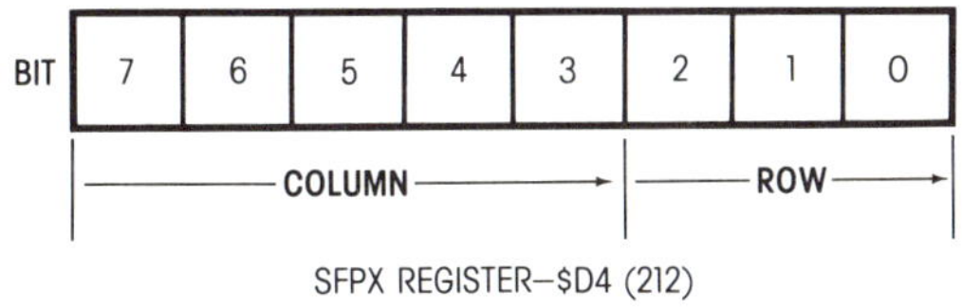

Fig. 10-2 Organization of the SFPX register in terms of column-row values from the keyboard matrix

by running the short program in Listing 10-1 and pressing the desired keys. End the program by striking the STOP key.

Listing 10-1

```
10 A=PEEK(212)
20 PRINT "$";RIGHT$(HEX$(A),2);A
30 GOTO 10
```

Six keys in the keyboard matrix do not appear as unique values in SFDX: the two SHIFT keys ($0F and $34), CONTROL ($3A), C=($3D), and ALT ($50). These keys are actually scanned separately by the nor-

Fig. 10-3 Hexadecimal and decimal values that appear in the SPFX register as a result of the given key presses

Key Code		Key	Key Code		Key	Key Code		Key
Hex	Dec		Hex	Dec		Hex	Dec	
$00	0	INST DEL	$19	25	Y	$32	50	] ;
$01	1	RETURN	$1A	26	G	$33	51	CLR HOME
$02	2	← CRSR →	$1B	27	(8	$34	52	
$03	3	F7	$1C	28	B	$35	53	=
$04	4	F1	$1D	29	H	$36	54	↑
$05	5	F3	$1E	30	U	$37	55	? /
$06	6	F5	$1F	31	V	$38	56	! 1
$07	7	↑ CRSR ↓	$20	32	) 9	$39	57	←
$08	8	# 3	$21	33	I	$3A	58	
$09	9	W	$22	34	J	$3B	59	" 2
$0A	10	A	$23	35	0	$3C	60	SPACE BAR
$0B	11	4	$24	36	M	$3D	61	
$0C	12	Z	$25	37	K	$3E	62	Q
$0D	13	S	$26	38	O	$3F	63	
$0E	14	E	$27	39	N	$40	64	HELP
$0F	15		$28	40	+	$41	65	8
$10	16	% 5	$29	41	P	$42	66	5
$11	17	R	$2A	42	L	$43	67	TAB
$12	18	D	$2B	43	−	$44	68	2
$13	19	& 6	$2C	44	> .	$45	69	4
$14	20	C	$2D	45	[:	$46	70	7
$15	21	F	$2E	46	@	$47	71	1
$16	22	T	$2F	47	< ,	$48	72	ESC
$17	23	X	$30	48	£	$49	73	+
$18	24	' 7	$31	49	*	$4A	74	−

Fig. 10-3 (cont.)

Key Code Hex	Key Code Dec	Key	Key Code Hex	Key Code Dec	Key	Key Code Hex	Key Code Dec	Key
$4B	75	LINE FEED	$50	80		$56	86	→
$4C	76	ENTER	$51	81	0	$57	87	NO SCROLL
			$52	82	.	$58	88	
$4D	77	6	$53	83	↑			
$4E	78	9	$54	84	↓			
$4F	79	3	$55	85	←			

= GRAY KEY

= CALCULATOR KEYPAD

Fig. 10-4 Summary of SHFL6 values that appear as a result of pressing the SHIFT, C=, CONTROL, and ALT keys

Key: SHIFT	C=	CONTROL	ALT	SHFLG–$D3 Hex	Dec
Up	Up	Up	Up	$00	0
Down	Up	Up	Up	$01	1
Up	Down	Up	Up	$02	2
Down	Down	Up	Up	$03	3
Up	Up	Down	Up	$04	4
Down	Up	Down	Up	$05	5
Up	Down	Down	Up	$06	6
Down	Down	Down	Up	$07	7
Up	Up	Up	Down	$08	8
Down	Up	Up	Down	$09	9
Up	Down	Up	Down	$0A	10
Down	Down	Up	Down	$0B	11
Up	Up	Down	Down	$0C	12
Down	Up	Down	Down	$0D	13
Up	Down	Down	Down	$0E	14
Down	Down	Down	Down	$0F	15

mal IRQ interrupt handler. Codes indicating the status of these keys appear in the SHFLG register at $D3 (211). See Figure 10-4.

SFDX indicates which of the basic keys is pressed and SHFLG indicates the current combination of SHIFT, C=, CONTROL, and ALT keys. Given those two registers, you can determine any combination of keystrokes. While you are pressing a CONTROL-H for example, SFDX holds $1D (29) and SHFLG holds $04 (4).

The BASIC routine in Listing 10-2 prints HELLO on the screen until the user does a custom keyboard operation—hold down the CONTROL and SHIFT keys while pressing the X key:

Listing 10-2

```
10 PRINT "HELLO ";
20 IF PEEK(211)=5 AND PEEK(212)=23 THEN END
30 GOTO 10
```

The combination of SFPX and SHFLG clearly suggests a great deal of flexibility with regard to programming keyboard control operations.

Working with the Non-Scanned Keys

Several keys are absent from the keyboard matrix: CAPS LOCK, 40/80 DISPLAY, SHIFT LOCK, and RESTORE. These keys are handled in different fashion from the others.

The current status of the CAPS LOCK key can be found in bit 6 of the R8510 register at $01 (1): 0 = key latched down, 1 = key up. You can check the status with a BASIC statement of this form:

```
PRINT PEEK(1) AND 64
```

This statement returns a value of 0 if the CAPS LOCK key is latched down and a value of 64 if it is up.

The flag for the 40/80 DISPLAY key is located at bit 7 in the MMU register at $D505 (54533): 0 = switch latched down, 1 = up. You can check the status with the following BASIC statement:

```
PRINT PEEK(54533) AND 128
```

It returns a value of 0 if the switch is latched down (80-column display) and 128 if it is up (40-column display).

The RESTORE key is connected to CIA #2 and is checked as part of the systems NMI interrupt routine. The SHIFT LOCK key is simply a push-on/push-off toggle switch that is connected in parallel with the SHIFT keys.

Using the Keyboard Queue and GETIN

The system's keyboard queue is a small, 10-byte buffer located from $034A through $0353 (842–851). The primary purpose is to hold keycodes that are arriving from the keyboard until they are dispatched in some fashion.

Keyboard character codes in the queue are handled on a first-in, first-out basis. A byte pointer, NDX at $D0 (208), points to the last character in the current queue or, from a different point of view, the pointer indicates the number of pending characters. Putting a new keyboard character into the queue advances NDX. Removing a character reduces the value of NDX.

The simplest way to reach the contents of the keyboard queue is by executing the Kernal's GETIN routine at $FFE4 (65508). As long as at least one character remains in the queue, GETIN pulls out the first character, places it in register A of the microprocessor and reduces the value of NDX. When the queue is empty, GETIN returns $00.

The keycodes in the keyboard queue are quite a bit different from those fetched from SFPX, however. Instead of being codes that indicate the column-row coordinate of a pressed key, the codes in the keyboard queue are adjusted according to the Commodore 128's ASCII character format shown in Figure 10-5.

Fig. 10-5 Hexadecimal and decimal keycodes that appear in the keyboard queue and main keyboard buffer

The first column indicates the key. The remaining columns show keycodes when the key is pressed alone, with the SHIFT key, with the CONTROL key, and with the C= key

Key	Alone		SHIFT		CONTROL		C=	
←	$5F	95	$5F	95	$06	6	$5F	95
1	$31	49	$21	33	$90	144	$81	129
2	$32	50	$22	34	$05	5	$95	149
3	$33	51	$23	35	$1C	28	$96	150
4	$34	52	$24	36	$9F	159	$97	151
5	$35	53	$25	37	$9C	156	$98	152
6	$36	54	$26	38	$1E	30	$99	153
7	$37	55	$27	39	$1F	31	$9A	154
8	$38	56	$28	40	$9E	158	$9B	155
9	$39	57	$29	41	$12	18	$29	41
0	$30	48	$30	48	$92	146	$30	48
+	$2B	43	$DB	219	$00	0	$A6	166
−	$2D	45	$DD	221	$00	0	$DC	220
£	$5C	92	$A9	169	$1C	28	$A8	168
CLR HOME	$13	19	$93	147	$00	0	$93	147
INST DEL	$14	20	$94	148	$00	0	$94	148
Q	$51	81	$D1	209	$11	17	$AB	171
W	$57	87	$D7	215	$17	23	$B3	179

Fig. 10-5 (cont.)

Key	Alone		SHIFT		CONTROL		C=	
E	$45	69	$C5	197	$05	5	$B1	177
R	$52	82	$D2	210	$12	18	$B2	178
T	$54	84	$D4	212	$14	20	$A3	163
Y	$59	89	$D9	217	$19	25	$B7	183
U	$55	85	$D5	213	$15	21	$B8	184
I	$49	73	$C9	201	$09	9	$A2	162
O	$4F	79	$CF	207	$0F	15	$B9	185
P	$50	80	$D0	208	$10	16	$AF	175
@	$40	64	$BA	186	$00	0	$A4	164
*	$2A	42	$C0	192	$00	0	$DF	223
↑	$5E	94	$DE	222	$1E	30	$DE	222
RUN STOP	$03	3	$83	131	$03	3	$03	3
A	$41	65	$C1	193	$01	1	$B0	176
S	$53	83	$D3	211	$13	19	$AE	174
D	$44	68	$C4	196	$04	4	$AC	172
F	$46	70	$C6	198	$06	6	$BB	187
G	$47	71	$C7	199	$07	7	$A5	165
H	$48	72	$C8	200	$08	8	$B4	180
J	$4A	74	$CA	202	$0A	10	$B5	181
K	$4B	75	$CB	203	$0B	11	$A1	161
L	$4C	76	$CC	204	$0C	12	$B6	182
[:	$3A	58	$5B	91	$1B	27	$5B	91

Fig. 10-5 (cont.)

Key	Alone		SHIFT		CONTROL		C=	
] ;	$3B	59	$5D	93	$1D	29	$5D	93
=	$3D	61	$3D	61	$1F	31	$3D	61
RETURN	$0D	13	$8D	141	$00	0	$8D	141
Z	$5A	90	$DA	218	$1A	26	$AD	173
X	$58	88	$D8	216	$18	24	$BD	189
C	$43	67	$C3	195	$03	3	$BC	188
V	$56	86	$D6	214	$16	22	$BE	190
B	$42	66	$C2	194	$02	2	$BF	191
N	$4E	78	$CE	206	$0E	14	$AA	170
M	$4D	77	$CD	205	$0D	13	$A7	167
< ,	$2C	44	$3C	60	$00	0	$3C	60
> .	$2E	46	$3E	62	$00	0	$3E	62
? /	$2F	47	$3F	63	$00	0	$3F	63
↑ CRSR ↓	$11	17	$91	145	$00	0	$91	145
← CRSR →	$1D	29	$9D	157	$00	0	$9D	157
SPACE BAR	$20	32	$A0	160	$00	0	$A0	160
1	$31	49	$31	49	$31	49	$31	49
2	$32	50	$32	50	$32	50	$32	50
3	$33	51	$33	51	$33	51	$33	51
4	$34	52	$34	52	$34	52	$34	52
5	$35	53	$35	53	$35	53	$35	53
6	$36	54	$36	54	$36	54	$36	54

Fig. 10-5 (cont.)

Key	Alone		SHIFT		CONTROL		C=	
7	$37	55	$37	55	$37	55	$37	55
8	$38	56	$38	56	$38	56	$38	56
9	$39	57	$39	57	$39	57	$39	57
0	$30	48	$30	48	$30	48	$30	48
.	$2E	46	$2E	46	$2E	46	$2E	46
+	$2B	43	$2B	43	$2B	43	$2B	43
−	$2D	45	$2D	45	$2D	45	$2D	45
ENTER	$0D	13	$8D	141	$8D	141	$8D	141
ESC	$1B	27	$1B	27	$1B	27	$1B	27
TAB	$09	9	$18	24	$18	24	$18	24
HELP	$84	132	$84	132	$84	132	$84	132
LINE FEED	$0A	10	$0A	10	$0A	10	$0A	10
NO SCROLL								
↑	$91	145	$91	145	$91	145	$91	145
↓	$11	17	$11	17	$11	17	$11	17
←	$9D	157	$9D	157	$9D	157	$9D	157
→	$1D	29	$1D	29	$1D	29	$1D	29
F1	$85	133	$89	137	$00	0	$89	137
F3	$86	134	$8A	138	$00	0	$8A	138
F5	$87	135	$8B	139	$00	0	$8B	139
F7	$88	136	$8C	140	$00	0	$8C	140

You can use the hybrid routine in Listing 10-3 to confirm the codes returned from the keyboard queue. Use the C= key to slow down the rate of listing and the STOP key to break out of the program.

Listing 10-3

```
10 FOR K=0 TO 5
20 READ D:POKE 3072+K,D
30 NEXT K
40 DATA 32,228,255,133,250,96
50 SYS 3072
60 A=PEEK(250)
70 PRINT "$";RIGHT$(HEX$(A),2);A
80 GOTO 50
```

Lines 10–40—Load the following machine language routine that fetches a character from the keyboard queue and saves it in zero-page register $FA (250):

```
F0C00  JSR $FFE4   ;CALL GETIN
F0C03  STA $FA     ;SAVE KEY IN $FA (250)
F0C05  RTS         ;RETURN TO BASIC
```

Line 50—Call the machine-language routine.

Line 60—Fetch the character code from $FA (250).

Line 70—Print the hexadecimal and decimal versions of the key code.

Line 80—Repeat until you press the STOP key.

A lot of internal processing takes place between the time you press a key and the corresponding codes appear in the keyboard queue. Pressing the function keys, F1 through F8 and the HELP key, does not print a simple keycode. Rather they stack the queue with the sequence of ASCII characters that spell out the command. Strike the F1 key, for example, and you see hexadecimal values 47, 52, 41, 50, 48, 49, and 43. Look up those codes in Table 10-5 and you will see that the sequence spells out GRAPHIC—the command normally assigned to function key F1.

Keycodes in the queue also take into account the influences of the SHIFT, CONTROL, and C= key. You don't have to refer to the SHFLG.

Keyboard entries resulting from BASIC's INPUT, GET, and GETKEY functions also use the keyboard queue but only on a pass-through basis. Such characters pass through the queue on their way to the systems major keyboard buffer described in the next section of this chapter.

Machine language counterparts of BASIC's GETKEY and GET functions take advantage of the keyboard scanning feature of the normal IRQ handler, the keyboard queue, and the Kernal's GETIN routine. The following example halts the execution of a program until the user enters a prescribed keystroke—CONTROL-X in this case:

```
FETCH   JSR $FFE4     ;CALL GETIN
        CMP #$18      ;CONTROL-X?
        BNE FETCH     ;IF NOT, FETCH AGAIN
        RTS           ;ELSE RETURN
```

The next example in Listing 10-4 emulates BASIC's GETKEY function by carrying out one series of operations until the user presses a specified key. The key in this instance is upper- or lowercase Y.

Listing 10-4

```
        LDA #$00      ;MAKE SURE THE KEYBOARD
        STA $D0       ;QUEUE IS EMPTY
LOOP    LDA #$40      ;@ CHARACTER
        JSR $FFD2     ;PRINT IT
        JSR $FFE4     ;GETIN
        CMP #$59      ;UPPERCASE Y?
        BEQ END       ;IF SO, END
        CMP #$D9      ;LOWERCASE Y?
        BNE LOOP      ;IF NOT, PRINT AGAIN
END     RTS           ;RETURN
```

Do not type the semicolons and any text following them when entering this routine through the miniassembler.

Using the Main Keyboard Buffer

The system's main keyboard buffer is a block of 161 bytes of RAM between $0200 and $02A1 (512–673). Virtually all characters typed at the keyboard are stacked into this buffer until certain kinds of actions dispatch the information elsewhere.

The main keyboard buffer is quite different from the simpler keyboard queue in several respects. One of the most obvious differences is that the main keyboard buffer is much larger—161 bytes as opposed to just 10. That fact leads to another major difference: the Kernal's GETIN routine not only fetches bytes from the queue but empties it as it goes along. Fetching bytes from the main keyboard buffer does not empty the queue. The data remains intact until the next keyboard operation writes new bytes over it.

Because the current sequence of keyboard codes simply writes over previous ones in the main keyboard buffer, it tends to become a messy warehouse of new and old information—bits and pieces of previous keyboard entries. However, the most recent entry always begins at the first location in the buffer and extends to the first occurrence of a $00 byte.

> *NOTE:* The current string in the main keyboard buffer begins at address $0200 (512) and extends to the first occurrence of a $00 (0) data byte.

Direct-mode keyboard operations insert the characters into the main keyboard buffer until the user presses the RETURN key. The system then inserts the 0—the end-of-string marker—at the end of the entry. Keyboard operations in response to BASIC's INPUT statement work the same way.

Other keyboard operations, such as those for BASIC's GET and GETKEY, also push a character into the main keyboard buffer. However, because they are single-key operations, the system accepts the character, inserts the 0 marker, and immediately dispatches the character to the designated string variable.

The main keyboard buffer is an attractive place to enter sequences of keystrokes required for machine language programs. A keyboard input routine at $4F93 (20371) makes it easy to enter characters from the keyboard into the main keyboard buffer. The routine shows the blinking cursor, accepts editing operations, and ends only when the user presses the RETURN key.

The machine language program in Listing 10-5 accepts the user's input from the keyboard and places it into the main keyboard buffer. After the user ends the entry procedure by pressing the RETURN key, the program copies the data into another block of RAM that begins at $1400.

Listing 10-5

```
        LDA #$93     ;CLEAR THE SCREEN AND
        JSR $FFD2    ;HOME THE CURSOR
        JSR $4F93    ;GET THE KEYBOARD INPUT
        LDY #$00     ;SET THE TRANSFER POINTER
NEXT    LDA $0200,Y  ;GET A CHARACTER
        STA $1400,Y  ;TRANSFER IT
        BNE NEXT     ;IF NOT DONE, XFER NEXT
        RTS          ;ELSE RETURN
```

Do not type the semicolons and any text following them when entering this routine through the miniassembler.

Using the Function Keys

The Commodore 128 features ten function-key operations. Pressing function keys F1, F3, F5, and F7 invoke functions 1, 3, 5, and 8. Holding down the SHIFT key while pressing those same keys invokes functions 2, 4, 6, and 8. The two remaining functions are related to the HELP key and SHIFT-RUN/STOP.

All ten function-key operations do their jobs by emulating commands the user would otherwise enter directly from the keyboard. Pressing the HELP key, for example, replaces the keyboard operation of typing HELP and pressing the RETURN key.

The function key commands are executed from a definition table located in a 246-byte block of RAM, $100A–$10FF (4106–4351). Examining this block shows the following default function-key assignments:

F1—GRAPHIC

F2—DLOAD"

F3—DIRECTORY <RETURN>

F4—SCNCLR <RETURN>

F5—DSAVE"

F6—RUN <RETURN>

F7—LIST <RETURN>

F8—MONITOR <RETURN>

SHIFT-RUN/STOP (Function 9)—Dp"* <RETURN>
RUN <RETURN>

HELP (Function 10)—HELP <RETURN>

BASIC's KEY statement makes rather easy the changing of functions assigned to keys F1 through F8. See the description of that statement in Chapter 2. Any of the ten functions can be changed by taking advantage of a Kernal routine accessed from $FF65 (65381).

The general procedure for altering any of the key functions is

1. Write the text for the desired function to a convenient location in RAM.
2. Write the LSB, MSB, and bank number of the text into three consecutive zero-page addresses.
3. Load the starting address of the zero-page locations to register A.
4. Load the function key number (1–10) to register X.
5. Load the number of characters in the text to register Y.
6. Call the Kernal routine at $FF65 (65381).

The Kernal routine must be used for altering the function-key assignments because the operation requires more than simply loading the desired text codes to the function-key assignment block. The problem is that all ten function-key assignments must be arranged in their numerical order and back-to-back in the RAM block. This means all new function-key assignments, except for function 10, require adjusting the RAM location of all the higher-numbered assignments.

The default function assigned to the SHIFT-RUN/STOP key can be annoying because it immediately loads the first disk file in the current directory. Accidentally making this keystroke wipes out any BASIC programming in the system at the time. The example in Listing 10-6 uses the general function-change procedure to change that key function to something less drastic—sounding the bell.

Listing 10-6

```
10 C$=CHR$(7)+CHR$(13)
20 FOR K=0 TO LEN(C$)
30 POKE 3072+K,ASC(MID$(C$,K+1,1))
40 NEXT K
50 POKE 250,0:POKE 251,12:POKE 252,15
60 SYS 65381,250,9,LEN(C$)
```

Line 10—Define the key function (sound the bell).

Lines 20–40—Load the text for the function, beginning from address 3072 ($0C00).

Line 50—Specify the address of the text:

LSB of the address to 250
MSB of the address to 251
Bank number to 252

Line 60—Call the Kernal at 65381 after, setting:

Address 250 to register A
Function number to register X
Length of function text to register Y

Listing 10-7 is an assembly language version of the same routine that looks like this:

Listing 10-7

```
             ;LOAD THE BELL COMMAND AT $C000
LDA #$07     ;BELL CHAR
STA $C000    ;TO $C000
LDA #$0D     ;CR CHAR
STA $C001    ;TO $C001
             ;SET UP ZERO-PAGE LOCATIONS
LDA #$00     ;LSB OF CHAR ADDRESS
STA $FA      ;TO $FA
LDA #$0C     ;MSB OF CHAR ADDRESS
STA $FB      ;TO $FB
LDA #$0F     ;BANK 15
STA $FC      ;TO $FC
```

Listing 10-7 (cont.)

```
        ;SET THE REGISTERS AND CALL
LDA #$FA        ;FIRST Z-P ADDRESS
LDX #$09        ;FUNCTION KEY 9
LDY #$02        ;NUMBER OF CHARS
JSR $FF65       ;CALL THE KERNAL ROUTINE
RTS             ;RETURN
```

Do not type the semicolons and any text following them when entering this routine through the miniassembler.

The general procedure for restoring the default function-key assignments involves copying the ROM version, $CEA8-$CEF4, to the function-key RAM table $1000-$104C.

A BASIC version of the procedure looks like this:

```
10 FOR K=0 TO 76
20 POKE 4096+K,PEEK(52904+K)
30 NEXT K
```

See Listing 10-8 for an assembly language implementation of the same operation.

Listing 10-8

```
        LDX #$4C        ;SET XFER POINTER TO 76 BYTES
XFER    LDA $CEA8,X     ;GET BYTE FROM ROM
        STA $1000,X     ;SAVE TO RAM
        DEX             ;DECREMENT THE POINTER
        BPL XFER        ;IF NOT DONE, XFER ANOTHER
        RTS             ;ELSE END
```

Do not type the semicolons and any text following them when entering this routine through the miniassembler.

11

Joystick, Paddle, Light Pen, and Mouse Procedures

Joysticks and game paddles have been a part of personal computing from the very beginning. Light pens have been used with business and scientific computing systems for several decades and are just now beginning to find their way into personal computing. The mouse is relatively new but is catching on fast.

These four peripheral devices have something in common as far as the Commodore 128 is concerned—they all use the same built-in device called CIA #1 (one of the complex interface adapters).

BASIC 7.0 deals directly with the joystick, paddles, and pen with its JOY, POT and PEN functions. No special BASIC functions exist for the mouse, but currently available information suggests that a mouse can be treated as a joystick function.

Joystick and game-paddle products and software routines are well-developed for the Commodore personal computers. This chapter describes BASIC and machine-language routines. Unfortunately, the Commodore 128 products and software documentation for the light pen and mouse are scanty at the time of this writing. Instead of guessing or attempting to generalize such information from Commodore's Amiga computer, we have decided to omit further references to light pen and mouse procedures. You will simply have to keep an eye open for developments described in future periodicals and books.

Joystick Procedures

The Commodore 128 can use up to two joystick assemblies at one time. They are plugged into the controller ports. The assembly plugged into port 1 is designated joystick 1, and the one plugged into port 2 is designated joystick 2.

As illustrated in Figure 11-1, the joystick hardware is configured so that it has nine discernible positions. The center position is labeled 0, straight right is 3, straight down is 5, down-right is 4, and so on.

Each joystick assembly also includes a "fire" pushbutton.

Fig. 11-1 Joystick positions and values returned by BASIC's JOY(*n*) function

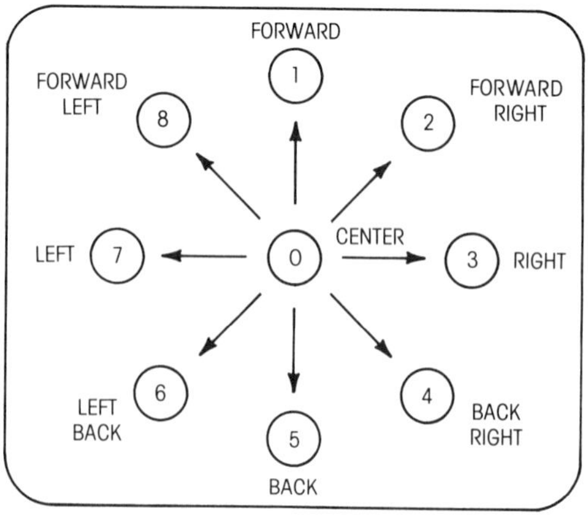

Using BASIC's JOY Function

BASIC's JOY function returns decimal numeric values that indicate the current joystick position—the same values shown in Figure 11-1. The general form of the function is:

JOY(*n*)

where *n* specifies one of the two joysticks, 1 or 2.

Regarding the "fire" pushbutton, the JOY function also returns values that indicate whether or not that button is pressed. When the pushbutton is pressed, JOY returns the stick-position values plus 128. Thus, if the stick is centered, but the pushbutton pressed, JOY returns a value of 0 + 128, or 128. If the stick is pushed to the right and the button is pressed, JOY returns a value of 7 + 128, or 135.

The program in Listing 11-1 prints values indicating the positions of the joysticks and an asterisk whenever the corresponding pushbutton is pressed. The program also uses the pushbuttons as control devices. Line 10, for instance, keeps the program in a "do-nothing" loop until a player presses the pushbutton on joystick 1. Once the program is started, it is ended only when both players press their respective pushbuttons at the same time.

Listing 11-1

```
10 IF JOY(1)<128 THEN 10
20 IF JOY(1)>=128 THEN J1=JOY(1)-128:B1$="*":ELSE B1$=""
30 IF JOY(2)>=128 THEN J2=JOY(2)-128:B2$="*":ELSE B2$=""
40 PRINT J1;B1$,J2;B2$
50 IF JOY(1)>=128 AND JOY(2)>=128 THEN END:ELSE GOTO 20
```

Working with the Joystick Registers

Working with joystick registers requires a somewhat different view of the joystick assembly. Figure 11-2 shows five switches. Four are operated by the stick and one by the pushbutton. For all practical purposes, these switches are connected directly to the five lower-order bit locations in two registers in CIA#1: $DC00 (56320) and $DC01 (56321).

You need to know that the switches and register bits are configured so that the bit value is 1 when a switch is *not* activated, and the bit takes on a value of 0 when the switch is activated.

JOYSTICK 1 Bits Reading from these bit locations completely defines the status of joystick 1.

Address: **$DC00 (56320)**

Fig. 11-2 Joystick switch positions

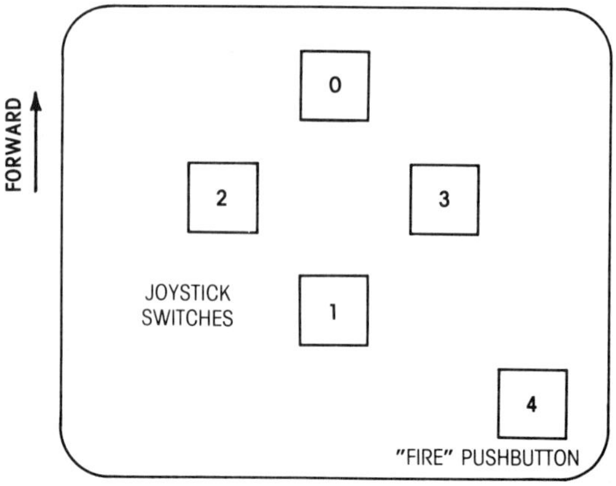

Data: 1 = switch open
0 = switch closed

Bit 0 = Joystick position switch 0
Bit 1 = Joystick position switch 1
Bit 2 = Joystick position switch 2
Bit 3 = Joystick position switch 3
Bit 4 = Pushbutton

JOYSTICK 2 Bits Reading from these bit locations completely defines the status of joystick 2.

Address: $DC01 (56321)
Data: 1 = switch open
0 = switch closed

Bit 0 = Joystick position switch 0
Bit 1 = Joystick position switch 1
Bit 2 = Joystick position switch 2
Bit 3 = Joystick position switch 3
Bit 4 = Pushbutton

Determining the position of joystick 1 is thus a matter of PEEKing into its register and isolating the four lower-order bits. Such a statement returns the decimal stick-position values shown in Table 11-1. For example:

```
J1=PEEK(56320) AND 15
```

Determining the status of the joystick pushbutton calls for PEEKing into the register and isolating bit 4. The result is either 0 or 16—0 if the button is pressed and 16 if it is not. That kind of operation can be done this way:

```
B1=PEEK(56320) AND 16
```

Table 11-1
Values Returned in Joystick Registers

Binary 3 2 1 0	Values Hex	Dec	Position
0 0 0 0	$0	0	—
0 0 0 1	$1	1	—
0 0 1 0	$2	2	—
0 0 1 1	$3	3	—
0 1 0 0	$4	4	—
0 1 0 1	$5	5	RIGHT, DOWN
0 1 1 0	$6	6	RIGHT, UP
0 1 1 1	$7	7	RIGHT
1 0 0 0	$8	8	—
1 0 0 1	$9	9	LEFT, DOWN
1 0 1 0	$A	10	LEFT, UP
1 0 1 1	$B	11	LEFT
1 1 0 0	$C	12	—
1 1 0 1	$D	13	DOWN
1 1 1 0	$E	14	UP
1 1 1 1	$F	15	CENTER

The same general procedure applies for machine language programs that use the joysticks. The example in Listing 11-2 carries matters a step further, however, by working the joystick-reading procedure into the IRQ interrupt handler. Once you execute the routine, zero-page registers $FA and $FB carry the five switch bits for joysticks 1 and 2, respectively. The advantage is that the system updates the status every 1/60th of a second, whether any other programming is running or not.

Listing 11-2

```
0D00   SEI            ;SET INTERRUPT DISABLE
0D01   LDA #$0D       ;LSB OF NEW IRQ
0D03   STA $0314      ;TO IRQ LSB VECTOR
0D06   LDA #$0D       ;MSB OF NEW IRQ
0D08   STA $0315      ;TO IRQ MSB VECTOR
0D0B   CLI            ;CLEAR INTERRUPT DISABLE
0D0C   RTS
0D0D   LDA $DC00      ;FETCH BYTE FOR JOY 1
0D10   AND #$1F       ;ISOLATE LOWER 5 BITS
0D12   STA $FA        ;SAVE TO REGISTER $FA
0D14   LDA $DC01      ;FETCH BYTE FOR JOY 2
0D17   AND #$1F       ;ISOLATE LOWER 5 BITS
0D19   STA $FB        ;SAVE TO REGISTER $FB
0D1B   JMP $FA65      ;JUMP TO NORMAL IRQ
```

Game Paddle Procedures

A single paddle assembly consists of a dial (actually a variable resistor) and a "fire" pushbutton. The Commodore 128 can work with four such assemblies at the same time—two at each of the controller ports.

Using BASIC's POT Function

BASIC's POT function returns decimal values proportional to the amount of turn on the dial. Assuming that the pushbutton is not pressed, the range of values is from 0 through 255—the larger the value, the greater the amount of clockwise turn. The same idea applies when the pushbutton is pressed but the values are increased by 256.

The general form of the function is:

POT(*n*)

where *n* specifies one of the four game paddles, 1 through 4.

The example in Listing 11-3 prints values indicating the positions of the dials on the four paddles. An asterisk beside the values indicates the corresponding "fire" pushbutton is pressed. The program runs in an endless loop, so you should do a STOP keystroke to end it.

Listing 11-3

```
10 FOR K=1 TO 4
20 J(K)=POT(K)
30 B$(K)="":IF J(K)255 THEN J(K)=-256:B$(K)="*"
40 PRINT J(K);B$(K),
50 NEXT K
60 PRINT
70 GOTO 10
```

Working with the "Pot" Registers

To read the game paddles from a machine language routine, you must work directly with the I/O format of CIA #1. The procedures described here are specified only in terms of hexadecimal notation. The reason is that one can POKE and PEEK the addresses but never obtain reliable results.

The procedure and example cited in the following text assume that you want to read all four pot positions and the status of all four "fire" pushbuttons.

1. Disable interrupts to freeze the A/D conversion for the pot values.
2. Save the current CIA#1 status so that its IRQ keyboard operations are not disrupted when the interrupts are enabled at the conclusion of the routine.
3. Set the data direction register, $DC02, for inputs from the pot lines, bits 6 and 7.
4. Write $80 to Port A register, $DC00, to read pots 1 and 3.
5. Do a short delay.
6. Fetch and save the positions of pots 1 and 3. Read from SID addresses $D419 and $D41A and save in available RAM.
7. Fetch the "fire" button status for buttons 1 and 3. Read from bits 2 and 3 of $DC00, shift them to bits 0 and 1, and mask them off. Save the result in available RAM.
8. Write $40 to Port A register, $DC00, to read pots 2 and 4.
9. Do a short delay.
10. Fetch and save the positions of pots 2 and 4. Read from SID addresses $D419 and $D41A and save in available RAM.
11. Fetch the "fire" button status for buttons 2 and 4. Read from bits 2 and 3 of $DC01, shift them to bits 0 and 1, and mask them off. Save the result in available RAM.
12. Fetch the original CIA#1 direction byte (saved in Step 2) and restore it to $DC02.
13. Enable interrupts.
14. Use the pot and pushbutton data as desired.

The routine in Listing 11-4 is a direct implementation of the procedure. It requires no set-up, but leaves the status of the paddles and buttons in the following address locations:

Paddle 1 position—**$0D02**
Paddle 2 position—**$0D01**
Paddle 3 position—**$0D04**
Paddle 4 position—**$0D03**
Button 1—Bit 0 of **$0D05**
Button 2—Bit 0 of **$0D06**
Button 3—Bit 1 of **$0D05**
Button 4—Bit 1 of **$0D06**

Listing 11-4

```
POTS SEI          ;DISABLE INTERRUPTS
     LDA $DC02    ;GET CURRENT DATA DIRECTION FOR PORT A
     STA $0D00    ;SAVE IT
     LDA #$C0     ;SPECIFY INPUT LINES 6 AND 7
     STA $DC02    ;SET THE INPUTS
     LDA #$80     ;SPECIFY UNIT A (POTS 1 AND 3)
     STA $DC00    ;ADDRESS THEM
     JSR DELY     ;DO A TIME DELAY
     LDA $D419    ;GET POT 1
     STA $0D02    ;SAVE IT
     LDA $D41A    ;GET POT 3
     STA $0D04    ;SAVE IT
     LDA $DC00    ;GET BUTTON STATUS FOR POTS 1 AND 3
     JSR SHFT     ;ISOLATE THE BUTTON BITS
     STA $0D05    ;SAVE BUTTON STATUS
     LDA #$40     ;SPECIFY UNIT B (POTS 2 AND 4)
     STA $DC00    ;ADDRESS THEM
     JSR DELY     ;DO A TIME DELAY
     LDA $D419    ;GET POT 2
     STA $0D01    ;SAVE IT
     LDA $D41A    ;GET POT 4
     STA $0D03    ;SAVE IT
     LDA $DC01    ;GET BUTTON STATUS FOR POTS 2 AND 4
     JSR SHFT     ;ISOLATE THE BUTTON BITS
     STA $0D06    ;SAVE BUTTON STATUS
     LDA $0D00    ;GET OLD DIRECTION
     STA $DC02    ;RESTORE IT
     CLI
     RTS

DELY LDY #$80
     DEY
     BPL          DELY
     RTS

SHFT ROR          ;SHIFT BITS 2 AND 3
     ROR          ;TO 0 AND 1
     AND #$03     ;ISOLATE BITS 0 AND 1
     RTS
```

12

Printer and Communications Procedures

The Commodore operating system does not include any commands specifically tailored for printer and communications (RS-232-C) operations. Rather, the system regards all ports as serial and deals with them in terms of serial-port commands such as OPEN, CLOSE, PRINT#, and so on.

Printer Procedures

A printer is a powerful accessory for personal computer systems because it makes possible the generation of permanent printouts of virtually anything that can be printed to the screen. The simplest printer arrangement uses one of the printers manufactured specifically for Commodore computers.

The printer should be daisy-chained from the computer's serial port and through other serial devices, such as disk drives, as shown in Figure 12-1. Other brands of printers use the same general connections but require a special adapter unit that should be available through your Commodore dealer.

Fig. 12-1 A daisy-chain arrangement from the serial port on the console through a disk drive and to a Commodore printer

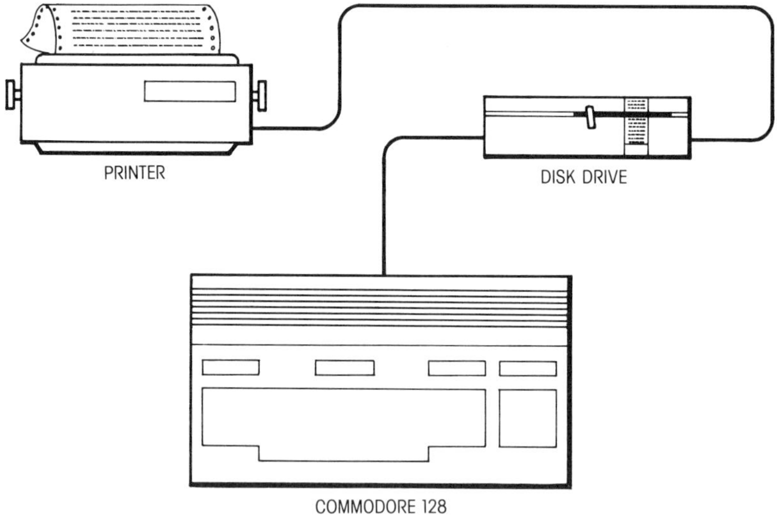

BASIC Commands for Printer Operations

Commodore 128 regards a printer as a serial output device: usually device number 4. So you don't need special commands because the usual serial output commands—OPEN, CLOSE, PRINT#, and CMD—are wholly adequate.

The OPEN statement, as applied to printer operations, looks like this:

OPEN *filenum*,4,*set*

The *filenum* parameter specifies the file number for information to be directed to the printer. As with any other application of the command, *filenum* can be any integer value between 1 and 255 that isn't currently used by any other file. The *set* parameter specifies whether a Commodore printer will use the uppercase/graphics character set (*set* = 0) or the uppercase/lowercase set (*set* = 1).

The following example opens a file for the printer, using file number 1 and specifying the uppercase/graphics character set:

```
OPEN 1,4,0
```

Once a file is open for the printer, use PRINT# statements to direct material to the printer. The general form is:

PRINT#*filenum*,*text*

The *filenum* parameter must be the same file number that was used for opening the printer file, and *text* is any numeric or string constant, variable, or expression.

The following example prints HELLO to the printer, assuming that the file was previously opened as file number 1:

```
PRINT#1,"HELLO"
```

When your printer operations are done, you must close the printer channel this way:

CLOSE *filenum*

where *filenum* is the file number you originally used for opening the printer file.

Listing 12-1 shows a couple of simple examples. The first example opens file 1 to the printer and directs the string constant, HELLO, to it. The second opens file 2 to the printer and uses a FOR. . .NEXT loop to print numerals 0 through 9.

Listing 12-1

```
10 OPEN 1,4,0
20 PRINT#1,"HELLO"
30 CLOSE 1

10 OPEN 2,4,0
20 FOR N=0 TO 9
30 PRINT#2,N
40 NEXT N
50 CLOSE 2
```

Once a file is opened for the printer, PRINT# statements that refer to the specified file number direct information to the printer. Ordinary PRINT statements in the program direct information to the screen, whether or not the printer file is open. These features make possible the direction of information to the screen, the printer, or both. Consider the example in Listing 12-2:

Line 10—Clear the screen and home the cursor.

Line 20—Print a string constant to the screen. The fact that the printer channel is not open isn't relevant.

Line 30—Open a channel to the printer as file 1.

Line 40—Direct a string constant to the printer.

Line 50—Define a string variable, M$.

Line 60—Print the content of M$, first to the printer, then to the screen.

Line 70—Close the printer file.

Listing 12-2

```
10 SCNCLR
20 PRINT "THIS IS GOING ONLY TO THE SCREEN"
30 OPEN 1,4,0
40 PRINT#1,"THIS IS GOING ONLY TO THE PRINTER"
50 M$="THIS IS GOING TO BOTH"
60 PRINT#4,M$:PRINT M$
70 CLOSE 1
```

An alternative procedure for directing information to the printer is to redirect all screen characters to the printer. The procedure makes impractical the sending of data to both the screen and printer but represents the most effective technique for printing program listings.

Redirecting all screen activity to the printer is a matter of opening a file for the printer, then executing this sort of command:

CMD *filenum*

where *filenum* is the file number assigned to the printer in the OPEN command. The following two-step operation sets up a program-listing operation:

OPEN *filenum*,4,0:CMD *filenum*

Closing a file that uses the CMD feature requires a two-step operation:

PRINT#*filenum*:CLOSE *filenum*

The same program-listing commands normally used for listing programs on the screen can be fit between those two operations.

Suppose that you have a BASIC program in memory that you want to list on the printer. A simple LIST command from the keyboard lists the program on the screen, and the following set of commands—also entered from the keyboard—lists the same program on your printer:

```
OPEN 1,4,0:CMD 1:LIST
```

When the listing is done, close the operation with this set of commands:

```
PRINT#1:CLOSE 1
```

Of course, you can list selected portions of a BASIC program by applying variations of the LIST command described in Chapter 2.

You also can direct the monitor's disassembler listings to the printer so that you can make a hardcopy listing of a machine language program. Begin the operation with this sort of operation:

OPEN *filenum*,4,*set*:MONITOR

This opens a file for the printer, directs screen operations to it, and sets the monitor mode. Next, enter the range of programming to be disassembled and printed:

D *strtaddr endaddr*

When the listing is done, press the X key to return to the BASIC interpreter and restore normal operations:

PRINT#*filenum*:CLOSE *filenum*

The following sequence of commands disassemble and print a machine language routine between $0C00 and $0CFF in bank 15:

```
OPEN 2,4,0:CMD 2:MONITOR
D $F0C00 $F0CFF
PRINT#2:CLOSE 2
```

Using the Special Printer Control Codes

Commodore printers support a small family of special commands as shown in Table 12-1. Assuming that a file is open to the printer, the technique for directing these codes to the printer takes this general form:

PRINT#*filenum*,CHR$(*code*)

where *code* is the decimal version of one of the printer control codes.

Table 12-1 Commodore Printer Control Codes

Control Character		Printer Response
Dec	**Hex**	
10	$0A	Line Feed
13	$0D	Carriage Return
14	$0E	Enable double-width character mode
15	$0F	Disable double-width character mode
18	$12	Enable reverse-character mode
146	$92	Disable reverse-character mode
17	$11	Enable uppercase/lowercase character set
145	$91	Enable uppercase/graphics character set

Using the RS-232-C Communications Feature

The Commodore 128 includes a built-in, RS-232-C communications feature—all the hardware and software required for exchanging data directly between two Commodore computers. Most users, however, would rather take advantage of existing telephone systems, and communicate with any kind of computer anywhere in the world. Connecting the Commodore 128 to a telephone, however, requires a special accessory called a *modem.*

The modem plugs into the User Port on the rear of the console unit, and a telephone jack-and-cable assembly connects the modem to the telephone system. The following discussions assume that you have installed a modem device specifically designed for the Commodore family of personal computers.

It is beyond the scope of this book to introduce the full range of RS-232-C communications. A number of good books currently are available on the subject and, in fact, some good software makes it unnecessary to know much about the details of communications. The following discussions deal with the most essential elements of RS-232-C communications as they apply to the Commodore 128.

The following terms and expressions are most important for setting up any useful RS-232-C link:

Baud rate—Rate of data transfer specified in the number of bits per second.

Number of stop bits—Number of bits, 1 or 2, that mark the end of a word.

Number of bits per word—Number of bits, 5 through 8, that make up a complete word or character.

Parity format—Scheme used for error-checking purposes.

Duplex format—Scheme (half- or full-duplex) that determines whether a character you sent to another system is echoed back to your screen. There is no echo in the half-duplex mode.

Handshaking lines—Number of electrical lines used for exchanging start/stop information between your computer and the other one.

Line feed after each CR—Send a line feed character after each carriage return character.

Setting Up a Communications Channel from BASIC

The OPEN statement for the RS-232-C channel satisfies most of the needs for setting up a communications link. Bearing in mind that the RS-232-C feature uses device number 2, the general form of the OPEN statement is:

OPEN *fileno*,2,*secaddr*,"*control*,*command*"

The file number parameter, *fileno*, serves two purposes. Like opening a file for any of the other channels, the file number simply serves as a reference number for subsequent I/O statements for that channel. Considering that you cannot work with more than 10 files at any given moment, the file numbers are generally numbers between 1 and 10. In the RS-232-C format, however, using file numbers between 128 and 255 serves a special purpose—it instructs the system to insert a line feed character after each carriage return.

> *NOTE:* If your communications format requires an automatic line feed after each carriage return, OPEN the RS-232-C channel with a *fileno* between 128 and 255. Otherwise, use the usual lower-valued numbers.

The second parameter in the OPEN statement is always the desired device number. The device number for RS-232-C communications is two.

The third term, *secaddr*, is the secondary address. It is normally used for specifying additional operating features but has no relevance in an OPEN statement for RS-232-C communications. The address can be any value between 0 and 255.

The final elements *control* and *command* are decimal values that specify a number of different communications formats. They are actually numeric values, but have to be fit into the OPEN statement as strings, either as *control,command* or CHR$(*control*)+CHR$(*command*).

The *control* term is a single numeric value that specifies the number of stop bits, word size and baud rate. Table 12-2 provides a convenient means for determining the value of the *control* term. One of the most common RS-232-C communications formats uses 1 stop bit, 8 data bits per word, and a transmission rate of 300 baud. The numeric values from the Add columns in the table are 0, 0, and 6. The sum of the three values is 6, so the value assigned to the *control* term would be 6.

Table 12-2
Guide for Determining Decimal Values for *control* Parameter in OPEN Statement for RS-232-C Operations

Select parity, number of stop bits, number of bits per word and baud rate options shown in three columns, then sum values in corresponding add columns

Number of Stop Bits		Number of Bits per Word		Baud Rate	
Number	Add	Number	Add	Baud	Add
1	0	8	0	user-def	0
2	128	7	32	50	1
		6	64	75	2
		5	96	110	3
				134.5	4
				150	5
				300	6
				600	7
				1200	8
				1800	9
				2400	10
				3600	11
				4800	12
				7200	13
				9600	14
				19200	15

The *command* term in the OPEN statement sets the parity, duplex, and handshaking formats. Table 12-3 shows the numeric values that can be summed to produce the appropriate value to be assigned to the *command* term. In most RS-232-C schemes, the parity is not used, there is no echo (half duplex), and the system uses the three-line handshaking scheme. Summing the corresponding values from the table: 0 + 0 + 0 = 0. Thus, 0 is the appropriate value for the *command* term.

Given the values described in the examples, an appropriate OPEN statement for RS-232-C communications looks like this:

```
OPEN 1,2,2,"6,0"
```

or

```
OPEN 1,2,2,CHR$(6)+CHR$(0)
```

Table 12-3
Guide for Determining Decimal Values for *comd* Parameter in OPEN Statement for RS-232-C Operations

Select parity, duplex, and handshaking options shown in three columns, then sum values in corresponding add columns

Parity	Add	Duplex	Add	Handshaking	Add
None	0	Full	0	3-line	0
Odd	32	Half	16	Other	1
Even	96				
Mark	160				
Space	224				

Those examples set up the following RS-232-C format:

- 300 baud
- 8 data bits with 1 stop bit
- No parity
- Half duplex
- No LF after CR
- Minimum handshaking

Executing an OPEN statement for RS-232-C applications automatically allocates a pair of 256-byte buffers, one for receiving data and another for sending it. The receive buffer is located in low RAM $0C00–$0CFF (3072–3327) and the transmit buffer is at $0D00–$0DFF (3328–3583). Obviously these blocks of RAM should be used for no other purpose while the RS-232-C channel is open.

A more subtle feature of the OPEN statement for an RS-232-C channel is that it automatically clears all specified variable values and closes any other channels that are open at the time. For this reason, a program usually opens the RS-232-C channel before using any variables and opening other kinds of channels.

> ***NOTE:*** It is recommended that you OPEN an RS-232-C channel before doing anything else in the program that uses that channel.

The BASIC commands that you use for sending and receiving data through an open RS-232-C Channel are PRINT# and GET#, respectively. The program in Listing 12-3 sets up a Commodore 128 as a "dumb" terminal—one that simply sends and receives keyboard characters:

Line 10—Open a communications channel with the specifications described in the previous example.

Line 20—Get a character from the RS-232-C receive buffer. If there is no character, go to line 40.

Line 30—If the GET#1 function finds a character in the receive buffer, print it on the screen.

Line 40—See if the user is pressing a key on the keyboard. If not, loop back to line 20.

Line 50—If the user is pressing CONTROL-Q, go to line 80 to end the program.

Line 60—Put the user's key character into the RS-232-C transmit buffer for output to the other terminal.

Line 70—Loop back to line 20 to check for another character in the receive buffer.

Listing 12-3

```
10 OPEN 1,2,2,"6,0"
20 GET#1,RX$:IF RX$="" THEN 40
30 PRINT RX$;
40 GET TX$:IF TX$="" THEN 20
50 IF ASC(TX$)=17 THEN 80
60 PRINT#1,TX$;
70 GOTO 20
80 CLOSE 1
```

Communicating with Other Computers

Many other kinds of computer systems use a character-coding format that is slightly different from that of the Commodore 128. Therefore, you need to translate characters being sent and received in order to avoid confusion.

Table 12-4 compares the standard ASCII codes, 0 through 127, with their Commodore counterparts from the uppercase/lowercase character set. The table clearly suggests the need for further character conversions, both before sending certain characters and upon receiving them.

Table 12-4 Comparison of Codes and Characters for Standard ASCII Character Set and Commodore Character Set

Codes		Standard	Commodore
Dec	Hex	Characters	Characters
0	$00	NULL	NULL
1	$01	SOH	—
2	$02	STX	—
3	$03	ETX	—
4	$04	EOT	—
5	$05	ENQ	white
6	$06	ACK	—
7	$07	BELL	BELL
8	$08	BS	—
9	$09	TAB	TAB

Table 12-4 (cont.)

Codes		Standard	Commodore
Dec	**Hex**	**Characters**	**Characters**
10	$0A	LF	LF
11	$0B	VT	disable set change
12	$0C	FF	enable set change
13	$0D	CR	CR
14	$0E	SO	set lowercase
15	$0F	SI	—
16	$10	DLE	—
17	$11	DC1	cursor down
18	$12	DC2	reverse on
19	$13	DC3	home
20	$14	DC4	DEL
21	$15	NAK	—
22	$16	SYN	—
23	$17	ETB	—
24	$18	CAN	set/clear tabs
25	$19	EM	—
26	$1A	SUB	—
27	$1B	ESC	ESC
28	$1C	FS	red
29	$1D	GS	cursor right
30	$1E	RS	green
31	$1F	US	blue
32	$20	SPACE	SPACE
33	$21	!	!
34	$22	"	"
35	$23	#	#
36	$24	$	$
37	$25	%	%
38	$26	&	&
39	$27	'	'
40	$28	(	(
41	$29	)	)
42	$2A	*	*
43	$2B	+	+
44	$2C	,	,
45	$2D	-	-
46	$2E	.	.
47	$2F	/	/
48	$30	0	0
49	$31	1	1
50	$32	2	2
51	$33	3	3
52	$34	4	4
53	$35	5	5
54	$36	6	6
55	$37	7	7
56	$38	8	8
57	$39	9	9
58	$3A	:	:
59	$3B	;	;
60	$3C	<	<

Table 12-4 (cont.)

Codes		Standard	Commodore
Dec	Hex	Characters	Characters
61	$3D	=	=
62	$3E	>	>
63	$3F	?	?
64	$40	@	@
65	$41	A	a
66	$42	B	b
67	$43	C	c
68	$44	D	d
69	$45	E	e
70	$46	F	f
71	$47	G	g
72	$48	H	h
73	$49	I	i
74	$4A	J	j
75	$4B	K	k
76	$4C	L	l
77	$4D	M	m
78	$4E	N	n
79	$4F	O	o
80	$50	P	p
81	$51	Q	q
82	$52	R	r
83	$53	S	s
84	$54	T	t
85	$55	U	u
86	$56	V	v
87	$57	W	w
88	$58	X	x
89	$59	Y	y
90	$5A	Z	z
91	$5B	[	[
92	$5C	\	£
93	$5D	]	]
94	$5E	^	↑
95	$5F	_	←
96	$60	'	(graphic)
97	$61	a	A
98	$62	b	B
99	$63	c	C
100	$64	d	D
101	$65	e	E
102	$66	f	F
103	$67	g	G
104	$68	h	H
105	$69	i	I
106	$6A	j	J
107	$6B	k	K
108	$6C	l	L
109	$6D	m	M
110	$6E	n	N
111	$6F	o	O

Table 12-4 (cont.)

Codes		Standard	Commodore
Dec	Hex	Characters	Characters
112	$70	p	P
113	$71	q	Q
114	$72	r	R
115	$73	s	S
116	$74	t	T
117	$75	u	U
118	$76	v	V
119	$77	w	W
120	$78	x	X
121	$79	y	Y
122	$7A	z	Z
123	$7B	{	(graphic)
124	$7C	|	(graphic)
125	$7D	}	(graphic)
126	$7E	~	(graphic)
127	$7F	DEL	(graphic)

The program in Listing 12-4 suggests a translation format for communicating with other systems that use the standard ASCII character format. A character code is transmitted and received as variable K.

Line 10—Set fast operation.

Line 20—Dimension the transmit/receive arrays.

Line 30—Set all values to 1–255 consecutively.

Line 40—Set 0–31 in the receive array to 0.

Lines 50 and 60—Align the uppercase and lowercase letters in both arrays.

Line 70—Set 128–159 in the receive array to 0.

Line 80—Adjust transmit array to send lower-valued codes.

Lines 90 and 100—Align backspace and DEL operations in both arrays.

Line 110—Restore normal speed.

Listing 12-4

```
10 FAST
20 DIM T%(255):DIM R%(255)
30 FOR K=0 TO 255:T%(K)=K:R%(K)=K:NEXT
40 FOR K=0 TO 31:R%(K)=0:NEXT
50 FOR K=65 TO 90:T%(K)=K+32:R%(K)=K+32:NEXT
60 FOR K=97 TO 122:T%(K)=K-32:R%(K)=K-32:NEXT
70 FOR K=128 TO 159:R%(K)=0:NEXT
80 FOR K=193 TO 218:T%(K)=K-128:NEXT
90 T%(20)=127:T%(157)=8
100 R%(13)=13:R%(8)=157:R%(127)=20
110 SLOW
```

The communications programming that you add to this routine transmits the character as T%(K) and prints a received character as R%(K). See a demonstration version in Listing 12-5. The example is intended to illustrate a principle and thus lacks the qualities of a truly useful communications routine.

Listing 12-5

```
10 OPEN 1,2,2,"6,0"
20 FAST
30 DIM T%(255):DIM R%(255)
40 FOR K=0 TO 255:T%(K)=K:R%(K)=K:NEXT
50 FOR K=0 TO 31:R%(K)=0:NEXT
60 FOR K=65 TO 90:T%(K)=K+32:R%(K)=K+32:NEXT
70 FOR K=97 TO 122:T%(K)=K – 32:R%(K)=K-32:NEXT
80 FOR K=128 TO 159:R%(K)=0:NEXT
90 FOR K=193 TO 218:T%(K)=K – 128:NEXT
100 T%(20)=127:T%(157)=8
110 R%(13)=13:R%(8)=157:R%(127)=20
120 SLOW
130 GET#1,RX$:IF RX$="" THEN 150
140 PRINT CHR$(R%(ASC(RX$)));
150 GET TX$:IF TX$="" THEN 130
160 IF ASC(TX$)=17 THEN 190
170 PRINT#1,CHR$(T%(ASC(TX$)));
180 GOTO 20
190 CLOSE 1X
```

13

Commodore 128 Memory Maps

Commodore 128 memory operations refer to three different kinds of locations that can be addressed: random-access memory (RAM), read-only memory (ROM), and device input/output (I/O) locations. Generally speaking, it is possible to read and write data to RAM locations but only read data from ROM locations. Such a generalization cannot be made about the I/O (memory-mapped) addresses, however, due in part to the fact that they are sometimes connected directly to peripheral devices.

The sixteen different combinations of memory configurations make the Commodore 128 an exceedingly fast and powerful personal computer. Because of the system's memory-banking operations, you will find that certain blocks of addresses serve more than one purpose in the overall memory map. For the same reason, you will occasionally find two different blocks of addresses serving the same apparent function. The memory-management operations described in Chapter 14 can go a long way toward resolving any practical difficulties in that regard.

The Lower RAM Addresses: $0000-$03FF

The lower RAM area is unique in several important respects. First, it is directly accessible from all sixteen bank configurations. That says something about its relative importance to the system. The only other equally accessible block of memory is the four MMU registers at $FF00-$FF04.

A second unique feature is that it includes the microprocessor's zero-page RAM—a segment of RAM that can be machine-language addressed with a single byte rather than the normal two-byte format. Just above the zero-page RAM is the microprocessor's stack area. The location and application of the zero-page and stack areas are dictated by the nature of the 8502 microprocessor.

Zero-Page RAM: $00-$FF

Registers in zero-page RAM can be addressed from a great deal of machine coding by means of single-byte addresses. A zero-page address that might otherwise be specified as $00A0, for instance, also can be specified as $A0.

The Commodore 128 makes extensive use of zero-page locations—virtually all of them at one time or another. The following memory map describes the locations that have clear-cut and potentially useful applications. The fact that the zero-page RAM is common to all bank configurations means that a programmer does not have to be concerned about switching banks in order to make use of it.

$00 **0**

D8510 8502 I/O data direction register.

$01 **1**

R8510 8502 I/O data register.

$02–$09 **2–9**

Bank and 8502 registers used during long JSR and long JMP routines. See JSRFAR at $02CD and JMPFAR at $02E3.

$02 (2) = Bank number
$03 (3) = MSB of program counter
$04 (4) = LSB of program counter
$05 (5) = P register
$06 (6) = Monitor A register
$07 (7) = X register
$08 (8) = Y register
$09 (9) = SP register

$0A **10**

ENDCHR Scan for quote at the end of a string.

$0B **11**

TRMPOS Column location of the previous TAB statement in the current line of BASIC programming.

$0C–$0E **12–14**

BASIC applications.

$0F **15**

VALTYP BASIC DATA type:

$00 (0) = Numeric
$FF (255) = String

$10 **16**

INTFLG Numeric data format:

$00 (0) = Floating-point
$FF (255) = Integer

$11–$2C **17–44**

Basic applications.

$2D–$2E **45–46**

TXTTAB Pointer to start of RAM Bank-0 BASIC programming.

$2D (45) = LSB of address
$2E (46) = MSB of address
Default address: $0C01 but set to $0401 when a graphics screen is allocated.

$2F–$30 **47–48**

VARTAB Pointer to start of RAM Bank-1 BASIC variable list.

$2F (47) = LSB of address
$30 (48) = MSB of address
Default address: $0400

$31–$32 **49–50**

ARYTAB Pointer to start of RAM Bank-1 BASIC arrays.

$31 (49) = LSB of address
$32 (50) = MSB of address
Default address: $0400

$33–$34 **51–52**

FRETOP Pointer to start of free RAM Bank-1 memory space.

$33 (51) = LSB of address
$34 (52) = MSB of address
Default address: $0400

$35–$36 **53–54**

STREND Pointer to end of RAM Bank-1 BASIC string space, plus 1.

$35 (53) = LSB of address
$36 (54) = MSB of address
Default address: $FF00

$37–$38 **55–56**

FRESPC Pointer to current string address in RAM Bank 1.

$37 (55) = LSB of address
$38 (56) = MSB of address

$39–$3A **57–58**

MEMSIZ Highest address used by BASIC in RAM Bank 1.

$39 (57) = LSB of address
$3A (58) = MSB of address
Default address: $FF00

$3B–$3C **59–60**

CURLIN Current BASIC line number.

$3B (59) = LSB of line number
$3C (60) = MSB of line number

$3D–$3E **61–62**

TXTPTR Pointer to address of the current BASIC text character.

$3D (61) = LSB of address
$3E (62) = MSB of address

$41–$42 **65–66**

DATLIN Current DATA line number.

$41 (65) = LSB of line number
$42 (66) = MSB of line number

$43–$44 **67–68**

DATPTR RAM address of the current DATA item.

$43 (67) = LSB of address
$44 (68) = MSB of address

$47–$48 **71–72**

VARNAM Pointer to address of current BASIC variable name.

$49–$4A **73–74**

VARPNT Pointer to address of current variable value.

$4B–$62 **75–98**

BASIC applications.

$63–$68 **99–104**

Floating-point accumulator #1.

$6A–$6F **106–111**

Floating-point accumulator #2.

$70–$7C **112–124**

Basic applications.

$7D–$7E **125–126**

BASIC run-time stack pointer.

$7F **127**

Program mode flag:

$00 (0) = Direct mode
$80 (128) = Program mode

$80–$8F **128–143**

Graphics parameters registers.

$90 **144**

STATUS Kernal I/O status byte, ST.

$91 **145**

STKEY STOP key flag:

$00 (0) = Key not pressed
$80 (128) = Key pressed

$92 **146**

SVXT Cassette timing constant.

Default value: $80 (128)

$93 **147**

VERCK Load/verify flag for disk and cassette operations:

$00 (0) = Load
$01 (1) = Verify

$94 **148**

C3P0 Serial output character-buffered flag.

$95 **149**

BSOUR Secondary address in the LISTEN mode, buffered character to send in TALK.

$96 **150**

SYNO Cassette synchronization number.

$97 **151**

Scratch register.

$98 **152**

LDTND Number of open files, file-table index. Reading from this register returns the number of files currently open.

Default value: $00 (0)

Do not write data directly to this register.

$99 **153**

DFLTN Default input device number. The default input device is the keyboard, so reading from this register returns a value of $00 (0). Be careful about writing other values to DFLTN.

$9A **154**

DFLTO Default output device number. The default output device is the screen, so reading from this register returns a value of $03 (3). Recklessly writing other values to DFLTN can create a lot of confusion.

$9B–$9D **155–156**

Cassette applications.

$9D **157**

MSGFLG Screen message flag:

$00 (0) = No message currently displayed
$40 (64) = Only error message(s) displayed
$80 (128) = Only control message(s) displayed
$C0 (192) = Control and error messages displayed

$9E–$9F **158–159**

Cassette error flags.

$9E (158) = Pass-1 status
$9F (159) = Pass-2 status

$A0–$A2 **160–162**

TIME Three-byte, free-running 60Hz counter.

$A0 (160) = High-order byte
$A1 (161) = Middle byte
$A2 (162) = Low-order byte

Reading from these registers returns the current count. Writing to them sets the counter.

$A3–$A4 **163–164**

Scratch registers. Do not use them.

$A5–$A6 **165–166**

Cassette applications.

$A7 **167**

INBIT RS-232-C input bit, also used by cassette routines.

$A8 **168**

BITCI RS-232-C input bit count, also used by cassette routines.

$A9 **169**

RINONE RS-232-C start-bit flag, also used as 0s counter for cassette routines.

$AA **170**

RIDATA RS-232-C input byte buffer, also used by cassette routines.

$AB **171**

RIPRTY RS-232-C input parity byte, also used by cassette routines.

$AC–$AD **172–173**

SAL Pointer to start of cassette input buffer. The difference between this pointer and TAPE1 at $B2 and $B3 is not clear.

$AC (172) = LSB of address
$AD (173) = MSB of address
Default: $0B00 (2816)

The registers are also used for text-screen scrolling operations.

$AE–$AF **174–175**

EAL Address of the end of a program or file block.

$AE (174) = LSB of address
$AF (175) = MSB of address

Reading from these registers after loading a program or file returns the highest RAM address used.

$B0–$B1 **176–177**

CMP0 Cassette timing constants.

$B2–$B3 **178–179**

TAPE1 Pointer to start of cassette buffer.

Default value: $0B00 (2816)

$B4 **180**

BITTS RS-232-C output bit count, also used by cassette routines.

$B5 **181**

NXTBIT RS-232-C output bit to be sent next, also used by cassette routines.

$B6 **182**

RODATA RS-232-C output byte buffer.

$B7 **183**

FNLEN Length of current file name. Reading from this register returns the number of characters in the last-referenced file name.

$B8 **184**

LA Current logical file number. Reading from this register returns the file number of the last-referenced file.

$B9 **185**

SA Current secondary address.

$BA **186**

FA Current device number.

$BB–$BC **187–188**

FNADR Address of the start of the current file name.

$BB (187) = LSB of address
$BC (188) = MSB of address

Use BANKF at $C7 to specify a bank number other than the default, Bank 0.

$BD **189**

ROPRTY RS-232-C output parity, also used by cassette routines.

$BE **190**

FSBLK Cassette input block counter.

$BF **191**

MYCH Serial character buffer.

$C0 **192**

CAS1 Cassette motor-switch control.

$C1–$C2 **193–194**

STA I/O start address.

$C1 (193) = LSB of address
$C2 (194) = MSB of address
Default address: $0100 (256)

$C3–$C4 **195–196**

VECTAB Address of start of vector restore table. Set to default value by the RESTOR Kernal: $E073 (57459)

$C5 **197**

CDATA Cassette read/write scratch register.

$C6 **198**

BANKB Bank number for the current block read, write, or verify operation.

$C7 **199**

BANKF Bank number of the current file name, used in conjunction with the file name address, FNADR, at $BB.

Default bank number: $00 (0)

$C8–$C9 **200–201**

RIBUF Address of the start of the RS-232-C input buffer.

$C8 (200) = LSB of address
$C9 (201) = MSB of address
Default address: $0C00 (3072)

$CA–$CB 202–203

ROBUT Address of the start of the RS-232-C output buffer.

$CA (202) = LSB of address
$CB (203) = MSB of address
Default address: $0D00 (3328)

$CC–$CD 204–205

KEYTAB Address of the start of the editor key tables.

$CC (204) = LSB of address
$CD (205) = MSB of address
Default address: $FA80 (64128)

$D0 208

NDX Number of characters remaining in the keyboard buffer, keyboard index pointer.

$D1–$D2 209–210

Keyboard applications.

$D3 211

SHFLAG Key flag for SHIFT, C=, CONTROL, and ALT keys:

$00 (0) = None of the following keys
$01 (1) = SHIFT key depressed
$02 (2) = C= key depressed
$04 (4) = CONTROL key depressed
$08 (8) = ALT key depressed
$0F (15) = CAPS LOCK is locked down

Sum the values to determine the nature of simultaneous key presses.

See Chapter 10 for more keycode details and applications.

$D4 212

SFDX Keyboard coordinate of current key pressed:

$58 (88) = No key pressed

$D5 **213**

LSTX Keyboard coordinate of previous key pressed.

$D7 **215**

SMODE 40/80-column screen mode:

$00 (0) = 40-column screen
$80 (128) = 80-column screen

Reading from this location returns the current screen mode. Writing to the location sets the designated screen mode.

$D8 **216**

GMODE Text/Graphics screen mode:

$00 (0) = 40-column text, GRAPHIC 0
$20 (32) = Standard full-screen graphics, GRAPHIC 1
$60 (96) = Standard split-screen graphics, GRAPHIC 2
$A0 (160) = Multicolor full-screen graphics, GRAPHIC 3
$E0 (224) = Multicolor split-screen graphics, GRAPHIC 4

Reading from this location returns the current text/graphics screen mode. Writing to the location sets the designated mode.

$D9 **217**

Image of bit 2 of the R8510 register at $01.

$DA–$DF **218–223**

Editor applications.

$E0–$E1 **224–225**

PNT Screen RAM address of the first column in the current text-cursor line.

$E0 (224) = LSB of address
$E1 (225) = MSB of address

$E2–$E3 **226–227**

USER Color RAM address of the first column in the current text-cursor line.

$E2 (226) = LSB of address
$E3 (227) = MSB of address

$E4 **228**

WINDBOT Bottom line of the current text window.

Range of values: $00–$18 (0–24)
Default value: $18 (24)

$E5 **229**

WINDTOP Top line of the current text window.

Range of values: $00–$18 (0–24)
Default value: $00 (0)

$E6 **230**

WINDLFT Left column of the current text window.

Range of values:
40-column screen: $00–$27 (0–39)
80-column screen: $00–$4F (0–79)

Default value: $00 (0)

$E7 **231**

WINDRGT Right column of the current text window.

Range of values:
40-column screen: $00–$27 (0–39)
80-column screen: $00–$4F (0–79)

Default value: $27 (39)

NOTE: The value is set to $4F (79) when the 80-column screen is invoked.

$E8 **232**

LXSP Logical line number for current input operation.

$E9 **233**

Logical column for the start of current input operation.

$EA **234**

INDX Logical column for the end of the current input operation.

$EB **235**

TBLX Current row location of the text cursor.

Range of values: $00–$18 (0–24)

$EC **236**

PNTR Current column location of the text cursor, relative to WINDLFT.

Maximum range of values:

40-column screen: $00–$27 (0–39)
80-column screen: $00–$4F (0–79)

$ED **237**

WINDLINS Number of available lines in the current text window.

Range of values: $00–$18 (0–24)
Default value: $18 (24)

$EE **238**

WINDCOLS Number of available columns in the current text window.

Range of values:

40-column screen: $00–$27 (0–39)
80-column screen: $00–$4F (0–79)

Default values:

40-column screen: $27 (39)
80-column screen: $4F (79)

$EF **239**

CURCHAR Character being printed.

$F0 **240**

LASCHAR Last character printed. Used as an ESC key flag.

$F1 **241**

COLOR Current text character color.

Range of values: $00–$0F (0–15)
Default value: $0D (13);

$F2 **242**

LASCOLOR Color of the previous character. Only the lower nibble (bits 0 through 3) are meaningful.

$F3 **243**

RVS Normal/reverse printing flag.

$00 (0) = Normal

Non-zero value = Reverse

Reading from RVS register returns the current status. Writing the values to the register sets the normal/reverse status.

$F4 **244**

QTSW Quote-mode flag.

$00 (0) = Quote mode off

Non-zero value = Quote mode on

$F5 **245**

QTSW Insert-mode flag.

$00 (0) = Insert mode off

Non-zero value = Insert mode on

$F6 **246**

INSRT Current number of insert-mode (INST) keystrokes.

$F7 **247**

MODE Enable/disable character-switch flag (SHIFT-C= operation):

$00 (0) = Enable switching
$80 (128) = Disable switching

$F8 **248**

SCROLL Enable/disable screen scrolling:

$00 (0) = Scroll enabled
$80 (128) = Scroll disabled

Reading from this register returns the current scroll status. Writing the values sets the scroll mode.

$F9 **249**

BELLS Enables/disables the normal beep (bell) tone.

$00 (0) = Bell enabled
$80 (128) = Bell disabled

Reading from this register returns the current bell status. Writing the values sets the bell status.

$FA–$FE **250–254**

FREKZP Five bytes of zero-page RAM available for user programs.

$FF **255**

BASZPT Top of zero page, BASIC scratch register.

System Stack RAM: $0100-$01FF

The 8502 microprocessor makes extensive use of the 256-byte block of RAM known as the system stack. The microprocessor handles data on a first-in, last-out basis. That is, bytes A and B might be pushed onto the stack in that order, but they have to be pulled off in the reverse order—byte B followed by byte A.

Stacking operations begin at the top of the stack area, $01FF, and work downward toward $0100. The Commodore 128 rarely uses more than half of the available stack area for routine stack operations. The system engineers appear to have good reason to believe the stacking operations will go no farther down than $0137. Some registers are dedicated to other applications in the range of $0100–$0136.

All things considered, try to avoid writing programs that load or POKE data into the range of $0100–$01FF (256–511).

Common Buffers, Vectors and RAM Routines: $0200-$03FF

The lower area of RAM, $0200-$03FF (512-1023), is dedicated to registers and program routines that must be accessible from all possible bank configurations. A cursory review of the following descriptions of the memory map ought to demonstrate the overall importance of the lower area of RAM to the fundamental operating system.

$0200–$02A1 **512–673**

Input buffer for BASIC and the monitor, 161 bytes.

$02A2–$02AE **674–686**

Kernal RAM code for fetching a byte from any bank. See the main Kernal at $FF74.

$02AF–$02BD **687–701**

Kernal RAM code for sending a byte to any bank. See the main Kernal at $FF77.

$02BE–$02CC **702–716**

Kernal RAM code for comparing bytes between any two banks. See the main Kernal at $FF7A.

$02CD–$02E2 **717–738**

Kernal RAM code for doing a JSR to any bank. See the main Kernal at $FF6E.

$02E3–$02F9 **739–761**

Kernal RAM code for doing a JMP to any bank. See the main Kernal at $FF71.

$0300–$0301 **768–769**

IERROR Vector to routine to print BASIC error message. Default version is called with the error number in register X.

Default address: **$4D3F**

$0302–$0303 **770–771**

IMAIN Vector to BASIC's warm start to a routine.

Default address: $4DC6

$0304–$0305 **772–773**

ICRNCH Vector to a routine that crunches BASIC text to BASIC tokens.

Default address: $430D

$0306–$0307 **774–775**

IQPLOP Vector to a routine that restores a BASIC token to text.

Default address: $5151

$0308–$0309 **776–777**

IGONE Vector to a routine that executes a BASIC token.

Default address: $4AA2

$030A–$030B **778–779**

IEVAL Vector to a routine that interprets a BASIC arithmetic function.

Default address: $78DA

$030C–$030D **780–781**

Vector to a routine that tokenizes two-character ESCAPE commands.

Default address: $4321

$030E–$030F **782–783**

Vector to a routine that converts an ESCAPE token to text.

Default address: $51CD

$0310-$0311 **784-785**

Vector to a routine that executes an ESCAPE token.

Default address: $4BA9

$0312-$0313 **786-787**

Vector to MMU in any bank.

Default address: $FF00

$0314-$0315 **788-789**

CINV RAM vector to hardware IRQ.

Default address: $FA65

$0316-$0317 **790-791**

CBINV RAM vector to BRK-instruction interrupt handler.

Default address: $B003

$0318-$0319 **792-793**

NMINV RAM vector to NMI interrupt handler.

Default address: $FA40

$031A-$031B **794-795**

IOPEN RAM Kernal vector to OPEN routine.

Default function: OPEN at address $EFBD

$031C-$031D **796-797**

ICLOSE RAM Kernal vector to CLOSE routine.

Default function: CLOSE at address $F188

$031E-$031F **798-799**

ICHKIN RAM Kernal vector to CHKIN routine.

Default function: CHKIN at address $F106

$0320–$0321 **800–801**

ICHKOUT RAM Kernal vector to CHKOUT routine.

Default function: CHKOUT at address $F14C

$0322–$0323 **802–803**

ICLRCHN RAM Kernal vector to CLRCHN routine.

Default function: CLRCHN at address $F226

$0324–$0325 **804–805**

ICHRIN RAM Kernal vector to CHRIN routine.

Default function: CHRIN at address $EF06

$0326–$0327 **806–807**

IBSOUT RAM Kernal vector to BSOUT routine.

Default function: BSOUT at address $EF79

$0328–$0329 **808–809**

ISTOP RAM Kernal vector to STOP routine.

Default function: STOP at address $F66E

$032A–$032B **810–811**

IGETIN RAM Kernal vector to GETIN routine.

Default function: GETIN at address $EEEB

$032C–$032D **812–813**

ICLALL RAM Kernal vector to CLALL routine.

Default function: CLALL at address $F222

$032E–$032F **814–815**

Monitor command vector.

Default address: $B006

$0330–$0331 **816–817**

ILOAD RAM Kernal vector to LOAD routine.

Default address: $F26C

$0332–$0333 **818–819**

ISAVE RAM Kernal vector to SAVE routine.

Default address: $F54E

$0334–$033D **820–829**

Editor key indirects.

$033E–$0349 **830–841**

Vectors to keyboard tables.

$034A–$0353 **842–851**

KEYD Ten-byte IRQ keyboard buffer, keyboard queue.

$0354–$035D **852–861**

Map of screen TAB stops, 10 bytes.

$035E–$0361 **862–865**

Map of screen line wraps, 4 bytes.

$0362–$036B **866–875**

LAT Logical file numbers for each open file, 10 maximum.

$036C–$0375 **876–885**

FAT Device numbers for each open file, 10 maximum.

$0376–$037F **886–895**

SAT Secondary addresses for each open file, 10 maximum.

$0380–$039E **896–926**

CHRGET RAM routine to fetch the next byte of BASIC text from Bank 0.

$0386 **902**

CHRGOT Entry point within CHRGET to fetch the previous byte again. See CHRGET above at $0380.

$039F-$03AA **927-938**

RAM routine: Fetch-indirect from Bank 0.

$03AB-$03B6 **939-950**

RAM routine: Fetch-indirect from Bank 1.

$03B7-$03BF **951-959**

RAM routine: Fetch-indirect from Bank 1. Index from zero-page $24-$25.

$03C0-$03C8 **960-968**

RAM routine: Fetch-indirect from Bank 0. Index from zero-page $26-$27.

$03C9-$03D1 **969-977**

RAM routine: Fetch-indirect from Bank 0. Index from zero-page $3D-$3E.

$03D2-$03FF **978-1023**

Miscellaneous applications.

The Upper RAM-Only Area: $0400-$3FFF

The upper RAM-only area includes important I/O buffers, a few routines, and a lot of video memory. It begins with the default text screen RAM at $0400 through $07FF (1024-2047). See Chapter 6 for a line-by-line map of the screen RAM.

BASIC Run-Time Stack: $0800-$09FF

The BASIC run-time stack serves as a first-in/last-out stack for interactive and nested BASIC operations. BASIC cannot run properly without access to this stack, and this suggests why there are no bank configurations that use BASIC ROM without RAM 0.

Everyone other than highly sophisticated BASIC programmers should avoid the run-time stack. PEEKing into the area—2048 through 2559—serves no real purpose, and POKEing into the area can be disastrous when you are using the BASIC interpreter.

Monitor and Kernal Variables: $0A00-$0AFF

$0A00-$0A01　　2560-2561

Vector to BASIC 7.0 warm start.

$0A00 = LSB of the address
$0A00 = MSB of the address
Default value: **$4003 (16387)**

$0A02-$0A04　　2562-2564

System status/video-configuration bytes.

$0A05-$0A06　　2565-2566

MEMSTR Pointer to the beginning of system-usable, Bank-0 RAM.

$0A05 (2565) = LSB of the address
$0A06 (2566) = MSB of the address
Default value: **$1C00 (7168)**

$0A07-$0A08　　2567-2568

MEMSIZ Pointer to the top of system-usable, Bank-1 RAM.

$0A07 (2567) = LSB of the address
$0A08 (2568) = MSB of the address
Default contents: **$FF00 (65280)**

$0A09-$0A0D　　2569-2573

Cassette registers, buffers, and flags.

$0A0E　　2574

Serial I/O flag.

$0A0F **2575**

RS-232-C flag.

$0A10 **2576**

M51CTR RS-232-C pseudo control register.

Bits 0-3 = Baud-rate code
Bit 4 = Always 1
Bits 5-6 = Word-length code
Bit 7 = Stop-bit code

See details in Chapter 12.

$0A11 **2577**

M51CDR RS-232-C pseudo command register.

Bit 0 = Handshake bit
Bits 2-4 = Not used (set to 0)
Bits 6-7 = Parity format (default NO PARITY)

See details in Chapter 12.

$0A12–$0A13 **2578–2579**

M51AJB Non-standard RS-232-C baud rate.

$0A14 **2580**

RSSTAT RS-232-C status register.

Bit 0 = Operating-mode bit
Bits 1-5 = Not used
Bit 6 = Line-feed format
Bit 7 = Echo format

See details in Chapter 12.

$0A15 **2581**

BITNUM Number of bits to be sent or received via RS-232-C.

$0A16–$0A17 **2582–2583**

BAUDOF RS-232-C baud-rate timer.

$0A18 **2584**

RIDBE RS-232-C index to the end of the receive buffer.

$0A19 **2585**

RIDBS RS-232-C index to the start of the receive buffer.

$0A1A **2586**

RODBS RS-232-C index to the start of the transmit buffer.

$0A1B **2587**

RODBE RS-232-C index the the end of the transmit buffer.

$0A1C **2588**

RS-232-C flag bit.

$0A1D–$0A1F **2589–2591**

TIMED Downcounting version of the three-byte, real-time clock at zero-page $A0 through $A2.

$0A1D (2589) = LSB of counter
$0A1E (2590) = Middle byte of counter
$0A1F (2591) = MSB of counter

$0A20 **2592**

XMAX Maximum size of the keyboard buffer.

Default value: $0A (10) bytes

$0A21 **2593**

Output stop flag generated by CONTROL-S key command.

$0A22 **2594**

RPTFLG Repeat-key flag.

$00 (0) = Disable repeat
$40 (64) = Space bar, INST/DEL, and cursor-movement keys repeat
$80 (128) = All keys repeat (default)

$0A23–$0A25 **2595–2597**

Repeat-key rates.

$0A26 **2598**

BLNSW Cursor blink enable/disable.

$00 (0) = Enable blinking effect (default)
$40 (64) = Disable blinking effect

$0A40–$0A5A **2624–2650**

Storage area for screen parameters swapped with zero-page $E0–$FA (224–250) when switching between 40- and 80-column screens.

$0A60–$0A6D **2651–2669**

Screen tab and line-wrap bit maps, swapped with $0354–$0361 (852–865) when switching between 40- and 80-column screens.

$0A80–$0A9F **2688–2719**

Monitor buffer.

$0AA0–$0AFF **2720–2815**

Reserved for general system applications.

Buffer Area: $0B00–$10FF

This Bank-0 area of RAM is set aside for sets of 256-byte buffers. The blocks are available for machine-language programs and files as long as they are not being used for their prescribed purposes.

$0B00–$0BBF **2816–3007**

TBUFFR Cassette I/O buffer. Also see $0B00 below.

$0B00–$0BFF **2816–3071**

DOS BOOT buffer.

$0C00–$0CFF **3072–3327**

RS-232-C receive buffer.

$0D00-$0DFF **3328-3583**

RS-232-C transmit buffer.

$0E00-$0FFF **3584-4095**

Sprite definition area. See details in Chapter 8.

$1000-$1009 **4096-4105**

Index, or number of characters, for commands assigned to the programmable function keys.

$100A-$10FF **4106-4351**

Current function-key assignments, up to 46 bytes.

General BASIC Usage: $1208-$121A

$1208 **4616**

Error number for BASIC's last error condition.

$1209-$120A **4617-4618**

Line number for BASIC's last error condition:

$1209 (4617) = LSB of line number
$120A (4618) = MSB of line number

$1210-$1211 **4624-4625**

Pointer to end of BASIC programming in Bank 0.

$1210 (4624) = LSB of address
$1211 (4625) = MSB of address

$1212-$1213 **4626-4627**

Pointer to highest available Bank-0 RAM for BASIC text:

$1212 (4626) = LSB of address
$1213 (4627) = MSB of address

$1218–$121A **4632–4634**

JSR to USR routine. Set LSB of the USR address in $1219 and the MSB in $121A.

Bit-Map Color and Screen RAM: $1C00–$3FFF

This block of RAM can be allocated for BASIC text or bit-map memory. See allocation details and line-by-line memory maps in Chapter 7.

$1C00–$1FFF **7168–8191**

Bit-map color memory.

$2000–$3FFF **8192–16383**

Bit-map screen memory.

BASIC ROM: $4000–$AFFF

The BASIC interpreter occupies $4000 through $AFFF when the system is configured for ROM in that block.

Critical BASIC Jump Vectors

$4000 **16343**

Jump instruction to BASIC's cold-start routine. The point executes a JMP instruction to $4023.

$4003 **16346**

Jump instruction to BASIC's warm-start routine. The point executes a JMP instruction to $4009.

$4006 **16349**

Jump instruction to BASIC's IRQ routine. The point executes a JUMP instruction to $A84D.

$4009 **16352**

Entry point to BASIC's warm-start initialization routine. Enter this routine from $4003.

$4023 **16419**

Entry point to BASIC's cold-start initialization routine. Enter this routine from $4000.

$7A85 **31365**

Entry point for a routine that transfers a numeric value from a designated location in RAM to Floating-Point Accumulator #1. Execute this routine from the jump table at $AF60.

See more details at $AF60.

$8AB4 **35508**

Entry point for a routine that transfers a numeric value from a designated location in RAM to Floating-Point Accumulator #2. Execute this routine from the jump table at $AF5A.

See more details at $AF5A.

$8C00 **35840**

Entry point for a routine that transfers a numeric value from Floating-Point Accumulator #1 to a designated location in RAM. Execute this routine from the jump table at $AF66. See $AF66 for more details.

$8C28 **35880**

Entry point for a routine that copies a floating-point value from FAC2 to FAC1. Call this from the FAC jump table at $AF69.

$8C38 **35896**

Entry point for a routine that copies a floating-point value from FAC1 to FAC2. Call this from the FAC jump table at $AF6C.

$8C47 **35911**

Entry point for a routine that rounds off a floating-point value by dropping all digits to the right of the decimal point. Use $AF4B to access it.

See ROFF at $AF4B for more information.

$8C84 **35972**

Entry point for the routine that executes BASIC's ABS function. Use $AF4E to access it.

See ABS at $AF4E for more information.

$8C57 **35927**

Entry point for a routine that determines the sign of a value in FAC#1. Use $AF51 to access it and read the indication of the sign in register A.

See SGN at $AF51 for more information.

$8E42 **36418**

Entry point for a routine that converts the current content of FAC1 into ASCII-coded text. Enter this routine from $AF06.

See $AF06 in the FAC jump table for more information.

$8FB7 **36791**

Entry point for the routine that executes BASIC's SQR operation to calculate the square-root of a floating-point value. Use $AF30 to access it.

See SQR at $AF30 for more information.

$8FFA **36858**

Entry point for the routine that negates a floating-point value. Use $AF33 to access it.

See NEG at $AF33 for more information.

$9409 **37897**

Entry point for the routine that executes BASIC's COS function. Use $AF3F to access it.

See COS at $AF3F for more information.

$9410 **37904**

Entry point for the routine that executes BASIC's SIN function. Use $AF42 to access it.

See SIN at $AF42 for more information.

$9459 **37977**

Entry point for the routine that executes BASIC's TAN function. Use $AF45 to access it.

See TAN at $AF45 for more information.

$94B3 **38067**

Entry point for the routine that executes BASIC's ATN function. Use $AF48 to access it.

See ATN at $AF48 for more information.

$AF03-$AF05 **44803-44805**

This entry point actually executes a JMP $793C.

$AF06-$AF08 **44806-44808**

Jump statement to a routine that converts a floating-point value in FAC1 into a ASCII-coded string, beginning from address $0100 (256).

Procedure:

1. Load the value to be converted into FAC1.
2. Set the Bank-15 configuration and call the routine:

```
LDA #$00
STA $FF00
JSR $AF06
```

3. Read the ASCII version from $0100 to the first occurrence of a $00 byte.

This entry point actually executes a JMP $8E42.

$AF09-$AF0B **44809-44811**

This entry point actually executes a JMP $8052.

$AF0C-$AF0E **44812-44814**

This entry point actually executes a JMP $8815.

$AF0F–$AF11 **44815–44817**

This entry point actually executes a JMP $8C75C.

$AF12–$AF14 **44818–44820**

This entry point actually executes a JMP $882E.

$AF15–$AF17 **44821–44823**

This entry point actually executes a JMP $8831.

$AF18–$AF1A **44824–44826**

This entry point actually executes a JMP $8845.

$AF1B–$AF1D **44827–44829**

This entry point actually executes a JMP $8848.

$AF1E–$AF20 **44830–44832**

This entry point actually executes a JMP $8A24.

$AF21–$AF23 **44833–44835**

This entry point actually executes a JMP $8A27.

$AF24–$AF26 **44836–44838**

This entry point actually executes a JMP $8B49.

$AF27–$AF29 **44839–44841**

This entry point actually executes a JMP $8B4C.

$AF2A–$AF2C **44842–44844**

This entry point actually executes a JMP $89CA.

$AF2D–$AF2F **44845–44847**

This entry point actually executes a JMP $8CFB.

$AF30–$AF32 44848–44850

SQR Jump instruction to a routine that returns the square-root of a value in Floating-Point Accumulator 1 (FAC#1).

Procedure:

1. Load the argument to FAC#1.
2. Call this routine, JSR $AF30.
3. Read the square-root value in FAC#1.

This entry point actually executes a JMP $8FB7.

$AF33–$AF35 44851–44853

NEG Jump instruction to a routine that switches the sign of a value in Floating-Point Accumulator 1 (FAC#1). In effect, it multiplies the value by −1.

Procedure:

1. Load the argument to FAC#1.
2. Call this routine, JSR $AF33.
3. Read the negated value in FAC#1.

This entry point actually executes a JMP $8FFA.

$AF36–$AF38 44854–44856

This entry point actually executes a JMP $8FBE.

$AF39–$AF3B 44857–44859

This entry point actually executes a JMP $8FC1.

$AF3C–$AF3E 44860–44862

This entry point actually executes a JMP $9033.

$AF3F–$AF41 44863–44865

COS Jump instruction to a routine that calculates the trigonometric cosine of a value in Floating-Point Accumulator 1 (FAC#1).

Procedure:

1. Load the angle in radians to FAC#1.

2. Call this routine, JSR $AF3F.
3. Read the cosine of the value in FAC#1.

This entry point actually executes a JMP $9409.

$AF42–$AF44 44866–44868

SIN Jump instruction to a routine that calculates the trigonometric sine of a value in Floating-Point Accumulator 1 (FAC#1).

Procedure:

1. Load the angle in radians to FAC#1.
2. Call this routine, JSR $AF42.
3. Read the sine of the value in FAC#1.

This entry point actually executes a JMP $9410.

$AF45–$AF47 44869–44871

TAN Jump instruction to a routine that calculates the trigonometric tangent of a value in Floating-Point Accumulator 1 (FAC#1).

Procedure:

1. Load the angle in radians to FAC#1.
2. Call this routine, JSR $AF45.
3. Read the tangent of the value in FAC#1.

This entry point actually executes a JMP $9459.

$AF48–$AF4A 44872–44874

ATN Jump instruction to a routine that calculates the trigonometric arctangent of a value in Floating-Point Accumulator 1 (FAC#1).

Procedure:

1. Load the argument to FAC#1.
2. Call this routine, JSR $AF48.
3. Read the arctangent of the value, expressed in radians, from FAC#1.

This entry point actually executes a JMP $94B3.

$AF4B–$AF4D 44875–44877

ROFF Jump instruction to a routine that rounds off a numeric value by dropping all figures to the right of the decimal point.

Procedure:

1. Load the argument to FAC#1.
2. Call this routine, JSR $AF4B.
3. Read the rounded value from FAC#1.

This entry point actually executes a JMP $8C47.

$AF4E–$AF50 44878–44880

ABS Jump instruction to a routine that calculates the absolute value of a number in Floating-Point Accumulator 1 (FAC#1).

Procedure:

1. Load the argument to FAC#1.
2. Call this routine, JSR $AF4E.
3. Read the absolute value from FAC#1.

This entry point actually executes a JMP $8C84.

$AF51–$AF53 44881–44883

SGN Jump instruction to a routine that returns a value which indicates the sign of a number in Floating-Point Accumulator #1 (FAC#1).

Procedure:

1. Load the floating-point value to FAC#1.
2. Call this routine, JSR $AF51.
3. Read the sign indication from register A:

   $01 (1) = Positive value
   $FF (255) = Negative value

This entry point actually executes a JMP $8C57.

$AF54–$AF56 44884–44886

This entry point actually executes a JMP $8C87.

$AF57-$AF59 44887-44889

This entry point actually executes a JMP $8437.

$AF5A-$AF5C 44890-44892

Jump instruction to a routine that moves a value from a specified location in RAM to Floating-Point Accumulator #2.

Procedure:

1. Load the LSB of the source RAM address to register X.
2. Load the MSB of the source RAM address to register Y.
3. Call this routine, JSR $AF66.

This entry point actually executes a JMP $8AB4.

$AF5D-$AF5F 44893-44895

This entry point actually executes a JMP $8A89.

$AF60-$AF62 44896-44898

Jump instruction to a routine that moves a value from a specified location in RAM to Floating-Point Accumulator #1.

Procedure:

1. Load the LSB of the source RAM address to register X.
2. Load the MSB of the source RAM address to register Y.
3. Call this routine, JSR $AF66.

NOTE: Use the routine described at $AF66 to move a value from FAC#1 to a location in RAM.

The entry point actually executes a JMP $7A85.

$AF63-$AF65 44899-44901

This entry point actually executes a JMP $8BD4.

$AF66-$AF68 44902-44904

Jump instruction to a routine that moves a value from Floating-Point Accumulator #1 to a specified location in RAM.

Procedure:

1. Load the LSB of the destination RAM address to register X.

2. Load the MSB of the destination RAM address to register Y.
3. Call this routine, JSR $AF66.

NOTE: Use the routine described at $FA60 to move a value from RAM to FAC#1.

This entry point actually executes a JMP $8C00.

$AF69-$AF6B 44905-44907

Jump instruction to a routine that copies the content of FAC2 to FAC1.

Procedure: Call the routine, JSR $AF69.

This entry point actually executes a JMP $8C28.

$AF6C-$AF6E 44908-44910

Jump instruction to a routine that copies the content of FAC1 to FAC2.

Procedure: Call the routine, JSR $AF6C.

This entry point actually executes a JMP $8C38.

$AF7B-$AF7D 44923-44925

This entry point actually executes a JMP $5A9B.

$AF7E-$AF80 44926-44928

This entry point actually executes a JMP $51F3.

$AF81-$AF83 44929-44931

This entry point actually executes a JMP $51F8.

$AF84-$AF86 44932-44934

This entry point actually executes a JMP $51D6.

$AF87-$AF89 44935-44937

This entry point actually executes a JMP $4F4F.

$AF8A-$AF8C 44938-44940

This entry point actually executes a JMP $430A.

$AF8D–$AF8F 44941–44943

This entry point actually executes a JMP $5064.

$AF90–$AF92 44944–44946

This entry point actually executes a JMP $4AF6.

$AF93–$AF95 44947–44949

This entry point actually executes a JMP $78D7.

$AF96–$AF98 44950–44952

This entry point actually executes a JMP $77EF.

$AF99–$AF9B 44953–44955

This entry point actually executes a JMP $5AA6.

$AF9C–$AF9E 44956–44958

This entry point actually executes a JMP $5A81.

$AF9F–$AFA1 44959–44961

This entry point actually executes a JMP $50A0.

$AFA2–$AFA4 44962–44964

This entry point actually executes a JMP $92EA.

$AFA5–$AFA7 44965–44967

This entry point actually executes a JMP $4DCD.

Screen Editor ROM: $C000–$CFFF

The screen editor ROM contains a number of jump instructions for Kernal and interrupt routines as well as some screen routines and buffers.

Screen Editor JUMP Instructions

The following ROM locations are composed of three-byte, machine language JMP instructions. Although you can access the Kernal and interrupt routines through these addresses, you should use the alternative RAM addresses that accompany the descriptions.

$C000–$C002 **49152–49154**

Jump instruction to CINT Kernal routine $C07B.

See CINT at Kernal $FF81 for more details.

$C003–$C005 **49155–49157**

Jump instruction to editor routine at $CC34.

$C006–$C008 **49158–49160**

Jump instruction to editor routine at $C234.

$C009–$C00B **49161–49163**

Jump instruction to editor routine at $C29B.

$C00C–$C00E **49164–49166**

Jump instruction to editor routine at $C72D.

$C00F–$C011 **49167–49169**

Jump instruction to SCREEN Kernal routine at $CC5B.

See SCREEN at Kernal address $FFED for more details.

$C012–$C014 **49170–49172**

Jump instruction to SCNKEY Kernal routine at $C55D.

See SCKKEY at Kernal address $FF9F for more details.

$C015–$C017 **49173–49175**

Jump instruction to editor routine at $C651.

$C018–$C01A **49176–49178**

Jump instruction to PLOT Kernal routine at $CC6A.

See PLOT at Kernal address $FFF0 for more details.

$C01B–$C01D **49169–49181**

Jump instruction to editor routine at $CD57.

$C01E–$C020 **49182–49184**

Jump instruction to editor routine at $C9C1.

$C021–$C023 **49185–49187**

Jump instruction to editor routine at $CCA2.

$C024–$C026 **49188–49190**

Jump instruction to editor routine at $C194.

$C027–$C029 **49191–49193**

Jump instruction to Kernal routine at $CE0C. Initializes 80-column character set.

See Kernal address $FF65 for more details.

$C02A–$C02C **49194–49196**

Jump instruction to Kernal SWAP routine at $CD2E.

See Kernal address $FF5F for more details.

$C02D–$C02F **49197–49199**

Jump instruction to editor routine at $CA1B.

Screen Editor ROM Routines and Buffers

$C065–$C07A **49253–49274**

ROM version of editor indirects that are loaded to RAM $0334–$0349 by the CINT Kernal routine.

$C07B **49275**

CINT Kernal routine for initializing the editor and screen parameters. Execute this routine by calling it from the main Kernal at $FF81.

See $FF81 for more details.

$C194–$C233 **49556–49715**

Editor's hardware interrupt handler, IRQ. Execute this routine by calling it at $C024.

$CEB2–$CFFF **52914–53247**

Function-key command buffer.

I/O, ROM, and RAM Block: $D000–$DFFF

The addressing block between $D000 and $DFFF (53248–57343) is by far the most complex in terms of bank-switching operations. It serves three entirely different kinds of functions, depending on the current bank selection.

The block serves I/O functions in bank configurations 4, 5, 6, 7, 8, 9, 10, 11, 12, 13, and 15. The same addressing block is used as character ROM in the Bank-14 configuration and is available as RAM in bank configurations 0, 1, 2, and 3.

I/O Block Map

Bank-configured as an I/O block, $D000 through $DFFF contains:

1. The VIC 40-column text and video chip
2. SID sound chip
3. A dynamic memory management unit (MMU chip)
4. The 80-column video chip
5. 40-column color memory
6. A complex interface adapter (CIA) for game paddles, joysticks, keyboard, and light pen
7. A second CIA chip for serial communications: printer and RS-232-C
8. Optional memory expansion controller

$D000–$D010 **53248–54271**

Sprite screen positions:

$D000 (53248) = Sprite 1 LSB of X position
$D001 (53249) = Sprite 1 Y position
$D002 (53250) = Sprite 2 LSB of X position
$D003 (53251) = Sprite 2 Y position
$D004 (53252) = Sprite 3 LSB of X position

$D005 (53253) = Sprite 3 Y position
$D006 (53254) = Sprite 4 LSB of X position
$D007 (53255) = Sprite 4 Y position
$D008 (53256) = Sprite 5 LSB of X position
$D009 (53257) = Sprite 5 Y position
$D00A (53258) = Sprite 6 LSB of X position
$D00B (53259) = Sprite 6 Y position
$D00C (53260) = Sprite 7 LSB of X position
$D00D (53261) = Sprite 7 Y position
$D00E (53262) = Sprite 8 LSB of X position
$D00F (53263) = Sprite 8 Y position
$D010 (53264) = 9th bit of sprite X positions

Bit 0 = Sprite 1
Bit 1 = Sprite 2
Bit 2 = Sprite 3
Bit 3 = Sprite 4
Bit 4 = Sprite 5
Bit 5 = Sprite 6
Bit 6 = Sprite 7
Bit 7 = Sprite 8

$D011 53265

VIC control register 1:

Bit 7 = Raster compare bit
Bit 6 = Extended color flag

0 = normal
1 = extended color

Bit 5 = Bit-map mode flag

0 = normal
1 = bit-map mode

Bit 4 = Blank screen flag

0 = normal
1 = blank with border color

Bit 3 = Text lines flag

0 = 24 lines
1 = 25

Bits 0–2 = Smooth Y scroll (0 through 7 dots)

$D012 **53266**

This register carries the number of video scan lines (0 through 255) for the bit-map portion of a mixed screen. See applications information in Chapter 7.

$D013 **53267**

Light pen latch for Y position.

$D014 **53268**

Light pen latch for X position.

$D015 **53269**

Sprite display flag register.

0 = sprite off
1 = sprite on

Bit 0 = Sprite 1 on/off
Bit 1 = Sprite 2 on/off
Bit 2 = Sprite 3 on/off
Bit 3 = Sprite 4 on/off
Bit 4 = Sprite 5 on/off
Bit 5 = Sprite 6 on/off
Bit 6 = Sprite 7 on/off
Bit 7 = Sprite 8 on/off

$D016 **53270**

VIC control register 2:

Bits 6-7 = Not used
Bit 5 = Always 0
Bit 4 = Multicolor flag

0 = standard
1 = multicolor

Bit 3 = 38/40 column flag

0 = 30 columns
1 = 40 columns

Bits 0–2 = Smooth X scroll (0–7 dots)

$D017 **53271**

Sprite 2X vertical expansion flags:

0 = normal
1 = expand

Bit 0 = Y-expand sprite 1
Bit 1 = Y-expand sprite 2
Bit 2 = Y-expand sprite 3
Bit 3 = Y-expand sprite 4
Bit 4 = Y-expand sprite 5
Bit 5 = Y-expand sprite 6
Bit 6 = Y-expand sprite 7
Bit 7 = Y-expand sprite 8

$D018 **53272**

VIC internal address vectors:

Bits 4–7 = Video matrix base address
Bits 0–3 = Character dot base address

$D019 **53273**

VIC IRQ flags:

0 = no
1 = yes

Bit 7 = Any IRQ
Bits 4–7 = Not used
Bit 3 = Light pen IRQ
Bit 2 = Sprite-to-sprite collision IRQ
Bit 1 = Sprite-to-figure collision IRQ
Bit 0 = Raster compare IRQ

$D01A **53274**

VIC IRQ Mask:

0 = interrupt disabled
1 = interrupt enabled

$D01B **53275**

Sprite-to-figure priority flags:

0 = sprite moves behind figures
1 = sprite moves in front of figures

Bit 0 = Sprite 1 priority
Bit 1 = Sprite 2 priority
Bit 2 = Sprite 3 priority
Bit 3 = Sprite 4 priority
Bit 4 = Sprite 5 priority
Bit 5 = Sprite 6 priority
Bit 6 = Sprite 7 priority
Bit 7 = Sprite 8 priority

$D01C **53276**

Sprite multicolor enable flags:

0 = standard
1 = multicolor

Bit 0 = Sprite 1 color mode
Bit 1 = Sprite 2 color mode
Bit 2 = Sprite 3 color mode
Bit 3 = Sprite 4 color mode
Bit 4 = Sprite 5 color mode
Bit 5 = Sprite 6 color mode
Bit 6 = Sprite 7 color mode
Bit 7 = Sprite 8 color mode

$D01D **53277**

Sprite 2X horizontal expansion flags:

0 = normal
1 = expand:

Bit 0 = X-expand sprite 1
Bit 1 = X-expand sprite 2
Bit 2 = X-expand sprite 3
Bit 3 = X-expand sprite 4
Bit 4 = X-expand sprite 5
Bit 5 = X-expand sprite 6
Bit 6 = X-expand sprite 7
Bit 7 = X-expand sprite 8

$D01E **53278**

Sprite-to-sprite collision detection flags:

0 = sprite not involved
1 = sprite involved:

Bit 0 = Sprite 1 collision
Bit 1 = Sprite 2 collision
Bit 2 = Sprite 3 collision
Bit 3 = Sprite 4 collision
Bit 4 = Sprite 5 collision
Bit 5 = Sprite 6 collision
Bit 6 = Sprite 7 collision
Bit 7 = Sprite 8 collision

See a complete table of values for all possible combinations of sprite-to-sprite collisions in Chapter 8.

$D01F **53279**

Sprite-to-figure collision detection flags:

0 = sprite not involved
1 = sprite involved:

Bit 0 = Sprite 1 collision
Bit 1 = Sprite 2 collision
Bit 2 = Sprite 3 collision
Bit 3 = Sprite 4 collision
Bit 4 = Sprite 5 collision
Bit 5 = Sprite 6 collision
Bit 6 = Sprite 7 collision
Bit 7 = Sprite 8 collision

See a complete table of values for all possible combinations of sprite-to-figure collisions in Chapter 8.

$D020 **53280**

Border color—Low-order nibble values are $0 through $F (0–15).

$D021 **53281**

Background color 0—Low-order nibble values are $0 through $F (0–15).

$D022 **53282**

Background color 1 for extended color mode—Low-order nibble values are $0 through $F (0–15).

$D023 **53283**

Background color 2 for extended color mode—Low-order nibble values are $0 through $F (0–15).

$D024 **53284**

Background color 3 for extended color mode—Low-order nibble values are $0 through $F (0–15).

$D025 **53285**

Sprite multicolor 1—Low-order nibble values are $0 through $F (0–15).

$D026 **53286**

Sprite multicolor 2—Low-order nibble values are $0 through $F (0–15).

$D027 **53287**

Sprite 1 color—Low-order nibble values are $0 through $F (0–15).

$D028 **53288**

Sprite 2 color—Low-order nibble values are $0 through $F (0–15).

$D029 **53289**

Sprite 3 color—Low-order nibble values are $0 through $F (0–15).

$D02A **53290**

Sprite 4 color—Low-order nibble values are $0 through $F (0–15).

$D02B **53291**

Sprite 5 color—Low-order nibble values are $0 through $F (0–15).

$D02C **53292**

Sprite 6 color—Low-order nibble values are $0 through $F (0–15).

$D02D **53293**

Sprite 7 color—Low-order nibble values are $0 through $F (0–15).

$D02E **53294**

Sprite 8 color—Low-order nibble values are $0 through $F (0–15).

$D400–$D401 **54272–54273**

Voice 1 frequency registers:

$D400 (54272) = LSB of voice-1 frequency
$D401 (54273) = MSB of voice-1 frequency

$D402–$D403 **54274–54275**

Voice 1 pulse width registers:

$D402 (54274) = LSB of pulse waveform
$D403 (54275) = MSB of pulse waveform, bits 0–3

NOTE: Bits 4–7 of $D403 are not used.

$D404 **54276**

Voice 1 control register:

0 = disable
1 = enable

Bit 7 = Random noise
Bit 6 = Pulse waveform
Bit 5 = Sawtooth waveform
Bit 4 = Triangular waveform
Bit 3 = Oscillator test bit
Bit 2 = Ring modulate 1 with 3
Bit 1 = Synchronize 1 with 3
Bit 0 = Start attack/sustain, decay gate: 1 = start attack/sustain, 0 = start decay

---

$D405 **54277**

Voice 1 envelope generator 1:

Bits 4–7 = Attack duration
Bits 0–3 = Decay duration

$D406 54278

Voice 1 envelope generator 2:

Bits 4–7 = Sustain volume level
Bits 0–3 = Release duration

$D407–$D408 54279–54280

Voice 2 frequency registers:

$D407 (54279) = LSB of voice-2 frequency
$D408 (54280) = MSB of voice-2 frequency

$D409–$D40A 54281–54282

Voice 2 pulse width registers:

$D409 (54281) = LSB of pulse waveform
$D40A (54282) = MSB of pulse waveform; bits 0–3

NOTE: Bits 4–7 of $D40A are not used.

$D40B 54283

Voice 2 control register:

Data:

0 = disable
1 = enable

Bit 7 = Random noise
Bit 6 = Pulse waveform
Bit 5 = Sawtooth waveform
Bit 4 = Triangular waveform
Bit 3 = Oscillator on/off: 0 = on, 1 = off
Bit 2 = Ring modulate 2 with 1
Bit 1 = Synchronize 2 with 1
Bit 0 = Start attack/sustain, decay gate: 1 = start attack/sustain, 0 = start decay

$D40C **54284**

Voice 2 envelope generator 1:

Bits 4–7 = Attack duration
Bits 0–3 = Decay duration

$D40D **54285**

Voice 2 envelope generator 2:

Bits 4–7 = Sustain volume level
Bits 0–3 = Release duration

$D40E–$D40F **54286–54287**

Voice 3 frequency registers:

$D40E (54286) = LSB of voice-3 frequency
$D40F (54287) = MSB of voice-3 frequency

$D410–$D4011 **54288–54289**

Voice 3 pulse width registers:

$D410 (54288) = LSB of pulse waveform
$D411 (54289) = MSB of pulse waveform: bits 0–3

NOTE: Bits 4–7 of $D411 are not used.

$D412 **54290**

Voice 3 control register:

Data:

0 = disable
1 = enable

Bit 7 = Random noise
Bit 6 = Pulse waveform
Bit 5 = Sawtooth waveform
Bit 4 = Triangular waveform
Bit 3 = Oscillator test bit
Bit 2 = Ring modulate 3 with 2
Bit 1 = Synchronize 3 with 2
Bit 0 = Start attack/sustain, decay gate: 1 = start attack/sustain, 0 = start decay

$D413 **54291**

Voice 3 envelope generator 1:

Bits 4–7 = Attack duration
Bits 0–3 = Decay duration

$D414 **54292**

Voice 3 envelope generator 2:

Bits 4–7 = Sustain volume level
Bits 0–3 = Release duration

$D415–$D416 **54293–54294**

Filter cutoff frequency:

$D415 (54293) = Low-order: bits 0–2
$D415 (54294) = MSB

NOTE: Bits 3–7 of $D415 are not used.

$D417 **54295**

Filter control register:

Bits 4–7 = Filter resonance: 0–15
Bit 3 = Filter external input: 0 = no, 1 = yes
Bit 2 = Filter voice 3: 0 = no, 1 = yes
Bit 1 = Filter voice 2: 0 = no, 1 = yes
Bit 0 = Filter voice 1: 0 = no, 1 = yes

$D418 **54296**

Filter mode and volume register:

Bit 7 = Voice 3 disable: 0 = no, 1 = yes
Bit 6 = Select SID high-pass filter: 0 = no, 1 = yes
Bit 5 = Select SID bandpass filter: 0 = no, 1 = yes
Bit 4 = Select SID low-pass filter: 0 = no, 1 = yes
Bits 0–3 = SID volume level

$D419 **54297**

A/D converter #1, values $00 through $FF (0–255).

$D41A **54298**

A/D converter #2, values $00 through $FF (0–255).

$D41B **54299**

SID oscillator 3 random number (noise) source.

$D41C **54300**

Envelope output for voice 3.

$D41D–$D41F **54301–54303**

Not used.

$D420–$D43F **54304–54335**

Image of $D400–$D41F.

$D440–$D45F **54336–54367**

Image of $D400–$D41F.

$D460–$D47F **54368–54399**

Image of $D400–$D41F.

$D480–$D49F **54400–54431**

Image of $D400–$D41F.

$D4A0–$D4BF **54432–54463**

Image of $D400–$D41F.

$D4C0–$D4DF **54464–54495**

Image of $D400–$D41F.

$D4E0–$D4FF **54496–54527**

Image of $D400–$D41F.

$D500 **54528**

Memory configuration register:

Bits 7-6 = RAM block allocation

00 = block 0
01 = block 1
10 = block 2 (identical to block 0)
11 = block 3 (identical to block 1)

Bits 5-4 = Allocation of blocks $C000-$CFFF and $E000-$FFFF4

00 = Kernal ROM
01 = Internal ROM
10 = External ROM
11 = RAM

Bits 3-2 = Allocation of $8000-$BFFF

00 = BASIC ROM
01 = Internal ROM
10 = External ROM
11 = RAM

Bit 1 = Allocation of $4000-$7FFF

0 = BASIC ROM
1 = RAM

Bit 0 = Allocation of $D000-$DFFF

0 = I/O
1 = Character ROM

See the RAM image of this register at $FF00 and more details in Chapter 14.

$D501-$D504 **54529-54532**

MMU Preconfiguration registers:

$D501 (54529) = Bank 0
$D502 (54530) = Bank 1
$D503 (54531) = Bank 14
$D504 (54532) = All block-0 RAM except I/O

See RAM images of this register at $FF01-$FF04 and more details in Chapter 14.

$D505 **54533**

Mode configuration register:

Bit 7 = 40/80 DISPLAY switch

$00 = switch down (80-column)
$80 = switch up (40-column)

Bit 6-5 = C64-mode cartridge switch
Bit 4 = Not used
Bit 3 = Fast disk flag
Bit 2 = Not used (?)
Bit 1 = Not used (?)
Bit 0 = Microprocessor select flag: 0 = Z-80, 1 = 8502

$D506 **54534**

RAM configuration register.

$D507-$D508 **54535-54536**

Starting location of virtual zero page.

$D509-$D50A **54537-54538**

Starting location of virtual page 1.

$D50B **54539**

System identification byte, $20 for the current Commodore 128.

$D50C-$D5FF **54538-54783**

Not used.

$D600 **54884**

80-column chip register number port.

$D601 **54885**

80-column chip data I/O port.

$D800–$DBFF 55296–56319

40-column color memory. See details in Chapter 6.

$DC00 56320

CIA#1 data port A—This port serves two different kinds of purposes, depending on whether the system writes to it or reads from it.

Writing to $DC00 specifies the keyboard column during keyboard scanning operations.

Reading from $DC00 provides game port information.

When using joysticks:

Bit 4 = Joystick 1 pushbutton (switch 4)

0 = pressed
1 = not pressed

Bit 3 = Joystick 1 switch 3 (right)

0 = activated
1 = not activated

Bit 2 = Joystick 1 switch 2 (left)
Bit 1 = Joystick 1 switch 1 (down)
Bit 0 = Joystick 1 switch 0 (up)

When using paddles:

Bits 7-6 = Select which paddle set

01 = set 1
10 = set 2

Bit 3 = Paddle 2 pushbutton

0 = not pressed
1 = pressed

Bit 2 = Paddle 1 pushbutton

0 = not pressed
1 = pressed

$DC01 **56321**

CIA#1 data port B—Data read from this port depends on the byte written to its data direction register at $DC03.

When reading the keyboard, data indicates the current keyboard matrix row value.

When using joysticks:

Bit 4 = Joystick 2 pushbutton (switch 4)

0 = pressed
1 = not pressed

Bit 3 = Joystick 2 switch 3 (right)

0 = activated
1 = not activated

Bit 2 = Joystick 2 switch 2 (left)
Bit 1 = Joystick 2 switch 1 (down)
Bit 0 = Joystick 2 switch 0 (up)

When using paddles:

Bit 3 = Paddle 2 pushbutton

0 = not pressed
1 = pressed

Bit 2 = Paddle 1 pushbutton

0 = not pressed
1 = pressed

When using the timers:

Bit 7 = Timer B pulse output
Bit 6 = Timer A pulse output

$DC02 **56322**

CIA#1 data direction register for port A.

$DC03 **56323**

CIA#1 data direction register for port B.

$DC04-$DC05 **56324-56325**

CIA#1 timer A.

$DC04 (56324) = LSB of timer
$DC05 (56325) = MSB of timer

$DC06-$DC07 **56326-56327**

CIA#1 timer B.

$DC06 (56326) = LSB of timer
$DC07 (56327) = MSB of timer

$DC08-$DC0B **56328-56331**

Time-of-day clock.

$DC08 (56328) = Tenths of seconds
$DC09 (56329) = Seconds
$DC0A (56330) = Minutes
$DC0B (56331) = Hours and AM/PM

Bits 3-0 = hours
Bit 7 = AM/PM flag

$DC0C **56332**

Synchronous serial I/O buffer.

$DC0D **56333**

CIA#1 IRQ controls.

$DC0E **56334**

CIA#1 control register A.

$DC0F **56335**

CIA#1 control register B.

$DC10-$DCFF **56336-56575**

Images of $DC00-$DCFF.

$DD00 **56576**

CIA#2 data port A:

Bit 7 = Serial data input
Bit 6 = Serial clock input
Bit 5 = Serial data output
Bit 4 = Serial clock output
Bit 3 = Serial ATN output
Bit 2 = RS-232-C output

$DD01 **56577**

CIA#2 data port B:

0 = no
1 = yes

Bit 7 = RS-232-C data set ready
Bit 6 = RS-232-C clear to send
Bit 4 = RS-232-C carrier detect
Bit 3 = RS-232-C ring indicator
Bit 2 = RS-232-C data terminal ready
Bit 1 = RS-232-C request to send
Bit 0 = RS-232-C data received

$DD02 **56578**

CIA#2 data direction register for port A.

$DD03 **56579**

CIA#2 data direction register for port B.

$DD04–$DD05 **56580–56581**

CIA#2 timer A.

$DD04 (56580) = LSB of timer
$DD05 (56581) = MSB of timer

$DD06–$DD07 **56582–56583**

CIA#2 timer B.

$DD06 (56582) = LSB of timer
$DD07 (56583) = MSB of timer

$DD08-$DD0B **56584-56587**

Time-of-day clock.

$DD08 (56584) = Tenths of seconds
$DD09 (56585) = Seconds
$DD0A (56586) = Minutes
$DD0B (56587) = Hours and AM/PM

Bits 3-0 = hours
Bit 7 = AM/PM flag

$DD0C **56588**

Synchronous serial I/O buffer.

$DD0D **56589**

CIA#2 IRQ controls.

$DD0E **56590**

CIA#2 control register A.

$DD0F **56591**

CIA#2 control register B.

$DD10-$DDFF **56592-56831**

Images of $DD00-$DDFF.

Character ROM Map

Using the Bank-14 configuration uses $D000 through $DFFF as bit-mapped character ROM.

$D000-$D3FF **53248-54271**

Normal uppercase/graphics character set.

$D400-$D7FF **54272-55295**

Reverse uppercase/graphics character set.

$D800-$DBFF **55296-56319**

Normal uppercase/lowercase character set.

$DC00-$DFFF 56320-57343

Reverse uppercase/lowercase character set.

Kernal ROM: $E000-$FFFF

$E000 57344

Entry point for the system initialization routine. Same as pressing the RESTORE key while holding down the RUN/STOP key.

User's programs should access the routine from the system RST vector: JMP ($FFFC)

$E04B-$E055 57419-57429

Table of initial values loaded to $D500-$D50A by the RST routine described previously.

$E056 57430

Entry point for C128 RESTOR routine—Restores the C128 Kernal vectors and includes the VECTOR routine described below. User's programs should access the routine from the RESTOR Kernal at $FF8A.

See $FF8A in the Kernal jump tables for more information.

$E05B 57435

Entry point for C128 VECTOR routine. Swaps C128 vectors between user-defined RAM and the Kernal vector tables at $0314-$0333. User's programs should access the routine from the VECTOR Kernal at $FF8D.

$E073-$E092 57459-57490

Table of default Kernal vectors loaded to RAM addresses by the RESTOR and VECTOR routines described above. Also see the details for the VECTOR routine at $FF8D.

$E093 57491

Entry point for C128 RAMTAS routine. Sets default RAM organization. User's programs should access the routine from the RAMTAS Kernal at $FF87.

See $FF87 in the Kernal jump tables for more information.

$E0CD **57549**

Entry point for an alternative NMI routine.

$E109 **57609**

Entry point for IOINIT routine. Initializes the I/O parameters. User's programs should access the routine from IOINIT at $FF84.

See $FF84 in the Kernal jump tables for more information.

$E24B **57931**

Entry point for GO64 routine. Sets up the C64 mode without the ARE YOU SURE prompting message. User's programs should access the routine from the GO64 Kernal at $FF4D.

See $FF4D in the Kernal jump table for more information.

$E33B **58171**

Entry point for the TALK routine. Sets I/O device to send data to the computer. User's programs should access the routine from the TALK Kernal at $FFB4.

$E33E **58174**

Entry point for the LISTEN routine. Sets I/O device to accept data from the computer. User's programs should access the routine from the LISTEN Kernal at $FFB1.

See $FFB1 in the Kernal jump tables for more information.

$E43E **$58430**

Entry point for the ACPTR routine. Fetches a byte of data from an open channel. User's programs should access the routine from the ACPTR Kernal at $FFA5.

See $FFA5 in the Kernal jump tables for more information.

$E4D2 **58578**

Entry point for the SECOND routine. Sends secondary address in LIS-

TEN. User's programs should access the routine from the SECOND Kernal at $FF93.

$E4E0 **58592**

Entry point for the TKSA routine. Sends secondary address in TALK. User's programs should access the routine from the TKSA Kernal at $FF96.

See $FF96 in the Kernal jump tables for more information.

$E503 **58627**

Entry point for the CIOUT routine. Sends a byte to a serial port. User's programs should access the routine from the CIOUT Kernal at $FFA8.

See $FFA8 in the Kernal jump tables for more information.

$E515 **58645**

Entry point for the UNTLK routine. Turns off TALK mode. User's programs should access the routine from the UNTLK Kernal at $FFAB.

$E526 **58662**

Entry point for the UNLSN routine. Turns off the LISTEN mode. User's programs should access the routine from the UNLSN Kernal at $FFAE.

See $FFAE in the Kernal jump tables for more information.

$E5FB **58875**

Entry point for the Kernal routine that sets fast disk drive I/O. User's programs should call this routine from $FF47.

See $FF47 in the Kernal jump tables for more information.

$EEEB **61163**

Entry point for the GETIN routine. Fetches the next character from the keyboard buffer. The system can be directed to a custom version by loading the LSB of the alternative address to Kernal vector at $032A and the MSB to $032B.

User's programs, whether default or custom, should access the routine from the GETIN Kernal at $FFE4.

See $FFE4 in the Kernal jump tables for more information.

$EF06 **61190**

Entry point for the CHRIN routine. Fetches a character from an open channel. The system can be directed to a custom version by loading the LSB of the alternative address to Kernal vector at $0324 and the MSB to $0325.

User's programs, whether default or custom, should access the routine from the CHRIN Kernal at $FFCF.

See $FFCF in the Kernal jump tables for more information.

$EFBD **61373**

Entry point for the OPEN routine. Opens a file. The system can be directed to a custom version by loading the LSB of the alternative address to Kernal vector at $031A and the MSB to $031B.

User's programs, whether default or custom, should access the routine from the OPEN Kernal at $FFC0.

See $FFC0 in the Kernal jump tables for more information.

$F106 **61702**

Entry point for the CHKIN routine. Opens a channel for input. The system can be directed to a custom version by loading the LSB of the alternative address to Kernal vector at $031E and the MSB to $031F.

User's programs, whether default or custom, should access the routine from the CHKIN Kernal at $FFC6.

See $FFC6 in the Kernal jump tables for more information.

$F14C **61772**

Entry point for the CHKOUT routine. Opens a channel for output. The system can be directed to a custom version by loading the LSB of the alternative address to Kernal vector at $0320 and the MSB to $0321.

User's programs, whether default or custom, should access the routine from the CHKOUT Kernal at $FFC9.

See $FFC9 in the Kernal jump tables for more information.

$F188 **61832**

Entry point for the CLOSE routine. Closes a file. The system can be directed to a custom version by loading the LSB of the alternative address to Kernal vector at $031C and the MSB to $031D.

User's programs, whether default or custom, should access the routine from the CLOSE Kernal at $FFC3.

See $FFC3 in the Kernal jump tables for more information.

$F222 **61986**

Entry point for the CLALL routine. Closes all files and channels. The system can be directed to a custom version by loading the LSB of the alternative address to Kernal vector at $032C and the MSB to $032D.

User's programs, whether default or custom, should access the routine from the CLALL Kernal at $FFE7.

See $FFE7 in the Kernal jump tables for more information.

$F226 **61990**

Entry point for the CLRCHN routine. Closes selected channels. The system can be directed to a custom version by loading the LSB of the alternative address to Kernal vector at $0322 and the MSB to $0323.

User's programs, whether default or custom, should access the routine from the CLALL Kernal at $FFCC.

See $FFCC in the Kernal jump tables for more information.

$F23D **62013**

Entry point for a Kernal routine that closes all files open to a specified device. See more details at $FF4A in the Kernal jump table.

$F265 **62053**

Entry point for the LOAD routine. Loads a program or file. User's programs should access the routine from the LOAD Kernal at $FFD5.

See $FFD5 in the Kernal jump tables for more information.

$F53E **62782**

Entry point for the SAVE routine. Saves a block of RAM to tape or disk. User's programs should call this from the SAVE Kernal at $FFD8.

See $FFD8 in the Kernal jump tables for more information.

$F5F8 **62968**

Entry point for the UDTIM routine. Updates the real-time clock. User's programs should access the routine from the UDTIM Kernal at $FFEA.

See $FFEA in the Kernal jump tables for more information.

$F65E **63070**

Entry point for the RDTIM routine. Reads the real-time clock. User's programs should access the routine from the RDTIM Kernal at $FFDE.

See $FFDE in the Kernal jump tables for more information.

$F66E **63086**

Entry point for the STOP routine. Scans the keyboard and responds to a STOP keystroke. The system can be directed to a custom version by loading the LSB of the alternative address to Kernal vector at $0328 and the MSB to $0329.

User's programs, whether default or custom, should access the routine from the STOP Kernal at $FFE1.

See $FFE1 in the Kernal jump tables for more information.

$F731 **63281**

Entry point for the SETNAM routine. Sets a file name. User's programs should access the routine from the SETNAM Kernal at $FFBD.

See $FFBD in the Kernal jump tables for more information.

$F738 **63288**

Entry point for the SETLFS routine. Sets file number, device number, and secondary address. User's programs should access the routine from the SETLFS Kernal at $FFBA.

See $FFBA in the Kernal jump tables for more information.

$F73F **63295**

Entry point for a Kernal routine that sets the bank configuration for save, load, and verify operations. User's programs should call this routine from $FF68.

See $FF68 in the Kernal jump tables for more information.

$F744 **63300**

Entry point for the READST routine. Reads the most recent I/O status. User's programs should access the routine from the READST Kernal at $FFB7.

See $FFB7 in the Kernal jump tables for more information.

$F75C **63324**

Entry point for the SETMSG routine. Sets the prompt/error message status. User's programs should access the routine from the SETMSG Kernal at $FF90.

See $FF90 in the Kernal jump tables for more information.

$F75F **63327**

Entry point for the SETMO routine. Sets device timeout format. User's programs should access the routine from the SETMO Kernal at $FFA2.

See $FFA2 in the Kernal jump tables for more information.

$F763 **63331**

Entry point for the MEMTOP routine. Sets the highest RAM address used by BASIC. User's programs should access the routine from the MEMTOP Kernal at $FF99.

See $FF99 in the Kernal jump tables for more information.

$F772 **63346**

Entry point for the MEMBOT routine. Sets the lowest RAM address used by BASIC. User's programs should access the routine from the MEMBOT Kernal at $FF9C.

See $FF9C in the Kernal jump tables for more information.

$F781 **63361**

Entry point for the IOBASE routine. Returns the base address of the system's memory-mapped, I/O device area. User's programs should access the routine from the IOBASE Kernal at $FFF3.

$F786 **63366**

Entry point for the Kernal routine that returns the file and device number for a designated secondary address. User's programs should access the routine from $FF5C.

See $FF5C in the Kernal jump tables for more information.

$F79D **63389**

Entry point for a Kernal routine that returns the device number and secondary address of a designated file. User's programs should access this routine from $FF59.

See $FF59 in the Kernal jump table for more information.

$F7A5 **63397**

Entry point for a Kernal routine that does stash, fetch, swap, and verify operations between C128 memory and expansion RAM. User's programs should access the routine from the $FF50.

See more details at $FF50 in the Kernal jump tables.

$F7D0 **63440**

Entry point for a Kernal routine that fetches a byte from any bank. User's programs should access the routine from $FF74.

See $FF74 in the Kernal jump tables for more information.

$F7DA **63450**

Entry point for a Kernal routine that stores a byte of data to an address in any other bank. User's programs should access the routine from $FF77.

See $FF77 in the Kernal jump tables for more information.

$F7E3 **63459**

Entry point for a Kernal routine that compares a byte in any other bank with the content of register A. User's programs should access the routine from $FF7A.

See $FF7A in the Kernal jump tables for more information.

$F7EC **63468**

Entry point for a Kernal routine that returns the MMU configuration of a designated bank. User's programs should access the routine from $FF6B.

See $FF6B in the Kernal jump tables for more information.

$F867 **63591**

Entry point for a Kernal routine that initializes a ROM cartridge and boots the disk drive. User's programs should access the routine from $FF56.

See more details at $FF56 in the Kernal jump tables.

$F890 **63632**

Entry point for the Kernal routine that boots a program from the current disk. User's programs should access the routine from $FF53.

See $FF53 in the Kernal jump tables for more information.

$FA17 **64023**

Entry point for the Kernal routine that prints a string of ASCII-coded characters to the screen. User's programs should access the routine from $FF7D.

See $FF7D in the Kernal jump tables for more information.

$FA80–$FC7F **64128–64639**

Editor tables.

$FC80–$FEFF **64640–65279**

Reserved for foreign-language ROM.

ROM $FF00-$FF04: Memory-Management Registers

$FF00 **65280**

Bank configuration register. See details in Chapter 14.

$FF01-$FF04 **65281-65284**

Bank preconfiguration registers. See Chapter 14.

ROM $FF05-$FF44: Interrupt Routines

$FF05 **65285**

NMI Processes the system's non-maskable interrupt as determined by an address vector at $0318. The routine can be altered by writing a different NMI routine and loading its starting address to that vector location. The default routine can be restored at a later time by executing RESTOR at $FF8A. See the NMINV vector listed under VECTOR at $FF8D.

It is recommended that user's programs access this routine by executing an indirect jump to the NMI vector at $FFFA: JMP ($FFFA)

$FF17 **65303**

IRQ Processes interrupts determined by address vectors at $0314 and $0316. Those vectors, and hence interrupt processing, can be altered as required and later restored to the default routines by executing RESTOR at $FF8A. See the CINV and CBINV vectors listed under VECTOR at $FF8D.

It is recommended that user's programs access this routine by executing an indirect jump to the IRQ vector at $FFFE: JMP ($FFFE)

$FF3D **65341**

RST Executes a system restart. Same as pressing the RESTORE key while holding down the RUN/STOP key.

It is recommended that user's programs access this routine by executing an indirect jump to the RST vector at $FFFC: JMP ($FFFC)

ROM $FF47-$FFFF: Kernal Jump Tables and Hardware Vectors

$FF47-$FF49 65351-65353

Kernal jump to a routine that sets fast disk drive input/output.

Procedure for setting fast input:

1. Clear the carry flag, CLC.
2. Call the routine, JSR $FF47.

Procedure for setting fast output:

1. Set the carry flag, SEC.
2. Call the routine, JSR $FF47.

This entry point actually executes a JMP $E5FB.

$FF4A-$FF4C 65354-65356

Kernal jump routine that closes all files open to a specified device.

Procedure:

1. Load the desired device number to register A.
2. Call the routine, JSR $FF4A.

This entry point actually executes a JMP $F23D.

$FF4D-$FF4F 65357-65559

GO64 Kernal—Converts the system to the C64 mode without asking.

Procedure: Jump to the routine, JMP $FF4D.

This entry point actually executes JMP $E24B.

$FF50-$FF52 65360-65362

Kernal routine for doing stash, fetch, swap, and verify between the C128 memory and expansion RAM.

Procedure:

1. Load LSB of C128 start address to $DF02.
2. Load MSB of C128 start address to $DF03.
4. Load LSB of expansion start address to $DF04.
5. Load MSB of expansion start address to $DF05.
6. Load bank number of expansion RAM to $DF06.
7. Load LSB of number of bytes to $DF07.
8. Load MSB of number of bytes to $DF08.
9. Load C128 bank number to register X.
10. Load command code to register Y:

    0 = stash
    1 = fetch
    2 = swap
    3 = verify

11. Call the routine, JSR $FF50.

This entry point actually executes JMP $F7A5.

$FF53-$FF55 65363-65365

Kernal jump to a routine that boots a program from disk, equivalent to BASIC's BOOT command.

Procedure:

1. Load the ASCII value of the drive number to register A ($30 = 0, $31 = 1).
2. Load the value of the device number to register X.
3. Call the routine, JSR $FF53.

This entry point actually executes JMP $F890.

$FF56-$FF58 65366-65368

Kernal jump to a routine that initializes any ROM cartridges and boots the disk drive.

Procedure: Call the routine, JSR $FF56.

This entry point actually executes JMP $F867.

$FF59-$FF5B 65369-65371

Kernal jump to a routine that returns the device number and secondary address of a designated file number.

Procedure:

1. Load the file number to register A.
2. Call the routine, JSR $FF59.
3. Read the device number in register X.
4. Read the secondary address in register Y.

It invokes a FILE NOT FOUND error if the file cannot be found.

This entry point actually executes JMP $F79D.

$FF5C-$FF5E 65372-65374

Kernal jump to a routine that returns the file and device numbers for a designated secondary address.

Procedure:

1. Load the desired secondary address to register A.
2. Call the routine, JSR $FF5C.
3. Read the file number in register A.
4. Read the device number in register X.
5. Read the secondary address in Y.

It invokes a FILE NOT FOUND error if the file cannot be found.

This entry point actually executes JMP $F786.

$FF5F-$FF61 65375-65377

SWAP Kernal—Each execution of this routine swaps the 40-column and 80-column text screen parameters.

Procedure: Call the routine, JSR $FF5F.

This entry point actually executes JMP $C02A.

$FF62-$FF64 65378-65380

Kernal jump to a routine that initializes the character set for the 80-column screen format.

Procedure: Call the routine, JSR $FF62.

This entry point actually executes JMP $C027.

$FF65-$FF67 65381-65382

Kernal jump to a routine that assigns a string to a function key. Similar to BASIC's KEY statement but can include HELP and SHIFT-RUN keys as well.

Procedure:

1. Load the desired ASCII string to a RAM location.
2. Load the following sequence of information to three consecutive zero page addresses:
   a. LSB of the string address
   b. MSB of the string address
   c. Bank number of the string address
3. Load the first of the three zero-page addresses to register A.
4. Load the function-key number to register X.
5. Load the length of the string to register Y.
6. Call the routine, JSR $FF65.

This entry point actually executes JMP $C021.

$FF68-$FF6A 65384-65386

Kernal jump to a routine that sets the bank configuration for save, load, and verify operations.

Procedure:

1. Use the SETNAM Kernal to set a file name (see SETNAM at $FFBD).
2. Load the bank number for the operation into register A.
3. Load the bank number of the file name to register X
4. Call the routine, JSR $FF68.
5. Call the SAVE or LOAD routines as desired (see SAVE at FFD and LOAD at $FFD5).

This entry point actually executes JMP $F73F.

$FF6B–$FF6D 65387–65389

Kernal jump to a routine that returns the MMU configuration of a designated bank number.

Procedure:

1. Load the bank number to register X.
2. Call the routine, JSR $FF6B.
3. Read the bank-configuration status from register A.

Following JSR $FF6B with STA $FF00 immediately transfers the system to that bank configuration.

This entry point actually executes JMP $F7EC.

$FF6E–$FF70 65390–65392

Kernal jump to a routine that does a JSR (jump-and-return) to a program in any other bank.

Procedure:

1. Load the destination bank number to $02.
2. Load the MSB of the destination address to $03.
3. Load the LSB of the destination address to $04.
4. Carry the desired 8502 registers to the destination routine:

   Status register to $05
   Register A to $06
   Register X to $07
   Register Y to $08

5. Call the routine, JSR $FF6E.
6. Recover the 8502 registers returned by the far routine:

   Status register from $05
   Register A from $06
   Register X from $07
   Register Y from $08

See examples in Chapter 14.

This entry point actually executes JMP $02CD.

$FF71-$FF73 65393-65395

Kernal jump to a routine that makes it possible to do a JUMP to another routine in a different bank.

Procedure:

1. Load the destination bank number to $02.
2. Load the MSB of the destination address to $03.
3. Load the LSB of the destination address to $04.
4. Carry the desired 8502 registers to the destination routine:

   Status register to $05
   Register A to $06
   Register X to $07
   Register Y to $08

5. Call the routine, JSR $FF71.

See Chapter 14 for examples.

This entry point actually executes JMP $02E3.

$FF74-$FF76 65396-65398

Kernal jump to a routine that fetches a byte from any bank. In essence, it executes a LDA(*addr*),Y to load register A with the indexed data.

Procedure:

1. Load the LSB and MSB of the target address, in that order, in a sequence of two zero-page locations.
2. Load the first of the two zero-page addresses to register A.
3. Load the destination bank number to register X.
4. Load the index value to register Y.
5. Call the routine, JSR $FF74.
6. Read the fetched byte in register A.

See examples in Chapter 14.

This entry point actually executes JMP $F7D0.

$FF77-$FF79 65399-65401

Kernal jump to a routine that stores a byte to an address in any other bank. The general equivalent is STA (*addr*),Y.

Procedure:

1. Load the LSB and MSB of the target address, in that order, in a sequence of two zero-page locations.
2. Load the first of the two zero-page addresses to $02B9.
3. Load the byte to store in register A.
4. Load the destination bank number to register X.
5. Load the index value to register Y.
6. Call the routine, JSR $FF77.

See examples in Chapter 14.

This entry point actually executes JMP $F7DA.

$FF7A–$FF7C 65402–65404

Kernal jump to a routine that compares a byte in any other bank with the content of register A in the current bank. It is equivalent to a CMP(*addr*),Y.

Procedure:

1. Load the LSB and MSB of the target address, in that order, in a sequence of two zero-page locations.
2. Load the first of the two zero-page addresses to $02C8.
3. Load the compare byte to register A.
4. Load the destination bank number to register X.
5. Load the index value to register Y.
6. Call the routine, JSR $FF7A.
7. Read the result in the processor status register.

See examples in Chapter 14.

This entry point actually executes JMP $F7E3.

$FF7D–$FF7F 65405–65407

Kernal jump to a routine that prints a string of ASCII data to the screen.

Procedure:

1. Load the JSR $FF7D coding into RAM.
2. Load up to 255 ASCII-coded characters into RAM, immediately following the instruction in Step 1.

3. End the string with a $00.
4. Call the starting address of the routine from the RAM address used for step 1.

This entry point actually executes JMP $FA17.

$FF81-$FF83 65409-65411

CINT Kernal—Initializes the screen editor and VIC device.

Procedure: Call the routine, JSR $FF81.

This entry point actually executes JMP $C000.

$FF84-$FF86 65412-6544

IOINIT Kernal—Initializes all input and output devices.

Procedure: Call the routine, JSR $FF84.

This entry point actually executes JMP $E109.

$FF87-$FF89 65415-65417

RAMTAS Kernal—Restores default RAM allocation.

Procedure: Call the routine, JSR $FF87.

This entry point actually executes JMP $E093.

$FF8A-$FF8C 65418-65420

RESTOR Kernal—Restores all default Kernal and BASIC vectors.

Procedure: Call the routine, JSR $FF8A.

This entry point actually executes JMP $E056.

$FF8D 65421

VECTOR Kernal—Swaps 16 alterable Kernal vectors between the system's Kernal vector table ($0314-$0333) and a user-defined block of RAM. Table 13-1 summarizes the vectors and their index values.

Procedure for transferring the current vector table to user RAM:

1. Load LSB of the user-RAM block address to register X.
2. Load MSB of the user-RAM block address to register Y.
3. Set the carry flag (SEC).
4. Call the VECTOR subroutine.

Table 13-1 Summary of Kernal Vector Addresses and User-RAM Addresses When Using VECTOR Routine

Vector Table Address	User RAM Address	Kernal	Default Vector
$0314	USER ADDR. + $00	CINV	$FA65
$0316	USER ADDR. + $02	CBINV	$B003
$0318	USER ADDR. + $04	NMINV	$FA40
$031A	USER ADDR. + $06	OPEN	$EFBD
$031C	USER ADDR. + $08	CLOSE	$F188
$031E	USER ADDR. + $0A	CHKIN	$F106
$0320	USER ADDR. + $0C	CHKOUT	$F14C
$0322	USER ADDR. + $0E	CLRCHN	$F226
$0324	USER ADDR. + $10	CHRIN	$EF06
$0326	USER ADDR. + $12	CHROUT	$EF79
$0328	USER ADDR. + $14	STOP	$F66E
$032A	USER ADDR. + $16	GETIN	$EEEB
$032C	USER ADDR. + $18	CLALL	$F222
$032E	USER ADDR. + $1A	USRCMD	$B006
$0330	USER ADDR. + $1C	ILOAD	$F26C
$0332	USER ADDR. + $1E	ISAVE	$F54E

Procedure for transferring the user-RAM version of the vector table to the standard vector-table location:

1. Load LSB of the user-RAM block address to register X.
2. Load MSB of the user-RAM block address to register Y.
3. Clear the carry flag (CLC).
4. Call the VECTOR subroutine.

Use the RESTOR routine to restore the default vectors.

The VECTOR entry point actually executes JMP $E05B.

$FF90 **65424**

SETMSG Kernal—Determines whether prompt and error messages are to be printed on the screen. If so, you can determine which, or both, are to appear. The system restores the default value, $C0 (192), when returning to the monitor or BASIC.

Procedure:

1. Set the desired code to register A.

$C0 (192) both messages
$80 (128) control messages only
$40 (64) error messages only
$00 (0) no messages

2. Call SETMSG

The routine actually does a JMP $F75C.

$FF93 **65427**

SECOND Kernal—Sends a secondary address to an I/O device when operating in the LISTEN mode.

General procedure:

1. Configure a device to LISTEN (see $FFB1).
2. Load the secondary address to register A.
3. OR immediate with $60.
4. Call SECOND.

This entry point actually executes JMP $E4D2.

$FF96 **65430**

TKSA Kernal—Sends a secondary address to a device in TALK.

General procedure:

1. Configure a device to TALK (see $FFB4).
2. Load the secondary address to register A.
3. Call TKSA.

This entry point actually executes JMP $E4E0.

$FF99 **65433**

MEMTOP Kernal—Reads and sets the highest RAM address to be used for programming by operating systems such as BASIC. The default value is $FF00 (65280).

Procedure for reading current top RAM address:

1. Set the carry flag (SEC).

2. Call MEMTOP.
3. Read the LSB of the address from register X.
4. Read the MSB of the address from register Y.

Procedure for setting a top RAM address:

1. Load the LSB of the address to register X.
2. Load the MSB of the address to register Y.
3. Clear the carry flag (CLC).
4. Call MEMTOP

This entry point address actually executes JMP $F763.

$FF9C 65436

MEMBOT Kernal—Reads and sets the lowest RAM address to be used for programming by operating systems such as BASIC. The default value is $1C00 (7168).

Procedure for reading current bottom RAM address:

1. Set the carry flag (SEC).
2. Call MEMBOT.
3. Read the LSB of the address from register X.
4. Read the MSB of the address from register Y.

Procedure for setting a bottom RAM address:

1. Load the LSB of the address to register X.
2. Load the MSB of the address to register Y.
3. Clear the carry flag (CLC).
4. Call MEMBOT.

This entry point actually executes JMP $F772.

$FF9F 65439

SCNKEY Kernal—Scans the keyboard and returns the code for any pressed key in register A. The routine returns $00 (0) if no key is pressed. The system's normal IRQ procedure (see $FFF17) calls this routine 60 times per second and places the character into the keyboard buffer. There is little point in calling SCNKEY without first redirecting IRQ.

This entry point actually executes JMP $C012.

$FFA2 **65442**

SETTMO Kernal—Sets/resets the device timeout format. The routine is not relevant in the C128 mode.

$FFA5 **65445**

ACPTR Kernal—Fetches a byte of data from a device on an open channel.

General procedure:

1. Open a channel for TALK (see $FFB4).
2. Call ACPTR.
3. Find the byte in register A.

This entry point actually executes JMP $E43E.

$FFA8 **65448**

CIOUT Kernal—Sends a byte of data from register A to a device on an open channel.

General procedure:

1. Open a channel for LISTEN (see $FFB1).
2. Load the byte to register A.
3. Call CIOUT.

This entry point actually executes JMP $E503.

$FFAB **65451**

UNTLK Kernal—Instructs a serial device to stop sending data. Turns off the TALK mode (see $FFB4).

Setup procedure: none

This entry point actually executes JMP $E515.

$FFAE **65454**

UNLSN Kernal—Instructs a serial device to stop accepting data. Turns off the LISTEN mode (see $FFAE).

Setup procedure: none

This entry point actually executes JMP $E526.

$FFB1 **65457**

LISTEN Kernal—Instructs a serial device to accept data from the computer.

General procedure:

1. Load the device number to register A.
2. Call LISTEN.

Use CIOUT ($FFA8) to send data and UNLSN ($FFAE) to turn off the mode.

This entry point actually executes JMP $E33E.

$FFB4 **65460**

TALK Kernal—Commands a serial device to send data to the computer.

General procedure:

1. Load the device number to register A.
2. Call TALK.

Use ACPTR ($FFA5) to receive data in register A and UNTLK ($FFAB) to turn off the mode.

This entry point actually executes JMP $E33B.

$FFB7 **65463**

READST Kernal—Returns the status of the last I/O operation. After calling the routine, register A returns the status codes.

This entry point actually executes JMP $F744.

$FFBA **65466**

SETLFS Kernal—Sets logical file number, device number, and secondary address for file operations.

General procedure:

1. Load the file number to register A.
2. Load the device number to register X.
3. Load the secondary address to register Y.
4. Call SETLFS.

This entry point actually executes JMP $F738.

$FFBD 65469

SETNAM Kernal—Sets the file name for file operations.

General procedure:

1. Load the file name as an ASCII character string at a selected RAM address.
2. Load the length of the file name string to register A.
3. Load the LSB of the file name string address to register X.
4. Load the MSB of the file name string address to register Y.
5. Call SETNAM.

This entry point actually executes JMP ($F731).

$FFC0 65472

OPEN Kernal—Opens a file previously defined by the SETLFS and SETNAM routines.

General procedure:

1. Set up and execute SETNAM (see Kernal $FFBD).
2. Set up and execute SETLFS (see Kernal $FFBA).
3. Call OPEN.

This entry point actually executes JMP ($031A).

$FFC3 65475

CLOSE Kernal—Closes a specified file.

General procedure:

1. Load the file number of the file to be closed to register A.
2. Call CLOSE.

This entry point actually executes JMP ($031C).

$FFC6 65478

CHKIN Kernal—Opens a channel for input operations.

General procedure:

1. Set up and execute OPEN (see $FFC0).
2. Load the file number—the same one used in the previous OPEN operation—to register X.
3. Call CHKIN.

This entry point actually executes JMP ($031E).

$FFC9 65481

CHKOUT Kernal—Opens a channel for output operations.

General procedure:

1. Set up and execute OPEN (see $FFC0).
2. Load the file number—the same one used in the previous OPEN operation—to register X.
3. Call CHKOUT.

This entry point actually executes JMP ($0320).

$FFCC 65484

CLRCHN Kernal—Clears all I/O channels currently open and restores the default channel configuration—keyboard input, screen output.

Procedure: Call the routine, JSR $FFCC.

This entry point actually executes JMP ($0322).

$FFCF 65487

CHRIN Kernal—Fetches a character from a previously opened input channel to register A.

General procedure:

1. Set up and execute CHKIN (see $FFC6).

2. Call CHRIN.
3. Use the character found in register A.

See keyboard applications in Chapter 10 and other I/O applications in Chapter 12.

This entry point actually executes JMP ($0324).

$FFD2 **65490**

CHROUT Kernal—Sends a character from register A to a previously opened output channel.

General procedure:

1. Set up and execute CHKOUT (see $FFC9).
2. Load the character to be sent to register A.
3. Call CHROUT.

See screen applications in Chapter 6 and other I/O applications in Chapter 12.

This entry point actually executes JMP ($0326).

$FFD5 **65493**

LOAD Kernal—Loads or verifies a block of data from an input device to a block of RAM. It is normally used for loading files from cassette and disk systems.

General procedure:

1. Specify device number, file number, and secondary address by executing SETLFS (see $FFBA).
2. Specify a file name by executing SETNAM (see $FFBD).
3. Load $00 to register A for a LOAD operation.

   or

   Load $01 to register A for a VERIFY operation.
4. Load $FF to registers X and Y if you want to load the file at the address that was specified when the file was originally saved.

   or

Load the LSB of the desired RAM address to register X and load the MSB of the desired RAM address to register Y.

5. Call LOAD.

See Chapter 3 for further details and specific examples.

This entry point actually executes JMP $F265.

$FFD8 **65496**

SAVE Kernal—Saves a specified block of RAM to an output device, usually disk or cassette tape.

General procedure:

1. Specify device number, file number, and secondary address by executing SETLFS (see $FFBA).
2. Specify a file name by executing SETNAM (see $FFBD).
3. Load the LSB of the starting address to $C1 (193).
4. Load the MSB of the starting address to $C2 (194).
5. Load the LSB of the ending address to $AE (174).
6. Load the MSB of the ending address to $AF (175).
7. Call SAVE.

See Chapter 3 for more details and specific examples.

This entry point actually executes JMP $F35E.

$FFDB **65499**

SETTIM Kernal—Sets the three-byte, real-time counter.

General procedure:

1. Load the high-order byte to register A.
2. Load the middle byte to register X.
3. Load the low-order byte to register Y.
4. Call SETTIM.

See the description of "jiffy" clock registers, $A0 through $A2. Use RDTIM ($FFDE) to read the clock.

This entry point actually executes JMP $F665.

$FFDE 65502

RDTIM Kernal—Reads the three-byte, real-time counter.

General procedure:

1. Call RDTIM.
2. Read the high-order byte from register A.
3. Read the middle byte from register X.
4. Read the low-order byte to register Y.

See the description of "jiffy" clock registers, $A0 through $A2. Use SETTIM ($FFDB) to read the clock.

This entry point actually executes JMP $F65E.

$FFE1 65505

STOP Kernal—Scans the keyboard and responds to a STOP keystroke. It is a meaningful routine only when executed immediately after calling the UDTIM routine (see $FFEA). If the STOP key is pressed, the routine concludes with a 1 in the Z-flag bit of the status register. Otherwise the Z-flag bit is cleared to 0.

General procedure:

1. Call UDTIM ($FFEA).
2. Call STOP.
3. Complete the routine by using a branch statement based on the status of the Z-flag bit, BEQ or BNE.

See the description of the default STOP routine ($F66E) for details on redirecting the operation to a custom version.

This entry point actually executes JMP ($0328).

$FFE4 65508

GETIN Kernal—Fetches the next character from an input channel, usually the keyboard buffer or RS-232-C buffer. The character is fetched to register A. If the buffer is empty, the routine returns a $00 (0).

General procedure:

1. Call CHKIN (see $FFC6) to open a channel for input.

2. Call GETIN.
3. Deal with the character in register A.

See the description of the default GETIN routine ($EEEB) for details on redirecting the operation to a custom version.

This entry point actually executes JMP ($032A).

$FFE7 **65511**

CLALL Kernal—Closes all files and channels.

Setup procedure: None

See the description of the default CLALL routine ($F222) for details on redirecting the operation to a custom version.

This entry point actually executes JMP ($032C).

$FFEA **65514**

UDTIM Kernal—Updates the real-time clocks. The system normally calls this routine 60 times each second on an interrupt basis. It is a useful programming tool only when devising custom interrupt routines that require clock updates.

Procedure: Call the routine, JSR $FFEA.

This entry point actually executes JMP $F5F8.

$FFED **65517**

SCREEN Kernal—Fetches the current text screen row-column parameters.

General procedure:

1. Call SCREEN.
2. Read the number of text rows from register Y.
3. Read the number of text columns from register X.
4. Read the number of text columns in the alternative text screen from register A.

This entry point actually executes JMP $C00F.

$FFF0 **65520**

PLOT Kernal—Sets or reads the current text cursor position.

Procedure for setting the text cursor:

1. Load the desired row number to register X.
2. Load the desired column number to register Y.
3. Set the carry flag (SEC).
4. Call PLOT.

Procedure for reading the position of the cursor:

1. Clear the carry flag (CLC).
2. Call PLOT.
3. Read the row number from register X.
4. Read the column number from register Y.

See Chapter 6 for specific applications and examples.

This entry point actually executes JMP $C018.

$FFF3 **65523**

IOBASE Kernal—Returns the base, or starting address, of the system's memory-mapped I/O space.

General procedure:

1. Call IOBASE.
2. Read the LSB of the address from register X.
3. Read the MSB of the address from register Y.

The memory-mapped base address for the current Commodore 128 system is $D000.

This entry point actually executes JMP $F781.

$FFF6–$FFF7 **65526–65527**

Not used.

$FFF8

Vector to $E224.

$FFFA

Vector to NMI routine at $FF05.

$FFFC

Vector to system reset (RST) routine at $FF3D.

$FFFE

Vector to IRQ routine at $FF17.

14

Memory Management Procedures

An 8502 microprocessor chip is the heart of the Commodore 128 computer. It is a high-speed, 8-bit processor that can work with a 64K address space at any given time. The Commodore 128, however, has 128K of RAM, more than 48K of built-in ROM, and 4K of memory-mapped I/O. The 8502 cannot deal with all those addressable blocks at one time, so Commodore had to build in some rather sophisticated bank-switching operations, operations that switch banks of memory in and out of the system so that the microprocessor is never working with more than 64K at any given moment.

Most bank-switching operations take place routinely and automatically. A programmer rarely has to give them much thought. However, you can do some custom bank switching in order to take advantage of the system's full range of memory.

This chapter describes the banks that are currently available, suggests some bank-switching procedures, and outlines some techniques for swapping information between different banks.

The Standard Bank Configurations

Table 14-1 summarizes the system's sixteen standard bank configurations, including the major address blocks and the functions assigned to them. You will notice that no references are made to expansion-RAM accessories. The reason is that those add-on products are not directly relevant to bank descriptions.

Table 14-1 Complete Summary of the Bank Configuration

Bank 0

Address Range		
Hex	**Dec**	**Function**
$0000 -$03FF	0–1023	RAM 0
$0400 -$3FFF	1024–16383	RAM 0
$4000 -$7FFF	16384–32767	RAM 0
$8000 -$BFFF	32768–49151	RAM 0
$C000 -$CFFF	49152–53247	RAM 0
$D000-$DFFF	53248–57343	RAM 0
$E000 -$FEFF	57344–65279	RAM 0
$FF00 -$FF04	65280–65284	RAM 0
$FF05 -$FFFF	65285–65535	RAM 0

Table 14-1 (cont.) *Bank 1*

Address Range Hex	Dec	Function
$0000 -$03FF	0-1023	RAM 0
$0400 -$3FFF	1024-16383	RAM 1
$4000 -$7FFF	16384-32767	RAM 1
$8000 -$BFFF	32768-49151	RAM 1
$C000 -$CFFF	49152-53247	RAM 1
$D000-$DFFF	53248-57343	RAM 1
$E000 -$FEFF	57344-65279	RAM 1
$FF00 -$FF04	65280-65284	RAM 0
$FF05 -$FFFF	65285-65535	RAM 1

Bank 2

Address Range Hex	Dec	Function
$0000 -$03FF	0-1023	RAM 0
$0400 -$3FFF	1024-16383	RAM 2
$4000 -$7FFF	16384-32767	RAM 2
$8000 -$BFFF	32768-49151	RAM 2
$C000 -$CFFF	49152-53247	RAM 2
$D000-$DFFF	53248-57343	RAM 2
$E000 -$FEFF	57344-65279	RAM 2
$FF00 -$FF04	65280-65284	RAM 0
$FF05 -$FFFF	65285-65535	RAM 2

The Commodore 128 has no additional RAM allocated for RAM 2, so RAM 2 is the same as RAM 0. As a result, the Bank 2 configuration is identical to Bank 0.

Bank 3

Address Range Hex	Dec	Function
$0000 -$03FF	0-1023	RAM 0
$0400 -$3FFF	1024-16383	RAM 3
$4000 -$7FFF	16384-32767	RAM 3
$8000 -$BFFF	32768-49151	RAM 3
$C000 -$CFFF	49152-53247	RAM 3
$D000-$DFFF	53248-57343	RAM 3
$E000 -$FEFF	57344-65279	RAM 3
$FF00 -$FF04	65280-65284	RAM 0
$FF05 -$FFFF	65285-65535	RAM 3

The Commodore 128 has no additional RAM allocated for RAM 3, so RAM 3 is the same as RAM 1. As a result, the Bank 3 configuration is identical to Bank 1.

Table 14-1 (cont.) *Bank 4*

Address Range		
Hex	**Dec**	**Function**
$0000 -$03FF	0–1023	RAM 0
$0400 -$3FFF	1024–16383	RAM 0
$4000 -$7FFF	16384–32767	RAM 0
$8000 -$BFFF	32768–49151	Internal ROM
$C000 -$CFFF	49152–53247	Internal ROM
$D000-$DFFF	53248–57343	I/O block
$E000 -$FEFF	57344–65279	Internal ROM
$FF00 -$FF04	65280–65284	RAM 0
$FF05 -$FFFF	65285–65535	Internal ROM

Internal ROM is not shipped with the Commodore 128. An empty ROM socket is provided on the circuit board for such a device, however.

Bank 5

Address Range		
Hex	**Dec**	**Function**
$0000 -$03FF	0–1023	RAM 0
$0400 -$3FFF	1024–16383	RAM 1
$4000 -$7FFF	16384–32767	RAM 1
$8000 -$BFFF	32768–49151	Internal ROM
$C000 -$CFFF	49152–53247	Internal ROM
$D000-$DFFF	53248–57343	I/O block
$E000 -$FEFF	57344–65279	Internal ROM
$FF00 -$FF04	65280–65284	RAM 0
$FF05 -$FFFF	65285–65535	Internal ROM

Internal ROM is not shipped with the Commodore 128. An empty ROM socket is provided on the circuit board for such a device, however.

Bank 6

Address Range		
Hex	**Dec**	**Function**
$0000 -$03FF	0–1023	RAM 0
$0400 -$3FFF	1024–16383	RAM 2
$4000 -$7FFF	16384–32767	RAM 2
$8000 -$BFFF	32768–49151	Internal ROM
$C000 -$CFFF	49152–53247	Internal ROM
$D000-$DFFF	53248–57343	I/O block
$E000 -$FEFF	57344–65279	Internal ROM
$FF00 -$FF04	65280–65284	RAM 0
$FF05 -$FFFF	65285–65535	Internal ROM

1. The Commodore 128 has no additional RAM allocated for RAM 2, so RAM 2 is the same as RAM 0. As a result, the Bank 6 configuration is identical to Bank 4.
2. Internal ROM is not shipped with the Commodore 128. An empty ROM socket is provided on the circuit board for such a device, however.

Table 14-1 (cont.) *Bank 7*

Address Range Hex	Dec	Function
$0000 -$03FF	0-1023	RAM 0
$0400 -$3FFF	1024-16383	RAM 3
$4000 -$7FFF	16384-32767	RAM 3
$8000 -$BFFF	32768-49151	Internal ROM
$C000-$CFFF	49152-53247	Internal ROM
$D000-$DFFF	53248-57343	I/O block
$E000 -$FEFF	57344-65279	Internal ROM
$FF00 -$FF04	65280-65284	RAM 0
$FF05 -$FFFF	65285-65535	Internal ROM

1. The Commodore 128 has no additional RAM allocated for RAM 3, so RAM 3 is the same as RAM 1. As a result, the Bank 7 configuration is identical to Bank 5.
2. Internal ROM is not shipped with the Commodore 128. An empty ROM socket is provided on the circuit board for such a device, however.

Bank 8

Address Range Hex	Dec	Function
$0000 -$03FF	0-1023	RAM 0
$0400 -$3FFF	1024-16383	RAM 0
$4000 -$7FFF	16384-32767	RAM 0
$8000 -$BFFF	32768-49151	External ROM
$C000-$CFFF	49152-53247	External ROM
$D000-$DFFF	53248-57343	I/O block
$E000 -$FEFF	57344-65279	External ROM
$FF00 -$FF04	65280-65284	RAM 0
$FF05 -$FFFF	65285-65535	External ROM

External ROM is an optional, external program cartridge that is specifically designed for use in the C128 mode.

Bank 9

Address Range Hex	Dec	Function
$0000 -$03FF	0-1023	RAM 0
$0400 -$3FFF	1024-16383	RAM 1
$4000 -$7FFF	16384-32767	RAM 1
$8000 -$BFFF	32768-49151	External ROM
$C000-$CFFF	49152-53247	External ROM
$D000-$DFFF	53248-57343	I/O Block
$E000 -$FEFF	57344-65279	External ROM
$FF00 -$FF04	65280-65284	RAM 0
$FF05 -$FFFF	65285-65535	External ROM

External ROM is an optional, external program cartridge specifically designed for use in the C128 mode.

Table 14-1 (cont.) *Bank 10*

Address Range Hex	Dec	Function
$0000 -$03FF	0-1023	RAM 0
$0400 -$3FFF	1024-16383	RAM 2
$4000 -$7FFF	16384-32767	RAM 2
$8000 -$BFFF	32768-49151	External ROM
$C000 -$CFFF	49152-53247	External ROM
$D000-$DFFF	53248-57343	I/O Block
$E000 -$FEFF	57344-65279	External ROM
$FF00 -$FF04	65280-65284	RAM 0
$FF05 -$FFFF	65285-65535	External ROM

1. The Commodore 128 has no additional RAM allocated for RAM 2, so RAM 2 is the same as RAM 0. As a result, the Bank 10 configuration is identical to Bank 8.
2. External ROM is an optional, external program cartridge specifically designed for use in the C128 mode.

Bank 11

Address Range Hex	Dec	Function
$0000 -$03FF	0-1023	RAM 0
$0400 -$3FFF	1024-16383	RAM 3
$4000 -$7FFF	16384-32767	RAM 3
$8000 -$BFFF	32768-49151	External ROM
$C000 -$CFFF	49152-53247	External ROM
$D000-$DFFF	53248-57343	I/O Block
$E000 -$FEFF	57344-65279	External ROM
$FF00 -$FF04	65280-65284	RAM 0
$FF05 -$FFFF	65285-65535	External ROM

1. The Commodore 128 has no additional RAM allocated for RAM 3, so RAM 3 is the same as RAM 1. As a result, the Bank 11 configuration is identical to Bank 9.
2. External ROM is an optional, external program cartridge specifically designed for use in the C128 mode.

Bank 12

Address Range Hex	Dec	Function
$0000 -$03FF	0-1023	RAM 0
$0400 -$3FFF	1024-16383	RAM 0
$4000 -$7FFF	16384-32767	RAM 0
$8000 -$BFFF	32768-49151	Internal ROM
$C000 -$CFFF	49152-53247	Kernal ROM
$D000-$DFFF	53248-57343	I/O Block
$E000 -$FEFF	57344-65279	Kernal ROM
$FF00 -$FF04	65280-65284	RAM 0
$FF05 -$FFFF	65285-65535	Kernal ROM

Internal ROM is not shipped with the Commodore 128. An empty ROM socket is provided on the circuit board for such a device, however.

Table 14-1 (cont.) *Bank 13*

Address Range Hex	Dec	Function
$0000 -$03FF	0–1023	RAM 0
$0400 -$3FFF	1024–16383	RAM 0
$4000 -$7FFF	16384–32767	RAM 0
$8000 -$BFFF	32768–49151	External ROM
$C000 -$CFFF	49152–53247	Kernal ROM
$D000-$DFFF	53248–57343	I/O Block
$E000 -$FEFF	57344–65279	Kernal ROM
$FF00 -$FF04	65280–65284	RAM 0
$FF05 -$FFFF	65285–65535	Kernal ROM

External ROM is an optional, external program cartridge specifically designed for use in the C128 mode.

Bank 14

Address Range Hex	Dec	Function
$0000 -$03FF	0–1023	RAM 0
$0400 -$3FFF	1024–16383	RAM 0
$4000 -$7FFF	16384–32767	BASIC 7.0 ROM
$8000 -$BFFF	32768–49151	BASIC 7.0 ROM
$C000 -$CFFF	49152–53247	Kernal ROM
$D000-$DFFF	53248–57343	Character ROM
$E000 -$FEFF	57344–65279	Kernal ROM
$FF00 -$FF04	65280–65284	RAM 0
$FF05 -$FFFF	65285–65535	Kernal ROM

Bank 15

Address Range Hex	Dec	Function
$0000 -$03FF	0–1023	RAM 0
$0400 -$3FFF	1024–16383	RAM 0
$4000 -$7FFF	16384–32767	BASIC 7.0 ROM
$8000 -$BFFF	32768–49151	BASIC 7.0 ROM
$C000 -$CFFF	49152–53247	Kernal ROM
$D000-$DFFF	53248–57343	I/O Block
$E000 -$FEFF	57344–65279	Kernal ROM
$FF00 -$FF04	65280–65284	RAM 0
$FF05 -$FFFF	65285–65535	Kernal ROM

Bank 15 is the default configuration for the C128 mode of operation. Casual users and programmers rarely have to give any special consideration to banking operations. The alternatives can provide more experienced programmers with some powerful programming tools.

A couple of facts go a long way toward simplifying the view presented in the table. First, RAM blocks 2 and 3 are not included in the

Commodore 128 as separate blocks. RAM 0 is one 64K block of RAM and RAM 1 is another—this adds up to the system's characteristic 128K capacity. Blocks 2 and 3 are included for future product expansion, most likely for a product that will be known as the Commodore 256.

Some authors are saying that RAM 2 and RAM 3 do not exist within the system, which is not exactly the case. RAM 0 and RAM 2 refer to the same set of memory devices within the system. Likewise, RAM 1 and RAM 3 refer to the second 64K block of RAM. Whatever appears in RAM 0 also appears in RAM 2, and whatever is written to RAM 1 is written to RAM 3 as well.

> ***NOTE:*** The Commodore 128 has only two RAM blocks:
>
> RAM 2 is the same as RAM 0
> RAM 3 is the same as RAM 1
>
> Thus:
>
> Bank 2 is the same entity as Bank 0
> Bank 3 is the same entity as Bank 1
> Bank 6 is the same entity as Bank 4
> Bank 7 is the same entity as Bank 5
> Bank 10 is the same entity as Bank 8
> Bank 11 is the same entity as Bank 9

For all practical purposes, one should avoid any notion of writing programs that refer to Banks 2, 3, 6, 7, 10, and 11.

Furthermore, the Internal ROM functions refer to a device that is not included in the Commodore 128 as it is shipped from the factory. The empty socket is available on the console's printed-circuit board, but nothing is there unless you provide a custom chip. Assuming you are not installing a custom internal ROM chip, bank configurations 4, 5, 6, and 7 provide no special features.

> ***NOTE:*** Unless you have installed a custom, internal ROM function chip, Bank 4, Bank 5, Bank 6, and Bank 7 serve no special purpose.

The addressing space allocated for External ROM refers to ROM cartridges available as optional accessories that are specifically configured for C128 mode. Existing C64 cartridges run on the Commodore 128, but they automatically reconfigure the system for C64 mode of operation. Some instances occur where you need to write programs that work in conjunction with a C128 cartridge. When this is not the case, you don't need to refer to bank configurations 8, 9, 10, 11, and 13.

> *NOTE:* Bank 8, Bank 9, Bank 10, Bank 11, and Bank 13 are meaningful only when working with an external ROM cartridge specifically designed for the C128 mode.

The foregoing discussions lead to an important notion that goes a long way toward simplifying a programmer's view of the bank-configuration scheme: configurations 0, 1, 14, and 15 are the only ones that allow universal programming applications, applications for systems that are not supported with special ROM accessories.

A comparison of bank configurations 14 and 15 shows that the only difference is that 14 provides direct access to the character-set ROM.

The remainder of the material in this chapter deals mainly with memory management procedures for bank configurations 0, 1, 14, and 15.

Bank-Switching Statements, Registers and Procedures

A number of procedures exists for switching between the standard bank configurations and making up a couple of non-standard configurations. The choice of a procedure often depends on the kind of programming environment you are using.

Using BASIC's BANK Statement

BASIC's BANK statement represents the simplest and most straightforward procedure for switching bank configurations in BASIC programs. The general form of the statement is:

BANK *bankno*

where *bankno* is the desired bank number, 0 through 15. After executing the statement, the system directs all address-related commands (PEEK, POKE, SYS, etc.) to the designated bank. The example in Listing 14-1 sends the ASCII characters for string HELLO from RAM 0 in Bank 15 to a RAM-1 location in Bank 1.

Listing 14-1

```
10 BANK 15
20 M$="HELLO"
30 BANK 1
40 FOR K=1 TO 5
50 POKE 32767+K,ASC(MID$(M$,K.1))
60 NEXT K
70 BANK 15
```

Line 20 defines the string in Bank 15 variable RAM space. Line 30 then specifies that subsequent POKE operations are to refer to addresses in the Bank 1 configuration—beginning from address 32768 ($8000) in this case.

After running the program, you can confirm that the operation has taken place as described. Enter the MONITOR command to get to the monitor mode, then examine the block of data beginning from $8000 in Bank 1. Recalling that the first character in the five-nibble monitor addresses indicates the bank number, enter this command:

```
>18000
```

The command returns this sort of display from ROM 1:

```
>18000 48 45 4C 4C 4F   :HELLO
```

You can confirm that the string was *not* sent to ROM 0 by examining the same address in Bank 15—by entering the >F8000 monitor command.

Using the MMU Configuration Register

The summaries of bank configurations in Table 14-1 show a five-byte segment of RAM 0 between $FF00 and $FF04 (65280–65284). Those registers, like zero-page RAM, are directly available in all bank configurations. That says something about their relative importance to the overall operation of the system—proper bank switching is impossible without them. They are the memory management unit (MMU) registers.

The first register in that group is especially important. It is the MMU configuration register. All bank-switching operations, whether executed automatically by the operating system or from user's programming, refer to it.

The MMU configuration register at $FF00 (65280) is actually a RAM version of the same register located in the MMU device at

$D500 (54528). They are the same registers for all practical purposes. Writing data to one of them automatically writes the same data to the other. It is recommended, however, that you work only with the RAM version at $FF00.

Writing data to the MMU configuration register immediately establishes the given bank configuration, and reading data from the register returns the current bank configuration. The data in the MMU configuration register is not a value identical to the Bank numbers 0 through 15. The register contains $00 when the system is in Bank 15, for instance, and $7F (127) for Bank 1. The breakdown of bit assignments in Figure 14-1 shows the rationale behind the coding in the MMU configuration register.

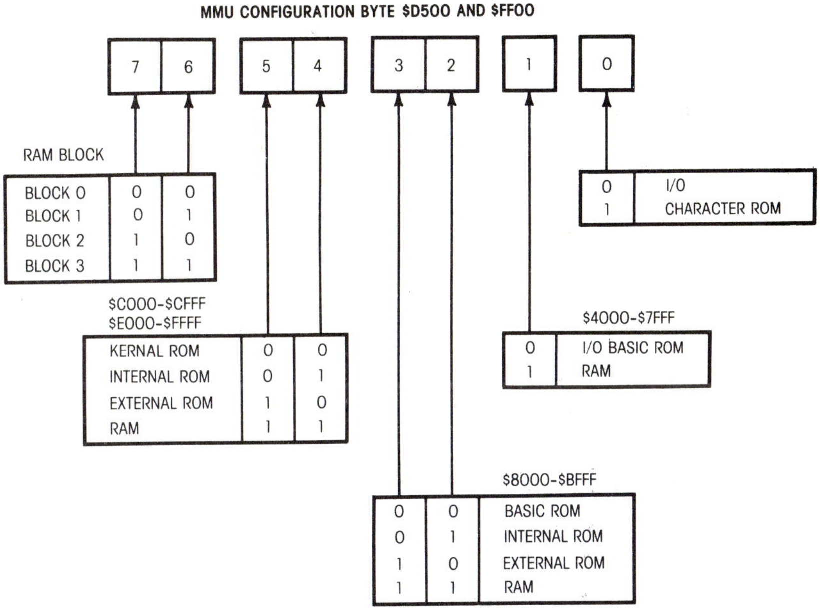

Fig. 14-1 Allocation of bits in the MMU Configuration Register at $FF00 (65280)

Bit 0 determines whether $D000-$DFFF is used for I/O or Character ROM. Bank 14 is the only standard bank configuration that uses a 1 in that location.

Bit 1 specifies the application of $4000-$7FFF: the lower portion of the ROM-based BASIC interpreter or RAM.

Bits 2 and 3 work together to specify the application of $8000-$BFFF: the upper segment of the BASIC interpreter, Internal ROM (the optional custom ROM chip), External ROM (C128 cartridge), or RAM.

Bits 4 and 5 fix the configuration of $C000-$EFFF and $FF05-$FFFF: Internal ROM, External ROM, or RAM.

Bits 6 and 7 specify the RAM block used when bits 2, 3, 4, and 5 indicate RAM usage. The four possible selections allow for RAM 0, RAM 1, RAM 2, and RAM 3. Bearing in mind that RAM blocks 2 and 3 are redundant, these bits are normally set at 00 or 01.

Table 14-2 uses this information to show the MMU configuration codes for each of the 16 standard bank configurations.

Table 14-2 Standard Bank Configuration Number and Codes Used by the MMU Configuration Register at $FF00 (65280)

Bank Number	MMU Configuration Code	
	Hex	Dec
0	$3F	63
1	$7F	127
2	$BF	191
3	$FF	255
4	$16	22
5	$56	86
6	$96	150
7	$D6	214
8	$2A	42
9	$6A	106
10	$AA	170
11	$EA	234
12	$06	6
13	$0A	10
14	$01	1
15	$00	0

An understanding of how the bits are allocated in the MMU Configuration Register invites the possibility of setting up some potentially useful, non-standard bank configurations. Consider the following binary value:

01000000

Loading this value, $40 or 64, to the MMU Configuration Register produces the following non-standard bank configuration:

$0000 -$03FF	RAM 0
$0400 -$3FFF	RAM 1
$4000 -$7FFF	BASIC 7.0 ROM
$8000 -$BFFF	BASIC 7.0 ROM
$C000-$CFFF	Kernal ROM
$D000-$DFFF	I/O Block
$E000 -$FEFF	Kernal ROM
$FF00 -$FF04	RAM 0
$FF05 -$FFFF	Kernal ROM

Using the MMU Preconfiguration Registers

During the normal course of system operations, the Commodore 128 has to switch continually between ROM programming and program

RAM space. It switches back and forth between particular sets of bank configurations, even when a user's program does not call for any special banking. For that reason, the MMU contains a set of four preconfiguration registers—registers that hold the most used MMU configuration codes.

Just as two locations exist for the MMU Configuration Register, $FF00 and $D500, so two sets of locations exist for the preconfiguration registers. The first contains the MMU configuration code for Bank 0, the second contains the code for Bank 1, and the third for Bank 14.

MMU Preconfiguration Register #1

Locations: $FF01 (65281)
$D501 (54529)

Default value: $3F (63) for Bank 0

MMU Preconfiguration Register #2

Locations: $FF02 (65282)
$D502 (54530)

Default value: $7F (127) for Bank 1

MMU Preconfiguration Register #3

Locations: $FF03 (65283)
$D503 (54531)

Default value: $01 (1) for Bank 14

The three preconfigurations serve their purpose in an unusual fashion: writing or POKEing any value to one of the registers invokes their bank configuration. The write operation is what is significant. Normal system-interrupt routines maintain the default values, no matter what you attempt to write to the registers.

You can use two ways to set up a Bank 1 configuration: POKE 127 to the MMU Configuration register or POKE anything to MMU Preconfiguration Register #2.

Here are some suggested procedures for using the MMU registers to switch among the four commonly used bank configurations.

Switching to BASIC's equivalent of Bank 15:

Method 1: `POKE 65280,0`
Method 2:
```
LDA #$00
STA $FF00
```

Switching to BASIC's equivalent of Bank 0:

Method 1: POKE 65280,63
Method 2: POKE 65281,0
Method 3: LDA #$3F
STA $FF00
Method 4: STA $FF01

Switching to BASIC's equivalent of Bank 1:

Method 1: POKE 65280,127
Method 2: POKE 65282,0
Method 3: LDA #$7F
STA $FF00
Method 4: STA $FF02

Switching to BASIC's equivalent of Bank 14:

Method 1: POKE 65280,1
Method 2: POKE 65283,0
Method 3: LDA #$01
STA $FF00
Method 4: STA $FF03

A fourth MMU preconfiguration register performs the same function as the preceding three registers but specifies a non-standard bank configuration.

MMU Preconfiguration Register #4

Locations: $FF04 (65284)
$D504 (54532)

Default value: $41 (65) for the following non-standard bank configuration

$0000 -$03FF	RAM 0
$0400 -$3FFF	RAM 1
$4000 -$7FFF	BASIC 7.0 ROM
$8000 -$BFFF	BASIC 7.0 ROM
$C000-$CFFF	Kernal ROM
$D000-$DFFF	Character ROM
$E000 -$FEFF	Kernal ROM
$FF00 -$FF04	RAM 0
$FF05 -$FFFF	Kernal ROM

Using the Bank 1 Configuration

Perhaps the most compelling reason for using the Bank 1 configuration is to provide a large amount of RAM that is protected from Bank 15 programming and vice-versa. RAM 1, accessible through Bank 1, can be a virtual storehouse of data and machine language programming that is called by BASIC programming in the RAM 0 area of the Bank 15 configuration.

Using Bank configurations 1 and 15 in that fashion requires some understanding of how data can be loaded to RAM 1 and later transferred or otherwise called by programming in RAM 0. The discussions in this chapter deal mainly with those two bank configurations, but the principles generally apply to other combinations.

Allocating Bank 1 RAM

The RAM 1 addresses that are uniquely available in the Bank 1 configuration begin at $0400 (1024) and run through $FFFF (65535) but with a five-byte gap for the MMU registers beginning at $FF00 (65280).

When Bank 1 RAM is used in conjunction with BASIC programming in Bank 15, however, you need to set a few minor limitations on how the Bank 1 configuration can be used. The difficulty is that BASIC programming which uses variables in conjunction with Bank 1 operations has to keep track of the values in a segment of the foreign RAM. The default starting address for variables and array values is $0400 (1024) in RAM 1.

The programmer can deal with the situation in two different ways. One is to make sure that any data or machine language programming in RAM 1 begins at an address that is well above $0400—at $0800 (2048) for example. The alternative is to move the variable pointers for RAM 1 into the upper addressing range, then use everything up to that point for data and machine language programs. $F000 (61440) is a good place to set the pointers.

VARTAB Pointer to start of BASIC variable list in Bank 1.

$2F (47) = LSB of address
$30 (48) = MSB of address
Default address: **$0400 (1024)**

ARYTAB Pointer to start of BASIC arrays in Bank 1.

$31 (49) = LSB of address
$32 (50) = MSB of address
Default address: **$0400 (1024)**

FRETOP Pointer to start of free memory space in Bank 1.

$33 (51) = LSB of address
$34 (52) = MSB of address
Default address: $0400 (1024)

STREND Pointer to end of BASIC string space, plus 1, in Bank 1.

$35 (53) = LSB of address
$36 (54) = MSB of address
Default address: $FF00 (65280)

MEMSIZ Highest address used by BASIC in Bank 1.

$39 (57) = LSB of address
$3A (58) = MSB of address
Default address: $FF00 (65280)

Remember that none of this has any relevance in situations where the system is not running BASIC programming in any form, so the allocation of BASIC usage in RAM 1 can be adjusted as described in the following text.

Assuming that you have decided to confine BASIC's usage of Bank 1 RAM to the area of $0400–$0800:

1. Make sure VARTAB, ARYTAB, and FRETOP are at the default values of $0400.
2. Set STREND and MEMSIZ to the highest address to be used by BASIC—$0800, for example.

A BASIC implementation of the procedure looks like the version in Listing 14-2.

Listing 14-2

```
10 BA=47
20 POKE BA,0:POKE BA+1,16          :REM VARTAB TO $0400
30 POKE BA+2,0:POKE BA+3,16        :REM ARYTAB TO $0400
40 POKE BA+4,0:POKE BA+5,16        :REM FRETOP TO $0400
50 POKE BA+6,0:POKE BA+7,32        :REM STREND TO $0800
60 POKE BA+8,0:POKE BA+9,32        :REM MEMSIZ TO $0800
```

On the other hand, you might wish to raise the VARTAB, ARYTAB, and FRETOP pointers so that you can use RAM 1 from $0400.

1. Set VARTAB, ARYTAB, and FRETOP to the lowest address they are to use—$F000 for example.
2. Make sure STREND and MEMSIZ are set to their default values, $FF00.

A BASIC routine for setting up this format looks like the version in Listing 14-3.

Listing 14-3

```
10 BA=47
20 POKE BA,0:POKE BA+1,240        :REM VARTAB TO $F000
30 POKE BA+2,0:POKE BA+3,240      :REM ARYTAB TO $F000
40 POKE BA+4,0:POKE BA+5,240      :REM FRETOP TO $F000
50 POKE BA+6,0:POKE BA+7,255      :REM STREND TO $FF00
60 POKE BA+8,0:POKE BA+9,255      :REM MEMSIZ TO $FF00
```

Composing, Saving, and Loading Procedures for Bank 1

Original machine language programs can be created in the monitor for the Bank 1 configuration just as easily as any other bank. Monitor commands that cite the five-character addresses should simply begin with a 1. Saving and loading blocks of RAM from the monitor and in the Bank 1 configuration requires a bit more attention to detail, however.

The monitor command for saving a block of RAM has this general form:

S "*filename*",8,*strtaddr*,*endaddr*

where:

filename—file name

strtaddr—starting address of the program

endaddr—ending address of the program

If the program was composed in the Bank 1 configuration, the starting and ending addresses must begin with a 1 digit. The default bank configuration for the monitor is 0, so if you omit that leading digit, the system saves data from the specified starting and ending addresses, but in RAM 0.

Suppose that you have used the mini-assembler to create a machine language program that runs from $10800 through $108FF—where the leading digit indicates the bank configuration number. This is properly saved on disk by this command:

```
S "PROG",8,10800,108FF
```

Unfortunately, the leading digit (bank configuration number) only specifies the bank that holds the program to be saved. It does not become part of the LOAD address in the file directory.

The general monitor command for loading a block of RAM from disk looks like this:

L "*filename*",8,*altaddr*

where *altaddr* is an alternative loading address. The alternative loading address is usually optional but certainly not when you want to load a file to a block of RAM in the Bank 1 configuration. In this case, the alternative address must be specified with a leading 1 digit.

A file originally saved from $10800 through $108FF, for example, will load to $00800 if you do not specify $10800 as the alternate starting address.

The same general idea applies to saving and loading binary files from BASIC. It is possible to pull a block of data from the Bank 1 configuration and save it on disk, even while running in BASIC's usual Bank 15 configuration. An appropriate form of the command in that case is:

BSAVE "*filename*,B*bankno*,P*strtaddr* TO P*endarrd*

where:

filename—file name

bankno—bank configuration number of the block to be saved (1 in most examples cited in this chapter)

strtaddr—decimal starting address of the block

endaddr—decimal ending address of the block

The following example operates under BASIC's usual Bank 15 configuration, but actually saves a segment of data, 2048 through 2323 in the Bank 1 configuration:

```
BSAVE "TRYIT",B1,P2048 TO P2323
```

Notice that the starting and ending addresses contain no information regarding the bank. The *bankno* parameter does that. Thus, when it is time to BLOAD the program, the statement must include a reference to the bank number but does not have to specify an alternative loading address. The statement, limited to the application under discussion here, looks like this:

BLOAD "*filename*",B*bankno*

This command loads a file called *filename* to the original address in the specified bank number. To load the file saved in the previous example:

```
BLOAD "TRYIT",B1
```

Because bank configuration 15 is the only one that supports the full range of BASIC operations, save commands such as DSAVE and SAVE and load commands such as DLOAD and LOAD are not appropriate for working directly with the Bank 1 configuration.

Summary of MMU Configuration Registers

$D500 **54528**

MMU configuration register, determines the current bank configuration.

Bit 0 = Content of $D000-$DFFF

0 = I/O Block
1 = Character ROM

Bit 1 = Content of $4000-$7FFF

0 = BASIC ROM
1 = RAM

Bits 2 and 3 = Content of $8000-$BFFF

00 = BASIC ROM
01 = Internal ROM
10 = External ROM
11 = RAM

Bits 4 and 5 = Content of $C000-$CFFFF and $E000-$FFFF

00 = Kernal ROM
01 = Internal ROM
10 = External ROM
11 = RAM

Bits 6 and 7 = RAM used

00 = RAM 0
01 = RAM 1
10 = RAM 2
11 = RAM 3

This chapter includes more details.

$D501-$D504 **54529-54534**

Bank preconfiguration registers.

$D501 (54529) = Bank 1
$D502 (54530) = Bank 2
$D503 (54531) = Bank 14
$D504 (54532) = Non-standard bank configuration:

$0000-$03FF RAM 0
$0400-$3FFF RAM 1
$4000-$7FFF BASIC 7.0 ROM
$8000-$BFFF BASIC 7.0 ROM
$C000-$CFFF Kernal ROM
$D000-$DFFF Character ROM
$E000-$FEFF Kernal ROM
$FF00-$FF04 RAM 0
$FF05-$FFFF Kernal ROM

This chapter contains more details.

Bank Switching Procedures

BASIC program text normally begins at one of two different addresses, depending on whether the graphics area is allocated for bit-mapped graphics operations. In either case, the system uses the RAM 0 block for BASIC text, and that text can extend well above $4000 (16384). The significance of this fact is that RAM-based programming often shares the same addressing range with the ROM-based BASIC interpreter. The computer handles the situation by switching between RAM 0 and BASIC ROM.

The only bank configurations that can handle BASIC properly are Bank 14 and Bank 15. For most practical purposes, BASIC programs are always executed in the Bank 15 configuration.

This is not to say, however, that you cannot use a different bank configuration in conjunction with a BASIC program. The BASIC programming must run from Bank 15, but you can load and retrieve data from a different bank. Bank 1 happens to be the most meaningful in that regard.

Once a BASIC program sets up the Bank 1 configuration, the system begins an elaborate bank-switching scheme that involves RAM 1 as well as the usual combination of RAM 0 and BASIC ROM. The switching scheme makes it necessary to use a bit of RAM 1 space for variables and strings that are generated while operating under the Bank 1 configuration. The pointers are located in zero-page RAM, locations $2F through $3A (47-58).

$2F–$30 47–48

VARTAB Pointer to start of RAM Bank-1 BASIC variable list.

$2F (47) = LSB of address
$30 (48) = MSB of address
Default address: $0400

$31–$32 **49–50**

ARYTAB Pointer to start of RAM Bank-1 BASIC arrays.

$31 (49) = LSB of address
$32 (50) = MSB of address
Default address: $0400

$33–$34 **51–52**

FRETOP Pointer to start of free RAM Bank-1 memory space.

$33 (51) = LSB of address
$34 (52) = MSB of address
Default address: $0400

$35–$36 **53–54**

STREND Pointer to end of RAM Bank-1 BASIC string space, plus 1.

$35 (53) = LSB of address
$36 (54) = MSB of address
Default address: $FF00

$37–$38 **55–56**

FRESPC Pointer to current string address in RAM Bank 1.

$37 (55) = LSB of address
$38 (56) = MSB of address

$39–$3A **57–58**

MEMSIZ Highest address used by BASIC in RAM Bank 1.

$39 (57) = LSB of address
$3A (58) = MSB of address
Default address: $FF00

The default values indicate that BASIC can work with the RAM 1 block from $0400 through $FEFF (1024–65279). The list also shows that the lower part of this RAM area is normally set aside for variables. POKEing data into the lower part of Bank 1 RAM can cause a lot of difficulties.

The options are to move the variable pointers to a higher address in RAM 1 or make sure that your BASIC programming doesn't POKE anything into that lower Bank 1 memory area. The latter option is the simplest. As a rule of thumb, $0800 (2048) is a pretty good lower limit on any information POKEed to Bank 1.

The program in Listing 14-4 illustrates a bank-switching operation:

Line 10—Open the door to RAM 1.

Lines 20–40—POKE letters of the alphabet to Bank 1, beginning from address 2048.

Line 50—Close the door to RAM 1 and return to the Bank 15 configuration.

Line 60—Clear the text screen (always a RAM 0 operation).

Line 70—Set up a FOR. . .NEXT loop.

Line 80—Point to RAM 1 and get a character as C from that bank.

Line 90—Return to RAM 0 and POKE the character to video RAM.

Listing 14-4

```
10 BANK 1
20 FOR K=0 TO 25
30 POKE 2048+K,K+129
40 NEXT K
50 BANK 15
60 SCNCLR
70 FOR K=0 TO 25
80 BANK 1:C=PEEK(2048+K)
90 BANK 15:POKE 1024+K,C
100 NEXT K
```

Two ways are available for POKEing bank configurations. One is to POKE the appropriate values to the MMU configuration register at decimal address 65280:

POKE 65280,0 = BANK 15
POKE 65280,1 = BANK 14
POKE 65280,127 = BANK 1

Consider the version of the program in Listing 14-5 that replaces BANK statements with POKEs.

Listing 14-5

```
10 POKE 65280,127                    :REM BANK 1
20 FOR K=0 TO 25
30 POKE 2048+K,K+129
40 NEXT K
50 POKE 65280,0                      :REM BANK 15
60 SCNCLR
70 FOR K=0 TO 25
80 POKE 65280,127:C=PEEK(2048+K)     :REM READ FROM BANK 1
90 POKE 65280,0:POKE 1024+K,C        :REM WRITE TO BANK 15
100 NEXT K
```

An alternative to POKEing bank-configuration codes to the MMU configuration register is to POKE any value to the preconfiguration registers:

POKE 65281,0 = BANK 0
POKE 65282,0 = BANK 1
POKE 65283,0 = BANK 14

A reference to Bank 15 is missing from that list, but it happens to work into the scheme quite naturally via the MMU configuration register:

POKE 65281,0 = BANK 15

A

Number-System Base Conversions

Just about any computer, including the Commodore 128, is essentially a binary machine. The 8502 microprocessor does all of its control, arithmetic, and logic operations in a base two (binary) number system. The 8502 works with eight-bit binary numbers—a full byte of them.

People do not think and work with binary numbers very well, however. Such numbers, being made up exclusively of 0s and 1s, are very cumbersome. One alternative to purely binary representations of numbers is *hexadecimal* numbers. The hexadecimal (base 16) number system looks at binary numbers in groups of four. Every group of four binary numbers (sometimes called a *nibble*) can be represented by a single hexadecimal number. Instead of having to work with strings of eight 0s and 1s in base-two binary, you can work with just two hexadecimal characters.

Although many machine-language programmers can learn to work with hexadecimal numbers with great proficiency, the general population still prefers the ordinary decimal (base 10) number system. For this reason, BASIC is built around the decimal number system exclusively.

As long as you work with BASIC in its most elementary fashion—doing no special addressing or machine-language work—you will not need to be aware of hexadecimal or binary numbers. Hexadecimal numbers, however, become quite helpful when you are doing extensive machine-language programming.

Thus, programmers who are working their way deeper into the Commodore 128 system will find themselves having to make conversions between decimal and hexadecimal numbers and, eventually, between binary and hexadecimal numbers. The purpose of this appendix is to make such conversion tasks as simple as possible.

There are many ways to approach the conversions between these three different systems. The following are the most straightforward.

Hexadecimal-to-Decimal Conversions

Data in the Commodore 128 system is carried as a one-byte (two-hexadecimal-number) code. Addresses are carried as one-byte codes for the zero-page memory and as two-byte codes for the remainder of the usable memory space. Table A-1 can be very helpful for translating hexadecimal numbers into their decimal counterparts. This sort of situation often arises when one is writing programs in both BASIC and machine language.

The table can be used for converting up to four hexadecimal places (nibbles) to their decimal counterpart. Notice that there are four major columns, labeled 1 through 4. These columns represent the relative positions of the hexadecimal characters as they are usually written, with the least-significant nibble on the right and the most-significant nibble on the left.

Table A-1 Hexadecimal-Decimal Conversion

MSB 4		3		2		LSB 1	
Hex	Dec	Hex	Dec	Hex	Dec	Hex	Dec
0	0	0	0	0	0	0	0
1	4096	1	256	1	16	1	1
2	8192	2	512	2	32	2	2
3	12288	3	768	3	48	3	3
4	16384	4	1024	4	64	4	4
5	20480	5	1280	5	80	5	5
6	24576	6	1536	6	96	6	6
7	28672	7	1792	7	112	7	7
8	32768	8	2048	8	128	8	8
9	36864	9	2304	9	144	9	9
A	40960	A	2560	A	160	A	10
B	45056	B	2816	B	176	B	11
C	49152	C	3072	C	192	C	12
D	53248	D	3328	D	208	D	13
E	57344	E	3584	E	224	E	14
F	61440	F	3840	F	240	F	15

To see how the table works, suppose that you want to convert the hexadecimal value $1A3F to its decimal format. The first character on the left takes a decimal equivalent shown in column 4—4096. The second character from the left takes on the value from column 3—2560. The last two figures get their decimal equivalents from columns 2 and 1—48 and 15, respectively. To get the true decimal value, add those decimal equivalents: 4096 + 2560 + 48 + 15, which equals 6719. In other words, hexadecimal $1A3F is equal to decimal 6719.

If you are converting a two-place hexadecimal number, use columns 2 and 1. Hexadecimal $C3, for instance, is equal to 192 + 3, or decimal 195.

Table A-1 is adequate for hexadecimal-to-decimal conversions for all the usual sort of work on the Commodore 128.

Decimal-to-Hexadecimal Conversions

When working back and forth between BASIC and machine-language routines, you often need to convert decimal data and addresses into hexadecimal notation. Table A-1 comes to the rescue again. The procedure is straightforward but involves several steps.

Suppose, for example, that you want to convert decimal 65 to its hexadecimal counterpart. First, find the decimal number on the table equal to or less than the desired decimal number. The decimal number in this example is 65, and the closest value less than 65 is 64. The 64 is equivalent to a hexadecimal $4 in column 2. Thus, the most significant number in the hexadecimal representation is 4.

Next, subtract 64 from the number that you are working with: 65 − 64 = 1. Look up the hexadecimal value of the 1 in the next-lower column of the table—column 1 in this instance. The hexadecimal version of that number is $1. Putting together those two hexadecimal characters, you get a $41. Indeed, decimal 65 translates to hexadecimal $41.

For a more involved conversion, suppose that you must convert decimal 19314 into hexadecimal notation. Looking through the columns of decimal numbers in the table, you find that 16384 is the next-lower value. It translates into hexadecimal $4 in column 4. Thus, you are going to end up with a four-digit hexadecimal number, with the digit on the left being a 4.

To get the next-lower place value, subtract the table value 16384 from 19314: 19314 − 16384 = 2930. The next-lower decimal value in this case is 2816 from column 3. That turns up a $B as the next hexadecimal character. So far, the number is $4B.

Now subtract the table value 2816 from 2930: 2930 − 2816 = 114. The next-lower decimal value from column 2 is 112, and its hexadecimal counterpart is 7. To this point, the hexadecimal number is $4B7.

Finally, subtract the table value 112 from 114: 114 − 112 = 2. From column 1, decimal 2 is the same as hexadecimal $2, so the final hexadecimal character is $2.

Putting this all together, the decimal 19314 is the same as hexadecimal $4B72. Figure A-1 summarizes the operation.

Fig. A-1 Converting decimal values to hexadecimal values

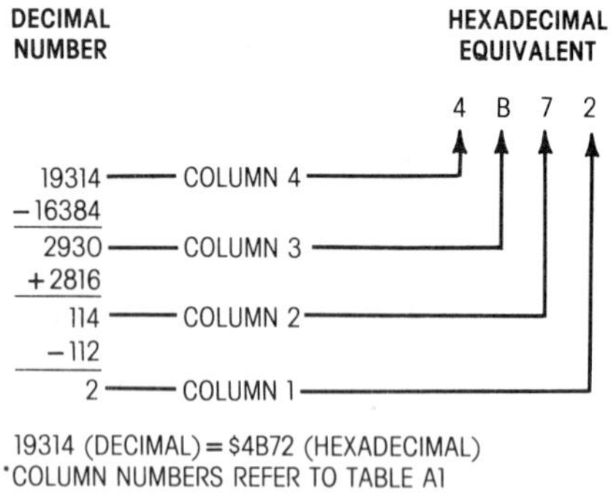

Conventional Decimal to Two-Byte Decimal Format

When POKEing addresses as two-byte numbers to memory, you need to convert the address to be affected into a two-byte format. In decimal, such an operation isn't easy but is all a part of setting up address locations in decimal-oriented BASIC.

By way of an example, suppose that you are to load a two-byte version of decimal address 1234 into memory addresses 16787 and 16788. That number to be stored, 1234, is too large for either of those two-byte addresses, so it has to be broken up into two parts: one for each of the address locations.

Before a decimal number can be divided into a two-byte version, it must be converted to hexadecimal form. Using the decimal-to-hexadecimal conversion described in the previous section, you find that decimal 1234 is equal to hexadecimal $04D2.

Next, you divide that hexadecimal version of the number into two bytes: the most-significant byte (MSB) is $04, and the least-significant byte (LSB) is $D2. Divide that way and you end up with two one-byte hexadecimal values: $04 and $D2.

Finally, convert those two sets of hexadecimal numbers into their decimal equivalents, treating them as two separate hexadecimal values. Thus, $04 converts to decimal 4 and $D2 converts to 210.

The two-byte version of decimal 1234 is thus 4 and 210, with 4 being the MSB and 210 being the LSB.

That takes care of the conversion of an ordinary decimal number into a two-byte version, also in decimal. Now you must POKE these numbers into decimal addresses 16787 and 16788.

If you place the LSB of the two-byte number into the lower-numbered address, the BASIC operation for satisfying the requirements of the example looks like this:

```
POKE 16787, 210  :  POKE 16788,4
```

Granted, it isn't a simple procedure to convert an ordinary decimal number to a two-byte decimal format, but it's the price that must be paid for working with a byte-oriented machine in a decimal-oriented BASIC language.

Two-Byte Decimal to Conventional Decimal Format

Suppose that you are analyzing a machine-language routine presented in a decimal-oriented, BASIC format. Under that condition, a two-byte address appears as a set of two decimal numbers. If you want to get that pair of numbers into a conventional decimal format, you have to play with them a bit.

Consider an instance where 223 turns up as the LSB in decimal and 104 is the MSB. What address, or two-byte decimal number, do they represent?

First, convert both sets of numbers to their hexadecimal counterparts: decimal 223 = $DF and decimal 104 = $68. Because $DF is the MSB and $68 is the MSB, the overall hexadecimal representation of that two-byte decimal format is $DF68.

All that remains to be done is to convert this hexadecimal number to its full decimal counterpart:

$DF68 = 24567 + 2048 + 208 + 15 = 26849

The combination of decimal numbers 223 and 104 actually points to decimal 26849.

Binary-to-Decimal Conversion

In practice, most binary-to-decimal conversions are carried out with one-byte (or eight-bit) binary numbers, although sometimes you need to do the conversion from two-byte (16-bit) numbers.

Figure A-2 shows the breakdown of an eight-bit binary number. The positions are labeled 0 through 7, with zero indicating the least-significant bit position. Each of those eight-bit locations contains either a 0 or a 1.

Fig. A-2 Organization of an eight-bit binary number

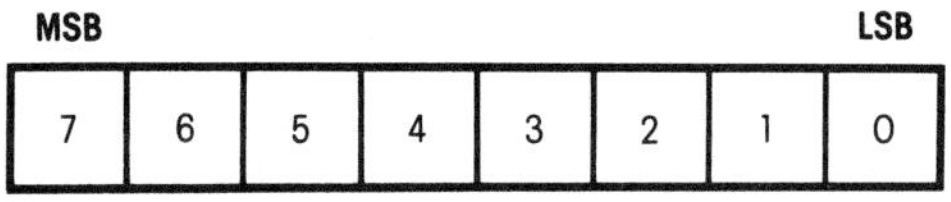

Suppose that you want to POKE 01101011. But you have to use a decimal version of that binary number from BASIC. Here is how to go about determining the decimal version.

First, multiply the 0 or 1 in each bit location by 2^n, where n is the bit place in each case. Then add the results. (See the example in Figure A-3.)

Fig. A-3 Converting binary values to decimal values

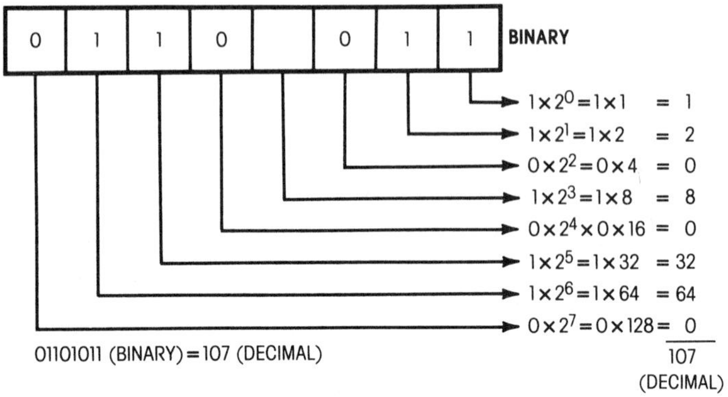

The same idea applies to converting 16-bit binary numbers to a decimal equivalent. The place values run from 0 to 15 in that case, and Table A-2 can help you determine those powers of two.

Table A-2
Powers of 2

n	2^n
0	1
1	2
2	4
3	8
4	16
5	32
6	64
7	128
8	256
9	512
10	1024
11	2048
12	4096
13	8192
14	16384
15	32768

Binary-to-Hexadecimal Conversion

Converting a binary number to a hexadecimal format is perhaps the simplest of all conversion operations. All you have to do is group the binary number into sets of four bits each, beginning with the least-significant bit. Then find the hexadecimal value for each group. Table A-3 helps with the latter operation.

Suppose the binary number is 10011101. There are two sets of four bits (or nibbles) here, 1001 and 1101. The hexadecimal equivalent is 9 for the first set and D for the second set, as Table A-3 shows. Therefore, the hexadecimal version of this eight-bit binary number is $9D.

The same procedure works equally well for 16-bit numbers. The only difference is that you end up with four hexadecimal characters rather than two.

Table A-3
Binary-Hexadecimal Conversion

Binary	Hex
0000	$0
0001	$1
0010	$2
0011	$3
0100	$4
0101	$5
0110	$6
0111	$7

Table A-3 (cont.)

Binary	Hex
1000	$8
1001	$9
1010	$A
1011	$B
1100	$C
1101	$D
1110	$E
1111	$F

Hexadecimal-to-Binary Conversion

Converting a hexadecimal number to its binary form is a simple matter of applying Table A-3 to change each hexadecimal character to the appropriate groups of four binary bits.

Example: Convert address $404D to a binary format. According to the table, this hexadecimal number can be represented as 0100 0000 0011 1101.

Decimal-to-Binary Conversion

Several algorithms are commonly cited for mathematically converting any decimal number to its binary format. A two-step procedure is simpler in the long run and probably more accurate.

The general idea is to convert the decimal number to its hexadecimal counterpart as described earlier in this appendix. Then convert the hexadecimal characters to their binary versions as described in the previous section.

As an example, convert 1234 decimal to binary. First, as described earlier, calculate the hexadecimal version of decimal 1234. Your answer should come out to $04D2. That hexadecimal number, expressed in binary (from Table A-3), is 0000 0100 1101 0010. Thus 1234 is equal to binary 10011010010. You may include the five leading zeros if you wish.

Complete Conversion Table for Decimal 0-255

For the sake of readers who have no heart for doing a lot of number-base conversions, Table A-4 can come to the rescue. It is impractical to tabulate the conversions for the entire memory range of the Commodore 128 system, but the range of values shown here will apply to any data byte.

Table A-4
Decimal-Hexadecimal-Binary Table for Decimal Values 0-255

Dec	Hex	Bin	Dec	Hex	Bin
0	$00	00000000	48	$30	00110000
1	$01	00000001	49	$31	00110001
2	$02	00000010	50	$32	00110010
3	$03	00000011	51	$33	00110011
4	$04	00000100	52	$34	00110100
5	$05	00000101	53	$35	00110101
6	$06	00000110	54	$36	00110110
7	$07	00000111	55	$37	00110111
8	$08	00001000	56	$38	00111000
9	$09	00001001	57	$39	00111001
10	$0A	00001010	58	$3A	00111010
11	$0B	00001011	59	$3B	00111011
12	$0C	00001100	60	$3C	00111100
13	$0D	00001101	61	$3D	00111101
14	$0E	00001110	62	$3E	00111110
15	$0F	00001111	63	$3F	00111111
16	$10	00010000	64	$40	01000000
17	$11	00010001	65	$41	01000001
18	$12	00010010	66	$42	01000010
19	$13	00010011	67	$43	01000011
20	$14	00010100	68	$44	01000100
21	$15	00010101	69	$45	01000101
22	$16	00010110	70	$46	01000110
23	$17	00010111	71	$47	01000111
24	$18	00011000	72	$48	01001000
25	$19	00011001	73	$49	01001001
26	$1A	00011010	74	$4A	01001010
27	$1B	00011011	75	$4B	01001011
28	$1C	00011100	76	$4C	01001100
29	$1D	00011101	77	$4D	01001101
30	$1E	00011110	78	$4E	01001110
31	$1F	00011111	79	$4F	01001111
32	$20	00100000	80	$50	01010000
33	$21	00100001	81	$51	01010001
34	$22	00100010	82	$52	01010010
35	$23	00100011	83	$53	01010011
36	$24	00100100	84	$54	01010100
37	$25	00100101	85	$55	01010101
38	$26	00100110	86	$56	01010110
39	$27	00100111	87	$57	01010111
40	$28	00101000	88	$58	01011000
41	$29	00101001	89	$59	01011001
42	$2A	00101010	90	$5A	01011010
43	$2B	00101011	91	$5B	01011011
44	$2C	00101100	92	$5C	01011100
45	$2D	00101101	93	$5D	01011101
46	$2E	00101110	94	$5E	01011110
47	$2F	00101111	95	$5F	01011111

Table A-4 (cont.)

Dec	Hex	Bin	Dec	Hex	Bin
96	$60	01100000	144	$90	10010000
97	$61	01100001	145	$91	10010001
98	$62	01100010	146	$92	10010010
99	$63	01100011	147	$93	10010011
100	$64	01100100	148	$94	10010100
101	$65	01100101	149	$95	10010101
102	$66	01100110	150	$96	10010110
103	$67	01100111	151	$97	10010111
104	$68	01101000	152	$98	10011000
105	$69	01101001	153	$99	10011001
106	$6A	01101010	154	$9A	10011010
107	$6B	01101011	155	$9B	10011011
108	$6C	01101100	156	$9C	10011100
109	$6D	01101101	157	$9D	10011101
110	$6E	01101110	158	$9E	10011110
111	$6F	01101111	159	$9F	10011111
112	$70	01110000	160	$A0	10100000
113	$71	01110001	161	$A1	10100001
114	$72	01110010	162	$A2	10100010
115	$73	01110011	163	$A3	10100011
116	$74	01110100	164	$A4	10100100
117	$75	01110101	165	$A5	10100101
118	$76	01110110	166	$A6	10100110
119	$77	01110111	167	$A7	10100111
120	$78	01111000	168	$A8	10101000
121	$79	01111001	169	$A9	10101001
122	$7A	01111010	170	$AA	10101010
123	$7B	01111011	171	$AB	10101011
124	$7C	01111100	172	$AC	10101100
125	$7D	01111101	173	$AD	10101101
126	$7E	01111110	174	$AE	10101110
127	$7F	01111111	175	$AF	10101111
128	$80	10000000	176	$B0	10110000
129	$81	10000001	177	$B1	10110001
130	$82	10000010	178	$B2	10110010
131	$83	10000011	179	$B3	10110011
132	$84	10000100	180	$B4	10110100
133	$85	10000101	181	$B5	10110101
134	$86	10000110	182	$B6	10110110
135	$87	10000111	183	$B7	10110111
136	$88	10001000	184	$B8	10111000
137	$89	10001001	185	$B9	10111001
138	$8A	10001010	186	$BA	10111010
139	$8B	10001011	187	$BB	10111011
140	$8C	10001100	188	$BC	10111100
141	$8D	10001101	189	$BD	10111101
142	$8E	10001110	190	$BE	10111110
143	$8F	10001111	191	$BF	10111111

Table A-4 (cont.)

Dec	Hex	Bin	Dec	Hex	Bin
192	$C0	11000000	224	$E0	11100000
193	$C1	11000001	225	$E1	11100001
194	$C2	11000010	226	$E2	11100010
195	$C3	11000011	227	$E3	11100011
196	$C4	11000100	228	$E4	11100100
197	$C5	11000101	229	$E5	11100101
198	$C6	11000110	230	$E6	11100110
199	$C7	11000111	231	$E7	11100111
200	$C8	11001000	232	$E8	11101000
201	$C9	11001001	233	$E9	11101001
202	$CA	11001010	234	$EA	11101010
203	$CB	11001011	235	$EB	11101011
204	$CC	11001100	236	$EC	11101100
205	$CD	11001101	237	$ED	11101101
206	$CE	11001110	238	$EE	11101110
207	$CF	11001111	239	$EF	11101111
208	$D0	11010000	240	$F0	11110000
209	$D1	11010001	241	$F1	11110001
210	$D2	11010010	242	$F2	11110010
211	$D3	11010011	243	$F3	11110011
212	$D4	11010100	244	$F4	11110100
213	$D5	11010101	245	$F5	11110101
214	$D6	11010110	246	$F6	11110110
215	$D7	11010111	247	$F7	11110111
216	$D8	11011000	248	$F8	11111000
217	$D9	11011001	249	$F9	11111001
218	$DA	11011010	250	$FA	11111010
219	$DB	11011011	251	$FB	11111011
220	$DC	11011100	252	$FC	11111100
221	$DD	11011101	253	$FD	11111101
222	$DE	11011110	254	$FE	11111110
223	$DF	11011111	255	$FF	11111111

B

Derived Trigonometric Functions

The functions shown in Table B-1 are not included in BASIC, but they can be executed by applying the corresponding expressions.

Table B-1 Derived Trigonometric Functions for BASIC

Function	Equivalent
Secant	1/COS(X)
Cosecant	1/SIN(X)
Cotangent	1/TAN(X)
Inverse sine	ATN(X/SQR(1 − X*X))
Inverse cosine	*k* − ATN(X/SQR(1 − X*X))
Inverse secant	ATN(SQR(X*X − 1))+SGN(X − 1)**k*
Inverse cosecant	ATN(1/SQR(X*X − 1))+SGN(X − 1)+*k*
Inverse cotangent	ATN(X)+*k*
Hyperbolic sine	(EXP(X) − EXP(− X))/2
Hyperbolic cosine	(EXP(X)+EXP(− X))/2
Hyperbolic tangent	(EXP(X) − EXP(− X))/(EXP(X)+EXP(− X))
Hyperbolic secant	2/(EXP(X)+EXP(− X))
Hyperbolic cosecant	2/(EXP(X) − EXP(− X))
Hyperbolic cotangent	(EXP(X)+EXP(− X))/(EXP(X) − EXP(− X))
Inverse hyperbolic sine	LOG(X+SQR(X*X+1))
Inverse hyperbolic cosine	LOG(X+SQR(X*X − 1))
Inverse hyperbolic tangent	LOG((1+X)/(1 − X))/2
Inverse hyperbolic secant	LOG((1 − SQR(1 − X*X))/X)
Inverse hyperbolic cosecant	LOG((1+SGN(X)*SQR(1+X*X))/X)
Inverse hyperbolic cotangent	LOG((X+1)/(X − 1))/2

The value assigned to variable *k* in these functions should be 1.570796 if using radians or 90 if using degrees.

Index